Portrait of the King

Theory and History of Literature
Edited by Wlad Godzich and Jochen Schulte-Sasse

Volume 57. Louis Marin *Portrait of the King*
Volume 56. Peter Sloterdijk *Thinker on Stage: Nietzsche's Materialism*
Volume 55. Paul Smith *Discerning the Subject*
Volume 54. Réda Bensmaîa *The Barthes Effect*
Volume 53. Edmond Cros *Theory and Practice of Sociocriticism*
Volume 52. Philippe Lejeune *On Autobiography*
Volume 51. Thierry de Duve *The Readymade: Marcel Duchamp, Painting and Modernity*
Volume 50. Luiz Costa Lima *The Control of the Imaginary*
Volume 49. Fredric Jameson *The Ideologies of Theory: The Syntax of History, Volume 2*
Volume 48. Fredric Jameson *The Ideologies of Theory: Situations of Theory, Volume 1*
Volume 47. Eugene Vance *From Topic To Tale: Logic and Narrativity in the Middle Ages*
Volume 46. Jean-François Lyotard *The Differend*
Volume 45. Manfred Frank *What is Neostructuralism?*
Volume 44. Daniel Cottom *Social Figures: George Eliot, Social History, and Literary Representation*
Volume 43. Michael Nerlich *The Ideology of Adventure, Volume 2*.
Volume 42. Michael Nerlich *The Ideology of Adventure, Volume 1*.
Volume 41. Denis Hollier *The College of Sociology*
Volume 40. Peter Sloterdijk *Critique of Cynical Reason*
Volume 39. Géza von Molnár *Romantic Vision, Ethical Context: Novalis and Artistic Autonomy*
Volume 38. Algirdas Julien Greimas *On Meaning: Selected Writings in Semiotic Theory*
Volume 37. Nicolas Abraham and Maria Torok *The Wolf Man's Magic Word: A Cryptonymy*
Volume 36. Alice Yaeger Kaplan *Reproductions of Banality: Fascism, Literature, and French Intellectual Life*
Volume 35. Denis Hollier *The Politics of Prose*
Volume 34. Geoffrey Hartman *The Unremarkable Wordsworth*
Volume 33. Paul de Man *The Resistance to Theory*
Volume 32. Djelal Kadir *Questing Fictions: Latin America's Family Romance*
Volume 31. Samuel Weber *Institution and Interpretation*
Volume 30. Gilles Deleuze and Félix Guattari *Kafka: Toward a Minor Literature*

For other books in the series, see p. xviii.

Withdrawn from
Davidson College Library

Library of
Davidson College

Portrait of the King

Louis Marin

Translation by Martha M. Houle
Foreword by Tom Conley

Theory and History of Literature, Volume 57

University of Minnesota Press, Minneapolis

The University of Minnesota Press gratefully acknowledges translation assistance provided for this book by the French Ministry of Culture.

Copyright © 1988 by the University of Minnesota.

Originally published as *Le Portrait du roi*, copyright © 1981 by Éditions de Minuit, Paris.

All rights reserved. No part of this publication may be reproduced, stored in a retrieval system, or transmitted, in any form or by any means, electronic, mechanical, photo-copying, recording, or otherwise, without the prior written permission of the publisher.

Published by the University of Minnesota Press
2037 University Avenue Southeast, Minneapolis MN 55414.
Published simultaneously in Canada
by Fitzhenry & Whiteside Limited, Markham.
Printed in the United States of America.

Library of Congress Cataloging-in-Publication Data
Marin, Louis, 1931-
  Portrait of the king.

  (Theory and history of literature; v. 57)
  Translation of: Le portrait du roi.
  Bibliography: p.
  Includes index.
  1. Louis XIV, King of France, 1638-1715.   2. Monarchy
—France   3. France—Kings and rulers.   I. Title.
II. Series
JN2369.L67M3713   1987   321.6'0944   87-19093
ISBN 0-8166-1603-5
ISBN 0-8166-1604-3 (pbk.)

The University of Minnesota
is an equal-opportunity
educator and employer.

Contents

Foreword: The King's Effects *Tom Conley*   vi
Introduction: The Three Formulas   3
Overture: The King, or Force Justified. Pascalian Commentaries   16
First Entrance: "The State Is Me," or the King's Narrative
    The King's Narrative, or How to Write History   39
    Interlude: The Discourse of the Flatterer, or the King's Eulogy   89
        The Fox's Tactics   94
        Racinian Strategies   105
Second Entrance: "This Is My Body," or the King by Sacrament
    The Royal Host: The Historic Medal   121
    Interlude: Royal Money and Princely Portrait   138
Third Entrance: "A Portrait of Caesar Is Caesar," or the King in His Frame
    The King and His Geometer   169
    The Prince's Palace   180
    The Magician King, or the Prince's Fête   193
    The King's Portrait   206
Finale: The Legitimate Usurper, or the Shipwrecked Man as King   215
Appendix: Donkey Skin   239
Notes   257
Bibliography   273
Index   285

Foreword
The King's Effects
Tom Conley

Le Portrait du roi is a hermetic book. Readers familiar with Louis Marin will immediately recognize its role in the evolution of his writing. Many of the articles, seminars, and projects included in this book develop from the sparkling research he initiated on ideology and space in *Utopiques: jeux d'espace* (1973) and *La Critique du discours* (1975). In the former he takes up the relations of ideology, politics, and topography in culture from the time of Thomas More to what he calls the "desperate" Utopias of Disneyland and Disneyworld. In his first book, collections of art, literature, cartography, and city planning inform his views of imaginary kingdoms. Three years later in the *Critique du discours*, Marin engages a protracted dialectical study of the central roles that Jansenist rhetoric and Pascal's logic had played in the formation of modern world-views. The two books underscore how the power of official modes of representation—whether in the logic of reason our times have inherited from schematic thinking in the wake of Descartes or in the spatial allegories of contemporary cities—work through human subjects when they practice their most innocuous activities. A person on foot in a modern city is no less indoctrinated than anyone writing a dissertation following the laws of usage that chart the frame of common sense.

Portrait of the King develops the methods and conclusions of the two former books to produce the most forceful, indeed accessible, of all his studies of the paradigms of power that the modern age has inherited from the archaic orders of the age of Louis XIV. A patient reading of Marin's work—and it does require patience and time—yields the conclusion that in the arts of representation are found the real origins and organs of social control.

In this respect Marin's work will find positive reception among followers of the anthropologist Clifford Geertz, Louis Althusser the political scientist, and Ernest H. Kantorowicz, a historian of theological rituals. Geertz discovered that in pre-modern and non-Western societies power is defined and managed through the relations held between a figure who produces a representation of itself and those who imitate it. Between the leader who makes displays and those who engage in them is established the difference separating a monarch from his subservient bodies. For as long as subjects *admire* by imitating the orders put to them in fields of ritualized life, a continuity of social distinctions can be held. Althusser, the political scientist whose austere readings of psychoanalysis and Marx inspired much of the ferment of May 1968, argued that the power of a society is often controlled by those who know how to handle ideology. By that term he meant not, as Webster has it, a science of the history and evolution of human ideas, but rather the state of idealism in which subjects bathe themselves in their everyday lives. Marin engraved Althusser's definition at the cornerstone of *Utopiques*. " 'The representation of the imaginary relations that individuals of a given society hold with their real conditions of existence' " (*Utopiques*: 18, quoting Althusser) might also figure at the beginning of *Portrait of the King*. Whoever institutes a collectively imaginary order monitors the desires and dreams of multitudes. Power is therefore enabled as much or more from control of ideas about life as from that of military forces or other visibly repressive agencies. Aesthetic displays bearing no ostensible relation with politics become instruments of force ensuring the strength of an order. Althusser labeled this an "institutional" mode of representation, one that historian of archaic behavior Ernest H. Kantorowicz studied in *The King's Two Bodies* (Princeton: 1957). He showed that the medieval conception of royalty used the Catholic theology of the *Corpus Mysticum* to elaborate juridical practice, to define the meaning of the crown and pattern ritual displays of kingship. Power was constituted through the "effect" of the Catholic mass when subjects unconsciously absorbed them in the secular areas of political life. As in the areas studed by Geertz and Althusser, an aesthetic activity grounded the shape and practice and power.

Marin's work develops from similar sets of matrices. A precious document for any study of the relations that have been held between art and power, it demonstrates that the West since the seventeenth century has its beginnings not only in the growth of capital economy but no less crucially in the "hidden" persuasions of public medias. Not that Marin is a Vance Packard: a logician in the line of the religious figures he studies, Marin suggests that France made decisive changes in the pageantry, literature, theater, and other archaic modes of display it had inherited from the medieval church and the dazzlement the Valois lineage had cultivated in the sixteenth century. In fact, with Colbert and Le Brun are the origins of the logic of contemporary medias. The correlations are so obvious and forceful that even the formal craft of *Portrait of the King* seems to mask the implications of its hypotheses both from itself and its readers.

Although closed in its design, the book's symmetries reveal much about the order and substance of its contents. The hermetic shape is arguably its own ideology. The book implies that the prismatic history of the "effects" of Louis XIV's aesthetic productions are extensions of our own relations with television, magazines, the fine arts in our best museums, and other phenomena that embody the range of popular and elite culture. Here the author appears as a staunchly Freudian historian—perhaps in the line of Michel de Certeau's last two chapters of *L'Ecriture de l'histoire* (1975)—by determining that our obsession with the past allows us to write of the present through the opening of an abyss of time at the basis of any historical investigation. What was then allows the here and now to be born of a return in movement to and from an imaginary object produced in the action of disinterring. For this reason the age of the Sun King of *Portrait of the King* is fraught with fear of the return of a totalitarian dictature. Clearly the order of Louis's age fascinates the author; he vivifies it through formal discourses of semiotics and psychoanalysis, but he also keeps it at bay, protecting both its aura and his obsessive identification with it from the tarnish of historical fact. It remains as a partial object, a wound of sorts, that the author caresses. He holds the force of its conclusions in the imaginary field of the seventeenth century that he unearthes and creates for us.

In its own synthetic shape are englobed and reflected the forms of power it studies. Three formulas, Marin asserts, dominate the logic of reason in seventeenth-century France. Soon after Louis XIV acceded to the throne on March 9, 1661, the king's motto was circulated. "L'état, c'est moi": no better expression could be forged to bear the stamp of its own self-willed authority. And no doubt because it rings and rhymes with both the Christian maxim of the Eucharist, *Ceci est mon corps* (*hoc est meum corpem*) and the Port-Royalists' utterance reflective of both the Gospels and numismatic style, "Le portrait de César, c'est César" (in chapter fourteen of the second part of the "Art of Thinking"). The three maxims are mutually self-informing. Their quasi-identity invokes the enigmas of power, of representation, of violence, and aesthetics of a world, although only 300 years past, that only appears to be light years away. It remains distant in its mix of medieval and archaic practices, to be sure; but Louis's world is uncannily near because orders of force used to produce human subjects and social contradiction have changed little in the passage from Louis to the modern state. Marin superimposes the three formulas to connote how such an alignment produced a triadic symbolic identity of state, truth, and god. Whatever pertained to one order was also of the others.

Symmetry is sovereignty. The tautology of each statement (or in terms of speech-acts, of their performative functions) incites exasperation and frustration mixed with admiration. They elicit a mix of contradictory responses which momentarily immobilize those to whom they are directed. (They are not unlike media-slogans which resound and redound with the same self-legitimizing circularity: "The Right Choice"; "We Do it Right"; "The World Is Going our Way.") All are forms of metadiscourse, expressions which produce their own truth in the closed symmetry of their formulation. The self-containment of "L'état, c'est moi," "Ceci est mon corps," and "Le portrait de César, c'est César" achieves what one century earlier, in the time of civil war preceding Henry of Navarre's ascendancy, was coined as the wish for a centralized and unified France: "Un roy, une loy, une foy" [one king, one law, one faith]. By the time of Louis XIV the orders of kingship, legislation, and religion, which had been only tentatively aligned at the turn of the century, are stamped into one.

They become the basis of an *official aesthetics*. In the wake of the vanguards of its early years, our century has been taught to spurn the idea of creative dictatures which impose on masses the ways that they must play, obey, live their public and private lives, and even imagine themselves in history and science. A careful reading of *Portrait of the King* will leave us with the uneasy feeling that, as in the Age of Louis, our entire lives are determined by institutional models of representation. Poetry and fantasy may indeed be aporias in the fearful symmetries of the discourses producing our names and bodies, but their creative elements are nonetheless contained within the overriding order of "dominant" modes of representation—that is, signs which are so pervasive that the distinction between dominant and dominated modes no longer has currency. Whether of 1660 or 1990, *all* modes of representation are dominant, and no less than the ways ideology, because it is unconscious, pervades all symbolic activity.

For this reason the hermetic order of *Portrait of the King* seems to pre-empt its conclusions. The reader is free to enter anywhere and everywhere but will inevitably be led back to its imposing triad of state, religion, and art. Each of the three maxims is used to subtitle one of the sections. Over the portal of the first "entry" is "L'état, c'est moi"; this section (roughly a third of the sum) deals with the writing of history immortalizing the young Sun King upon his accession to the throne. In this first third of the book Marin examines Pellisson's "Rapport à Colbert exposant un projet de l'histoire de Louis XIV," a blueprint for an aesthetic biography destined to yield "immortal effects." Before the advent of the secular state, historiography created itself through encomium. Epideictic rhetoric assigned itself the task of immortalizing its patron by comparing the king to myths wrought in complex symmetries and geometrical figures. Emblematic and heraldic combinations of language and image gave moral substance to contingency. Placed in simultaneously logical, tabular, discursive, and allegorical configurations, facts were carved from orders where design could lend a stable and hermetic appearance to the confusions of contingency. Future events could be included in the pregiven structures divinizing the king's human origins.[1] In this way the historical project depended upon an almost entirely visual frame of narrative focalizing its diverse or divergent elements of narration toward a unique vanishing point. "The king is placed on the horizon of the perspectival field, right where every appearance swoons in vision" (French edition: 69-70). History, he implies, turns into a picture; its beginning and end radiate in the figure of both the king and the light of God. An optical conversion is insinuated in Pellisson's discursive "project", and the resulting movement from language to Albertian perspective and back and forth again produces confusion. Therein the representation generates its "representation-effect," that is, its dazzlement. Cast in terms of history, the past arches toward this identity of origin but according to optical laws; when they pass through a convex lens, rays of light converge toward a focal point before they invert and are sent outward. Absolute power is figured through the perfection of a self-inverting symmetry; it is therefore established by virtue of the convincing order of its geometrical projection.

Marin locates the modes of production of such effects in what the classical age drew from Aristotle's pages on circumstantial rhetoric in the *Poetics*. Through an alert reading of La Fontaine's "Fox and the Crow," he examines how flattery might operate in the king's court. He shows that regal power is based and displayed solely in and through representations of language. Nothing exists beyond the shimmer of its performance. Merely staged as communication—hence bearing the myth of exchange where none exists—the courtesan's discourse becomes an art of seduction which uses simulacra to lure the interlocutor into belief or to fall into the trap of credulity. The person flattered is tricked into *seeing himself seen* in a "desire for absolute power." The crow of La Fontaine's celebrated poem thirsts for the image of omnipotence that the fox displays in the transparency of words. The crow's *desire* is tantamount to his will to power, but the mirror image in which he contemplates himself as total sovereign—like Louis beholding himself in his Hall of Mirrors—allows the fox to lure the crow's regard away from the world to the infinite self-reflection of narcissism. Caught in the specularity of his own desire, the bird loses power when he forgets to hold the lump of cheese in his beak. The moment of self-fascination or self-simulation leads the black bird to its demise. The fable treats of the narcissistic captivation that is not confined to Versailles. La Fontaine employs totemism to shunt the "discursive representations" of a political field onto a miniature scale where the theoretical consequences can be seen in clearer perspective. Like the structure of politics in the reign of the monarch, a chiasm—identical to the focal inversions that Marin located in Pellisson's writing—reveals that power is a function of desire. The latter is embodied in fascination, which exists only in optical shapes that the aesthetic technocracy holds over its subjects. Marin never indicates exactly how the revolutions science had been achieving in visibility are related to centralization, but he does suggest that the study of the history of objectivity cannot be dissociated from that of political practice. They are more than merely metaphors of each other.

The Sun King's desire for absolute power is embodied in the dialectical effects left by the impression of self-containment in the utterance, "L'état, c'est moi." Such is the tenor of Marin's first "entry" into *Portrait of the King*. Now his second entry mimes the first. "Ceci est mon corps" maddens us into believing in an adequate, a plenary and motivated relation between the world and language (that perhaps had been current since Innocent III's pronouncement adequating sign and referent in 1217, but which was under revision during the Council of Trent). Marin takes up the issue in a more recent and secular context, in Rascas de Bagarris's *Discours qui montre la nécessité de rétablir le très ancien et auguste usage public des vrayes et parfaites médailles* (1602), in which state counsel advises the king to stamp commemorative coins for the sake of immortalizing (often dubious) historical contingency. Bagarris tells his monarch to use graven images in order to transform discourse miraculously into history. The strategy is both very old and quite modern: whoever beholds a commemorative coin is entreated to look and to read. And because the medallion compounds language with figures, the viewer's attention is divided between an order of intellection and gaze. Like La Fontaine's crow at the moment he sees himself idealized in the words of the flattering fox, the beholder is caught in a momentary double bind and split between two modes of apprehension. That instant produces the historical subject; it is the moment of interpellation reenacting and reestablishing ideology.

Here the reader discovers a focal point of Marin's study, that of a chiasm between the first "entry" devoted to history and the third panel that deals with cartography, painting, and pageantry. In the latter, under the motto of "Un portrait de César, c'est César," Marin studies the centralizing perspective in seventeenth-century maps of Paris, the semiotics of display at Versailles soon after its inauguration, and Félibien's project for a portrait of Louis XIV. The visual enterprises detailed at the end of the book correspond to his extended study of Pellisson's narrative at the beginning. The flip side of the king's history, the panel visualizes the heroic discourse of the king as a function of representation in painting. The logic of its placement in Marin's overall scheme also indicates that *Portrait of the King* embodies strategies of power no less covertly than those which are studied within its contents. On one side, writing turns to painting while on the other, painting turns in the direction of writing.

Readers are free to enter the book anywhere, encounter any given problem, but everywhere, as in a hall of mirrors, we affront the same ensemble of paradoxes. The book invites and excludes, and it necessarily fascinates and frustrates its beholder. *Portrait of the King* does not fail to insist obsessively on the same crucial issues in various ways. For one, in the aesthetic domain the king's power is engendered only by virtue of his *effects*. The "king-effect" dazzles and arrests because it divides the spectator (or reader). Marin depends on the principle of the torn conscience (or *la conscience déchirée*, a formula he draws directly from

Hegel) for his identification of the multifarious relations of power in official forms of art. The monarch is made, ennobled, and immortalized through the artistry of what and whoever represents him in language and image. But in part it is *we*, the author suggests, who are baited into producing these effects.

In this fashion Marin's study stands at a crucial chapter in the history of the medias. Readers will no doubt find many similarities linking the "strategies" that Félibien, Racine, or Pascal deploy and the construction of "effects" of everyday life as we know them in the world of contemporary forms. The principal difference between the seventeenth century and now is apparent in the decentralizing strategies which, as we shall observe, multiply a reduced number of effects everywhere. The central point of reference is scattered, the overall pattern holds true. He notes that power exists only in and through the fields of representation. These elicit the sense of the "self" and the "subject" through what he repeatedly describes as *effects of representation*. The glossy impressions which official means of simulation leave upon spectators—whether by direct address or through modes appealing to collective distraction—tear attention asunder; they force the viewer or consumer into a glazed state of astonishment. Subjects are produced when they lose critical or historical conscience; when they succumb to dazzlement or charm of any origin.

The archaic side of the work surfaces in the scatter of the king's body. Marin writes, "The king is embodied in his image because the king's world is set free in the infinity of each of his subject's representations," where "the orders of reality are inverted and mixed in an incessant and universal reflexivity" (French edition: 249-50). When the king's body can be refracted everywhere throughout the state, as a fragmentary presence that flickers and sparkles about the order of reality it produces, its permanence can only be grounded in the fascination it elicits from the public. Hence the symbolic activity of statehood becomes its *raison d'être*. The fabrication of presence yields only a gloss of omnipotence. Is this not analogous to the media blitz that creates subjectivity in our time when we are lured into "having it our way"? The king's means of control are not those of a repressive agency, but rather as multifariously autonomous but homologous styles of aura. In contemporary terms these might be seen between the relation of articles and photos in *People* Magazine, soap operas, political events and their analysis, summit meetings, investigations of Iranian scandals on morning TV after Donahue, first-run cinema, high school and college curricula, articles in both the *New York Times* and *USA Today*. The various configurations of meaning that link the information yield a fake continuity of daily travail. The king's effect produced it consciously, whereas today it falls through the warp of the fabric of myriad shapes of received communication. An ensemble of limited impressions from many origins results in the same, often unsettling conclusion to the effect that the contemporary subject wafts in a flow of controlled sensory impressions regulated by a market economy that projects an impression of controlled chaos to maintain the dynamics of global economy. Such seem to be the "effects" of the aesthetic agencies as they have been transformed from the world of Louis XIV to that of consumer culture.

At this juncture the relation of Marin's work and Marxian analysis becomes clearer. *Portrait of the King* suspends the power of representation in the official aesthetic program of the classical age. A protracted reading of Marin's articles tells us that the king's effects were no doubt not that many, at least insofar as all in fact fall under the dominion of each of the three metadiscursive formulas. A Marxist would discover that LeBrun's or Félibien's project of history, akin to what the French Academy accomplished in its radical impoverishment of the French language in the years 1630-1660, entails a massive reduction of sensory experience among the subjects in his realm. All variety of life is aimed toward the figure of the leader's godlike irrepresentability as the ultimate Subject of all Representation.

Options of life and language are diminished in favor of an ostensive presence of the model of "state policy" in every sphere of life.[2] The subject is encouraged to idolize the king's omnipotence in all orders of everyday life, to contemplate the extensiveness of his presence, and to live in fascinated astonishment before the empty sign of Louis. Marin's own Marxian moment, although of intensely theological cast, imbues the conclusion of his introduction. Summarizing the relation that Pascal derives from a comparison of justice and power, he detects how Pascal envisages an efficient means of controlling a national imagination through universal respect of established order. Marin remarks, "Thus the general diversity of the institutions of power and of the power in their discourse takes as its exact corollary the *suppression of all possible diversity in the institutional orders of a given society* (French edition: 46, our stress). Were the remark applied to the early modern *sensorium*, by which Father Walter Ong defines the register of bodily sensations that we can imagine in a past epoch, expressed through the associative wealth in the heritage of its linguistic register,[3] or to the fabulously rich complex of archaic social orders before the age of "state policy" under Louis XIV, the organic continuum—in other words the resilient and supple dynamics of language and the body in the pre-Cartesian world—Marin would be locating a first crucial moment in the material history of modernity. There the task of the centralizing dictature would have been one of reducing the imaginary options a world of subjects kept for its imagination and health. The operation is not different from what Jacques LeGoff discovered at work in early Christian times, when the monotheistic order had to make the simple and ruseful clarity of its theology to repress the myriad structures of residual pagan cultures. At stake was a need to reduce drastically the range of both real and imaginary fields of sensation that had characterized lay, rural and Gallo-Roman and other local populations. From the second to the fifth century the model of state policy was set in place.[4] Colbert surely knew the design and transposed it to an entirely secular plane but in the authoritarian garb of religious vestments.

Marin does not specify exactly what worlds of experience are lost with the advent of official aesthetics. He offers the paradigm of religious politics that determines the limits of the public imagination in general, both in the classical age and, as we must surmise because of the high categorical type of the concepts informing his study, in our own period as well. In the latter a broad sensorium is no more than the media-effect glossing over a general reduction of the ranges of experience and language. The loss of the senses in the aura of their extension is engineered by technocracies that make modes of sensation available "at the touch of a finger." They ultimately figure in the same global impoverishment because all meaningful life is relegated to simplicity, efficiency, or clarity. Such reduction operates in the time of Louis XIV through the ubiquitous imprint of the king's signature on all public surfaces, but today the ostensible origin is, like ideology itself, both everywhere and nowhere.

Marxian innuendo tells readers that Marin is arguing for only a theoretical overview of the classical age. A classicist might label the book as a political history without events or policy. In Marin's plan effects are born and maintained through representation, and as such they supersede narratives—or lived stories—based on contingency and circumstance. In this respect *Le Portrait du roi* differs from much of the empirical historiography associated with the *Annales* or with the names of American counterparts.[5] Marin's grasp of an "event" is informed by both discursive formations and fields of logic which are said to precondition fact or experience. His intent therefore also includes reduction of the panoply of forms (marking the history of the period) to an invisible dynamic of representation. No doubt informed by Heidegger's pregnant remarks about the seventeenth century wishing to reduce the great wealth of world history to a "world-picture,"[6] it opts for a mix of invisibility with the sparse and enthusing severity of classical diction. Forged by official aesthetics, imaginary conditions of life become functions of dialectical reason. Pragmatic scholars might balk at Marin's attempt to write a history with a minimum of events, of dates, names, or of places; whether it succeeds or fails imports less than the vision that discerns a universal motivation, what he baptizes as the desire for power and the desire to see that power embodied in the simultaneous presence and absence of a play of effects—in the interrelations of aesthetics and kingship.

The limits Marin assigns to his endeavor are narrow, and the measure of its results owes much to the very austerity of his style. The book surpasses its own frame most "effectively" in engaging the paradoxes at the bottom of the monarch's effigy. In the central chapter devoted to a medallion cast for the Sun King, Marin speculates on one of the basic chiasms that embody art and power in the difference of reading and seeing. In numismatics power is engendered by combinations of two absolutely different modes of intellection. One, which reads language in the invisibility of what its symbols convey, is contrasted by the other, of lines and relief which appeal to the eye and touch. The latter qualities he associates with the *imaginaire*, a Lacanian term designating the world before consciousness or language; it only anticipates exchange, discourse, or symbolic regions in general. A mix of confused impressions that the mind has not yet semanticized, it partakes of sensation and is "semiotic" rather than "symbolic,"[7] and it does not yet know oedipal laws of constraint. It persists in a sensuous view of colors and shapes. That it is a *view* indicates where it is isolated from language, or the former. Now Marin aligns language with the invisibility of discourse. When the visible crosses into the field of the invisible, and vice-versa, transgression occurs.

Marin treats it as chiasm, in which the *reading* of a medallion points to a view of its concrete texture, whereas a viewing of the portrait in the field on the averse (or reverse) veers toward a *reading*. Similar emblematic reasoning informs the book everywhere. "Relating the narrative of the king in a story effectively means making it visible. Showing the narrative of the king in his icon means having it told" (French edition: 147). Narrative therefore moves toward visibility when its totality shows us the tableau of the king's facts and deeds, all the while a visible object embodying the king—a painting, a sculpture, a relief, or an image stamped on a medallion—induces its beholders to tell or remind themselves of the legendary narrative of the exploits that guarantee the posterity before their eyes. A tale "makes us see" a tableau, and a tableau "makes us tell" a narrative. Through the ploy of the king's simultaneous absence and presence spectators are forced to divide their faculties and to move back and forth between one mode and another. "A boundary has been drawn between reading and viewing [*lisibilité et visibilité*] but only in order to be endlessly crisscrossed" (French edition: 147): thus begins a logic of transgression, hence of oedipal design in which the king plays the role of the father. As soon as he draws the line between the two faculties (which may not have been so easily divided in the early modern sensorium or even in the texture of Descartes's language of sensation when such divisions would appear to be initiated), Marin establishes their utter difference and imbues the aesthetic world with a logic of guilt. A Christian mode initiates and informs a psychogenetic model. In this fashion both the daring beauty and suspended perfection of Marin's system become congruent with the cultural effects he studies. Its appeal resides in its resilience, for the bases of all official forms of art that we know today are propounded—willfully, it can be suggested—on what is implicitly legislated to be a distinction between reading and seeing. All medias tend to *oedipalize*, in other words, they produce subjectivity by holding as a firm law the unstated point that to read is not to see, and vice-versa, but always at the very time they invite the world to transgress the borders their aesthetics have created.

The May 15, 1987 issue of *People* Magazine offers a stunning image of Donna

Rice recumbent on a beach. She stares at the readers, inviting us to partake in the ventures for which the medias had just crucified Gary Hart. The caption of the emblem-cover, *Hart Stopped*, aims the eye toward the visibility of its writing in the pun on (Gary) Hart and (the spectator-buyer's) heart. At the check-out counter it is *we* who are stopped, *we* who are inculpated and arrested in a forbidden act of commingling reading and seeing in a moment of captivation and imaginary lust. The political contender loses not simply because of tact, fact, or event than for reason of the unconscious drives that an official narrative has produced through the same chiasms of visible and symbolic forms. The media industry, the world of Colbert in our time, owes much to the strategies that the great economist's commercial artists (Le Brun, Pellisson, André Le Nôtre, Jouvenet, and later, Hyacinthe Rigaud) had been using to blueprint the king's sovereignty over his subjects.

This "incessant crisscrossing" from one world to the other leaves chiasms everywhere in the double relation between a sign of state and its beholder. Marin draws upon the logic of emblems in whose difference of image and text is located an evanescent mark—perhaps a χ—of death. The medias impose a frightening figure of the unknown and capitalize on its effects for the instauration of their power. Such were the ineffable effects in the official aesthetics of Louis's realm, and such are their almost timeless presence today. In linking the realm of aesthetics with those of language and power, patient readers will discover that Marin's portrait of the Sun-King's world is disquietingly—even astonishingly—modern.

Notes

1. Marin draws much from the allegories of mottoes and devices as Edgar Wind explains them in *The Pagan Mysteries of the Renaissance* (New York: Norton, 1958). And Erwin and Dora Panofsky's conclusions about the open-ended allegories in their "Iconography of the Galerie François Premier at Fontainebleau," *Gazette des Beaux-Arts*, 11 (1958) mark a classically mannered moment in the study of history, aesthetics, and politics which furnishes a backdrop to Marin's project. Although Marin's method seems to combine casuistry with semiotics—hence both the exhilaration and fatigue it can elicit together—its conclusions have much in common with what Angus Fletcher likens to the political structure of allegory. "Ideological power-structures" that veer from discursive to diagrammatical or schematic configurations, allegories entrap their readers by the dazzling closure and efficaciousness of their explanations: they attempt to ply anything and everything into their own design. See the first two chapters of Fletcher's *Allegory: Theory of a Symbolic Mode* (Ithaca: Cornell University Press, 1964), a book that has lost little of its original force over the past two decades.

2. How Louis's epoch established an overweaning reason imbued with religiosity is the topic of Michel de Certeau's study of "la raison d'état" or state policy which is implanted in seventeenth-century France when highly centralizing bureaucratic procedure is enacted in the name of the Catholic church. Marin is virtually studying the same topic from within aesthetic confines and with an inductive method. Readers might compare Marin's literary approach to reason with de Certeau's history of religious structures in *L'Ecriture de l'histoire* (Paris: Gallimard, 1975): ch. 4, parts 1-2.

3. Father Ong associates touch and sight with the aural dimension of language. "Cultures vary greatly in their exploitation of the various senses and in the way in which they relate their conceptual apparatus to the various senses"; he adds that "some cultures make more of taste than do others," in *The Presence of the Word* (Minneapolis: University of Minnesota Press, 1981): 3-4.

4. "Clerical Culture and Traditions of Folklore," in *Social Historians in Contemporary France* (New York: Harper, 1972): 131-40, especially 135-37.

5. Readers might compare Marin's intense study of the discourses purporting events that are planned to happen (such as Pellisson's project) to both Natalie Z. Davis's pervasive documentary bent in *Society and Culture in Early Modern France* (Stanford: Stanford University Press, 1975) and Donald Kelley's tendency to turn a theoretical problem (ideology) toward facts and dates of a history of ascending (Protestant) consciousness [in *The Beginning of Ideology: Consciousness and Society in the French Reformation* (Cambridge: University Press, 1981)]. The two historians aim at describing mental structures, while Marin stays within the aesthetic and political discourses that anticipate or, he would argue, precondition those very facts and structures.

6. "Humanism first arises," he speculates, "where the world becomes picture," in "The Age of the World Picture," Part III of *The Question Concerning Technology and Other Essays*, tr. William Lovitt (New York: Harper, 1977): 133.

7. Two different ideolects are used. Marin draws much from a schematic reading of Lacan's triad of the imaginary, the symbolic, and the real to demarcate the intelligible from the visible. Readers no doubt find that the distinction is less clearly drawn in Lacan's French and that Marin may also be drawing on Julia Kristeva's derivative schemes which are elaborated in *Semiotikè* (Paris: Seuil, 1969). His language is not, however, that distant from Sartre's highly provocative distinction between "poetry" (visible language) and "prose" (through which forms are understood narratively, in content, in the invisible world of the intellect) offered in *Qu'est-ce-que la littérature* in 1946.

Theory and History of Literature

Volume 29. Peter Szondi *Theory of the Modern Drama*
Volume 28. Edited by Jonathan Arac *Postmodernism and Politics*
Volume 27. Stephen Melville *Philosophy Beside Itself: On Deconstruction and Modernism*
Volume 26. Andrzej Warminski *Readings in Interpretation: Hölderlin, Hegel, Heidegger*
Volume 25. José Antonio Maravall *Culture of the Baroque: Analysis of a Historical Structure*
Volume 24. Hélène Cixous and Catherine Clément *The Newly Born Woman*
Volume 23. Klaus Theweleit *Male Fantasies, 2. Male Bodies: Psychoanalyzing the White Terror*
Volume 22. Klaus Theweleit *Male Fantasies, 1. Women, Floods, Bodies, History*
Volume 21. Malek Alloula *The Colonial Haren*
Volume 20. Jean-François Lyotard and Jean-Loup Thébaud *Just Gaming*
Volume 19. Jay Caplan *Framed Narratives: Diderot's Genealogy of the Beholder*
Volume 18. Thomas G. Pavel *The Poetics of Plot: The Case of English Renaissance Drama*
Volume 17. Michel de Certeau *Heterologies*
Volume 16. Jacques Attali *Noise*
Volume 15. Peter Szondi *On Textual Understanding and Other Essays*
Volume 14. Georges Bataille *Visions of Excess: Selected Writings. 1927-1939*
Volume 13. Tzvetan Todorov *Mikhail Bakhtin: The Dialogical Principle*
Volume 12. Ross Chambers *Story and Situation: Narrative Seduction and the Power of Fiction*
Volume 11. Edited by John Fekete *The Structural Allegory: Reconstructive Encounters with the New French Thought*
Volume 10. Jean-François Lyotard *The Postmodern Condition: A Report on Knowledge*
Volume 9. Erich Auerbach *Scenes from the Drama of European Literature*
Volume 8. Mikhail Bakhtin *Problems of Dostoevsky's Poetics*
Volume 7. Paul de Man *Blindness and Insight: Essays in the Rhetoric of Contemporary Criticism* 2nd ed., Rev.
Volume 6. Edited by Jonathan Arac, Wlad Godzich, and Wallace Martin *The Yale Critics: Deconstruction in America*
Volume 5. Vladimir Propp *Theory and History of Folklore*
Volume 4. Peter Bürger *Theory of the Avant-Garde*
Volume 3. Hans Robert Jauss *Aesthetic Experience and Literary Hermeneutics*
Volume 2. Hans Robert Jauss *Toward and Aesthetic of Reception*
Volume 1. Tzvetan Todorov *Introduction to Poetics*

Portrait of the King

Introduction
The Three Formulas

The present work is, in a sense, the follow-up and consequence of *La Critique du discours: Etudes sur la Logique de Port-Royal et les Pensées de Pascal*.[1] While researching that book I was struck by the prominence that the grammarians and logicians of Port-Royal gave to the notion of representation, as well as by the general equivalence they posed or presupposed between it and the notion of sign at whatever level on which they analyzed language (term, proposition, discourse) and in whatever domain that language belonged (verbal, written, iconic).

I placed this equivalence in question by inquiring into the Port-Royalist definition of sign as representation in two domains where the signifying function had to play an essential role, domains that nonetheless escaped to a certain extent the constraints of its rules of functioning. These were the exegetic domain, the discourse of God to man, and the rhetorical domain, the discourse of man to man. Representation in both cases ceased to represent, because in it began the play of figures. From that point on the analysis of language could no longer be purely and simply its description; surreptitiously, the analysis became its regulation, or rather its normalization. The Port-Royal *Logic* then appeared to me to be the exemplary text in which fact and right, observation and prescription, the given and the ideal—if not to say the ideological—intermingle indissolubly.

It was a question, then, of bringing to light an endeavor at work inside the theoretical and practical model of representation and sign, an endeavor that two indications animating the text itself were found to suggest. The first indication concerned the place and function of the Pascalian citations that intervened at key points in the theory of language as a countermodel to what the Port-Royalists were proposing. This countermodel, far from being imported from the outside as a heterogeneous element, was none other than that of Port-Royal, but only to the extent that it had begun to work in its articulations, in the play of its parts, in its pretexts as in its margins.[2] Pascal called this internal endeavor, this flip side of the logicians' analytic mastery of language, not its hidden face, but rather the processes it deployed to accomplish itself, designating its critique in the same gesture.

I found the other indication while examining the additions made in successive editions of the *Logic* between 1662 and 1683. These additions concerned again two key problems in the representational model. On the one hand was the structure of the sign-representation, where the question of distinction and confusion between meaning and referent was raised, confusion being able to appear, paradoxically, as the mark of a true language and distinction, as that of error. On the other hand was the structure of the sentence-judgment, where the questions of its alethic and existential values was raised.[3] Now in these texts, both occasional and essential, I encountered an example that, although privileged from the point of view of logico-grammatical theory, seemed to emerge from a domain outside of it. It concerned the formula that simultaneously presents, accomplishes, and summarizes the Catholic dogma of real presence, "This is my body," put in question by Calvinist ministers in the name of an "erroneous" linguistic interpretation of the word of Jesus Christ. This utterance, a speech act that leads toward a deictic by an ontological affirmation, a predicate that is the body of the subject of enunciation—is not this utterance a figure? Or else does the thing shown become in and through the speech act the act itself, that is to say, the body-subject? The question of the Eucharist from then on lost its status as additional and circumstantial example, as application of the theory of sign as representation, while founding, centrally, the representational model and, at the same time, putting it to work, challenging it, and ultimately producing its internal critique.[4]

We still find today in this work both Pascal in his eminently quotable text and the Eucharist in its Catholically repeated formula. The work was dedicated, while playing a bit on words and on the rhetorical figure of the chiasmus, to the representation of the king and to the king of representation, dedicated, in other words, to the relationships between power and representation. These relationships could be reformulated as two questions: what about power and its representations and, inversely, what about representation and its powers? The expression of the conjunction of power in general with representation is uttered here as reversible into that of a double and reciprocal subordination, and that is what the present work explores in the field of politics. The first relationship is that the institution of power appropriates representation as its own. It gives itself representations, and it produces its own representations of language and image—to what ends? The second relationship is that representation, or the framework of representation, produces its power and produces itself as power—what are the powers of representation? These questions would remain empty, however, if the one or the many meanings of representation or of power were not made more specific.

What is re-presenting, if not presenting anew (in the modality of time) or in the place of (in the modality of space)? The prefix *re-* introduces into the term the value of substitution. Something that was present and is no longer is now represented. In the place of something that is present elsewhere, a given is present here. At the place of representation then, there is a thing or person absent in time or space, or rather an other, and a substitution operates with a double of this other in its place. Thus the angel at the tomb on the morning of the resurrection: "He is not here, he is elsewhere, in Galilee, as he had said he would be"; thus the ambassador in the foreign country. Such would be the first effect of representation in general: to do as if the other, the absent one, were here and the same; not presence but effect of presence. It is surely not the same, but it is as if it were, and often better than, the same. Thus the photograph of the deceased on the mantelpiece; thus the narrative of the battle of the past by the narrator of today. Alberti, in the second book of his treatise *On Painting*, was already writing that "painting contains a divine force which not only makes absent men present, as friendship is said to do, but moreover makes the dead seem almost alive. Even after many centuries they are recognized with great pleasure and with great admiration for the painter."[5] A marvel of representation, this effect is its power, a power (a divine force, going along with Alberti) with a hold on the transitive dimension of representation; this thing that is other, the simulacrum of the same, is the direct object of *to represent*.

But we also read in the dictionary: "To represent: to exhibit, to expose to sight. To 'represent' one's license, one's passport, one's birth certificate. To 'represent' someone, to make him appear personally, to put him in the hands of those who had put him in our trust."[6] To "represent," then, is to show, to intensify, to duplicate a presence. It is no longer a question of being someone's herald or ambassador in order to represent him, but to exhibit or show him in the flesh to those who ask for a reckoning. The prefix *re-* no longer introduces into the terms a substitution value but, rather, an intensity or frequency. The dictionary examples are revealing in their archaisms: they all concern to one degree or another the exhibition of a title. Thus, by the "representation" of one's passport at the border the bearer not only presents himself really but also presents his legitimate presence by the sign or title that authorizes or permits, not to say compels, his presence. Representation lies here in the element of sameness that it intensifies through duplication. In this sense it is its reflection, and to represent will always be to present oneself representing something. At the same time representation constitutes its subject. Such would be the second effect of representation in general, to constitute a subject through reflection of the representational framework: it is as if a subject were producing the representations, the ideas he has of things; it is as if there were neither world nor reality except for and through a subject, the center of that world. This "idealistic" production and centering would be only substantivized simulacra of the framework's functioning, and of the diversified effects resulting both from the reflection of the framework onto itself and from the intensification through redoubling of its functioning.

The first effect of the representational framework and the first power of representation are the effect and power of presence instead of absence and death; the second effect and second power are the effect of subject, that is, the power of institution, authorization, and legitimation as resulting from the functioning of the framework reflected onto itself. If, then, representation in general has indeed a double power—that of rendering anew and imaginarily present, not to say living, the absent and the dead and that of constituting its own legitimate and authorized subject by exhibiting qualifications, justifications, and titles of the present and living to being—in other words if representation reproduces not only de facto but also de jure the conditions that make its reproduction possible, then we understand that it is in the interests of power to appropriate it for itself. Representation and power share the same nature.

What do we say when we say *power*? Power is, first, to have the ability to exert an action on something or someone, not to act or to do but to have the potential of doing so, *to have* the force to do or to act. Power, in the most vulgar and general sense, is to be capable of force, to have—and I must insist on this property—a reserve of force that is not expended but that is in a *state* of being expendable. But what, then, is a force that is neither manifested nor exerted? As Pascal says, it is master only of external actions. As potential, power is also valorization of that potential as an obligatory constraint, generating duties as law. In this sense *power* means *to institute* potential as law, the former conceived as the possibility and capacity of force. And it is here that representation plays its role, in that it is at once the *means* of potential and its *foundation*. Hence the general hypothesis that supports the whole of the present endeavor, that the representational framework operates the transformation of force into potential and of force into power, and that twice, on the one hand by *modalizing* the force as potential and on the other by *valorizing* potential as a legitimate and obligatory state, and by justifying it.

How can representation carry out this transformation? On the one hand representation puts force in signs (as we put a boat in water) and on the other hand it signifies force in legal discourse. It carries out the substitution for the exterior act, where a force is manifested in order to annihilate another force in a struggle to the death, of signs of force, which need only be *seen* as a force to be *believed*. Representation in and through its signs represents force: as delegates of force, signs are not the representatives of concepts but rather the representatives of force, which can be grasped only in their representational effects:[7] the power-effect of representation is representation itself.

But what does a force do? We can grasp what it does in all clarity in the process of struggle of one force against another, and this process—even if it is a question of abstraction, it has the value of an ideal model of intelligibility—has no other objective than destruction. A force is force only through annihilation, and in this sense all force is, in its very essence, absolute, since it is such only to annihilate all *other* forces, to be without exterior and incomparable. Such is the struggle to the death of forces that we find in all political reflection on the origins of the state by Machiavelli, Hobbes, or Pascal, continuing to Hegel or Clausewitz, where this struggle signifies a rising to the extreme and a tendency toward the absolute of all force.

From then on, the placing in reserve of force in signs—which is power—will be at once the negation and conservation of the absolute of force: negation, since force is neither exerted nor manifested, since it is at peace in the signs that signify and designate it, and conservation, since force through and in representation will give itself as justice, that is to say, as law that obligatorily constrains under pain of death. Power is the tendency toward the absolute of the infinite representation of force, the desire for the absolute of power. From then on, representation (whose effect is power) is at once the imaginary satisfaction of this desire and its real deferred satisfaction. In representation that is power, in power that is representation, the real—if one understands by "real" the always deferred satisfaction of this desire—is none other than the fantastic image in which power will contemplate itself as absolute. If it is of the essence of all power to tend toward the absolute, it is in its reality never to console itself for not being so. Representation (of which power is the effect that, in turn, permits and authorizes it) would be the infinite work of force's mourning of the absolute. It would operate the transformation of the infinity of a real lack into the absolute of an imaginary that takes its place. The whole of my study—from the "Overture," which, with Pascal, treats the univocal rapport between *heterogeneous* force and justice, to its Finale, dedicated, again with Pascal, to the strange figure of the legitimate usurper of a kingdom whose king was by chance found to be absent—aims to follow the path of the transformation, in diverse fields and on diverse objects, of infinity into the absolute, the infinite representations of the prince in the imaginary absolute of the monarch. The whole of this endeavor attempts to sketch a portrait of the king (a representation of power) in this philosophical *frame* that would be the monarch himself (power as representation).

To represent, I have said, is to make the dead man come back as if he were present and living, and it is also to redouble the present and to intensify presence in the institution of a subject of representation. How, then, is representation the satisfaction of the desire for the absolute that animates the essence of all power, if it is not by being the imaginary substitute for this satisfaction, that is, by being its image? The portrait of the king that the king contemplates offers him the icon of the absolute monarch he desires to be, to the point of recognizing and identifying himself through and in it at the very moment when the referent of the portrait absents himself from it. The king is only truly king, that is, monarch, in images. They are his *real presence*. A belief in the effectiveness and operativeness of *his* iconic signs is obligatory, or else the monarch is emptied of all his substance through lack of transubstantiation, and only simulacrum is left; but, inversely, because *his* signs *are* the royal *reality*, the being and substance of the prince, this belief is necessarily demanded by the signs themselves; his flaw is at once heresy and sacrilege, error and crime.

If the present and presence of the prince signify the desire for the absolute of power, representation will also be the reflexive redoubling of this very desire — the production of a subject of representation animated by it: the prince is penetrated by the poignant care for his glory. The event and, indeed, the accident have no other reason and meaning than to be occasions for manifesting this concern and appeasing its uneasiness through exploits. But the great deed will always be insufficient to satisfy the thirst for glory. Hence this other paradox: that the reflection of presence always accuses more intensely, in the subject of representation that is its effect, the desire for the absolute of being a lack to fill, of being that empty place Pascal speaks of precisely with respect to the king, which is satisfaction always deferred. The king is first of all the movement of will or desire in the diversions of war, hunting, and ballet. The desire for the absolute of power, for the *incomparable* glory of the monarch, will take the form of time. The subject of representation, to realize itself as the subject of absolute power — the absolute monarch — will be produced as the effect of narrative representation, of narrative, and of the narrative of history, where is constructed, in the present of the prince's extraordinary act itself, the memorial of the memory of the king, a memorial that completes time in a past that is an eternalized present.

On the one hand, then, we have an icon that is the real and "living" presence of the monarch; on the other, a narrative that is his tomb and subsists forever. Representation as power and power as representation are a sacrament in image and a "monument" in language where, exchanging their effects, the dazzled gaze and the admiring reading consume the radiant body of the monarch, the former by narrating his history in his portrait and the latter by contemplating one of his perfections in a narrative that eternalizes his manifestation. As we know, representation is at once the action of putting before one's eyes the quality of being a sign or person that holds the place of another, an image, a political body, and an "empty coffin on which one stretches a cloth for a religious ceremony."[8]

In addition, the philosophical and historical reflections that this work attempts on the relationships of power and representation lead directly, in the fields that this relationship articulates — that is, the political imaginary and symbolism of the absolute monarch — to finding again the Eucharistic motif. In my work on the Port-Royal *Logic* I showed the central and roundabout role that this motif plays in the theory of the sign and the practical philosophy of the discourse that prolongs and crowns the *Logic*. This encounter could appear to be the effect of chance or the illusion of a theoretic and philosophic obsession if Ernest H. Kantorowicz's great book *The King's Two Bodies: A Study in Mediaeval Political Theology* had not demonstrated in the most rigorous fashion the fundamental function, as juridical and political model, played by the Catholic theology of the *Corpus mysticum* in the elaboration of the theory of royalty and of the royal crown and dignity.[9] But maybe it would have been fruitful to scrutinize with more refined instruments the complexities and displacements of a theology of the sacrament that, as Henri de Lubac has shown, refers simultaneously to a ritual and a liturgy, to a commentary and an exegesis, to a narrative and a history, and to an institution and a society, while being by definition and essence the repetition of a sacred mystery of the sign and of the secret.[10] Such a wealth of signification could not but furnish orientations of thought and action and of conceptions and paradigms throughout a history that elaborates, from the imperial and pontifical notion, the national and secular state whose head is the king and whose members are an institutional framework of power, claiming for their own account that very perpetuity that had formerly been attributed only to the church and the vicar of Jesus Christ, and to the Holy Roman Empire and its emperor. Kantorowicz's work explores these models and these paradigms, which are all suspended, in one fashion or another, on the diverse functions of a unique utterance, "This is my body," spoken in a community that this utterance founds and makes such as it is.

We could also, from this point of view, consider the present study as attempting to examine the various domains of language—historical narrative and eulogistic discourse—or of image—historical tableau, medal, or portrait—as expansions of the utterance "This is my body" that the mouth of the prince would proffer, thus transforming his representations in their various modalities into so many signs of the political sacrament of the state in the real presence of the monarch. If the Eucharistic formula in its Catholic sense as applied to the king constitutes the center of the work, its whole development has consisted in fact in articulating with the sacramental theological utterance two other propositions: the political-juridical one, which was spoken in Parliament in April 1655 by the young Louis XIV, *"L'état, c'est moi"*; and the other, semio-semantic one, written between 1662 and 1683 by the logicians of Port-Royal in chapter 14 of the second part of their *Logic*, "The portrait of Caesar is Caesar," where "Caesar" is the generic name of the prince (that is, the portrait of Louis is Louis). A minute analysis, semantic and pragmatic, of the first proposition (formed notably in relation to the words that Louis XIV, in fact, said) would show that the essence of the state is not defined there either by a concept or by an individual. It resides neither in the king (or the royal dignity) nor in Louis XIV, but it *is* none other than the proper name ("me") of the "I" that utters, "The state is me." A text of Hegel's in the *Phenomenology of Spirit* shows that there lies the key moment of absolutism: "For it is in the name alone that the *difference* of the individual from everyone else is not *presumed*, but is made *actual* by all. In the name, the individual *counts* as a pure individual, no longer only in his consciousness, but in the consciousness of everyone."[11] And, as Vincent Descombes writes in his commentary: "Naming does not consist in finding a word for someone who is already there [*a natural body*] . . . , the unique being of him who is alone in being who he is. It makes of the difference between the one and all others a real difference. . . . It is the word of the Other which makes the subject emerge."[12]

And there is the essential function of the discourse of flattery. "The state is me"—thus does the absolute monarch pose himself: the monarch, or power in its singularity; and the absolute, or power in its universality. We discover, then, the paradox of the proposition where some sentences about the young Louis are summarized: if "me" is the proper name of him who says here and now, "The state is me," then he who utters it localizes himself as a singular body in time and space. But the proposition, in the same verbal gesture, identifies him with the state, that is, with universal power in all places and at all times, everywhere present. In other words, the body present here of him who speaks now is none other than one body everywhere and always. Now a body at once local and translocal is precisely what the sacramental host realizes for Jesus Christ in the universal community of the church. But maybe it would be appropriate to say the reverse as well, and we would be approaching what René Demoris calls the obsession of classical discourse: never to utter the place where the king is not,[13] which in the extreme would render all discourse of and about the king impossible, since to say that the king is here is to say that he is not elsewhere. To be everywhere and always present, is it not to make that presence equal, always and everywhere, to that retreat and secrecy that Pascal considers precisely as the fundamental trait of the Eucharistic body?

In the same way that the theory of the sign as *representation* was fashioned from the inside by the Eucharistic utterance "This is my body," which was its apparent application, the juridico-political "This is my body," that is, "The state is me," fashions the representations of the prince at once in order to make of them the real presence of a monarch and to reveal his phantasmal power.

"The portrait of Caesar is Caesar." As a matter of fact, when the Port-Royal logicians formulate this utterance in the fourteenth chapter of the second part of their *Logic* as an echo of the fourth chapter in the first part, where maps and portraits exemplify their definition of the sign as representation, their explicit purpose in using it as an example is to show that the person who utters it is understood by all as speaking "in signification and in figure." This is a simple way of speaking, which does not demand other preparation or manner, "because the visible rapport between these sorts of signs [*natural signs whose prototype is the mirror image*] and things shows clearly that, when one affirms of the sign the thing signified, one does not want to say that that sign is really that thing"[14] but only its figure, its representation. The portrait of the king remains a portrait, his sign.

Hence the utterance "That is Louis," spoken in front of a portrait of Louis, is three or four times figure: It is a type of metaphor.[15] Such would be the "visible rapport," of which the logicians speak, between the sign and the thing, which then authorizes that the name of the thing be given to the sign. But it is also a type of metonymy.[16] The visible rapport would then concern less the actual or supposed resemblance of the portrait of Caesar to Caesar than the manifest and evident relationship between the existence and the manner of a portrait and him whose portrait it is. It is also a type of synecdoche, that said of an individual, or autonomasy.[17] The spectator of a portrait of Caesar, common "name" of a species, would designate it by the proper name of an individual, the name of "Caesar" whom the portrait represents.

The question posed by the logicians with the portrait of Caesar does not concern the linguistic description of a grammatical and semantic usage but a rule, or rather a norm. When does one have the *right* to give to signs the name of things? With the king's portrait this right is a natural right, because the portrait in general, and that portrait in particular, is a natural sign, and the three tropes of metaphor, metonymy, and synecdoche that are condensed in it are immediately *justified* by resemblance, correspondence, and connection (to use Fontanier's words), that is to say, simultaneously by a mimetic rapport, a rapport of internal dependency, and an external relationship. To name the king in front of his portrait is to say at once that the portrait resembles him, that he owes his existence to it, and that it includes his name.[18]

However, the introduction at the beginning of Chapter 14 of the example of the king's portrait and of the proposition uttered in front of it by its spectator, "It is the king," has no other objective than to found the validity, at the end of the same chapter, of another utterance pronounced by Jesus Christ and repeated throughout the earth, "It [this] is my body" (*"c'[eci] est mon corps"*). Just as "without preparation and offhandedly," we will be authorized to say of a portrait of the king that "it is the king," without preparation and offhandedly Jesus Christ was able to say of the bread, "It is my body." But whereas in the first case the visible rapport between the portrait and the king marks clearly that we mean that the king's portrait is, in signification and in figure, the king, in the second "the apostles not looking at the bread as a sign and not being at any pains as to what it signified, Jesus Christ would not have been able to give to the bread as sign the name of the signified thing, his body, without speaking against the usage of all men and without deceiving them."[19] Consequently, we cannot hear "This is my body" in the sense of figure, but rather, "All the nations of the world are brought *naturally* to take these words in the sense of reality."[20] There is a remarkable proximity between the two utterances and a no less remarkable distance in their interpretation: the same natural right authorizes the subject viewing the prince's portrait to give to the representation the name of him whom it represents, and to be understood as speaking in figure; and the faithful taking the body of Jesus Christ in communion are understood as making of the bread that body and as understanding the words of Jesus in the sense of reality, namely, that this bread here is his body. Between the Eucharistic symbols of Jesus Christ and the political signs of the monarch, Port-Royal underlines a contiguity but traces an insuperable boundary. It is this boundary that the desire for the absolute of power crosses with the fantastic representation of the absolute monarch in his portrait and in his name, traits legitimized by the utterance of just one name, a unique name authorized by the representation of the prince: a named portrait, the name of an image that is the presentation in which the monarch grasps himself as absolute.

To summarize schematically the Eucharistic model in its major articulations and to show how it was able to function as a juridical and political model, one could consider that in the utterance of the formula "This is my body" is produced *a sacramental body visible as the real presence of Jesus Christ* on the altar, a body present in reality that the symbolic species of the bread and wine dissimulate at the end of the performing act of language. But it should be added that the transformation of the bread and wine into the flesh and blood of Jesus Christ is the starting point of a commemoration of the historical sacrifice of the body of Jesus Christ such as it is told in the Scriptures: a repeated and recited narrative that constitutes the consecrating ritual. On the altar is therefore also produced *the absent historical body of Jesus Christ as narrative representation*. Finally, this same transformation of bread into the body of Jesus Christ, serving "to conceive how Jesus Christ is the food of our souls and how the faithful are united among themselves,"[21] that same body defines the communion place of the faithful and poses the signification of the spiritual work that is constructed in it: *ecclesiastical body as symbolic fictive society at once visible and invisible*.[22]

If we attempt to transpose the remarkable structure of the theological body into the juridical and political domain, a transposition that brings to light the historical gesture of absolutism, we can consider that the king's portrait—"It is Louis"—constitutes the sacramental body of the monarch who, as the visible host on the altar refers back to the transcendence of the word in the mystery of the Father, manifests and seals at once the unfathomable invisibility of Louis, the *arcana imperiium*, and the mysteries of the royal substance.[23] But we must also notice that the king's portrait in its very dimension as sacramental, as presence of the king's body in painted, sculpted, or written currencies, is also and indissolubly a narrative and historical representation. There is a dimension of narrative and of recitation in the royal portrait that is also the celebration of the king's historical body, his monumental tomb in and through the representation of history. Finally, the king's portrait envelops the king in his name as his law embraces his image: the king as right, the king as state, the symbolic fictive body of the kingdom in his head and soul. Thus the portrait as sacramental body of the king operates the historical body represented in the political symbolic body and lifts the historical body of his absence and imaginary in the symbolic fiction of the political body. The body of the king is thus visible in three senses: as sacramental body it is visibly *really present* in the visual and written currencies; as historical body it is visible as *represented*, absence become presence again in "image"; as political body it is visible as *symbolic fiction signified* in its name, right, and law. And the tension that could be historically described and analyzed between the name of the living king—the seal of his law—and the effigy of the dead king displayed in his representation—the majesty of royal dignity—*the portrait of the king as absolute monarch* resolves this tension in its triple dimension, at once presence, "imaginary" representation, and symbolic name.[24]

We must return to the formula "The state is me," which was not spoken but which summarizes and symbolizes, in an utterance both juridical and political, the royal discourse that Voltaire's historical narrative reports to us, and whose effect he describes as the king's body, a portrait-effect that is no doubt essential. Instead of a formula, then, this:

> When in 1655, after the suppression of the civil wars, after his first campaign and his coronation, the Parliament again wanted to assemble on the subject of some edicts, the king left Vincennes in his hunting costume, entered the Parliament in great boots, whip in hand, and spoke these few words: "We see the misfortunes your assemblies have produced. I order that those that have begun on my edicts cease. Mister First President, I forbid you to allow any assemblies and all of you to call them."

To which Voltaire adds: "His majestic bearing, the nobility of his features, and the tone and air of mastery with which he spoke were more commanding than the authority of his rank, which until then had been little respected."[25] The prince's speech given here to be read in its immediate authenticity—"his own words"—taken however from a narrative of history as one of its sequences, produces, in the very text of the narrating historian and in the name of a glossing commentary, *an iconic effect*: the body of young Louis, but in truth constituted as royal body—majestic bearing, nobility of features, tone and air of master—by the *reported* speech and the circumstances that frame it. *Louis suddenly becomes king as the portrait of a king*, by a manifestation of will that resembles, in many respects, an inverted parody of the ceremony of the *lit de justice* where, ten years earlier, the king had been recognized king by Parliament in the days that followed the death of Louis XIII.[26] The king's portrait would thus be the framework whereby absolute order is represented through an individual in the text and makes of him its representative, the foundation of its power. Absolute order is incarnated in a body and becomes a *body in the historical narrative*. But the king's portrait is also, and inversely, the terminal product of a narrative operation that gives *absolute order as already inscribed in narrated reality*, which offers reality to be read as already articulated by it.[27]

According to this perspective, my endeavor aims to understand the real presence of the king in the currency of his portrait—his sacramental body—as an operator of exchange between image and name, narrative and law, reality and norm. The sacramental body of the king, the portrait of the king as absolute monarch, signifies and shows this place of transit between the name, where the body has become signifier, and the narrative, the story, through which law has become body. To prolong in all modesty the work accomplished by Kantorowicz for the Middle Ages, my study would propose the following hypothesis for "classical" absolutism: the king has only one body left, but this sole body, in truth, unifies three, a physical historical body, a juridico-political body, and a semiotic sacramental body, the sacramental body, the "portrait," operating the exchange *without remainder* (or attempting to eliminate all remainder) between the historical and political bodies.

In 1662, in his sermon on the duties of kings, Bossuet states that,

> To establish this power [*puissance*] that represents His own,
> God places a mark of divinity on the forehead and face of
> sovereigns. . . . God has made in the Prince a mortal image of
> His immortal authority. You are gods, says David, and you are
> all children of the Almighty. But, oh gods of flesh and blood, oh
> gods of earth and dust, you will die as men. It does not matter. You
> are gods even though you die, and your authority does not die. This
> spirit of royalty passes in its entirety to your successors and
> imprints everywhere the same fear, the same respect, and the same
> veneration. The man dies, it is true; but the king, we say, never dies:
> the image of God is immortal.[28]

Some years previously, on a little piece of paper, Pascal had analyzed the mechanisms of representational frameworks, describing the effects they produce and discerning their reason in the configurations they draw on political, juridical, and theological planes:

> The custom of seeing kings accompanied by guards, drums, officers,
> and all those things that bend the machine toward respect and terror,
> causes their face to imprint on their subjects respect and terror even
> when they appear by themselves, because one does not separate in
> thought their persons from the retinues with which they are ordinarily
> seen. And the world, which does not know that the effect comes
> from this custom, thinks that it comes from a natural force; and from
> that come these words: "The character of Divinity is imprinted on
> his face, etc." (25-308).[29]

Pascal's thought, as if it were paraphrasing and parodying Bossuet's apostrophes, brings to light power as representation and representation as power in the phantasm of a royal body, of a prince's portrait, named "absolute monarch."

My study also has the difficult ambition of pursuing the critical dialogue between the Catholic theologian who enters the court and the Jansenist moralist who leaves the world, in the form of and according to the structures of one of those court ballets that Louis XIV loved to produce for himself:[30] a staging in representation of an episode of the history of representation and power in three entrances, but where the interludes would have the ironic function of showing the inner springs of the machines whose effect is the great spectacle of absolutism.

Overture
The King, or Force Justified.
Pascalian Commentaries

What about discourse when it is that of power, or when it is itself power? What, then, about power when a discourse expresses it, or when it defines the discourse itself? In the universe of genres of discourse is there a specific discourse, that of power, where discourse in general possesses, in and through itself, a power that is its "own"? And what is the relationship *between* this power, "belonging" to discourse in general, and power in general, which appropriates a discourse for itself and is uttered in a particular discourse that would be its "own"?

Here are two propositions:

1. Discourse is the mode of existence of an imaginary of force, an imaginary whose name is "power."
2. Power is the imaginary of force when it is uttered as discourse of justice.

How does force become power? How does it survive itself as power, *if not by holding forth* the discourse of justice? How does the discourse of justice become power, then, *by "holding" the place* of the effects of force? How does discourse in general operate the effects of force that are *held* to be just, to be justice itself?

"To hold forth discourse," "to 'hold' the place of," "to be held to be" — these are three stages in the movement of the imaginary by which force has become justice, that is to say, power, three degrees of the imaginary through which discourse has become power, that is to say, strong on its own.

It is in this way that we encounter Pascal at the edge of our analysis, unavoidable.

I. Force and Justice

"It is just to follow the just" (103-298): a categorical imperative, justice does not prescribe its commandment by virtue of anything other than itself. A just prescription is not deduced from Being, from the Good, from a speculative or theoretical proposition. A just prescription is just on its own without arguments of utility or of acceptability. *Justicia jussus sui*. And there is no degree of justice. There is no more or less just: it is all or nothing.

> Justice and truth are two points so subtle that our instruments are too blunt to touch them exactly. If they do make contact, they dull the point and press all around it, more on the false than on the true (44-82).

That which does not coincide with the point is unjust. Even when indiscernible, this point of the "just" does not admit of subtle degradations from the just to the unjust.

"It is necessary to follow the strongest" (103-298). Force is necessary. It is impossible not to follow the strong: it is a material, mechanical, and physical necessity. The strong is not imperative. It is not obligatory. The strong is absolute constraint, or else one dreams, imagines, fantasizes; the violence of force. But there are degrees of force: only the *strongest* is necessarily followed. To obtain this, the strongest still must manifest its force, but how, if not by confronting the other forces and annihilating them. It shows in this way—without words—that it is necessarily the strongest. The strongest is such only at the conclusion of a war of forces, at that of a conflict of forces when there is only one force left, the one that has reduced the other forces to nothing. The strongest is such only at the pure moment of the manifestation of its force, at the abstract moment of the destruction of the other forces. Such would be both the originative and instantaneous geneses of the institution in the fiction of a state of nature.

> The strings attaching men's mutual respect are in general strings of necessity; for there must be differences of degree, all men wanting to dominate and all not being able to, but some being able. Let us imagine, then, that we see these strings beginning to form. There is no doubt that men will fight each other until the stronger party oppresses the weaker (828-304).

"Justice without force is impotent; force without justice is tyrannical" (103-298). It is just to follow the just. But how to oblige, indeed, how to oblige *oneself* in a gesture of autonomy to follow the just, since a just prescription has no other right to prescribe than its own justice? Justice is impotent in its essence, for it does not dispose by itself and in itself of a force that would be that of justice, except in the utopia of a justice that would be strong only by being the zero degree of force, a utopia realized *once* by someone:

> It would have been useless to Our Lord Jesus Christ to come in splendor as king in his reign of sanctity; but he truly came with the splendor of his order. It is indeed ridiculous to be scandalized by the lowliness of Jesus Christ as if this lowliness were of the same order as the greatness that he came to show (308-793).

Force without justice is tyrannical. Justice is without force and is in itself impotent: the zero degree of force. Tyranny is an excess of force and as such is force without justice: *too* strong. More precisely, here is uttered the essence of all force as the fantastic desire to be the greatest force or, which amounts to the same thing, as the desire for the destruction of all other forces, as the desire for death.

> Tyranny consists of the desire for domination, universal and outside of its own order. There are various categories of men—the strong, the handsome, the sensible, the pious—with each reigning in his own area, not elsewhere. And sometimes they meet, and the strong and the handsome fight, stupidly, over who will be the master of the other; for their mastery is of different kinds. They do not understand each other, and their fault is to want to reign everywhere. Nothing is able to do so, not even force; it can do nothing in the kingdom of the savants and is master only of external actions. . . .
> Tyranny is wanting to have by one avenue what can only be had by another (58-332).

Here are two definitions of tyranny, that is, of force without justice that is force itself and absolute violence. The strong man in his infinite desire to be the absolute degree of force—an infinite paradox proportional to his desire—is the desire for homogeneity, let us say the desire for the destruction of all heterogeneity: thus all force is, in its tyrannical essence, universal entropy.

"Justice without force is contradicted, because there are always evil men. Force without justice is denounced" (103-298). Here is the key moment of the return of the apparent symmetries of force and justice: the negative moment of a leap into the field of discourse. Justice, which is without violence and with no force, is contra-*dicted*. Discourses express the contrary of what the just prescription prescribes—the just prescription, which has no right to be prescription other than by what comes from itself. In a word, discourses speak that the just is unjust. I note this upheaval of the discourse of contradiction of the just, where the just is uttered as unjust. That discourse is fact, accident, and event, and it arrives unexpectedly to overturn the just prescription in and through its utterance. Why? Because *there are always* evil men. The accident, the event of this singular discourse, is always already produced, it has always already taken place. Without explanation or justification. There are always evil men. A discourse of evil, a presence of the fact of evil in its discourse, is always already *there*. It is not a question here of a speculative or theoretical fiction, that of the cunning genius that would permit the founding of the just and its prescription. There has always been a discourse of evil. But evil is only a discourse, and that discourse is powerless to engage the just prescription, the justice of the just prescription. Evil is that discourse that negates and contradicts the just.

Force without justice is accused. But there is also another discourse, symmetrical and parallel to that of the evil men who contradict: the discourse of the accusation of tyranny. Two discourses are then confronted: that which contradicts justice and that which accuses force. But if we know who have always contradicted justice without force, the evil men, we do not know who accuses force without justice. The just man on his cross facing the tyrant on his throne, would he be the one who *holds* forth the discourse of accusation? Unless there is only accusation of tyranny through the silence of the accuser, or unless this silence in the accusation is the secret, the inaudible mark of the just man.

"Force and justice must therefore be joined together, and to do that, the just must be strong and the strong just" (103-298). Conclusion. Until now the motifs of force and of justice have worked independently of each other, starting from two initial propositions: "It is just to follow the just; it is necessary to follow the strongest" (103-298), starting from the opposition of the obligatory and the necessary of which two propositions had twice formulated the consequences by the double exclusion of the justice of force and of the force of justice. But this double exclusion, conforming to the general principle of Pascalian method of reasoning, which negates the contrary of the truth to be demonstrated,[1] permits the recording of a double displacement. As a first displacement, in what concerns justice from which force is excluded, we have come up against the observation that justice is absolutely deprived of all force; while in what concerns force (from which justice is excluded) we discover the universal desire for domination in all ways. In other words, justice without force *cannot commit* [*pouvoir faire*] an act of justice—it is impotent—whereas force without justice *commits an act of force* outside of its "own" domain constituted by external actions. As a second displacement we have entered the field of discourses—the one that contradicts justice and the one that accuses force—discourses that reciprocally operate a remarkable turning back of their modalities. Indeed, the discourse of contradiction turns the initial prescriptive utterance, "One must follow the just because it is just," back into a constative utterance, "The just is not just," or "The just is nonjust," of which the implicit consequence would be the negation of the prescription posed at the beginning: "It is unjust to follow the just [*since the just is said to be nonjust*]." The discourse of accusation operates a detour, since the initial constat of the necessity of following the strongest is implicitly transformed into a negative prescriptive utterance: "It is unjust to follow the strongest."

Whence the conclusion in the form of pragmatic principle and consequence, to resolve the disorder and confusion of the discourses of contradiction and accusation. For the contradiction of the just is itself *contradictory* ("It is unjust to follow the just"), and the accusation of the strongest is itself—*in the discourse*—a transgression of order, perfectly homologous to the tyrannical transgression of force. By converting an observed necessity into a negative prescription ("It is unjust to follow the necessary"), the discourse of accusation is, to use a Pascalian term, *ridiculous*.[2] "Force and justice must therefore be joined together" (103-298), since it is demonstrated by reasoning on the contraries that justice without force and force without justice end up either at contradiction (the contradictory discourse) or at ridiculousness (the discourse of accusation). The displacement of the initial utterances that, in Pascalian discourse, speak the silence of necessary force or of categorical justice, makes the contradiction of a discourse of force or the ridiculousness of a discourse of justice appear. Justice and force taken together must then permit the escape from both.

But it is worthy of notice that this conclusion takes, in Pascalian discourse, the enunciative form of a prescriptive: force and justice "must therefore be joined together" (103-298); a prescription for which an act—a "doing" [*faire*]—will be the means of accomplishment, the instrument of realization: "and to do that" (103-298).

It is indeed a question here of a pure prescriptive, dependent in the form of an ellipsis on the grammatical form of obligation (must [*il faut*]), at once in the ethical order and in the operative instruction of a command that carries in itself the cognitive conditions for the success of the action it requires. And this action aims at nothing less than an identification of two terms that the principle had juxtaposed by maintaining them in their exteriority. But it is there that the initial opposition of the categorical imperative of the just and of the mechanical necessity of the strongest reappears. It reappears in the form of two mutually disjunctive propositions of the process of identification between force and justice. The identity to be realized between the two is not inert, and their conjunction is not static, as $x = y$ is not equivalent to $y = x$. The identification between force and justice is a dynamic process that can operate according to two mutually exclusive orientations: either that the strong becomes an attribute qualifying justice or that the just becomes a determining quality of force. Between what is strong and what is just, which is, of the two exchanges, the possible one? Which substitution is realizable?

The demonstration:

"Justice is subject to dispute; force is easily recognizable and undisputed" (103-298). Justice can always be discussed and disputed. The essential notion of justice is the object of polemical discourses. Why? Certainly, the just is imperatively categorical: "It is just to follow the just" (103-298). But what *is* just? The very nature of the prescriptive of the just as deontic "tautology" appears to have to imply an inquiry into the ontological determination of justice. It would seem that this inquiry would, in turn, refer back necessarily to deducing the just prescriptive starting from a constative and theoretical proposition, posing the being of justice as the Good, Nature, and God. These are philosophical discourses, a war and confusion of discourses, and interminable disputes as regards the ontological determination upon which the imperative of the just would depend in order to have its full validity as imperative. That which it must be [*son devoir-être*] would find its duty [*devoir*] in a being [*être*]. But how to determine it without dispute? "Justice and truth are points so subtle that our instruments are too blunt to touch them exactly" (44-82). Through its very nature as value, the just prescription has no foundation other than itself, but—and this is a subtle and almost indiscernible point—it appears that a discourse will always seek to determine the just as a palpable quality and ontological predicate of the being of justice. Justice will not escape from the war of discourses, nor can it avoid being the object of philosophical discourses in mutual clash and repugnance.

On the other hand, force is very recognizable and without dispute. One cannot avoid seeing it, as it imposes itself through its very manifestation as the mechanical necessity of the strongest. It follows that force cannot, necessarily, be the object of discourse. We do not speak of force: we submit to it or exert it. But, you will say, is it not possible to accuse tyrannical force? Certainly, but this discourse is ridiculous, for it is "literally" without object, that is to say, without effect on its subject. It is an impotent discourse, for it will always be suspended from the absolute threat of death: "Be quiet, or I will kill you because I am stronger." The reason of the strongest is always the best. "Thus one was able to give force to justice." The conclusion here grabs hold, and it is surprising: force is given to justice. There was the power to submit force to justice! Here, then, is justice fortified, as politics has become morality and the political has been identified with the ethical. We have read badly. Let us reread: "Justice is subject to dispute. Force is easily recognizable and undisputed" (103-298). We expected the conclusions: "Thus one was able to give justice to force." But it is there that the order was not kept, to speak like Pascal.[3] The main clause and that which comes at the beginning of the sentence is only an effect of the causal subordinate clause that follows it, and the effect of this effect in the reading is very exactly the mark of the reversal of the true order. That the political is the ethical implies, by abrupt and instantaneous mutation, the reverse. *Coup de force* of the force that is a *coup de discours*.

"Thus force could be given to justice, because force has contradicted justice saying that it is unjust, and that it itself is just" (103-298). Force could be given to justice because force, which is and yet cannot be the object of discourse, gave itself the right to speak. It constituted itself as subject of discourse, produced language, and passed into signs. Such is the "true" zero point of force: the mute violence is suddenly mutated into meaning without losing its thanatocratic character. Force takes possession of the signs, language, and discourse through this universal desire for infinite domination outside of its own order (external bodies and actions), which constitutes its tyrannical essence as force. Seizing language, force is reflected in discourses and represented in signs. It is converted into meaning. And we will wonder with Pascal if all discourse, is not already and has not always been a force that is reflected, represented, reactive, and reactivated in signs and if the signs themselves, or the symbolic function in general, are not re-marked traces of force, that is, delegated representatives of force, and the foundation of their power.[4] As subject of discourse, force speaks. And the force that is represented in signs is the force that autonomizes and institutes itself and issues the edict that is its law and legitimates and authorizes itself. This position is a position of the self through which the pure manifestation of force, in this movement of self-reflection, institutes itself as power of a legitimate and autonomous order: power of discourse, discourse of power, identity, and reciprocal appropriation.

The discourse of force, discourse of self-institution and of self-legitimation, discourse that *is* power, includes a double dimension, a double negative and positive side: one might say it is a two-stroke machine whose strokes are simultaneous. Force has contradicted justice and said that it is unjust. Force does not argue to find out what is justice and what is just. It is the concern of the interminable speculative philosophical discourses. Force contradicts, and all the more surely that it is very recognizable and without dispute, and with all the more certainty that behind its representation, its reflection in discourse, will always be profiled the possibility of the absolute threat, that is to say, that of coming back to the silence or to the inarticulated cry of violence without words: "Justice is unjust. I speak truly, and you recognize the certainty of this truth under pain of death." Force contradicts justice by uttering pure contradiction: A is non-A, the just is nonjust, justice is unjust. But contradiction, the contra-dicting of the contradiction, is resolved without mediation or dialectic, *immediately*, for when force says that justice is unjust, it says *at the same time* that it is itself that is just. By uttering the contradiction of the nonjust just, force takes possession of justice, appropriates the just, and the strong is properly the just. And, with the same blow [*coup*], at one blow and only one, a *coup de force* that is a *coup de discours*, the strong one (the strongest one), by saying that it is just, is such. This is a felicitous performative whose enunciative situation makes its felicity, since it is not possible to contradict, because to contradict the discourse of force, that is, of power, is at once to be unjust and to expose oneself to force and to the strongest, which/whom one must follow. At the zero point where the mute violence of force, power, is canceled, the discourse of force *is* the force of discourse that does by saying and that, by saying it is just, makes itself just. At the same blow, we discover who the evil men are who, a little while back, were contradicting justice (without force): it is the strong who start to speak, that is, to hold forth a speech instead of striking and killing. Evil, the fact of evil, is the discourse of the strongest, that is, power, and far from politics being morality, it is ethics that at a single blow has become political. There is no morality, there is only politics.

"And thus being unable to make the just strong, the strong has been made just" (103-298). This is a second conclusion, which doubles back on and displaces the first. What was indicated in the first conclusion as a possibility (to give force to justice), because force in its discourse, power, had become justice, is revealed to be, in the second, an impossibility and a negative necessity: it is impossible to make the just strong, that is, to give force to justice, except in "words," by an infelicitous discourse that says without doing, a discourse both impotent and without effect, a ridiculous discourse. It is impossible to give force to justice: this negative necessity is but the reverse side of the positive necessity, very recognizable and without dispute, to follow the strongest, a necessity that in the discourse of force, in power, has become the power of discourse, a powerful and felicitous discourse, and the justification of force.

The initial constative of the necessity to follow the strongest is transformed, in and through the discourse of force, and in and through power (the discourse of power and power of discourse), in this final prescription: it is just to follow the strongest, because the strongest has called himself just, and it is just to follow the just. "The strong has been made just" (103-298). This final doing [*faire*] is a performative of language, an act of discourse of which Pascal's thought in its entirety has established the conditions of success and of pragmatic validity. All politics is discursive (the discourse of power), and it could well be that all discourse is political (the power of discourse). And yet Pascal holds forth a speech, he has spoken the violent silence of force, he has said the discourse of force appropriating justice for itself. Discourse and metadiscourse—who speaks in this way [*tenir ce langage*], who, that we call by the name of "Pascal"? What is his power? Is it political? And for what power does he speak?

II. The Clever Man and the Thought in the Back of the Mind

Such is the clever discourse of the clever man. "The reason of effects.—We must have a secret *thought* and judge everything accordingly while *speaking*, however, like the people" (91-336, my emphasis). To be clever is—before knowing how to do things [*savoir faire*] and being capable of applying one's knowledge to situations—to be disposed, able to act, alive, alert, agile, and ready to act in an instant; such is feeling, the nucleus of judgment with respect to reason:

> Reason acts slowly and with so many views on so many principles that must always be present, that at all hours it grows drowsy or strays. . . . Feeling does not act that way: it acts instantly and is always ready to act (821-252).

The clever man is agile like the great soul that traverses in an instant, at an infinite speed, all the between-two of extremes in an infinite agility whose *effect* is that of a firebrand, the illusion, there again, of a continuous and immobile line binding the "one" and the "other" with an immobile stroke.[5] In this sense the infinite distance between the point of the secret thought and the place of the common utterance has for *effect* an infinite proximity, a near-identity, a near-coincidence.

The labile position of the agile clever man is that of an utterance whose enunciation is *that of the infinite to the infinite*—the utterance, common opinion, and ordinary discourse whose *enunciation is of the infinite*: there is no true fixed and indivisible point, and there is no true totalizing and instantaneous position. All these "points," all these "wholes," are figures of the same fiction, because the order of size is animated by a continual flux from the whole to nothingness and from nothingness to the whole without the power to calm down, to rest in nothingness or in the whole always infinitely distant. And that for no other reason than the arbitrariness or the custom of a common error of placing, here or there, the indivisible, the fixed, the instant, and the zero. It is the discovery of the clever man: "When the truth about a thing is not known, it is a good thing that there is a common error that fixes the mind of men" (744-18), the thought in the back of the mind [*pensée de derrière*][6] that is not a common error but the constat that it is good that there be one.

To utter to infinity that there is no true position, no fixed position, is to place this utterance at the point of the whole or nothing, *to jump* outside of the order of size into an order that is different from it. The thought from the infinite to the infinite has the effect of indetermining all true fixed, totalizing, and indivisible positions. In itself, this thought is deprived of all determined content: it does not think of itself as content. Whatever the clever man thinks, whatever *his* thought is, it is immediately dissolved, destroyed, and indetermined by the function of the utterance whose discourse the clever man cannot "hold." While talking like the people, like everyone, of fixities, indivisibilities, and totalities, the clever man does not fix himself there. The fixed position, on the one hand, and the thought of the infinite, on the other, mark the dissolution of all place of truth, whether theoretical or practical. It is at once the place of the event of meaning in knowledge and the impossibility of expressing that meaning as such in a discourse that would be that of meaning. Meaning draws itself infinitely away from its discourse.

It is a clever, agile mind, a spirit of destruction in ceaseless movement, that is never at the place it utters; it is a spirit of rhythm oscillating in the continual reversal of the for and against; it is a spirit of mockery that talks like the people but judges everything with a thought in the back of the mind that is the point of the infinite to the infinite, a point that *in its discourse* can only be the "nothing-everything" of which his thoughts are never anything but effects momentarily and randomly distributed in the field of his thought. The clever man is the infinite spirit of irony dissolving all place of rest of thought. It is in this way that to mock philosophy is really to philosophize. Such is the thought in the back of the mind: not at all "dynamic" in its destructive place of work, it is the reason for the effects as simultaneous conjunction-disjunction of force and "meaning," the fantastic potential power of this figure that must be well understood.

For finally, if this thought is in the back of my mind, that signifies that I will never see it in the modality of the "see-in-my-thought" that is reflecting: a thought that I do not and cannot see as one of *my* thoughts, as *my* thought; a thought that is always outside of my head, that is not mine like my property, an attribute of my being, but that arrives unexpectedly *a tergo* and grasps hold of me. And if this thought is a thought from the back [*de dos*], always at my back, there is no use in turning my head to grasp hold of it: it is useless to turn around and do violence to oneself. There is no conversion possible toward it such as that which inaugurates the discovery of the principles of geometry.[7] It will always be unperceived, nonreflected, nonthetic, but it is through it that I am pushed and put into movement. It is a strangely secret force of which my judgment is the effect and my thought the place of its manifestation in the place of my discourse, when I speak like the people.

What, then, is this *other* force, different with an absolute difference and *completely other* than the one that inscribes itself in the discourse (of) power of which the power (of) discourse would only be the reproduction? Would it be the force of justice—which is without force of truth—which can do nothing in the kingdom of external actions?

> If it had been possible, force would have been put into the hands of justice, but force does not let itself be handled as one wants because it is a palpable quality, whereas justice is a spiritual quality that is disposed of as one wants: and thus we call just that which force observes to be so. Hence the right of the sword, because the sword gives a true right. Otherwise [*if it were not thus, if to carry a sword did not give a true right to be honored and respected by those who do not carry it*], we would see violence on one side and justice on the other. End of the twelfth *Provincial Letter* (85-878).

Precisely at the end of the twelfth letter the author challenges the Jesuit fathers in these terms:

> You believe you have force of impunity, but I believe I have truth and innocence. It is a strange and long war in which violence tries to oppress truth. All the efforts of violence cannot weaken the truth, and they only serve to exalt it the more. All the light of truth can do nothing to stop violence, and it only further irritates it. When force combats force, the more powerful destroys the lesser; when discourse is opposed to discourse, that which is true and convincing confounds

and dispels that which is only vanity and lies: but violence and truth can do nothing against each other. Let it not be supposed from this, however, that these things are equal; for there is this extreme difference, that the course of violence is limited by God's order, which leads its effects to the glory of the truth it attacks; whereas truth subsists eternally and ultimately triumphs over its enemies, because it is as eternal and powerful as God himself.[8]

III. Discourse-Power-Discourse: The Signs of Force

Sound opinions of the people. — To be elegant is not overly vain, for it shows that a great number of people work for one. It is to show by one's hair that one has a personal valet, perfumer, etc., by one's bands, thread, braid, etc. But it is not simply superficial, nor is it a simple harness, to have several arms [in one's service]. The more arms one has, the stronger one is. To be elegant is to show one's force (95-316).

This fragment effects an ironic pathway of meanings with the help of a double play on words: the people are *sound* [*sain*] in their opinions, and the elegant man [*le brave*] not too *vain* in his costume. For the elegant man is at once he who affronts danger courageously, the valiant and the valorous, and he who is dressed and adorned with care. This is an ironic pathway of meanings, because the relative vanity of the "elegant man" is turned back or shifted in value; meanwhile, value remains vanity, but it is a sound vanity, since the fragment explains the reason for the vanity and shows that its effect, in the opinion of the people who admire "elegant men" as valorous, is sound, for this "opinion conforms to reason and morality." To be elegant is at first *to show*, an ostentation that is the empty essence of vanity, since, by this show, the elegant man has value only in his appearance to others. To be elegant is to be one's appearance, to present oneself to others and by that *to represent* oneself through one's image in the gaze of others. But here suddenly the "classical" analysis of the effect of "vanity" by the moralist skids and slips toward the reason for the effect, for to be elegant is not only to show and be shown but also to show that a great number of people work for one. Thus the vain man is not as vain as the half-clever moralist thinks, for his vanity *makes* meaning. The elegant man, by showing himself, shows that he has several arms, or servants, and the more arms one has, the stronger one is. In this plurality there is force: "Plurality is the best avenue because it is visible and has the force to make itself be obeyed" (85-878).

How else to show that *one* has plurality for oneself — that is, the force of several arms — that a great number of people work for one, if not by signs? Hair, embroidery, ribbons, and the like: signs that are less those of beautiful adornment and noble appearance in the eyes of the people than effects of forces. The signifiers of this discourse—that is, the costume of the gentleman—refer back certainly to the signified of "quality," but as representatives or delegates of a force that, at this juncture, is that which is at work [*à l'œuvre*] in work. Signs are the effect of a force, but enslaved by a greater force: a sign of work and in work. A second angle of the analysis of force is indicated here. The stronger man, as we have seen, is stronger only through the annihilation of the less strong man, but the stronger man is also such only by enslaving the latter, that is, by *making* him *work* for him. The slave is a producer, for the master, of goods, which in turn are signs of the mastery of the master, and he can be considered by that as the operator of the transformation of the dominating force into the sign of that force, a transformation whose inner spring is the dominated force. From then on a discourse, understood as a particular system of signs, indicates at once a dominating force put into representation, a force reserved in and through the signs and a dominated and enslaved force that is the operator or producer of those signs. But whether it is a question of a force that annihilates or of one that enslaves, the signs always indicate a moment of domination, a plus factor that is a maximum of force. The stronger man "speaks" only to express his triumph. He could well say, "Justice is unjust"; his utterance *shows* his domination. The utterances of the discourse signify quite diverse meanings, but all show the same point, and all the significations will never be other than digressions with respect to the unique point that all these utterances point to, that is, the *right* of the stronger to signify. In other words, all discourse harbors an indication of violence beside or on top of its signification.

To be elegant is to have several arms: the individual organic body, the naked and hidden body, never seen in its nudity except in illness or death, is multiplied by signs into a social or political body. The visible body of the noble, the valorous and elegant man, is a body of signs, a being of discourse, but one whose signs show *real* multiplication and augmentation. The lace, bands, thread, braid, and hairstyle designate and indicate this multiplication and augmentation as body of power. It is in this way that the signs of the discourse acquire a signifying plus-value and through that an increase of force, precisely a power. In this sense signs, the effects of force put into representation, are themselves forces to the extent that they not only show force but also multiply it as effects, and they operate this multiplication and acquire the signifying plus-value of power only by being shown. It is in this representation, in this exhibition, that they become in their turn forces, to the extent to which they are submitted. To use signs is to show them, for they always designate, as if obliquely, the moment of force.

"But it is not simply superficial, nor is it a simple harness, to have several arms [in one's service]" (95-316). The clothes, the lace, the ribbons, the wig and its curls are not an addition, supplement, ornament, or decoration of the body. It is the body that is multiplied, the organic "instrument" that, passing into the architecture of the signs that cover it, acquires through it an ordered, instituted, and legitimated plurality, a power. "The more arms one has, the stronger one is." This equation formulates, in its rigor, the law of the rhetorical and political pleonasm of power and its institution. The accumulation of signs is none other than an accumulation of force reflected, represented, and reserved in power in proportion to the infinite desire of domination that is its essence.

From there comes the conclusion, in all the power [*puissance*] of its ambiguity, that to be elegant is to show one's force. To be elegant is to be valorous, to manifest one's force at the risk of violent death; meanwhile, to be vain (to be dressed and adorned with studied care) is equally to show it, but as power. Vanity simultaneously presents the "originary" value of the master who has run the risk of a struggle to the death and exhibits force multiplied in the signs of its representation: power.

The more arms *one* [*on*] has, the stronger *one* is: the strange subject of power, an anonymous indefiniteness. The representative system, the signs of force, produce the subject of power, but they also produce its object. To show one's force "absolutely" is always to show it to someone who acquires no other consistency than that of submitting to the power-signs, themselves effects of force. Produced by the discourse of force, which is power, the "people," in turn, hold forth their discourse in respectful and obedient behaviors or in the utterances that at once generalize their behaviors and justify them, whose generalization is their justification. The people's discourse is the recognition of justified force and its legitimation through the respect for obedience and for the self-legitimation of force in its power-discourse.

The Discourse of Respect

"Respect is to 'inconvenience yourself.' This appears vain, but it is quite right, for it amounts to saying: 'I would surely inconvenience myself if you had need of it, since I do so even when it does not serve you'" (80-317). The prescription of respect is reflexive: "Cause discomfort or unease [*malaise*] for yourself"; but it is not I who say to myself, "Inconvenience yourself," it is respect, and respect is none other than this prescription: "Inconvenience yourself." The prescription is without subject or object, unlike what it would be in autonomy where, giving to myself the prescription of respect, I would be at once he who decrees the order and he who obeys it. And yet that is saying too much, for respect does not even speak. *It does not say, it is*: "Inconvenience yourself." A reflexive mechanism here is internalized and autonomized, and only its effect is perceptible as a discomfort contrary to all natural finality or all empirical utility. Respect is vain, since it is of no use, either to him who is its object or to him who is its subject: it is a simple sign of a subjugation without cause, motive or finality.

However, the behavior of respect harbors a final implication [*implicature*]:

"'I would surely inconvenience myself if you had need of it, since I do so even when it does not serve you'" (80-317). But this implication, which is declared only by the "clever man" who analyzes the reason for the effect "respect," this implication of a subjugation that, having for cause the need of the one and the finality of the behavior of the other, is displaced onto the absolute, since respect is free, self-sufficient, without cause or end—this implication is unconscious. I inconvenience myself because respect is "Inconvenience yourself." "Law is law and nothing more. Custom is the whole of equity, for the sole reason that it is received; that is the mystic foundation of its authority" (60-294).

But the clever man adds: "Furthermore, respect is to distinguish the great. Now if respect meant sitting in an armchair, we should be showing everyone respect, and then there would be no way of marking distinctions; but by inconveniencing ourselves we make the distinction quite clear" (80-317). The effect is at once supplementary and bound to immediate prescription (respect is "Inconvenience yourself"), but *furthermore*, and *all the more so as* it prescribes without justification, it serves to distinguish. A sign of subjugation without cause or finality of usage, respect is such all the more so as it has for finality an immediate discernment. I distinguish spontaneously a great man all the more so as I inconvenience myself spontaneously in front of him. The dialectic of master and slave works well, but it is empty. Unlike the production of goods for the master's use, in which the slave "inconveniences himself" because the master needs them, this production of the use-value includes a plus-value but of signs, the plus-value of discourse and of power. In effect, these goods (bands, thread, braid, hairstyle, and so on) are less of use than of significance. They indicate, furthermore and all the more so, the mastery of the master, that it is a question of products of behavior without natural finality or empirical usefulness.

The reasons for the effects. "Sound opinions of the people" (95-316): the opinions of the people, utterances of beliefs, the discourse of ordinary language. "The reasons for the effects.—We must have a thought in the back of the mind and judge everything accordingly, while speaking, however, like the people" (91-336). The discourse of political belief is one of multiple discourses of belief: it is the discourse of the effects of force, and beliefs are the representation-effects of force. How can signs become forces? How are signs reflected forces, which are represented by and producers of their subject-object? How does the discourse (of) power institute itself in the power (of) discourse? How does power equal discourse, and discourse, power? What is the function of the imagination in the institution of power and discourse, of discourse-power, of power-discourse?

"Imagination.—It is the dominant part of man, the master of error and falsity.... This superb potential power, the enemy of reason, which it likes to control and dominate to show how much it is capable of in all things, has established a second nature in man" (44-82). The dominant part, a master of error, the superb potential power that controls and dominates, imagination, which occupies in the man-individual the position of force in the sociopolitical world, operates in the soul the same transformations that force operates in the world, the former accomplishing itself in custom or second nature, the latter in power. Just as the state of nature is a fiction of origin, a natural being of man is a fiction of the imagination that, by another turn, denies itself to better constitute its empire. "What gives respect and veneration to persons, works, laws, and the great, if not this imagining faculty? How inadequate are all the riches of the earth without its approval!" (44-82). It is then that the clever man, who judges of everything through a thought in the back of the mind, all the while talking like the people, constructs an ideal-typical scene, a scenario that "models" [*modelise*] the power of the imagination on souls and bodies: that of a magistrate attending a sermon. We must read this paragraph well and understand it correctly, not as a simple vignette illustrating one of the commonplaces of moralistic criticism through anecdote but as a rigorous experimental model whose calculated operations will produce a theoretical and practical result, as a near-demonstration of forces through their effects. At the first the chain, the strings of the people's respect for the magistrate, of the magistrate's for reason and of reason's for the divine word of charity:

> Would you not say that this magistrate, whose venerable age imposes respect on a whole people, governs himself with a pure and sublime reason and judges of things by their nature without stopping at those vain circumstances that wound only the imagination of the weak? See him enter during a sermon to which he brings a devout zeal, reinforcing the solidity of reason with the ardor of his charity. There he is ready to hear it with an exemplary respect (44-82).

Respect of the people for a venerable old age, respect of the noble old man for the government of pure reason that consists of judging the true essence of things without stopping at their accidental circumstances, respect finally of this subject of pure reason for the word of God made public by his mouthpiece. But see here how the singular circumstances of the predicator's discourse of charity, at the point where the chains and strings of respect in their universal generality hook on solidly, in an instant, in a burst of laughter, will undo the discourse-powers—the circumstances or effects of nature, art and chance: "At the appearance of the predicator, if nature has given him a hoarse voice and an odd sort of face, if his barber has shaved him badly, or if by chance he is not too clean, whatever great truths he may announce, I wager the loss of seriousness of our senator" (44-82). One should question this laugh, and this wager made by the clever man that a laugh will shake the grave personage. But what matters here is only to mark the functioning of the "experimental" framework that the clever discourse of the clever man has constructed: if the "negative" and singular effects of nature, art, and chance undo, in and through imagination and in one instant, the chain of the respect of the people for venerable old age, for pure reason that judges the nature of things, and for the ardor of charity for the divine word, it is then that old age, reason, and charity are only "positive" effects of the imaginary potential. The model demonstrates, with a successful mental experiment, the general positive effects and their reason through the singular negative effects of a same potential that can be grasped only through them and in them. It is in this way that there is no law and, even less, rules of imaginary effects. There are only effects and the reasons for these effects, of which the discourse of the clever man does not utter the truth but limits itself to declaring the strong probability: "I wager the loss of seriousness of our senator" (44-82).

The imagination is a potential, a dominant potential. But what about the force of this potential that puts a price on things by making signs of them, signs whose power to make the people believe [*faire croire*] is immediate and irresistible? Is it specific and particular, this force whose field of effects we are told is universal?

> This mystery has been well known to our magistrates. Their red robes, their ermines in which they wrap themselves like furry cats, the courts where they judge, the *fleurs de lis*, all this august apparel was very necessary, and if physicians did not have their cassocks and slippers and learned doctors their square bonnets and robes that are too large, never would they have duped the world which cannot resist such an authoritative show. If the magistrates had true justice and if the physicians had the true art of healing, they would have no use for square bonnets. . . . But having only imaginary sciences, they must take on these vain instruments that strike the imagination with which they are concerned, and through that, in effect, they attract respect toward themselves (44-82).

Disguises, affectations, and masks: all these vain instruments have that much more effect by being even more vain and that much more force by being simple signs with no value other than that of marking the quite empty place of true justice or science, of taking their place and, by doing that, of justifying their imaginary justice or truth by striking the imagination. This is where we perceive that the imaginary is at once in the subject and the object, or rather that through the play of signs, the effects of forces, and those of the forces of beliefs, the subjects—those who have only imaginary sciences—and the object—the imagination they are dealing with—are produced through the very functioning of the imaginary, for it is signs, those *vain* instruments, that entail irresistibly the respect of those who submit to them for those who wear them. The essential thing here is neither the just sentence of justice nor true science, not even the unjust man or false knowledge; what is at stake in the play of signs, in the play of discourse, is making people believe [*faire croire*] the reality of simulacra. "Through that, in effect, they attract respect toward themselves" (44-82). Signs are power, and power is only the irresistible force of their discourse or, rather, the effect of that force.

"Only men of war have not disguised themselves in this way, because in effect their part is more essential; they establish themselves through force, the others through affectation" (44-82). The *particular quality* of the warrior, even in the pomp of a parade — "these armed troops . . . , the trumpets and drums that walk ahead" (44-82), the guards, the scarred veterans, the forty thousand janissaries of the Great Lord — is to signify or to recall the "originary" violence of force, and even more so the absolute threat of the mortal danger that constitutes the limit of the discourse that is power. And if the king, our king, does not disguise himself, if he does not mask himself with extraordinary clothes to appear extraordinary, it is because his majesty is none other than the armed troop that surrounds him, like the discourse of signs that belong to him. For this troop has hands only for him, and they are enslaved forces, productive not of force but of signs: "The more arms one has, the stronger one is." The scarred veterans, trumpets, drums, and legions are to the king what the bands, thread, braid, and wig are to the elegant man. They are the king's *costume*, which *designates* his body as a body multiplied in majesty. Majesty is venerable only through it. The force of his guards is the form of his affectation, the ferocity of his men-at-arms, his disguise, the scarred veterans, his amusement; they assign him his power with drums and trumpets. "One's reason would have to be quite refined to be able to gaze upon the Great Lord as upon another man [*as upon any man*], surrounded in his superb seraglio by forty thousand janissaries" (44-82). Such is the concern of the people and of the clever man, who speaks like the people and who watches the royal pomp pass. Here is the concern of the thought in the back of the mind by which the clever man judges everything; here is the brief fiction that he proposes: "That it be put to the test: leave a king entirely alone [*reduced to the royal substance, whatever qualities be there*], with nothing to satisfy the senses, with no care to occupy his mind, with no company or diversion, with complete leisure to think about himself, and we will see that a king without diversion is a man full of misery" (137-142). The omnipotence of the absolute monarch that the young Louis XIV's discourse summarizes in the formula of the power of all power, "The state is me," is subject to the same analysis as is the ego by itself, in a metonymic transaction of qualities that, in the field of the imaginary, become signs, effects of force that make believe [*faire croire*], reactive forces presented in representation.

The "Genesis" of the Institution

> The strings attaching man's mutual respect are in general strings of necessity; for there must be differences of degree, all men wanting to dominate and all not being able to, but some being able.
> Let us imagine, then, that we see these strings beginning to form.

OVERTURE □ 33

There is no doubt that men will fight each other until the stronger party oppresses the weaker, and there is finally a dominant party. But once that is determined, then the masters, who do not want the war to continue, ordain that the force that is in their hands will pass down as it pleases them; some put it to the choice of the people, others to succession by birth, etc.
 And that is where the imagination begins to play its role. Until then, pure force did it: now, force is maintained by imagination in a certain party, in France by gentlemen, in Switzerland by commoners, etc.
 Now, these strings that attach respect to this or that person in particular are strings of imagination (828-304).

This fragment draws in its very movement the process of power's genesis, whose *terminus a quo* would be force in its generality and necessity and the *terminus ad quem*, representation in its imaginary particularity. "The strings attaching man's mutual respect are in general strings of necessity [*and it is necessary to follow the strongest*]. Now these strings that attach respect to this or that person in particular are strings of the imagination. [*Force has contradicted justice, saying that it is unjust and that it itself is just. And thus . . . one has made the strong just.*]" (828-304; 103-298). But, whether as point of departure or of arrival, the same term comes back: the strings that attach respect; and with this transit of the same between two heterogeneous things is given an explanation of the genetic process of power. The effects of force become a system of signs, that is to say, still a force, but heterogeneous from the former, a force in representation. The heterogeneity is marked here by the transformation of the generality of respect — the necessary expression of endured force — into the particularity or diversification of imaginary respect, a diversity that is in its turn the "institutional" mark or, rather, trace of the arbitrariness of force as represented in the signs that force appropriates for itself. The process that the fragment describes, in its structure as in its content, makes the relationship between the imagination (representation as the imaginary of force) and the arbitrariness of the discourse of force (power) appear [*faire apparaître*], but as well that between the diversification of the institution of force as power (the diverse types of constitutions and frameworks of state) and the self-legitimation of representation where force institutes itself (political power).
 Respect — we saw it above, and this fragment stresses it — is the social bond par excellence. It is what holds individuals together in a group as a society. Why, then, does respect have this originary social function? Why, rather than friendship or pity, is it posed here as the origin of social function in general? If for no other reason than that respect is the most general expression of the mechanical necessity of force and that the *socius* is, first of all, a mechanistic physics of forces. The image of the "string" realizes, in its brutal figure, the relationship

manifested by one force to another, by the stronger to the less strong, by the dominant to the dominated force. "The strings attaching men's mutual respect are in general strings of necessity; for there must be differences of degree" (828-304). What is uttered here is not an obligatory description in which a hierarchy or a structure of order is valorized but, rather, a physical necessity producing a "vertical" diversification, in which the differences between quantities of force are the reason by composition. The axiom on which this social physics of respect is founded is that of tyranny, the "universal desire for domination, outside of its own order" (58-332): "all men wanting to dominate and all not being able to, but some being able" (828-304). Man in general is defined by his desire to be the strongest, that is, the absolutely strong. But the satisfaction of this infinite desire for death, for the homogenization of heterogeneities, is infinitely deferred, and this *difference* between the universal will [*vouloir*] to dominate and the individual abilities [*pouvoirs*] to realize it is "synchronically" constitutive of the necessary differences in the "degrees" of human society in general and in the bonds, the "strings of respect," that organize it. All men want to dominate, all are not able to do so, but only some. This satisfaction by some of the infinite desire to dominate is not yet power but only potential power, and the highest degree of potential is then the dominant force with respect to the dominated forces. Force in its manifestation of potential is not the annihilation of other forces but the differentiated enslavement of them where they are "reserved" for the use of the strongest.

How, then, is such a discourse possible? "Let us imagine, then, that we see these strings beginning to form" (828-304). It is indeed a question of the description of a process of constitution. The clever man positions himself outside the described situation as theoretical subject, as "savant" who contemplates the social genesis. Still, this genetic theory of society is only a fiction: it is not a real story that is described but, there again, an experimental model, built to reveal and explain the physics of the *socius* in general. Meanwhile, this figure, by its "theoretical" implications, signifies that there is no state of nature and *then* a civil state but that there has always been society and, consequently, power; and the theoretical fiction of a genesis of the social state from the state of nature has no other function than to reveal, not an origin of power in general and of political power in particular, but the transcendental condition of power and of the institution in general. And the condition that all institutions presuppose theoretically is that of violence, struggle, and war between men. All institutional, instituting, or instituted discourse is made only by marking the traces of violence, of violence that is never other than trace, that appears as violence only by being marked and repeated, and that the discourse of the clever man in its theoretical function re-marks.

"There is no doubt that men will fight each other until the stronger party oppresses the weaker, and there is finally a dominant party" (828-304). In the struggle of the forces and at the moment of its triumph, the stronger force, a part of the dynamic composition of the forces in conflict, is transformed by this very struggle into the dominant party, an instance no longer physical or mechanical but political and already institutional. For the violent conflict of forces is already substituted a hierarchy of the potential powers of graduated enslavement. Let us picture, then, the evening of victory, that very moment that determines who is the strongest and that, in the universal desire for domination that some realize in this instant, is once, but *for always and ever after*, the moment of domination, of the end of the war and of the definition of the strongest part as the dominant party. "Then the masters—who do not want the war to continue" (828-304), who want to transform the "once," the "once" of victory, into a "for always," the mark, the strongest perhaps, of the universal desire for tyranny outside of the *proper order* at the struggle of the forces that is the present and unique instant of triumph—the masters pose themselves as institutors of continuity through a double will. First, a negative will: they do not want the repetition of the violent moment of the confrontation of the forces; they do not want, through a cowardice as fundamental as their worth and its desire for glory, to risk death again. A positive will next: "They order that the force that is in their hands succeed as pleases them." This is a discourse of prescription that institutes a definitive order, a realized will or desire, *but in the discourse*, which is the place for cowardice not to risk potential power again. From then on the always possible, aleatory, and empirical continuity of war is transformed into institutional, obligatory, and legitimate succession.

This movement of mastery described in the fragment as necessary movement has nonetheless for final content an arbitrary decision. "Force must, *say* the masters, *succeed* force; force must repeat my force as the strongest." But how is it possible without a new violent trial in which, with no other discourse, they risk their force to manifest it once again as the strongest? So that force can continue to be exerted without risk, *a rule for the succession of force as just rule and equitable law, whatever this rule or law is, must be uttered.* "And we *can* do it, continue the masters, *now*, since we are the strongest in this evening of victory."[9] The arbitrariness of the decision that rules the succession of force reflects the force of the masters, but not as force, which would necessitate the repetition of its manifestation in the struggle to the death. The arbitrariness of the rule's prescriptive decision reflects force in signs that are its delegates and placeholders, where it is converted into a representation whose function is at once to indicate and reserve it. Force is reflected in institutional discourse and in political power. With the arbitrariness of the decision of the masters—the discourse-power—is discovered the root of the diversification of force in general and of its necessity. Their discourse of order—of prescription and commandment—which institutes the succession of force, can only be an arbitrary decision, since it has no other foundation than their current force and since the foundation is of an order other than what it founds. This is where the diversity of institutions comes from, which is none other than the diversification of the discourse of the "justice" of force. "An amusing justice that is, limited by a river! Truth on this side of the Pyrenees, error on the other" (60-294).

"And that is where imagination begins to play its role" (828-304). The discourse of the masters reflects in its signs the force that is in their hands; and we understand indeed the force of its prescription at the moment it is uttered, since then the masters triumph because they are the strongest and because the threat of death—without words—that weighs on those who would like to contradict or accuse is then fully efficacious. But everything becomes shaky in time. In truth, what makes of force's discourse an obligatory discourse, and what gives power to power's discourse, is the imagination's own potential power in its relationship to custom in particular, and very precisely the internalization of this discourse of the arbitrariness of the decision of the masters as representation of obligatory belief. Of the power of power's discourse Pascal gives the definitive formula: "It is force that is held by the imagination in a certain party" (828-304), in a word, respect for the established order. Thus the universal diversity of the institutions of power and of the power of their discourses has for exact corollary the suppression of all possible diversity in the instituted order of a determined society.

The discourse of the imaginary buttressed by the discourse of force and giving it its force of obligation, its justice—such is the ethico-political institution. Power of discourse and discourse of power, the institution is only the means of conserving force outside of its application in the representation of belief.[10]

"Vain opinions of the people": they are such because in the discourse that the people hold forth—their belief—where power (the discourse of force) is really applied, the effect of this preserved, reserved, and reflected force is expressed in an imaginary system of signs. The people speak truly when they say that gentlemen *must* be honored, but they are wrong in taking the imaginary for the real, the effect for the reason for the effect: birth is an effective advantage. Birth is not a natural real advantage, but it is an effective advantage; it is the real effect of an institution, a power and a belief bound by reciprocal buttressing. It is the forgetting, through the people's discourse, of the institutional imaginary that very exactly makes the reality of the effect of the institution.

"Nobility is a great advantage that, at eighteen years of age, gives a man the standing, recognition and respect that another man could have merited at fifty. It is thirty years won with no effort" (104-322). It is indeed thus that the clever man speaks—like the people—by judging everything with a thought in the back of the mind.

First Entrance
"The State Is Me," or the King's Narrative

The King's Narrative,
or How to Write History

Let us suppose a text written around 1670:

Project for the History of Louis XIV
To M. Colbert

The design I have had the honor to talk to you about, although a little confusedly, is to write down the whole of this last war.

I would not understand this to be done in the form of a journal, or of an account and simple Memoirs, or of eulogies or panegyrics, which are all of different characters and styles and must be distinguished from one another. It would rather be as a great History in the manner of Livy, Polybius, and the other Ancients.

The state of all Europe, and particularly that of the two Kingdoms of France and Spain, would have to be represented from the very beginning. It is a fine field for speaking in abbreviated form of all the King's virtues, and for enabling [the reader] to well conceive [*bien faire concevoir*] of his greatness in all sorts of ways, through the secret comparison that the reader will himself make between His Majesty and all the other Sovereigns.

Next, the Historian and not the lawyer must explain the causes of the rupture and the King's just claims. A summary, but well-distilled and -studied narrative of the reasons the two Crowns allege, written in chosen terms and reduced to the expression of natural meaning, would enable the least enlightened persons to understand what the cleverest have difficulty unraveling in great volumes. At the end I would refute, but always in the same style of narration, the principal grounds of the *Bouclier d'Etat* [the Shield of State], which is the work of a clever man and which is creating a stir among foreigners.

All of this section, as it demands some degree of knowledge and must equally avoid both length and obscurity, would not be the easiest. I have, however, reflected sufficiently upon it and would hope to emerge from it to my honor.

Next I would work on what few modern historians have known how to do well, and almost no Frenchman: that is, the principal Actors in this war would have to be made known while supposing that no one yet knows them. For we write for posterity, which will not have seen them, and it is not even always true that to see them is to know them.

These sorts [*manières*] of portraits or characters, when they are well touched up, must be neither too great in number nor all in succession, but dispersed and placed with a certain degree of art and diversity. They must report in four words their birth and remarkable actions; they must subtly penetrate the talents and influence of each; they should say neither too little nor too much about them; and when one knows how to always convey much more than what is said about them, an admirable effect is produced. This is one of the great secrets for animating history and preventing it from ever dragging or tiring. The mind of the Reader, once he forms these different ideas and then sees each person fulfill them, makes a very delightful spectacle of it for himself.

From among all these characters, that of His Majesty must burst forth.

The King must be praised everywhere but, so to speak, without praise, by a narrative of all that he has been seen to do, say, and think. It must appear disinterested but be lively, piquant, and sustained, avoiding in its expressions all that veers toward the panegyric. In order to be better believed, it should not give him the magnificent epithets and eulogies he deserves; they must be torn from the mouth of the reader by the things themselves. Neither Plutarch nor Quintius Curtius praised Alexander in any other way, and he was well praised. It would no doubt be hoped that His Majesty approve and accept this design, which can almost not be well executed without him. But he must not seem to have accepted, known about, or ordered it.

History overlooks many circumstances that journals and Memoirs report. It does not concern itself with by how many paces a trench has been moved forward or which regiments mount the guard every day, when nothing extraordinary resulted. But in compensation, when it is a question of the Master and of an informative example of his value, firmness, and great sense, of which our King has given us a thousand, history lifts and makes the most of many little things about actions and principal persons that journals and Memoirs are accustomed to neglect. History puts all the great things it encounters in a better light through a nobler and more composed style, which encloses a lot in a little space with no wasted words.

Short and sensible reflections; particular discourses; military harangues; secret motives; the Princes' interests; negotiations; councils; the various sentiments of the public; agreeable descriptions of countries, cities, peoples, and their mores, of encampments, works, and the marches of armies: everything finds its place there. If one does not know how to melt and alloy all of this together into a solid body, full of a variety of forces and brilliance, how to paint rather than tell, how to make the imagination see [*faire voir*] everything that is put on paper, how to attract the readers by that, and how to interest them in what is happening, it is no longer History. It is at most a register, or chronicle.[1]

I. Traps

"To M. Colbert: The design I have had the honor to talk to you about, although a little confusedly, is to write down the whole of this last war."

Thus opens the report Pellisson addresses to Colbert, setting forth a project for Louis XIV's history. It hinges in its first sentence on a reflection, a reference "outside of the text," a dialogue, two alternating voices that have evoked, by fits and starts, a project—but maybe more if one accepts the double meaning of "design": it is a plan of production or enterprise, but also a representation, sketch, or schema of the history itself.[2] In this reminder, effected in good administrative order, Pellisson's design is twofold: to construct the paradigm and define the norms and rules of History in general, but also to draw the plan of the future product and trace the articulations of the great syntagm of the king's history, or at least its first sequence—"the whole of this last war." From the very beginning, therefore, in this reminder, there is a hesitation or, rather, a twofold understanding: it is simultaneously a question of determining a *manner* and, with it, a normative system—how *should one write* History? And to sketch a *matter*, and with it a structure or plan: *what I, Pellisson, will write*, the king's history, the king "made-written" as history. This double folding-back of the paradigm and syntagm, of which the text carries the traces throughout its development, will permit, in the end, the definition of a new object. Thanks to the confusion between the universal utterer who promulgates the rules of historical discourse and the single utterer who proposes to tell the historical narrative, the historical writing of *Louis XIV*—because it has precisely the king for object—will transform the paradigm "History" into a particular *narrative* and, inversely, make of this narrative a universal *model*. Louis XIV makes history, but it is history that is made in what he does, and at the same time his historian, by writing what he does, writes what must be written.

This introductory sentence, then, draws a certain representation of "history"—*Historie* and *Geschichte*[3]—at a time when Versailles is being built and organized, when the royal sun is climbing to the French and European zenith, and when the power of state, to speak in Hegelian language, is being universalized in a single "ego." A representation of History, no doubt, but one that indicates a twofold strategy of the power whose place of convergence and articulation, History, can be named along with the tradition of absolutism. I propose, therefore, to read the report, addressed by Pellisson to Colbert and setting forth the project of Louis XIV's history, as an example of the power of representation. A paradigmatic example.

Double Trap

An example that is paradigmatic to the extent of the reversibility of the expression "power of narrative" as "narrative of power." An emblematic text of the perfect—or what wishes itself to be perfect—correspondence of narrative and power: hence the absolutism of both narrative and power, which is not evaluated as a degree, or determined quantity, of force but is evaluated according to the characteristic of complete recuperation, of total coextensivity of power and narrative. There is neither excess nor lack, and no smudging, at least in Pellisson's project. Hence also, on these two three-centuries-old pages, it is possible to make some reflections that are not without practical value today on the relationships between the writer and political power, between the intellectual and the state.

It is a text that is a memoir, report, or memorandum of a writer to a politician, the obligatory mediator between him and power itself, the king—but one that, at the same time, aims to persuade the minister to intervene with his master so that the official responsibility of this writing will be accorded to the man of letters. It is a discourse on history and on the norms and rules of this particular kind of narrative, but it must be effected only in the persuasive framework of the person who will be its object, and it alone has the power, and all the power, to constitute him as subject of this narrative.

All of the "address" is thus a trap, but it is there only in order to expose another trap. What will bring about the king's favorable decision to name Pellisson royal historiographer is the efficacy of a plan, of a narrative machine susceptible of trapping the future readers of the royal history's narrative, of constituting them as subjects of the king and of subjugating them to his power as history's subject. Nevertheless, in order to acquire the position of having the power to write this narrative and, this being done, to make those who will read it fall into the trap of the history, it is less important for Pellisson to persuade Colbert and, through him, Louis XIV, that he possesses all the necessary knowledge, and it is less important for him to make it known to his omnipotent interlocutors that he knows how to write [*savoir écrire*], than it is to dismantle in front of them the mechanisms of the historical narrative's power over its readers, and the frameworks and techniques of manipulating the reader by the power of a narrative of absolute power that the king incarnates and that his minister personifies by delegation.

In all of this business Pellisson is, no doubt, in the position of importunate beggar; but the dispatch of the report founds a subtle tactic aimed at establishing a contract of services, a tactic in which the situations of power and force between the man of letters and the man of power are exchanged, inverted, and overturned from equally shared presuppositions and implications: "Give me the reponsibility of being 'your' historiographer. I will give you a history, 'yours,' but with the precondition that 'I *can*not write your history if I do not receive the office from you.'" This condition is understood, and it implies, in return, a certain number of specific characteristics concerning the historian's position, at once with respect to the history he plans to write and with respect to the king and his actions, which are its object.

In other words, Pellisson, a friend of Fouquet's, a prisoner recently released from the Bastille—a beggar of the royal power for the favor of the office of writer, exerts in his turn a formidable power on the latter to the extent that he reveals himself to the king as potentially having a power equal to his own.[4] To write the history of the royal power is to give to this power the means necessary for it to exert itself as absolute by signifying to it, in two pages, the equality or reciprocity of the power of historical narrative and the power of historical action, and of the power of the narrator of the royal history and the power of the actor in that history.

In this way political omnipotence, paradoxically, is absolute only on the condition that it divide itself, but *equally*, in perfect representation. The project presented to Colbert is the first "thrust" [*coup*] in an inaugural match whose conclusion will be the naming of Pellisson to the official position of king's historiographer; it is the scission between an action in which political omnipotence is manifested and a narrative of this action that must operate its omnipotent effects; it is representation, certainly, but not mirrored,[5] because it is perfect only in that it is constructed through the exchange and permutation of the positions of power; it is a representation whose structure is not that of reflection but of a technical-tactical machine that converts heterogeneous forces without loss or supplement: the historian "needs" the king, because he can tell the king's history only if the king calls him to his side and gives him the power to write [*le pouvoir-écrire*]. He "needs" the king, because he can produce the narrative only by applying (in the sense that one speaks in mechanics of the point of application of a force) the force of political power to a certain use of language, discourse, or writing. But the king "needs" the historian, because political power can find its completion, *its absolute*, only if a certain use of force, its concrete expression, is the point of application of the force of narrative power. In this way operates the chiasmus between political and discursive power, an exchange whose operator is the project presented by Pellisson and whose final product must be the total and perfect narrative representation of the history that Louis XIV makes and the one that Pellisson describes.

"It would no doubt be hoped that His Majesty approve and accept this design, which can almost not be well executed without him. But he must not seem to have accepted, known about, or ordered it." Appoint me official historiographer, but do not make that appointment official. The only, practical, quality of a trap is to be neither seen nor known by the prey that must fall into it. But I cannot set the trap of the historical narrative if the king does not give me the power to do so. The only outlet is for both sides to keep the secret of this complicity. Thus Pellisson, in his turn, traps the king and forces his decision while seeming to respect the freedom of his omnipotence. The historian "positions" the king as actor of the history, not only as the unique object of the narrative to come but also as the necessary and sufficient condition of its narration: the narrator-historian and the actor-king are the closest possible to each other and nearly indiscernible. But it is no less necessary, for the narrative to be able to function to the absolute of its power, that the strange enunciative structure be erased from the utterances it produced—that structure being the historian-narrator of the narrative as double and simulacrum of the actor-king of the history in general and in particular of that event of the history that consists of writing it. The whole of Pellisson's tactic rests, therefore, on the king's evaluation, in terms of political power, of the strategy of a narrative not yet written, a strategy that he sets forth in terms of stylistic and rhetorical tactics whose ensemble constitutes the narrative instance. Therefore, the *Project* indicates a double instance of discourse: one is the tactical, present, and punctual instance of Pellisson as author of the *Project for the History of Louis XIV*, addressed to Colbert and aimed at obtaining the office of historiographer; the other is the strategic, future, conditional, and uncertain instance of Pellisson as narrator of the narrative of Louis XIV's history, carrying out in this way the functions attached to his office. But the tactic of Pellisson as author is and can be effective for the king only through the evaluation that the latter will make of the strategy of Pellisson as narrator. Now this strategy, in its turn and inversely, can be effective only if the tactic succeeds—hence the necessity of slipping the drawing surreptitiously into the design, the narrative into the discourse, and the matter of the history into the manner of the narrative; better yet, by making this slippage a decisive factor in the success of the strategy, he also makes it a key element in the success of the tactic. These two instances of discourse hinge on each other, govern each other reciprocally, and have different objectives and addressees, but they are both in situations of interaction—the king with the reader, and the office of historiographer with the writing of history. The instances are all the more solidly linked as their dynamic relationship bestows political and narrative power on an exchange and transformation whose reversibility relies on a complex manipulation of the past and future by the subject of the enunciation. It is indeed a question of *making* the august addressee of the *Project read* the futures as pasts. Of course, the history has yet to be written, and Pellisson's report is not, in any way, a sample of it, but it is as if it were, because the manner of writing it is valid for the matter of what could be told. It is a question, inversely, of transferring the modality of the past utterance—necessity—to the future enunciation—probability.

The benefit drawn from the transformation is evident: history exists, in essence, in the mode of universal injunction; its application and realization can only necessarily flow from it. The paradigm of the ideal kind of history has been substituted for the historic real narrative syntagm to-be-written and the contingency of probable futures, a contingency reduced under the nontemporal necessity of an analytic deduction without risk. Consequently, the injunction can disappear, and the discourse of the manner of writing can be pursued and completed in the mode of a description of what is history: it already exists—"My history is made; all that remains is to write it."

It is not surprising, then, that to the double instance of the "locutor" corresponds a double instance of the "allocutee": the king (through Colbert), who is the necessary and sufficient condition of the narration of the history addressed to him, and the reader, who is the immediate and future addressee of the narrative-to-be-written. But Pellisson (tactical instance) addresses the king less by speaking of the history that he has made his project than by discoursing on the reader whom he will address once he has written it (strategic instance). Better yet, the most effective means of addressing the king now is precisely to speak only of the potential and future reader whom the king's history will address. So Pellisson, author of the project for the royal history to be transmitted to the king, stages himself as narrator of the narrative by staging his reader, his addressee, and by constructing *for the king* a representation of the reader who would result from the effects of his manner of writing the king's history. Whence, once again, comes the strange structure of the text's addressee, who is never placed as a "you" but always as a "he," the "he" of majesty or the manipulated "he," a structure in which, however, the latter is the means of manipulation of the former and the former the power that permits the operation of which the latter is the result. It is a question then, for the "addressor," of obtaining from his omnipotent "addressee," His Majesty, a transfer of power authorizing him to write his narrative, but he can obtain it only through the *simulation* of a reader of this narrative-to-be-written. This reader can only be a *simulacrum*, since the narrative does not exist, but he has the immense advantage of functioning as a *lure* for that political power whose fundamental aim is absolutism. Now this simulation, whose product is the "mannequin"-addressee, is none other than the discourse of the manner of writing history substituted for the narrative of the historical matter, that is, the display of the effects of this manner in a possible narrative, effects that form a system and constitute the "simulacrum"-reader, who, from that point on, cannot not be that subject (at once political and narrative) perfectly and absolutely subjugated to the power of the historian-king.

Bad Narrative Genres

It is no doubt not without interest to specify the theoretical and practical stakes involved in the continuous operation of closure of historical narrative representation—and that for two reasons. The first concerns the determination of that specific manner of writing called "history" or "great history," a definition of a genre of writing that is obtained through complex "cut-outs" across other different stylistic modes. The second is perhaps even more essential to my purpose. If this specific manner of writing a narrative and this strategic construction of the simulacrum-reader are one and the same, it is probable that the analysis of this cut-out of historical genres will permit us to approach the *principle* of Pellisson's strategy, the *discursive law* ruling his successive thrusts, their distribution, and the progressive composition of the effects of force that this strategy brings into play.

The initial movement of the author of the *Project* consists, as we have seen, of disqualifying two types of historical writing: chronicles and registers, on the one hand, journals and memoirs, on the other. There is his "attack," and it will furnish him, in the end, with two decisive thrusts at the conclusion of the match he has engaged in.

What is brought into question here, from beginning to end of the operation, is at once a certain type of subject of history and a certain notion of historical time. The surface criticism of journals and memoirs no doubt rests on the fact that this genre of writing history gets lost in base and common circumstances, details and ordinary things. But this bringing into question is founded on a more essential interrogation, which is perceived in the text only *a contrario*. Indeed, journals and memoirs imply, by definition, a reference to a subject who writes *his* history—the history of what has happened *to him* and that of which he has been spectator, witness, or actor. Journalistic and memorialistic accounts, by definition, pose their own subjects, and the circumstances spoken about in the text of the *Project* are those surrounding an action by an individual who affirms that the things—the events—occurred just as he writes about them: a singular history, in reference to a singular subject, who is inscribed in the narrative itself as producer both of the narrative and of the action that the narrative tells about. Pellisson, therefore, disqualifies a particular type of autobiography or discourse whose narrativity is subordinated to the explicit position, in the narrative itself, of the narrating subject who says "I." This is a problem at once theoretical and political: theoretical, because what is the difference between history and the historical narrative written in the first person? And political, because what is the significance of restraints when cast onto *subjects* of history? The theoretical question of historical narrative is that of its pragmatic value: how can a narrative pose a reference or make it be believed [*faire croire*]? How, while reading a historical narrative, do I pose, suppose, or presuppose that *this happened*, that this (the past event) took place, in all autonomy, independently of the subject who says so? Or, more precisely, how is it that, while reading the history, do I pose, suppose, or presuppose not only that it actually happened in that way but also that it is true for everyone universally?

On this point, precisely, hinges the political problem. If this presupposition (or position) of reference and truth is possible, it is because the subjects of the history do not exist or *no longer* exist. It is less because—to paraphrase Benveniste's famous formula—the events seem to tell themselves to the extent to which they were produced on the horizon of history,[6] than because henceforth there is no longer more than *one* universal subject and one absolute actor of the History, and because this sole actor of History is one with the subject writing the history of the absolute subject, which is universality and truth, obtained through the fictive identification of the historical actor with the historian-writer.

It is this fiction or simulation that is at the bottom of the tactical enunciative instance in the *Project*. It is through this fictive appropriation, producer of universality and truth, that the narrator is able not to appear in the narrative he writes.

From this comes the disqualification of a certain type of historical temporality, that of the register or chronicle. If History is not made by a plurality of subjects or agents independent of one another or in a position of having reciprocal interactions but by a unique and universal Subject, it is evident that the factor of temporal unification of historical actions and events can only be the temporality of this subject. It is the specific structure of his actions that will define the chronological envelope of the historical events and actions taken into consideration in the succession of narrative utterances that his historian produces. The narrator could not hold back the cutting up of chronological time into years or months, that is, into fixed and predetermined temporal containers—in a frame transcending the actions and events that take their places there—since the absolute Subject of the History is necessarily, by his very action, the producing principle of historical temporality. Hence the question (perhaps the fundamental question) that Louis XIV's "official" historical narrative poses: what representation does the king, who conceives and wants to conceive of himself as absolute Subject of History, have of his political will and actions [*son agir*]? What representation of his historical actions will his historiographer offer him—or what does he desire his historiographer to offer him—for the conception of his historical action? Not that the absolute power with which a single individual, the king, identifies himself is deprived of those representations, schemes, or projects that structure and orient his enterprises inside or outside the kingdom, that which is called "royal politics." What I question here is an operation that is more complex and of a different nature: How does a power that desires itself [*se désirer*] to be absolute think itself [*se penser*]? What is the phantasmatic in and through which the politics of this desire is rationalized? What is the imaginary of absolutism, and what are the role and function of the historiographer in constituting this phantasmatic and in constructing this imaginary?

Pleas and Panegyrics

Two other exclusions mark the *Project* of Louis XIV's history, the plea [*plaidoyer*] and the panegyric. The first has the simple function of signaling a reference to a paradigm of discourse that the whole text seeks to transgress and displace; the second appears only in order to be better developed, transformed, and negated at the heart of the text. The plea: "Next, the Historian and *not the lawyer* must explain the causes of the rupture and the King's just claims"; and the panegyric: "I would not understand this [the account of this last war] to be done in the form of a journal, or of an account and simple Memoirs, *or of eulogies or panegyrics*, which are all of different characters and styles and must be distinguished from one another." But the panegyric and eulogy excluded from History at the beginning return—and with what force—to the focal point of the *Project*, the *place of the king*: "*The King must be praised everywhere but, so to speak, without praise*, by a narrative of all that he has been seen to do, say, and think."

We will not stop at the exclusion of the judiciary plea except to stress that, behind the refusal of the confused and encumbered artifical and "technical" style of the jurists—the very ones whom power sent into the provinces and abroad to gather acts, testaments, and archival documents destined to be used by French diplomacy to define the king's just claims—is the author of the *Project's* reference to the typology of the genres of discourse formulated by Aristotle in the *Rhetoric*. There Aristotle distinguishes three forms of oratory discourse, judiciary, deliberative, and epideictic: the lawyer's *plea*, the politician's *discourse*, and the orator's *panegyric* (or *eulogy*).[7] These three forms possess the same enunciative structure, linking the person who speaks to the person he is speaking to and both of them to a subject about whom the locutor speaks to the allocutee, the latter constituting the end of the uttered discourse, the objective and goal of the orator. It is thus by a classification of auditors that Aristotle introduces the differential definitions of the three forms of oratory discourse and diversely bestows enunciation's formal apparatus on the triangular structure.

Now, Aristotle proposes a classification of "auditors" that does not correspond to that of the genres of oratory discourse: to the trichotomy of genres responds a binary typology of allocutees, who can be either judges [*kriteis*] or spectators [*theoroi*]. It is the typology of the objects of discourse that will restore the tripartite division corresponding to the judiciary, deliberative, and epideictic genres. In the first two the auditor *judges* the content of *what is said* according to the two great forms of time, the past and future. In the deliberative genre—the political oratory discourse—the orator, the statesman, counsels his auditors with a view to what is useful, that is, to what *will be* for the common good and to what *is to be done* in view of everyone's interest. The auditors pronounce on the discursive utterance according to the future. In the judiciary genre—the plea—the lawyer-orator accuses or defends. He speaks of *past*, already completed acts, and he speaks of them in view of the just and the unjust; and his auditor judges, according to the temporal category of the past, of existence or nonexistence, insofar as it is just or unjust, of the completed act. In return, in the genre of the eulogy and the panegyric, the enunciative structure is applied in a radically different manner: the auditor is spectator, he "contemplates" the speech being given "theoretically," and, when he judges, he does not pronounce himself on what is said but on the potential (the talent) of the person speaking, not on the content of the speech but on the way in which it is given. We understand, consequently, that in the eulogy or the panegyric the temporal form that governs the theoretical contemplation of the auditor as well as the enunciation of the operator is the present; better yet, the tense of the discursive account can only, in this "genre," be the present, since what is judged by the auditor-spectator is the *enunciation* itself: a judgment of praise in terms of beauty, "the beauty of virtue," writes Aristotle.

Is that to say that the discourse of praise is deprived of all content, since what determines its worth is the manner in which it is spoken? No. In the eulogy the auditor is spectator in that he judges the manner in which the orator makes him see, here and now in the speech he gives, the *beauty* of what he is speaking about. But often, adds Aristotle, orators make use in panegyrics of past things by evoking their memory and of things to come by conjecturing them. Nevertheless, the thing that will make the beauty of the speech and that will place the auditor in the position of spectator of this beauty is the speech act—the enunciative act—through which the orator will extract the beauty of what he is speaking about. It is through the *present* act that he will bring about [*faire être*] the beauty of his object, whether the latter is present, past, or future. If one of the essential transformations of the official position of the historiographer with Louis XIV's absolute was to be scriptor of the present of the reign, of the actuality of the king; if one of the most characteristic traits of this new position, which is inaugurated with Pellisson and will be pursued, a few years later, with Racine and Boileau, was the presence of the historiographer at the king's side in his battles and campaigns; then one can understand the interest of Pellisson's implicit reference to the Aristotelian paradigm: the king's historian must be the person who, in the present presence of the written utterance, *will bring about the permanent beauty* of the royal act and virtue for the reader's future memory. When the king's great deed, present today, *will* have *be*come *past*, it will be important to safeguard this present for posterity, and that only through a certain manner of writing by the historian, who must bring it about as beautiful at every present moment of the reading of the history. That reading must perform history's solar greatness in such a manner that all possible readers, present and future, cannot but be its admiring spectators.

Whence, no doubt, the necessity of attempting to unite in the same present the manner of the discourse and the matter of the narrative, the beauty of the writing and the beauty of the act. What is impossible, strictly speaking, in the present instant — which will always be split between the before of the act and the after, the hindsight, of the writing, can be realized practically, at once by the presence at the historic actor's side of the *narrator*-to-come of his action, and by the (repetitive) *permanence* of the *performativity* of a manner of writing, of a discourse in the narrative, and the always-present force of its effects.

Whence also the paradox, in the *Project*, of an inclusion-exclusion of the epideictic in the new and grandiose historic narrativity: "to write down the whole of this last war. I would not understand this to be done in the form of . . . eulogies or panegyrics . . . [and yet] the King must be praised *everywhere* but, so to speak, without praise, by a *narrative* of *all* that he has been *seen* to do, say, and think." We can now formulate the principle of Pellisson's strategy, the discursive law regulating his successive *coups*, and the progressive distribution and composition of the effects of force that this strategy brings into play. In the field of narrative freed by the exclusion of journals, memoirs, registers, and chronicles, the king's history should *displace* epideictic discourse — the eulogy and panegyric of the king — in order to produce the effects characteristic of the only paradigmatic form of discourse *absent* from his strategic calculations, the *political* discourse. In short, the displacement of the epideictic in the narrative at once takes the place of political discourse, and is a political operation.

II. Field of Forces, Field of Discourse

> The state of all Europe, and particularly that of the two Kingdoms of France and Spain, would have to be represented from the very beginning. It is a fine field for speaking in abbreviated form of all the King's virtues, and for enabling [the reader] to well conceive of his greatness in all ways, through the secret comparison that the reader will himself make between His Majesty and all the other Sovereigns.

Simulation-Simulacrum

A representation, a picture at the beginning of the historical narrative—that is the easiest response to the question dreaded by all writers: How to begin? It is dreaded even more by the historian-narrator, who must originate the chain of successive narrative utterances cited as instances in the linear development of chronological time: the zero point of the origin-beginning will be a synchronic picture, a *state* understood as the immobile composition of the forces confronted throughout Europe, a backdrop. But against this background the two facing figures of the protagonists of the imminent conflict stand out already: the two kingdoms of France and Spain. It is a "field" that is thus deployed all at one time: the field of war, the strategic map where political power has just maneuvered its armies, which is what *made* all of this "last war" in its unfolding—represented in terms of intentions, projects, and calculations, of *possibles*, but yet inscribed in European space. A whole past is completed, placed and constructed in its own space, *its field*, but like a future, and doubly so, in the utterance and the enunciation, since the narrative of this near past has not yet begun and since, when it does begin, it will be written in the future tense, a future where the field of completed action will open up. Such is the picture of the "past-future" war in the historian's narrative: it is the beginning of a writing but, at the same time, a retrospective origin; and it is a strategic map represented in the form of a tableau whose synchronic character of stasis before the storm is only, when all is said and done, the retrospective projection of the calm that has returned. This is an essential trait that all historical narratives share and, with them no doubt, all narrative in general.

But this turning around of the temporal categories of past and future, operated by the *representation* of the strategic calculation implied by all political enterprise, is here turned away. The space of the conflict is not, at first and essentially, the space of the representation of the calculations of the protagonists, the kingdoms of France and Spain. It is the space of a discourse, that is, of another strategy whose calculation at this point grabs hold and that will be specific to this narrative: an enunciative project that does not consist, at first, of describing the projects and intentions of the future adversaries but, rather, of formulating a project concerning the addressees of the narrative (to-be-written)—an overdetermination of the initial picture that aims for a double effect, on the king and on the reader. The description of the field of conflict will be a fine field for speaking about all the king's virtues, and this field of discourse *is* the first act, the first thrust, whose result is to construct the simulacrum-reader. It is indeed remarkable that this discourse of the historian not only refers to an object whose content he articulates, "all the King's virtues," but also poses the allocutee toward whom he directs his message as pure *effect* of his discourse. The message that "I" sends not only is in reference to an object that has a signifying existence only in and through it but also constitutes or constructs the addressee of this message as pure and simple pragmatic consequence: "It is a fine field for speaking . . . of all the King's virtues, and for enabling [the reader] to well conceive of his greatness in all sorts of ways."

Such is the first *coup* played by Pellisson in the match, and the general principle of his strategy, which he will dissimulate to the end—a *coup* he will repeat, different each time but each time linked to the preceding thrust and to the sum of the thrusts already played. He will position the addressee-reader as effect of the message sent and as the consistent series of successive effects and, by the same *coup*, write a text that would be, through and through, the simulation of the reading of this text, a text that would be to itself its own reading. A direct consequence would be to make this simulation be taken [*faire prendre*] for a metadiscourse and the simulacrum-reader for the real reader and to *make* his text be read [*faire lire*] as if his addressee were in front of him, a substantial "I," equal and symmetrical—in short, to make his discourse be read as a metadiscourse, as the display of a specific process of communication and exchange. Let us understand well that Pellisson's metadiscursive position concerning the narrative of the king's history is, in fact, already this narrative and this history. It is already History, the universal history of the formal apparatus of the enunciation. It is such only in order to dissimulate the operation of force necessarily implied by speaking. Representation is such only as the effect of representing, an operation that is taken to its greatest power in writing.

Speaking and Enabling [the Reader] to Conceive

This operation-of-force of speech is found, in our text, to be bound in a specific structure. It is, therefore, power of language. This structure is exposed by the syntactic and semantic structure of the sentence that the author of the *Project* devotes to it: "It is a fine field for speaking . . . of all the King's virtues, and for enabling [the reader] to well conceive of his greatness in all sorts of ways." On this strategic front of the attack, Pellisson gives the formula, precisely the *equation*, of his calculation, which is none other than the equation of the representative framework. The first side of the equation is "sending," with its three syntactically linked terms: (1) speaking, (2) of all the virtues, and (3) of the king. It is regulated by a "manner of saying" that is abbreviation, a process of shortening by condensation rather than by suppression, whose importance we will see in the discursive strategy and the construction of the reader-mannequin. This first articulation is presented as equal to the second—that is the value of the conjunctive "and"—that of "reception," also with three syntactically linked terms that I propose to rewrite in inverted fashion in order to bring out the operation of simulation-reading that the writer carries out: (3) of the king, (2) greatness in all sorts of ways, and (1) enabling [the reader] to conceive. To speak is to enable someone to conceive; but between going and coming back, between sending and reception, both sides of the equation of strategic calculation, a transformation has been operated: "all the King's virtues," *the referential object of the addressed discourse*, have become "his greatness in all sorts of ways," *the referential object of the received discourse*. No doubt, the term *King*, which is at once the name-term of the process of sending and the name-origin of the process of reception, remains the fixed pole of the whole operation; but what was referred to in the addressed discourse as a plurality of virtues belonging to it is read—in simulation—in the received discourse as the complex and infinitely diversified unity of a unique quality, greatness, a complexity that is, in fact, the diversification of the representation of the reader-simulacrum as much as of royal greatness. In other words, although it is presented or displayed as the perfect equation, without excess or residue, of two equal and symmetrical sides—the first corresponding to the sent and the second to the received discourse—between which there is neither loss nor production of meaning, in fact, the structural equation, which seems to define in all rigor the process of communication, operates a transformation where I read the simulation and strategy of power as constitutive of "representation" through which *what* the addressed discourse speaks *about—its matter—*is posed, in the text, by doubling and substitution, as *manner* of conceiving and understanding and as *form* of reception of the referred object. Figure 1 traces the model of the strategic operation and enunciative structure.

In this schema of the field of conflict and discourse, all the terms and relationships of the strategic calculation are represented in the "representation" of the narrative stage, with the exception of the thrust in the *match* that Pellisson is playing, the first sketch of the reader-simulacrum.

Indeed, if the discourse of representation of "the state of all Europe, and particularly that of the two Kingdoms of France and Spain," is the field where all the king's virtues are represented, and if the whole operation that will be executed in the narrative has for effect "enabling [the reader] to conceive of his greatness in all sorts of ways," only the introduction of an operator into the strategic calculation permits the transforming framework—the model of simulation-reading—to *function* and, in short, to make a machine and a trap out of the representative structure. The operator is "the secret comparison that the reader will himself make between His Majesty and all the other Sovereigns," a comparison that sets in motion a good conception of the king's greatness in all sorts of ways, a conception that, in turn, is itself only the simulated projection (by virtue of the received discourse) in the reader (reader-simulacrum) of the whole of the discourse addressed by the locutor. This remark, which is essential, obliges us, then, to extend the strategic model of the enunciation that we have just constructed and to take into consideration the principle of its functioning, which

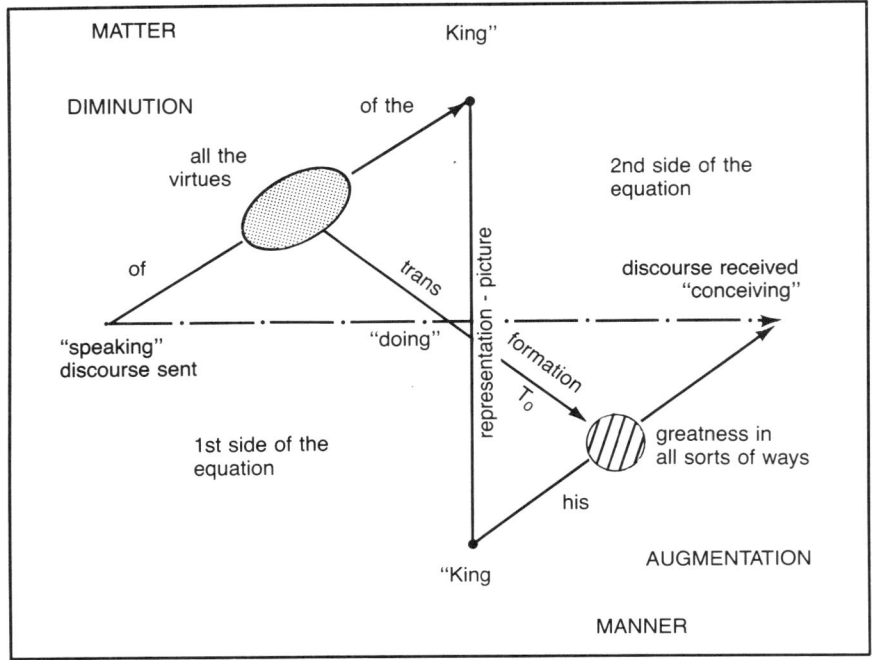

Figure 1. Field of the conflict

alone authorizes us to consider it as a machine-trap, as a model not only structural but also strategic.

For this it suffices to add a complementary term to the beginning and end of the representational process and to verify that this term obeys the transformation that we have put forward, which is indeed the case. This complementary term is precisely the initial stasis of the history's narrative, the description of the balance of political and military forces in Europe and, in particular, of those forces in the kingdoms of France and Spain. This is a good example of focalization, starting from the background picture, of the figures of the war's protagonists. This framing, in the iconic (photographic or pictorial) sense of the term, is operated through progressive *diminution*: (1) the state of *all* Europe, (2) the state of the *two* kingdoms of France and Spain, (3) *all the virtues*, (4) *of the* king, or, by abbreviation, *all* the kingdoms, *two* kingdoms, *one* king who is the King. Now on the level of the received discourse and the simulation-reading, this complementary term is indeed transformed, since the *focalization* effected in the first side of the equation, on all the virtues of the king starting from the *state of all Europe*, is inverted, in the second side, when comparing the royal greatness with *all the other sovereigns*. Europe (all the other sovereigns), the two kingdoms of France and Spain, and the balance of forces have all become there the simple undifferentiated and unitary term of a comparison of which His Majesty is the other term. Hence Figure 2, which marks the extended model of the strategic structure of enunciation.

Therefore, all the elements and relationships defined in sector A indeed find themselves, through duplication, to be the *same* in sector B—and how could it be otherwise, since there is only *one discourse* written (projected) by Pellisson, since this unique discourse is without "answer," since he takes and keeps the floor from beginning to end, and since he has and will have the last word? But at the same time, because Pellisson *simulates the reading* of the discourse that he projects writing and constructs a matrix for it, all of the elements and relationships of sector A are found to be transformed or substituted for sector B: referential objects and material are substituted for there by manners and forms of reception; the dynamic of focalization and framing in one term is substituted for by the inverted dynamic of the comparison of this term with an indefinite group that is relative to it; and the process of abbreviation or diminution is overturned in the process of augmentation and amplification. But once again the whole of this complex construct is only a lure: the narrative of this last war does not yet exist, and even if it were to exist, it would remain without an answer. A reading does not write itself, or if it does so, it ceases to be reading in order to constitute itself, in turn, as text. But a discourse—and there perhaps lies the strategy of the enunciation-power and the trap that it sets, the ruse of its discourse—can simu-

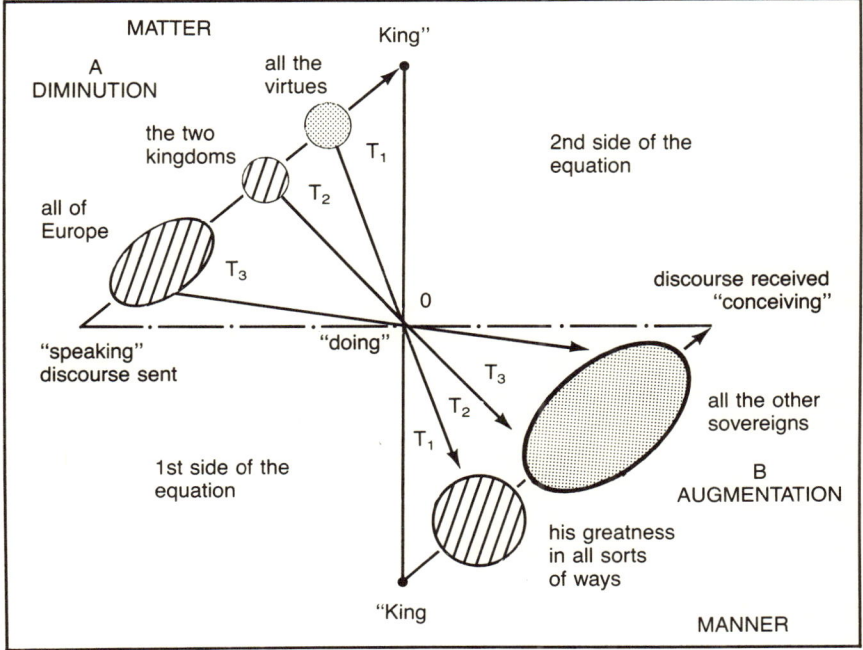

Figure 2. Extended field of the conflict

late its own reading and constitute or write itself from its own reading, and this is what is called "metadiscourse," the discourse on codes. Metalanguage is only a simulation and the critique of discourse, the simulacrum of its reader who nourishes it.

What are the stakes of this operation? I have already stated them: to share or, rather, to identify oneself fictively with the power of state. Clearly stated, the stakes are to become the king's historiographer. The inner spring of the whole framework is "the secret comparison that the reader will himself make on several occasions between His Majesty and all the other Sovereigns," its secret.[8] This term, which will reappear on several occasions expressly or substantively in the text of the *Project*, is ambiguous. In effect, it signifies in the context that the sender of the discourse *will keep* the comparison between the king of France and all the other sovereigns *hidden* but that the effect of his discourse upon all the king's virtues will infer the representation of the royal greatness in all sorts of ways, by a comparison that will be an effect of reading. But it signifies also that this unexpressed comparison will be neither penetrated nor even seen by the reader himself and that, at the same time, the complex and total representation of the royal greatness will be the conscious spot of an underside that, itself, will not be conscious. To the secret of the sender-narrator would correspond a secret of the receiver-narratee, but inverted. That which the narrator keeps *hidden* operates on the narratee *without his knowledge*. The former dissimulates a judgment or proposition in a term — what is a proposition, if not a comparison of two or several representations among themselves? And the latter, by transforming a representation corresponding to this term — what is a representation, if not the form or manner by which we represent a thing to ourselves by the term that signifies it? — will formulate, *without knowing it*, a judgment touching upon the thing represented. Without his knowledge, he will affirm that the thing — the king, at this juncture — is really what he conceives it to be.

But this comparison, dissimulated on the one hand, unknown or unconscious on the other, the double secret of this judgment — the will or desire that the things be my representations and my representations, the things themselves — which circulates from the addressed discourse to the received discourse, from the narrator to the narratee, from the addressor to the addressee, has the immense advantage, because it is secret (dissimulated or forgotten), of constituting a representation, not only complex and total, diverse and one, but also *absolute*, the only representation in which absolute power can *see itself* as absolute, for the simple reason that the absolute always supposes a "relative" with which it must be compared in order to be greater than all greatness, but that the forgetting or the dissimulation of this relative alone permits it to pose itself as *absolutely* absolute. In short, a comparison between the absolute and "the others" is necessary so that the absolute can see and pose itself as incomparable. But if, to repeat it once more, this whole subtle edifice of effects of inferred representations and hidden judgments is nothing but the projection of the writing itself of the history, overturned and inverted into a reading supposed true and a reader supposed "real," then we perceive how the exposition of Pellisson's discursive-narrative strategy is the first act of the tactical instance at the same time that it is the lure and trap that he sets for the addressee of the *Project*, that is, the absolute power of the state incarnated and singularized in the king. The mannequin-reader that he sketches from the very first sequence of his narrative-to-come is that much more powerful that he not only offers power, the king, the assurance of his exercise and application on the king's subject—the reader—but also sets the lure where he recognizes himself in his absoluteness and, at the same time, the trap for his own desire for omnipotence.

Iconic Translation

It is as if we were assisting, in a few lines, at the construction of the perspectival network of narrative representation and at the disposition of its figures in the illusorily deep space on the surface of the open stage. At first the narrator-painter, placed at the point of view, distributes the characters he is staging with regular and progressive diminution with respect to the vanishing point, a relationship regulated between two points structurally placed as equivalent: the state of all Europe, that of the two kingdoms of France and Spain, and all the virtues, finally, of the king. The historiographer has placed his eye at the peephole of the framework, and the king is situated on the horizon of the perspectival field, where all appearances fade from sight. "Prospect," as Poussin said, is the office of reason, the "theory" of true representation: the process of sending.[9] But from this point-hole on the horizon, appearances return toward the eye of the spectator, substituted in an instant for that of the painter—appearances, meaning, manners of seeing and receiving in which represented objects are regularly converted. All the figures thus perceived in their distribution on the stage order themselves with respect to a central figure in order to constitute the complex total unity of the pictorial representation. This representation indeed implies, in the immediacy of contemplation and spectacle, the secret comparison of the parts with the center and their encirclement in the general arrangement.

But at the same time this sequence is the introduction of the whole narrative to come, at once its beginning and the origin of the story it tells. Also, the construction of the "floor" of the narrative stage, the placing of simulated conditions for effectiveness of the narrative representation, is valid for the entire narrative, the whole finality of the projected narrative consisting of comparing representation with the effects of representation, narrative with picture. Thus the "initial picture," the first sequence of the whole narrative, functions as metonymy. It has the value of the transcendence of all of history, its battlefield and its field of origin, its enunciative matrix, operating the equivalency between history and the discourse on the narrative of the history to-be-written, and between war and enunciation.

Consequently, we are no longer surprised by the conclusion of the *Project*:

> If one does not know how to melt and alloy all of this together into a solid body, full of a variety of forces and brilliance, *how to paint rather than tell, how to make* the imagination *see* everything that is put on paper, how to attract the readers by that, and how to interest them in what is happening, it is no longer History. It is at most a register or chronicle.

Casus Belli, Occasio Mirifica

Second *coup* of the match; second scenario in the strategic calculation; second sequence in the narrative of History. After the description of the stasis of the balanced forces, after the construction of the field where the war will unfold and of the field of the discourse in whose forms the narrative of the war will be told, comes the explanation of the "rupture," the moment of the mechanical and dynamic disequilibrium, the moment of movement and change. "*Next*, the Historian . . . must explain the causes of the rupture." There again, it is a question of climbing upstream of the event that has taken place, the *occasus* of the history, in order to pick up the *casus belli*, to follow [*parcourir*]—to discourse on [*discourir*]—the line of time, but against the grain and a little beyond the event to be expressed, precisely in order to be able to express it, to tell it, certainly, but, as I say, by taking things from a little higher up, in short, to pose the aporia of the beginning and of the origin. We must, since the war has taken place and the event has henceforth all the de facto necessity of a completed past, seek in the stasis of balanced forces, in the static of equilibrium, the potential dynamic of the rupture and the war that will take place. But everything in its (narrative) time: first, the description of the equilibrium; next, the explanation of the causes of the rupture. And we must read well: the explanation of the causes of the rupture and not the explanation of the rupture. Pleonasm? No. To explain means to make something appear, to unfold it, to lay out the fabric of history, to iron out its folds until the crumpled thick fabric becomes the smooth and plain surface of the text of the historical narrative. We will see that in this sequence it is a question only of this: "a summary, but well-distilled and -studied narrative, written in chosen terms and reduced to the expression of natural meaning." At that moment the fabric of history must not have creases, and that is the function of narrative.

That is why, if the term *explanation* has been well understood, the narrative of the causes of the rupture is also that of the "King's just claims"; that is also why it is not a question of a "plea" but of "history." The explanation of the causes *is* the explanation of the "King's just claims." The *occasus* of history, the *casus belli*, is not and cannot be simply the disequilibrium of antagonistic forces in Europe, which could be the object of a de facto description. The objective report of the forces present, their conflict and the outburst of this conflict, is one with the justice and right—of the king. To explain the causes of the war is to unfold the "political will" [*vouloir politique*], that is, the will of history's agent, the king. Naturally, this will to power [*volonté de puissance*] has for itself justice and right; this goes without saying, and Pellisson does not come back to it. Neither Colbert nor the king needs to be persuaded or convinced. To insist would be to displease by implicitly signifying doubt. To base oneself on this right and this justice would indicate that by aiming to persuade others it is oneself that one seeks to convince. Whence the exclusion of judiciary discourse and of the plea in favor of narrative and history. To explain the *causes* of the rupture is to explain the cause of the king, not with the just and the unjust in mind—he is that by definition. It must simply be said as cause of the war; one must tell—unfold, explain—his will to power, or even his *desire for History*, in short, tell the history and, on the way, "always in this narrative style," justice and right will be expressed—their cause understood, in the end, along with the victory and glory of the king, and the judgment given, in all justice, by History itself.

The problem, therefore, is not there. It concerns, once again on this point, the reader and the process of reading, and

> would enable the least enlightened persons to understand what the cleverest have difficulty unraveling in great volumes. At the end I would refute, but always in the same style of narration, the principal grounds of the *Bouclier d'Etat* [the Shield of State], which is the work of a clever man and which is creating a stir among foreigners.[10]

The author of the *Project* puts into place here a "typology" of readers, readers classified "all along the scale of knowledge," (possible) modes of reading, and publics toward whom he directs the narrative of the causes of the rupture and the cause of the king. The characteristics of this narrative—to come—and the distinctive traits of its style have no other coherence than the characteristics and traits of the publics to whom it will have to be addressed. The reader-simulacrum sketched above reacts on the stylistic description of a narrative of explanation that does not yet exist. The imago of the potential readers sends very diverse "species," which, however, altogether produce imaginarily not the narrative but its qualities, not the narrative substance but its attributes, not of language but of style and ornaments.

What, then, are its stylistic characteristics? On the one hand, it must be *summary*, reduced to the limit of *natural* meaning: a brief, clear, ordinary language [*langue*] is one that everyone understands. But on the other hand, it must be well *distilled* and *studied*, written in chosen terms: studied, worked, ordered, and brought to maturity by a whole labor of writing and art. How can it be both one and the other? It is the secret of a knowing-how-to-do [*savoir-faire*] and of a knowing-how-to-write [*savoir-écrire*] that Pellisson will come back to, with insistence, in order to forestall the resistance and scepticism of his addressee. How to reconcile irreconcilables? Art and nature, science and simplicity, the effort of composition and clarity, complexity and naturalness? "Let me do it. I know how. I am perhaps the only person among all Frenchmen to know how to do it. Just as I do not contest as advocate or lawyer the justice of the cause of the king, in return, do not bring into question my art as writer. I believe you on your word. Believe me on my history project." Such is Pellisson's tactical thrust, exposing the second stage of his strategy: the play of reversal. The ensemble of the stylistic qualities of his narrative-to-come, whose application [*mise en œuvre*] and reunion in and through that narrative are presented as the mysterious effect of a *science* of the writer, is in fact only the projection onto the nonexistent narrative of the various degrees of science and knowledge held by the supposed readers and of the various modalities (alethic and epistemic) of the reading of the narrative by its addressee.

There are, first of all, those who do not know, "the least enlightened"; next there are those who know, but obscurely and confusedly, "the most clever," who are incapable of "unraveling [the truth] in big volumes"; there are, finally, those who believe they know the truth but who, in fact, are plunged in error, the readers of the *Bouclier d'Etat*. For the first, the narrative reduced to the limit of natural meaning, brief and clear; for the second, the well-distilled and -studied narrative, written in chosen terms; for the third, finally, the refuting narrative, the return of the excluded advocate, but in the form of a narrative that will cumulate all the preceding characters: brevity, clarity, simplicity, complexity, science, reflection, order, selection, and art. The operation that the author of the *Project* had effected in the preceding paragraph is reproduced here, but displaced and made more complex. Above, the narrator kept a judgment, a comparison, *hidden* in a term whose narratee formed the representation by formulating, *without knowing it*, the corresponding judgment. Now, the narrator keeps his knowledge and studied and chosen reflections *hidden*, thanks to his art of writing, beneath the simplicity and naturalness of the narrative of the causes of the war that the narratee, *who does not know* (or who knows badly, or who believes to know), *reads* as a simple narrative of the events while learning the king's reasons and claims, his cause as the just cause in the war. The complexity of what the narrator of the History must do (write) — the causes of the war as the good cause of the king — brings him to simulate a simple and natural reading of his narrative, to operate a reading-simulation that inverts the characteristic of his writing project, and thus to transfer the complexity of the writing onto the simulacrum of a complex reading. It is in this way that, in the exposition of the strategic calculation of the text *to come*, the contradictions of the strategy of the *completed* history and of the ideology of its completion can be resolved: those of force and justice, of the fact of the king's power [*puissance*] and the right of his cause, and of power and value. The strategic calculation of the project of the man of letters in the service of the strategy of the power of state doubles and reproduces that strategy, after the fact, in the stylistic and rhetorical effects of a narrative that takes it into account—while effacing that much more easily its contradictions as the writer's discourse limits itself to defining a project of narrative in terms of simulated effects, whose ensemble, in the form here named simulacrum-reader, takes the place of the real-possible reader. Thus the man of letters lures power with the lure of his instrument, discourse, metadiscourse, and its figures. Thus, simultaneously, he obtains from power—and with his trap—the power of the power of the discourse that he holds.

III. Portraits and Scenarios

Field of forces and field of discourse, causes of the war and cause of the king— a third stage opens, then, in the *Project* of the narrative of history, that of the "actors" of the war and of the agent of the History.

> Next I would work on what few modern historians have known how to do well, and almost no Frenchman: that is, the principal Actors in this war would have to be made known while supposing that no one yet knows them. For we write for posterity, which will not have seen them, and it is not even always true that to see them is to know them.

The entrance upon the stage of the vectors of the forces, the putting into place of the figures of the narrative representation, but also a new scenario of the strategic calculations.

I have remarked that, at the two previous moments of the *Project*, the definition of the place of the narrative stage was effected through negation, exclusion, or disqualification—journals, accounts, memoirs; eulogies and panegyrics; pleas and, with them, judiciary discourses—even if this negation was revealed to be, in fact, a (de)negation, because operating on the limits of the space of the narrative to-be-constituted. The excluded and negated, because excluded and negated, could then return to the field that it had contributed to enclosing. Until now, however, this (de)negation was coining a genre or mode of discourse or of narrative. While approaching, in this third stage, the part of the historical narrative that concerns the actors of the war, the author of the *Project* does not hesitate to play, but *explicitly*, a thrust of a different nature; the tactical instance here is enunciated in the disqualification of the authors who are his contemporaries, in a simple statement of fact. I do not believe that Pellisson hazarded this critical remark at this point in his discourse on Louis's history by chance: contemporary historical agents have not had the historical authors who were appropriate for them, and if—as we will see—there exists, in fact and by right, only one unique agent of History, the critical gesture signifies clearly that Louis XIV does not have the historiographer he deserves to have. Also, *a contrario*, since Pellisson is capable of writing and, soon, of justifying his critique, he poses himself as this absent historiographer: a remarkable tactical thrust—not to say "bluff"—because, in truth, the historical narrative that would show the difference between them and him from this point of view does not yet exist. Only the manner in which it should exist is said. But there is more. At this point, with this thrust, begins the connivance between the man of letters—the author, the historian—and the king—the actor and the historical agent—a complicity that will appear fully, several lines further on, when the possible historiographer exacts secrecy from the king on the design of having his own history written, a complicity that not only is a discursive intrigue but also carries away with it a specific model of the relationship between political and literary power. It is this model that the author of the *Project* will strive to construct, precisely by discoursing on the narrative staging of the "principal actors of this war."

Litotes and Intensification

One must thus make the principal actors of the war known and make them *well* known. But until now only the principle of the operation has been given: to simulate a universal and future reader who expects the historian to *really* make them known to him. How? By substituting, thanks to this epistemic and pragmatic subterfuge, one knowledge for another.

What then are, in the *Project*, the operators of this substitution?

> These sorts [*manières*] of portraits or characters, when they are well touched up, must be neither too great in number nor all in succession, but dispersed and placed with a certain degree of art and diversity. . . . An admirable effect is produced. This is one of the great secrets for animating history.

Just as in the first phase of the strategic calculation, the possible generator of the future narrative, the passage through the simulacrum of the universal reader permits and realizes the transformation of the principal actors of the war into types of portraits or characters, forms-of-reception, representations, or ideas in the process of reading. There again, the essential rule of this transformation rests upon the equivalence of two discursive, symmetrical, and inverted movements, of which the second is the representation of the first, and its dynamic effect: a *litotes*,[11] the abbreviation or diminution of the object of the sent discourse whose effect in the received discourse is expansion and *augmentation*. The litotes operates the transformation of the referential or the matter of the discourse into the manner or form of its reception.

Thus do the historical actors become portraits or characters, through reduction in the narrative of what they are in History. Again we must understand that these portraits are processes, microsystems of inverted effects of augmentation and expansion, little simulating machines, frameworks of transformation of the forces of the history not only into characters of the narrative but also—and that is indeed the goal of the operation—into manners of its reception, in a word, into simulacra. These are indeed "models" obtained mimetically through reduction and selection, but these models, or programs, are constituted only through the *simulation of the effects* of the narrative or discourse that contains them, when this last is imaginarily thought as read, heard, and received. The metadiscourse that Pellisson formulates on the narrative he projects, and where he makes his goals, intentions, and aims as effective narrator explicit, is not the description of the *real* rhetorical and persuasive effects of his narrative. It is entirely made up, in the metadiscourse itself (the metadiscourse is no doubt only that), of the *simulation* of those effects—the production, then, of the simulacrum of a reader in the narrative, where it is expected that the real reader will come, in the end, to fill the mannequin.

In order to realize their effects, these types of portraits or characters must be well "touched up," a technical term of painters that designates the gesture by which they pose and extend the colors on the picture, the closest possible to the expressive body, and which refers less to the mimesis of the object on the canvas than to the manner of the subject producing the representation. They must next be chosen and disposed of in the field of the picture, on the floor of the stage. Thus the figures that the painter distributes in the perspective network are placed as a function of the expressive and representative totality that he aims to produce and of their effects-affects on the reader-spectator. Finally, portraits or characters must be constructed according to the greatest economy of means, without falling into the obscurity of Tacitean *brevitas* but while avoiding at any cost an abundance and prolixity in which the design-drawing of the whole would be lost.[12] If "mannequin" is "the name that painters and sculptors give to a figure in wood or wax that they use to display the drapery of their works," then what Pellisson proposes here, with these portraits or characters of the historical actors, is none other than a mannequin that is a little more complex, that serves to determine not only the draping of each figure but also the "clothing" made of qualities such as birth, great deeds, and capacities that summarize the historical being of the man of war. But whatever the procedures of the delineation, construction, and disposition of the figures in the narrative representation, it is characteristic that, while referring to "real" persons, Pellisson presents these narrative figures in his design as a conjunction or combination of effects, the effects of the means of the historian-painter in his picture, and the effects on the reader-spectator of the picture. These are figures of simulation, of the *savoir-faire* of the future narrator, and of the credibility or persuadability of the universal-potential reader whom he imagines at the place and in the place of the real reader. In the end, the figures of his narrative are the figurative (rhetorical) diversification at once of the simulated narrator of the projected narrative and of the simulacrum-narratee of its reading.

These effects are cumulated into only one, that of the litotes: making always much more than what one says about something understood. To cite Fontanier, the litotes is a "particular kind of metalepsus that, instead of affirming something positively, negates absolutely the contrary thing or *diminishes* it more or less, in the aim of giving more energy and weight to the positive affirmation that it disguises."[13] In this way the discounted effect of the diminution is an augmentation, an intensification: "An admirable effect is produced. This is one of the great secrets for animating history. . . . The mind of the Reader . . . makes a very delightful spectacle of it for himself." Such is the remarkable narrative function of portraits and characters; such is the major effect of the simulacrum; such is the power of the intensification and augmentation of the rhetorical-narrative figure. Certainly, the portrait is a representation of the historical actor, but this representation must be conceived as a fiction, that is to say, as a matrix, a *functioning* model—precisely, a machine or framework for transforming the *matter* and movement in spectacle into the *manner* of perceiving and the *simulacrum* of reality.

What, then, is the great secret of historical narrative, of the narrative machine? Simply this: the narrator represents historical agents with mannequins that resemble them. And for this he limits himself to selecting a certain number of references (birth, remarkable actions, talents, and the import of each one) and to proposing that these reduced models be read in certain well-chosen places of the great narrative syntagm. This is easy for him, since he alone has *seen* them act in war, since this vision has been posed as the correct one, the real knowledge that only he possesses, and since, in contrast, the reader has been previously defined as the posterity that will not have *seen* them and that, necessarily, does not yet know them. This narratee who does not know because he does not see, or who would not see even if he had the eyes to see, reads, then, the portraits and characters of the actors and *next* reads the narrative. He fills these already prepared matrices and scenarios of actions with the actions of the history that the narrator tells. He discovers a history that the narrative produces, sequence after sequence, but he discovers also that the historical actions that he reads one after the other conform exactly to the reduced models his reading has been equipped with. The narrative representation in its newness, its surprises and its accidents, is thus perfectly coextensive with what it represents. It is as if the narratee-spectator, once endowed with a competence, were himself producing, through his reading, the narrative that is told to him; and beyond the narrative, it is as if he were producing the history that the narrative takes into account. Realizing the models in truth, applying, in fact, the portraits and characters to the actions of which history is and has been made, the reader in the imaginary of his reading produces and completes the narrative, makes history, and is its agent, sequence after sequence. The reader through his reading simulates the actor in his action, just as the text read simulates the completed history.

It is as if the construction, in the narrative, of the relationship between the historical character and his matrix-portrait, as the author of the *Project* presents it, were furnishing in its turn the model, or paradigm, of the relationship between the historical action of political power and the structure of that power. Far from *conceiving* actions in the world as consequences of rational *deliberation* and calculation that determine, as rigorously as possible, the relationships between existing forces and the means adequate to these relationships in order to attain a clearly and distinctly represented objective, what emerges in filigree from Pellisson's theoretical discourse is, on the contrary, to imagine the construction of an essence or idea of the power of the historical agent, a structure of power that is indissolubly a possibility and a potential power that the action will come to fill and bring to existence through the deployment of its internal energy. The only thing left, then, is to *simulate* this deployment of essence into existence, of representation into action, of possibility-potential into reality-act, this a priori analytical relationship in the form of an a posteriori empirical synthetic relationship, and to fold it back onto the temporal form of causality in order to obtain history itself.

Narrative is the operation of this simulation, an operation by which history (*Historie*) is produced as the effects of story (*Geschichte*). Narrative is not, then, the taking into account of history through narration but the operator of the simulation of history through narration; history is the *representational effect* (and not the *referential origin*) of narrative, the result of an imaginary structure of power. But once this imaginary structure is found to be ex-plicated in the empirical form of time thanks to which all differences reappear between conception and expression, expression and effectuation, means and the attainment of the objective, then history is produced, a simulacrum of the referential origin of the narrative that narration tells.

Delights of the Spectacle

What is left is to find out why this effect of representation operates, why the effect of narration is the affect of the narratee, why "the mind of the Reader . . . makes a *very delightful spectacle* of it for himself" and, at the same time, is caught in the simulacrum of the reference and reality of history.

The effect of representation—the simulacrum—operates only because it gives pleasure. What desire does this pleasure satisfy in and through the reading? It is as if the reader were repeating for his part the operation of simulation and producing, in its turn, the simulacrum of history, but secretly and without knowing it: his pleasure—the pleasure of reading the narrative—comes from there, from the astonishing conformity of the "unforeseeable" contingent and aleatory actions of the historic actors and from the matrical schemes, models, or scenarios of those actions constructed in their portraits and characters. It is as if history were already contained in the model-portraits of its agents: the paradoxic pleasure of surprise at the conformity, surprise that the expectation (the foresight) was not disappointed, that the narrated event did not come to belie or weaken the potential foresights implicit in the model, that reality gives reason to the idea.

A strange pleasure, for the actions of the historical character are not, "in truth," already inscribed in his representation, but in the reading it is as if they were already: from the scenario of the possibles implied in the narrative of the acts explained, a distance is preserved without which the narrative would disappear, for everything would have already been said before the curtain could rise on the spectacle. However, it is necessary that at a certain level this distance be erased. A distance posed and canceled: the one that exists between the possible and the real, a plural generality and unique particularity; but the possibles are the possibles of that reality, and the generalities are those of that particularity. The pleasure of reading is born in this contrariety, in this coming and going of representation and the represented; the rhythm of expectation-foresight and of surprise-newness; the surprising familiarity, the foreknowledge of the known; the desire for mastery and power [*puissance*] being fulfilled in the imaginary of reading; the pleasure-trap of narrative. It is as if the reader-spectator were himself pulling the strings of the puppet-mannequin that the narrator has furnished him with, as if he were presiding over the historical destiny of the characters, as if he were operating sovereignly, necessarily, the hazards and contingencies of their actions, as if, after the manner of the Platonic gods, he were pulling the strings of the narrative's mannequins, and as if at each gesture of the puppe he were discovering—divine surprise of contingency—the effect of his own gesture.

Brilliance [Eclat(s)]: The Place of the King

Everything will be said in the following line: if the whole strategic calculation of Pellisson, future historiographer of the king, is concentrated in one clause, it is because it is there that are found the stakes of the *Project*, its center of gravity, the point where tactic and strategy cross and are identified: *the place of the king*. "From among all these characters, that of His Majesty must burst forth [*éclater*]." In Louis's history-to-be-written, the king's portrait must occupy a central place. This decision is not and cannot be the object of discussion or material for modalization, as it is for the principal actors in this war, who "*would have to be made known while supposing that no one yet knows them*." Among them there is an originary actor, an actor who is the agent of the history to be told, the king, as archactor. And in the same movement, in the same thrust that is played here, there *must* likewise be a portrait, a character, a model that would contain and integrate all the others. The figures of the narrative are concentrated and condensed toward this vanishing point: from this point of view they are born, leave, and develop. Such is the place of the king, the fulguration of his sun, the brilliance of his eye, the instantaneous flash of his gesture in the space of European history and in the topos of the narrative that tells it: point of supreme intensity—explosion, brilliance, burst. Simultaneously, the king's portrait *must* "strike, with the intensity of its light, the eyes and minds" and also fill in an instant the whole space of the narrative stage with his brilliance and his presence, dispersed in all his places and shared among all the characters and portraits.

As source producing all light, unbearable to the eye and the gaze, the king's portrait is not only the sun in the central place of the narrative but also the light that spreads out everywhere and that lands in bursts on all and on everyone and *makes* them be seen.

At this point in our reading of Pellisson's text we must reread the fifth part of Descartes's *Discourse on Method*.[14] Like the sun in the discourse of physics, the king's portrait is in and of itself the brilliant and privileged moment of the narrative stage, and, like Cartesian light, it is also that which brings to light and shows all the actor-subjects of the history to the reader-spectator by striking them with its brilliance. As archactor of the narrative, the king's portrait is also, and in a very particular sense, its metanarrator, since it is through it that, properly speaking, the history of this last war can and must be told. In this central and decisive *coup* of the match, strategic calculation and tactical operation cross and are identified. For the king to occupy the position of agent of history in the historical representation, he must—and that is what the preceding paragraph has demonstrated—also be its metanarrator. But for the king to be the metanarrator of the historical narrative, the author of the *Project* must be his historiographer, because only he knows "the great secret for animating history and preventing it from ever dragging or tiring."

The king must be the metanarrator, but in a very particular sense. For he does not tell his own history, he makes it. But he is the condition of possibility of all historical narrative, since there is no historical narrative that is not his own history: the principal actors of this war are put into movement and action only through his movement and his action. He is their prime mover. It is in him and through him that they have being, mass, size, and movement. It is through him that they emerge from the wings of the European theater, enter the stage, and fulfill the gestures he exacts from them by his own action. They do not act, they react. The absolute of power is the absolute of the power to act, the absolute of an acting that has no source other than an internal one. It is this privileged actor that the narrator must put on stage as archactor, originary and unique in the very structure of his absolute acting [*son absolu d'agir*]. He must tell him and show him [*faire voir*]. He must therefore start by reducing him to a portrait, constructing a model of him, and defining the matrix of his action. But this reduction, construction, and definition was in fact begun with the initial representation of the state of all Europe, such that when the narrator announces that next he must work toward making the principal actors of this war known, the portraits and characters that must be touched up and dispersed with art and diversity are already placed in the field of the king's discourse, in the abridgment of all his virtues. The character of His Majesty contains, from now on, the portraits and characters of the actors; he envelops them in the unity of his field, in the brilliance of his light. Not only does the king make the others of the history act through his own action, not only does he call them to the stage of history through his own absolute acting, but he is that stage itself, the luminous space of their representation. In a word, the king, archactor of history, is, in and through the narrative of his narrator, *the simulacrum of the simulacra*.

It is as if Louis were pulling the strings of the puppet-actors in the theater of his action, their actions filling up the different ideas of them that he himself put into representation. But at the same time, since all this theater, the field of his stage, and the characters that move and re-act to absolute action in it, are the product and effect of the representation staged, play after play, by the narrator, *the great simulator of the simulacra of history is himself simulated*: he is the simulacrum that contains all the simulacra in the great simulation of his history that still waits to be written, of which the narrator offers him, in the form of a *lure*, the project of a history already written in its *fiction*. Consider, therefore, this play of shadows and reflections on the surface of the picture from which results the effect of historical representation. The relationship of the portrait to the character simulates that of the reader to the narrative and, at the same time, produces the reader in a simulation of reading: the *Project* that exposes what Louis's history must be simulates that history for His Majesty; the king himself lets himself be caught (or rather he must be) by his own simulator; and the narrator himself simulates with respect to the king the relationship of simulation in which he is caught with his reader. In an unending circle of enunciations and utterances, the uttered enunciations and the utterances of enunciation, the ceaseless referring back of the spectator to his image, of his image to the image he sees and of the images he sees, to his own position, without the carousel of shadows and reflections ever being able to stop and without the surface of the mirror where the play is occurring ever being itself visible.

But it is as if the narrative told by the "project-sick" narrator were the loyal representation of the History that has just taken place. And all is well thus, as the effect of representation really has been produced, since Pellisson will be named king's historiographer. Yes, we must here—once again—reread Descartes.

The narrative of the history of the universe and that of the history of the war are constructed according to the same strategic principles and the same tactical exigencies. In both cases the narrator as physicist-philosopher and the narrator as historian-man of letters aim to trap an absolute authority, God and his theologians, the king and his minister, and in order to do this both of them use the same tactical procedure: to expose the strategic-narrative calculation of an invisible and inaudible narrative, the great treatise of cosmogenesis written but not published, and the "Great History" of the king projected but not written. It is a question then, for both, of producing the simulacrum of this unparalleled narrative in such a way that the absolute authority, which all of this discourse refers to and addresses, authorizes and legitimates it, in advance or after the fact, at the sight and reading of its simulation. If power enters into the play of the writer, whether the physicist-philosopher or the historian-man of letters, it is because power finds, in the discourse addressed to it, its own figure, the simulacrum of the great simulator, the fiction of God the creator, in the imaginary spaces of a little matter and movement, the fiction of the king, the prime mover, in the European theater, of all the historical actors. This is fiction, figure and simulacrum, whose effect is the perfect representation of earth's real universe and of man in its theoretical center, of history in general, and of the history of the last war and of the king in its political center. It is because, in both cases, light and its source, the sun, play in the mirrors of physics and history, a play of brilliance and shadows, reflected and refracted, relayed and transmitted from figures to portraits, from planets and stars to character and characters, dispersed and placed with art and diversity on the whole surface of the picture and in the whole space of the stage, and yet focalized and centered at a point where the theoretical and political subjects both take on the strange appearance of an omnipotent and nonexistent form, which can only point to the great phantasmagoria of "classical" representation.

IV. The Epideictic Narrative, or the Historical Eulogy

The King must be praised everywhere but, so to speak, without
praise, by a narrative of all that he has been seen to do, say, and
think. It must appear disinterested but be lively, piquant, and
sustained, avoiding in its expressions all that veers toward the
panegyric. In order to be better believed, it should not give him the
magnificent epithets and eulogies he deserves; they must be torn
from the mouth of the reader by the things themselves.

Once the place of the king, the center of gravity of the text, has been conquered, the author of the *Project* can strike with a double strategic and tactical thrust: on the one hand, to the reader-addressee of the history to be written, on the other, to the supreme addressee of the *Project*, the king, addressor of the office of historiographer. He can exploit, in a word, his potential victory by occupying the conquered territory and by realizing the stakes of the play of simulation. As I have already noted, at this focal point the *Project* changes meaning and nature. The pathway of the narrative design, sequence after sequence, gives way to that of the historical paradigm in two stages, first that of its norms and next that of its functioning, the deontic modalities of the History clearing the way for the verbal forms of the present tense and for the instructions of its regulated operations. The crossing of the "place of the king" has permitted the decisive gain, that, henceforth, the narrative-to-be-made whose simulated narrator was being produced by the author of the *Project* is no longer exposed in its syntagmatic articulations but has become the object of a discourse that produces its stylistic and rhetorical qualities and that describes its attributes and characteristic dimensions. The narrative-to-come has become fulfilled narrative in the paradigm that underlies it.

The assurance that the persuasive victory is obtained is so strong that the "discursive" tactical instance can be declared: "It would no doubt be hoped that His Majesty approve and accept this design"—clearly, to name me his historiographer—for the decisive reason that it "can almost not be well executed without him." Better yet: the tactician does not hesitate to manipulate his omnipotent addressee and to formulate demands concerning him: "But he *must* not seem to have accepted, known about, or ordered it." The simulacrum functions alone and functions like a trap, a trap with a double trigger, a violent one concerning the supposed real reader of the historical narrative and one of complicity, but even more imperious, with respect to the king.

The calculation is the following: it is indeed a question of writing a narrative, and only a narrative, but whose unique object is the king; and it is a question of writing it in such a manner that its reading will be that of a discourse of praise. It is a question of fabricating a history whose effect will be and cannot be other than a panegyric of him who is its brilliant actor. We have noted that, from the very beginning of the text, Pellisson pronounces the exclusion from History of a certain number of modes of discourse: some types of narrative—journals, memoirs, and accounts—as well as the great Aristotelian discursive forms—the judiciary plea and the panegyrical discourse. The crossing and conquest of the place of the king permit the return of the excluded in the form of the epideictic, a return doubly simulated: first because the narrative that must manifest it is not written but could be; next and above all because the eulogy and panegyric of the king must reappear in the king's narrative, not in some of its points or in this or that of his places but by constituting it from one end to the other. If the history of this last war can only be the narrative of its unique agent, this narrative can only be the king's eulogy. The epideictic discourse must return after having been excluded from the conception of the Great History; it must return by the very nature of this history to be told, a History with a unique omnipotent, omniscient, just, irresistible, and the like, agent, not, however, as eulogic discourse but as narrative. It is *by avoiding* the panegyric that the panegyric extends its empire to the totality of the narrative thing, that *it* is the narrative itself. This mechanism, this machination, rests on a perfectly integrated double framework that the *Project* points to in its very formulation: "The King must be praised *everywhere . . . by a narrative of all that he has been seen to do, say, and think*"; such is the first inner spring of the trap in simulation. "The King *must be praised* everywhere *but*, so to speak, *without praise*, by a narrative"; such is the second inner spring of the trap, a spring that unleashes the first in the instantaneity of a same thrust.

Hence the double effect of the narrative thus produced: a narrative that will appear disinterested but that will be lively, piquant, and sustained. That the whole framework rests on this praise without praise is shown by the insistence Pellisson brings to this paradox and the precautions he takes in order to present it. Insistence and prudence: Pellisson is aware that this point is essential as much to the strategic calculation of his history as to his tactic as future historiographer. What, then, is praise that does not manifest itself as praise, since it is the very essence of praise to *say* that it is such, and since its "truth" is a praising way of saying? Similarly it will say *itself* to be praise, but this saying will not be the narrator's but his reader's. Henceforth we well understand that once the magnificent eulogy of the king is proffered and performed by the reader, its simulacrum will be definitely completed. This expresses the importance of the stakes of this thrust.

Scopic Machinations

First inner spring of the framework: "The King must be *praised* everywhere [*partout*] . . . *by* [*par*] [a narrative of] *all* [*tout*] that he has been seen to do, say, and think." If History is made by actors and if, among these actors, there is an agent through whom they receive being, life, and movement, the narrative of History can be only the narrative of this agent and of all he does, says, and thinks. His acts, words, and thoughts—and only they—define the absolute and universal space of History and of the narrative of history: the king must therefore be praised everywhere, in all that he does, says, and thinks. But this totality that admits of no remainder, that is without exteriority and is totalitarian, is also a space of total visibility and of absolute representability. This *all* is the all of History and of the narrative of History. To suppose in this space a nonvisible place would be to admit a "corner" of the royal universe where a kingly act, word, or thought would not be representable, would not be praisable, would not be sayable or writable in the form of narrative-praise, a private place, at once privatized and faltering, a fissure in the absolute sphericity of absolute power and its absolute representation-in-representation. From this point on the pure and simple internal demand of totalitarian power, which is the pure and simple demand of the absolute, takes away with it—analytically—the demand of its totalitarian and absolute narrative, without remainder and without exteriority. History, his story [*Historie*], is and can be none other than the text, his text, his narrative

[*Geschichte*]. Yes, the king really is the archactor of History and the metanarrator of his narrative. The narrator's gaze, the historiographer's eye, smashes the totalitarian correspondence of History and its text; it introduces a double polarity into the present presence of the royal act unto itself, that of doing [*faire*] and of seeing something being done [*voir faire*], a first scission of the subject of the history; a first difference that is immediately followed by another, between seeing and writing, a scission of time in the scission of the subject, a present split in the representation of an old present. Here is, in one movement, the difference opened up in the totalitaran identity: the king must be praised everywhere, (1) by all that he does, says, and thinks; (2) by all that he has been seen to do, say, and think; and (3) by all that he has been seen to do, say, and think (and that I will write, I, Pellisson, when I am named king's historiographer): "It would no doubt be hoped that His Majesty approve and accept this design, which can *almost* not be well executed without him." In the minute fissure of the "almost" erupt both the gaze of the historian present at the king's side and the retrospective writing of this gaze in the narrative of the royal history.

Nevertheless, it would be a mistake to think that this position brings the king back to the position of seen object. In fact, it is the reverse. This position is none other than to be under the king's gaze, in the optical beam of his eye.[15] The gaze of the "I-one [*on*]" is the plural, indefinite, and nonpersonal eye in the sovereign gaze, the bursting sun and burst light of His Majesty. This is the asymmetrical reciprocity of eyes and gaze, of eyes, which see what the king does, says, and thinks, and of gaze, which makes them see what he does, says, and thinks; a perfect representation without excess or loss in this play of reflections or of recognition, despite the double polarity of the historical agent and the narrator of his narrative, but that operates its effects only at the price of the simulation of this spectacle. For the anonymous eye of the court, the diffusion in the space of the absolute power of the "I" of the narrator (while waiting to be its condensation at the point of the narrative writing), does not see all that the king does, says, and thinks. Only *all* that "one" will have seen of the doing, saying, and thinking of the king will be told, said, and written by the pen of the "I" of the narrator.[16]

Such is indeed the principle of spectacular simulation, to produce in order immediately, not to dissimulate but fill with its effects and occupy with its simulacra of images and words the necessary gap of vision and contemplation that is the condition of possibility of the narrative of History—the gap where the *theoros* finds the place, not of its admiring listeners, as in the *Rhetoric*,[17] but of its seeing, saying, and writing. Because the king can be seen, his history can be told, and all that he will have been do, say, and think will be written—but can all be seen? No, since he can be seen only to the extent that he looks at us, since one contemplates only when taken and seized in the limits of *his* scopic beam. Such is the potential of simulation whose effect is narrative representation. But all painters well know that the perspective structure of vision—the prospect, rule, and norm of aspect—permits and defines the re-presentation of things themselves on the surface of the picture, but also that the counterpart of this fascinating effect is that there is necessarily something hidden in the represented, and that luminous vision always conceals in order to unfold itself, *"d'ombre, une morne moitié"* [of shadow, a gloomy half]; in short, that the eye is theoretical only on the condition of being seized in and by the gaze of what it sees. The very condition of the perfect correspondence of presence and the represented, of history and narrative, is a lack to be represented, an obscure reserve of light, a nocturnal face of the royal sun. Perfect representation is the effect of this imperfection.

It would be a mistake, from this point of view, to understand the insistence with which Pellisson poses the vision-contemplation, by the possible narrator, of the acts, words, and thoughts of the historical agent as a simple tactical weapon in the success of his petition. It is that, certainly. But the vision—aspect and prospect—and the position of the narrator's eye at the fixed point of the bringing into perspective of the narrative representation is also—and this time necessarily—an essential element in the strategic calculation of the narrative. It is indeed important that the eye of the narrator of the narrative be, in time and space, in the moment and the place, placed the closest possible to the gaze of the archactor and metanarrator of the History; that it participate in a way in its power [*puissance*], sun and light, which at once sees all there is to see and gives to sight all that is visible to those who see only through it; that it *almost* identify itself with the omnipotence of the master in order for the representation of all that he will have been do, say, and think to be almost equal to the originary presence; and that thus the identity and tautology of absolute power be safeguarded.

It is quite certain that there Pellisson takes up the ancient exigency of the autopsy as guarantee of the authenticity of the narrative of the past event and the absent place:[18] the presence of the present of the narrator, at the event that he tells of as *having taken place* in the oneness and immediacy of a vision once again in the spoken or read text, constitutes the *etymon* of the narrative, the truth of what is said and the veracity of the person who says it; vision and presence verify the narrator as witness and martyr: "I have seen it, with my eyes seen it, what is called seeing." But for the king's future historiographer this presence at His Majesty's side on a campaign has implications more vast and deep than the simple "cognitive" demand of truth. To see the historical event at the place of the king, to be placed in this supreme—or almost—position, is to see the coming of History itself, since the king is its unique agent. And since the gaze of the absolute master sends the light that gives sight and produces what is to be seen, to be present at his side is to participate in his gaze and to share, in a fashion, his power: to double and substitute for him in the narrative-to-come that this past presence not only authenticates but permits and authorizes. The king's history is really, then, original history in Hegel's sense; it is the narrative of the origin of

History, History seized by the narrator at the origin of the historical event, worthy of being noted and retained at the very moment of its production by its agent.[19]

But to the extent that this potential power thinks itself and wants itself to be supreme, to be absolute, though an element of the place of this power and this potential, the historian does not participate in it: he does not take part—by definition—in the act, in the word, and in the thought of the absolute agent of the History. Hence the strange value of the ancient autopsy in modern royal history: it signifies, certainly, the truth of the event and the veracity of the witness who tells it. But this witness is more than a witness. *He is at the place of the point of view and of the point of origin*, both producers of the event, but he has no part in it, under penalty of relativizing this point of view and this origin. And yet it is not the absolute agent of the History who is its narrator. As archactor, he is its metanarrator through an interposed person. It is not he who will write, *veni, vidi, vici*, the minimal historical narrative of absolute political power. It is the historiographer who will note, *venit, vidit, vicit*. The passage from the first to the third person signals the theoretical gap of the narrator with respect to the archactor and metanarrator. In other words, the position of the historian at the side of absolute political power, as close as is possible to that power but without taking any part in it, is very precisely *its fiction as the subject of the theoretical representation he gives of it*, its fiction, that is, its double, its simulacrum: the person political power needs in order to represent *itself*, in order to represent its own past in the future—maybe because the present of the absolute, because it is absolute, is forever opaque to it, perhaps because it is of the very essence of the absolute not to be able, without relativizing itself, to reflect *itself* such, to be conscious of itself in an immediacy without distance. It is as if, thanks to this fiction, absolute power were itself telling its own history through the anonymous voice and writing of the "I-one" of the narrator who only sees what it gives him to see. The historian is thus the simulacrum of the king, his narrative, the simulation of the sovereign's history whose effect is perfect narrative representation without excess or loss.[20]

That is why only the simulation of history and its representational effect has the power to write the present of absolute power, not as the present moment of its act, of its word, of its thought, but as future-past.[21] What Pellisson said of the principal actors in this war goes a fortiori for its unique and necessary agent. By writing all that he is seen to do, say, and think, History can write only what has already been seen, and by that it writes what one *sees* in order to show [*faire voir*] those who will not have seen and even those who, seeing, do not know. In other words, through its writing, which will always follow the present moment of the act, absolute power, in the fictive position that it gives itself in its simulacrum, reveals and writes itself, makes itself known in the future perfect [*futur antérieur*]: it will act, say, and think as having acted, said, and thought.

But at the same time, and by a reverse movement, this temporal identity, this identification of the two great categories of the past and the future in the present of the sovereign act, is none other than the effect of the simulation of history, for this present is never expressed: it could not be so except in writing, and writing, in its very effectuation, will constitute it in an old present, in a represented present. Never will the miraculous instant of the absolute be able to inscribe itself as such. If we compared Racine's travel journal, the notes written between Paris and Gand at the king's side in the winter of 1678, with the corresponding narrative of the royal historiographer in *L'Eloge historique du roi*,[22] we would see the lived opacity of the miracle, at once perpetual and successive, unfolding itself in the clarity and intelligibility of the narrative representation of the past become monument for posterity: the power of simulation that the absolute needs in order to constitute *itself* absolutely.

Paradoxical machinations

Second inner spring of the framework: "The King *must be praised* everywhere but, *so to speak, without praise*, by a narrative." If the historical narrative is as I have said, it is identified with the panegyric. In this way is constituted and written what Racine will call the historical eulogy [*éloge historique*], Racine who noted, like Pellisson and after him, in the margins of his *Lucien*: "Panegyric and history are as remote from each other as the heavens are from the earth."[23] In Pellisson, nevertheless, narrative weaves eulogy but does not speak it: "[It must avoid] in its expressions all that veers towards the panegyric," and yet "the King must be praised everywhere but, so to speak, without praise, by a narrative." Even attenuated, the rhetorical figure in the *Project* remains audacious, and doubly so, in the expression and its destination if one considers that the memorandum will be read by the king; "paradoxism,"

> figure of expression through reflection where the ideas uttered reflect back on those that are not, at the same time as they awaken them in memory; alliance of words or expressions; artifice of language by which ideas or words ordinarily contradictory or opposed to each other find themselves brought together and combined in such a way that, while seeming to fight and exclude each other reciprocally [*panegyric and history are as remote from each other as the heavens are from the earth*], they strike the intelligence by the most astonishing accord and produce the most true as well as the most profound and most energetic meaning.[24]

It could very well be that Fontanier gives us here, with the figure of paradoxism, the most exact definition of simulacrum as effect of representation. For the idea uttered, by being reflected in its contrary that is not uttered (thus praise and narrative), produces it nonetheless through this very reflection.

We must note here that the author of the *Project* reveals to his addressee the rhetorical mechanism that the text must, in order to be effective, remain dissimulated: indeed, the movement and force of the figure rest on the fact that, of the two contrary ideas that are brought together and combined, one is not uttered by the writer but is produced in the memory of his reader by the reflection of the other on its absence in the discourse—thus the narrative-to-come of the king's history that Pellisson proposes to Colbert. But it is this mechanism that Pellisson describes later on, and by describing it he reveals it and cancels out its effect. The king's history must be told in a "neutralized" narrative that, by being reflected in the mind of the reader onto its contrary, the panegyric, awakens it in "such a way that, while seeming to fight and exclude each other reciprocally" (to praise is not to tell, nor is to tell, to praise), panegyric and narrative "strike the intelligence by the most astonishing accord and produce the most true as well as the most profound and most energetic meaning," and, in short, tear the magnificent meaning, epithets, and eulogies from the mouth of the reader by the things themselves. In other words, the production of a term by the narrative of the king's history, by its enunciated object, its matter, and by its enunciating subject, its manner, can only be the eulogy of the king. In this way is constructed the contemplation [*theoria*] of the royal act as the beautiful, eternal monument to his power [*puissance*]. From that point on the narrative of the history of the king—if such be the king, supreme power, if such be his acting [*agir*], saying, and thinking, if such be his narrator—can only produce, by reflection onto the praise absent from the text, the panegyric of royal virtue "in all sorts of ways" to its supposed reading. In the same movement and gesture the king, archactor of History and metanarrator of the historical narrative, can only produce the narrative of his own history through his future historiographer, by the reflection of his praise that is the text of the *Project* onto the absence of the narrative this text takes away with it.

Nevertheless, his author formulates, in a few clauses, the way of writing the king's historical narrative by simulating the effects of representation of his history: "[a narrative that] must appear disinterested but be lively, piquant, and sustained, [tearing] from the mouth of the reader the magnificent epithets and eulogies [the king] deserves"—but that his narrator does not utter. The manner of writing the king's history is constructed around a double opposition, that of appearance and being, on the one hand, that of disinterest and interest, on the other, with, nonetheless, a characteristic distortion. For the narrative that the reader, simulated by the author of the *Project*, will read is, in fact, constructed in its simulacrum at the intention of the interested king while being *interesting*— alive, piquant, and sustained—for the reader; but at the same time it is *in the king's interest*, while he *appears disinterested* to the reader. In other words, the opposition of appearance and being functions in a heterogeneous fashion in the *Project* and in the history-to-be-written and, at the same time, permits the slippage of the term *interest* from one meaning to another. The historical narrative *is* an interested one for the king, who is its object and subject to the extent that he aims at and attains a *political* objective, the subjugation of the reader to the sovereign subject and his absolute power. Thus the king, addressee of the *Project* of his history, is engaged in its design because of a political and ideological interest. The narrative-to-be-written has for end a *utility*, as Aristotle would say, defining political discourse with the deliberative mode.[25] But in the structure of absolute power, in the economy of absolutism, the means, the machination for attaining this goal and realizing this utility, is the eulogy of the Subject by his subjects, the epideictic and not the deliberative.

Nevertheless, the eulogy cannot be given and declared such by the historiographer, and that for two reasons: The first, fundamental, arises from the tactical instance of discourse of the author of the *Project* destined for the king; for by becoming panegyric, the narrative would reveal Pellisson's interest: the office of royal historiographer. The second, no less essential, refers back to the strategic calculation defining the narrative-to-be-written, for the explicit eulogy would not be able to induce, in his supposed addressee, the effect of representation that the narrative mode takes away with it, namely, the representation of the thing itself, in its reality of old present, attested to and verified by the narrator-witness. This is why the historical narrative, in its simulation, must *appear disinterested* to its supposed reader, whether he be the royal Subject or the king's subject, but the king will understand this appearance for the sake of his subject explicitly and politically, and the subject, taking the appearance for being, will understand it from the narrator of the narrative and from the narrative he tells itself. By appearing disinterested, the historical narrative will aim to position the reader as spectator of the king's history and to make the reader position the narrator as spectator— which he also *is*, as we have seen.

The historical narrative must not, then, involve the reader through a *political interest*, for example, by showing what is the actual case with the great questions that, according to Aristotle, political discourse debates in the deliberative mode and that have bearing on the community of citizens and on its real existence.[26] The narrative must be narrated as if the narrator supposed that no one among his readers was interested in these practical questions of politics. He must position the reader as spectator in a theatrical distancing, as subject of representation. Or rather, to use Aristotle's language, the narrative must put its reader in the listening position of the panegyric in the epideictic mode. But how could he, since this discursive mode is expressly pushed aside under pain of revealing to the subject-reader the interest of the royal Subject and, to the latter, the singular interest of the narrator? Quite simply by writing an interesting narrative, a lively, piquant, and sustained narrative, by using the secrets that animate history and prevent it from ever dragging and tiring, a narrative that interests the readers in what is happening and attracts them by making them see in the imagination all that is put on paper. But of course it will consist of a whole other interest: no longer political but esthetic, no longer of practical utility but of theoretical pleasure.

Thus the double opposition articulating the formulation of the manner of writing the king's history manifests a sort of complex chiasmus of appearance and being on the one hand, of politics and aesthetics on the other, of appearance and reality, of practice and theory, of the simulated and the represented, of utility and pleasure, between utterance and enunciation, narrator and narratee.

In the end, the inner spring of the discursive trap constitutive of the narrative panegyric is the pleasure of history, where is applied what La Fontaine calls the "power of fables."[27] By detouring politics toward aesthetics, interested practical interest toward disinterested theoretical interest, the political power of "the state-me," the political absolute, produces and realizes, in the narrative of its history, *the* politics that is its own, the absolute subjugation of the subjects to the Subject where this power is incarnated.

Denegating Violence

"In order to be better believed [by the reader], it should not give him [the king] the magnificent epithets and eulogies he deserves; they must be torn from the mouth of the reader by the things themselves." Here the paradox of the narrative panegyric is resolved; here its trap is dismantled. Since the utterances characteristic of the epideictic mode — the epithet and the eulogy — are excluded from the narrative, the reader believes in what the narrative *represents*, in all that the narrator (= one [*on*]) has seen of the king; the reader sees the king as if he had been at his side, in his place: he sees — he believes he sees — the thing itself, and from then on this vision-contemplation, this aspect-prospect, this theoretic eye, performs words and thoughts of magnificent epithets and eulogies, the very ones the king deserves. The simulacrum as effect of representation thus permits the transfer of the said, not to speech but to reading; the narrative utterance, the "represented" of the royal act, is performed by the reader of the narrative in representation. But in this movement between sending and receiving a supplement appears that is precisely the effect of representation: for what is not said at the sending (epithets and eulogies) is — necessarily — said at the reception. That which is not represented in the narrative and by the narrator is so at the narratee's reading, in the name of effect of the narrative. And in that way the absolute sphere of absolute power, encroached upon for a moment by the totalitarian narrative of its history, is reconstituted as total and sufficient unto itself: a supplement that is violence, the very violence involved in the formal apparatus of enunciation, whose effectuation perfects the construction of the mannequin-reader by comparing it with the real reader.

It is a question, then, of explaining a mechanism — a machine — that our previous schemata have only described. Why is it that the king's narrative, uttered by the narrator, puts the "reader" in the position in which he not only gives the king's eulogy but also cannot not give it—a *necessary* performance, that is to say violent, which brings with it an increase of praise? The whole problem is articulated around an aporia: (1) How can the reading of a historical narrative be, at the same time, the reading of nonpraise? (2) How, moreover, can this reading produce the missing discourse, and that with a supplement that neither the uttered nor the avoided term contained? The question is radical. A first way of approaching, if not of resolving, it would be to consider history and panegyric as constituting a sort of antithetical structure of waiting for "the reading of the king." They are linked by their difference, which is determined by the two terms it separates. Consequently, while reading the history's narrative I link with it the contrary term that is coupled with it, the panegyric, but I read it as absent, as nonpraise, and I can do that only to the extent that this absence is brought into relation with its possible *presence*. But this approach only puts back and postpones the aporia: indeed, how has this differential structure of waiting been *constituted*? Does this structure of the narrative and epideictic modes have a historical or transcendental genesis that links them to each other through their difference? But even when the genesis of this structure could be brought into prominence, the production of the epideictic *supplement* would still need to be explained, starting with the narrative mode itself, which is perceived as the negation of its contrary.

If to tell a story, a history, consists in the narrator *suppressing* himself in what he tells, of denegating, through the narrated, the act of the narrative's production in favor of the acts this narrative gives to be read—act-events that seem to tell themselves—on the horizon of the history as they occur, when these act-events are those of the king, the unique and absolute agent of the history, when the history itself is nothing other than this perpetual and successive miracle through which the royal substance deploys itself in time and space, and when the narrative of this history by the historiographer is the fiction of his ex-plication, then what the reading of such a history and such a narrative brings back—and, necessarily, what it cannot *not* bring back—is the subject of enunciation *denegated-suppressed* by the narrative of the history, not however as *narrator, act producing the narrative, narration*, but as history itself and its absolute agent, performed in the discourse of the reader that much more strongly, more powerfully, more absolutely because the uttering subject, the narrator, has been more radically and more completely excluded and denegated in the narrative. The whole process we are seeking to explain here rests on a double denegation: the denegation of the subject of the narrative enunciation through which all narrative is constituted as such in its modality of production; and the (de)negation of the subject of the enunciation of the history's narrative (the historian) through which the history is constituted as the product of *one* agent, and as the totality of the acts, words, and thoughts of that agent. Consequently, the reading will only be able to manifest the return of this twice-denegated subject with all the power [*puissance*], all the force, all the violence of this double (de)negation. The first effect of this violence "corresponding" to the (de)negation of the historian is the discourse of praise for the king performed by the reader of the narrative. The second effect "corresponding" to the more profound (de)negation of the narrator is the discourse of hyperbolic praise for the king performed by the reader of the history. Here is produced a "veritable" hallucination of reading: the magnificent epithets and eulogies that the king deserves and that the historical narrative has denied him are torn from the mouth of the reader by the things themselves. For the eulogy must be given all its content and value: not a simple ornament of narrative or an embellishment of the history, it is the very power [*puissance*] of speech [*parole*] that confers being and reality on the agent; it is efficacious speech, the very efficaciousness of the speech, the absolute performative. Saying is doing irrevocably and immediately. "A living thing and a natural reality that grows and gets bigger with it, it is the praised man who gets bigger, for man is his very praise."[28] Thus the king in Racine's eulogy: "The road of negotiation is indeed short under a prince who, having power [*puissance*] and reason always on his side, needs only to declare his wishes [*volontés*] for them to be executed." If such is, in its full sense, "eulogy," if such is the king's eulogy, by avoiding eulogy in narrative the king's eulogy is constituted in narrative as the phantasmatic of his own reading of the narrative.

Now we understand the decisive *political* stakes of praise in the narrative of the king's history: involved is nothing less than the king's power, than the absolute of his power. A decisive match of the *political* game is being played here, and it is the decisive thrust of this decisive match that the author of the *Project* is explaining to the king, by giving the principle of the strategic calculation that regulates (or should regulate) the narrative-to-be-written of his history. The first move of the thrust: as (de)negation of the narrator of the narrative and (de)negation of the subject, the historian of the history, the act-events of the absolute historical agent occur, in the text, through their own telling with no locutor to say them. No one speaks here. The king tells himself in his history — as a strange effect of forgetting the act of saying in order for what is said to be inscribed as memory — and that is what is essential for the essential of the narrator's "repression" to persist. In this sense historical narrative is very much the biggest machination of political power for *preserving* power. By (de)negating the utterer, the king gives himself a proper memory through the simulation-fiction of a history told by itself: the satisfaction of power's desire for power.

The second move: but this eulogy is not said. Only the history is, where the king does not receive "the magnificent epithets and eulogies that he deserves." Nonetheless, the narrative is read in an inverted enunciation. Reading is an enunciation that would be entirely transfixed in the utterer's taking on of speech and writing, if the subject of enunciation were not denegated, erased, and suppressed by or in favor of the subject of the utterance, the absolute agent of the total history. The erased subject-utterer then returns—in the publication of the narrative—as subject-utteree, but under the law of the enunciation, in its subjugation, in an inversion of the poetic potential power of the speech [*parole*] of eulogy into its contrary. The utteree will not say the eulogy that would give him power over the hero of the history: he will not say the magnificent epithets and eulogies that the hero deserves. They *will be torn* from his mouth by the acts, words, and thoughts of the king. The things themselves *will say themselves* in his mouth. The reading of the narrative as *hyperbolic* eulogy of the actor of the narrative is thus the effect of the simulation narrative, effect or inverted satisfaction of power's desire for power where, *in the simulacrum*, its potential is intensified up to the absolute, that is, in the reader, the total and necessary subjugation of the performing word to the law of the absolute agent of the history whose narrating law is fiction.

The Tactical Stakes

The tactical instance of Pellisson, author of the present *Project*, can now be made explicit in the strategic calculation of Pellisson, future historiographer. By exhibiting the strategic calculation of the narrative-to-come, the author of the *Project* could not but eulogize the king, since this eulogy was the objective of that calculation. But the king, reader of the *Project*, that is to say, of his own eulogy, will not fail to produce the historical narrative that corresponds to this panegyric. Thus, by inverting the formula written above, the king's history (still to be written) is constituted in the eulogy that the *Project* expresses as the royal phantasmatic of his own reading (of the *Project*).

Thus by dismantling for the king, here and now in the *Project*, the trap set for the reader in the design of the future narrative that the *Project* exhibits, Pellisson—tactical instance—sets [*monte*] with this very dismantling [*démontage*] another trap for the king, reader of the *Project*: the king will fall in. He will name Pellisson *his* historiographer. Quite a pragmatic articulation of utterance and enunciation, subject-narrator and subject-narratee, addressor and addressee of the coupled potential powers of being and appearance, potentials that, linked and appropriated by both sides, become powers; powers confronted, abandoned only to be better kept or recovered, traps discovered, dismantled only to be more efficaciously set; games terribly operatory of simulation and of effects of representation; politico-military functioning of an elementary structure of signification that, in and through this functioning, becomes framework of power by defining the conflicting positions of force of those who act, speak, think, write, or read, who constitute them as subjects of power or of "unpower" on the diverse levels of enunciation and utterance. Even more precisely, subjects of power constitute themselves as subjects by occupying these diverse positions and as subjects of power by appropriating for themselves the forces of which these positions are the resultant, or the point of application. We could then ask ourselves if the elementary structure of signification where the coupling of appearance and being is logically developed is not purely and simply the speculative abstraction of the "relationships of forces," whether these be material, physical, or discursive; the theoretical extraction, that is, the consolidation and conservation of a speculative-theoretical power, applied post hoc to the relationships of forces and to their field; in short, the theoretical reason for the "reasons for the effects" of force, for which Pascal drew up the pragmatic model in a series of thoughts and fragments, with bearing on the Cartesian theory of the mechanism of causes and physical effects as on the political relationships of force and justice.[29]

V. Narrative Hypotyposis, or the Symbolic of Power

History overlooks many circumstances that journals and Memoirs report. It does not concern itself with by how many paces a trench has been moved forward or which regiments mount the guard every day, when nothing extraordinary resulted. But in compensation, when it is a question of the Master and of an informative example of his value, firmness, and great sense, of which our King has given us a thousand, history lifts and makes the most of many little things about actions and principal persons that journals and Memoirs are accustomed to neglect. History puts all the great things it encounters in a better light through a nobler and more composed style, which encloses a lot in a little space with no wasted words.

Exemplification

Just as the eloquence of eulogy excluded at the beginning of the *Project* returned in his text at the place of the king, so, once again, do journals and memoirs, but in order to mark negatively the specificity of the historical narrative mode. It is indeed no longer a question of discovering the rules and matrix of the functioning of the historical narrative signaled by the scansion of the instructions of writing and composition of the narrative-to-come on the textual surface of the *Project*. These instructions, which were so many more and more assured *coups* in the engaged match, have led Pellisson—a subtle player—to transform the design of the narrative-to-be-written into the drawing of the narrative already completed in his strategic matrix, the decisive operator of this transformation being at the focal point of the text, the placing of the king in all the structural positions of the enunciation and the utterance. It is henceforth a question of describing the immobile paradigm of the Great History that already exists in the perfect simulation of the narrative syntagm that will realize it, and consequently the bad narrative genres of the history will be evoked only in order to mark the specificities of the good paradigm. They are bad, as I have said, because they implicitly refer back to a certain position of the subject of the narrative representation in the represented and to a certain conception of the historical subject of the History, on the one hand, and, on the other, to a certain structuring of the time of the narrative and to a certain conception of historical temporality. We already know why the initial exclusion of the "bad" narrative genres will be maintained: if there is only one agent of History and if, for that reason, historical temporality is only and can only be the articulation of its time, then there can be only one subject writing the history, a double or fiction of this absolute agent whose characteristic will necessarily be not to appear in the narrative that he will write, to denegate himself as subject producer of the narrative representation in favor of the subject represented.

While moving on to the description of the paradigm of the Great History from this double exclusion, the author of the *Project* furnishes his supreme addressee with the dimensions essential to *his* subject and *his* temporality in the narrative and, at the same time, the temporality of his history taken into account in this narrative. The specific mark of the Great History is the extraordinary. It is the position of this criterion and its definition that will lead the future historiographer to pose and define the historicity of the event as its exemplarity.

What is it, then, that distinguishes the extraordinary from the ordinary? It is not a dimension of greatness or of exception belonging to the event, act, or word that would render it worthy of being reported. An event in its reality is neither ordinary nor extraordinary. It could be that the number of steps by which a trench was moved forward at a certain siege or that the mounting of the guard on a certain day by a certain regiment was extraordinary. Little things can be great, just as great things can be small. How do events produce the extraordinary? And if the extraordinary is the specific mark of Great History in its narrative, how does narrative produce the historical event? The answer is simple: all the other actors of history, excepting the king, cannot but produce ordinary things. Certainly, there is no actor of History who is its agent apart from the archactor, the unique and absolute agent of History, which signifies that all the king does, says, and thinks is extraordinary and, therefore, that the narrative of history is indeed the compendium, and only the compendium, of all that he has been seen to do, say, and think: "The King's history . . . is a continual chain of the marvelous deeds that he himself begins, that he himself completes. . . . In short, miracles follow closely upon other miracles."[30] All the king's actions are miracles. His history is a continued marvel, and the other actors of the history exist only, through their acts, words, and thoughts, in order to mark the perpetual miracle, the permanent and successive marvel of the king and his being in action. In exchange for the loss of the singular event, of detail, of the "small true fact," of their incoherent and insignificant teeming where the "real" is given and is lost, history offers the miracle of the event-example, the marvel of meaning, the gesture [*le geste*]—the medieval gest [*la geste*]—of the king who produces history and, by producing it, gives meaning to all reality.

We will have noted the remarkable term *master* linked to *example*. The "Master" is the king who bursts forth by his gaze-light on the principal actions and persons—at once point of view, vanishing point, central moment, and focal figure of the narrative representation—toward whom they all lean as toward their center, in whom they are summarized and integrated, through whom they are totalized. Master in this sense, he is also the master of meaning. Political mastery is inseparable from the magistery of knowledge: articulation of a mastery to a magistery, of politics to ethics, with the historiographer as operator. It is he who *makes* the meaning of courage, of firmness, of value, and of rationality *known* [*faire savoir*] in the act of political and military mastery, who says and writes the moral instruction that this act conceals as its essence. It is he, the writer, who will transform, through the narrative, the perpetual royal miracle into something extraordinary that doubles it and gives it meaning, rationalizing intelligibility and ethical instruction. More precisely still, it is the historiographer, the fictive double in the narration of the agent of the History, who infuses the act of this agent with a meaning and who, in the end, produces the *extraordinary* in the ordinary that the journals and memoirs are accustomed to neglect. This meaning is the meaning of History, not as the ensemble of its immanent laws but as the revelation, in the actions of the king that produce historical events, of a great moral and intellectual idea. The description of the paradigm of the History projected in the narrative syntagma is, in the *Project*, the announcement of this revelation. Such is the historical act of the history, its historical function as figure of the king: to produce the exemplarity of the event through the inscription of this event as act of the king in the narrative it recounts of his history.

The example is composed, at this juncture, of a double dimension: speculative and pragmatic.[31] In the single action is revealed a universal essence of which the action is the representation. Whence the "vertical" structure of the historical action in the context that is ours. Each royal action that the historian recounts, the most minute of these actions, on the condition that the narrative narrates it and converts its ephemeral event into a monument, is, through that, the singular revelation of a universal essence, an attribute or perfection of the royal substance. Consequently, the historical, political, and military action, each one of the acts that successively constitutes its strategic deployment, is not caught in the explicating-describing text of the causes and effects that the historical narrative would weave diachronically or "horizontally." This narrative, by transforming the event of the royal act into a sign, is the revealer of this act as the instantaneous point of insertion, in time and space, of a permanent and universal attribute of the king, of his substance, which is and can only be an absolute universal will.

But the whole has also a pragmatic value at once as cognitive instruction and as normative prescription. It is because the royal history thus conceived can only be repeated in the succession of the act-events of the willing substance that these acts, on the condition of being converted by history into signs, have an instructive value, that of constituting cognitive models of the future, of its contingencies and hazards. Indeed, to the extent that historical narrative, as projection of the paradigm of history onto the narrative syntagma, is the exemplary-exemplifying exposition of a structure or program of the royal will in each of his acts, it possesses through that an anticipatory value. It *says* what is to come in and through the narration thus understood of the past: it functions therefore as a kind of praxologic model, simulator of the future. But it is a question of a remarkably "monotonous" model, since, far from predicting the new, it only reproduces in exemplification the permanence of universal essences, of the immobile perfections of the royal substance. Also the cognitive instruction of the example refers back to the king as ethico-theological model. Its pragmatic value is essentially that of normalization: the king in his will is the model of omni-sapience, omni-beneficence, and omni-potence. Each one of his acts and thoughts is at once proof and realization of this model.

But this prescription is, in turn, strange, since each one of his acts, words, and thoughts is at once exemplary and inimitable—very exactly, extraordinary. It refers back to an unattainable transcendent norm. It cannot be generator of a conduct and practice that would reproduce the royal conduct and practice. The pragmatic value of the example, its normative and prescriptive "form," is to necessarily produce an epideictic performance. A miracle, be it permanent, is not imitated. It tears admiration from the mouth of the reader by the historical fact itself. If, therefore, the praxologic model is constitutive of the deliberative mode and, through that, is the essential of political discourse, we perceive how the narrative of the king's history by his historiographer is its substitute in an institutional structure of power where the state is identified with the willing substance of the king: a substitution operated by the displacement of the epideictic model into the narrative mode, with no reference to the narrator who denegates himself there in order to let the events themselves occur in the utterance, events that are and are only the acts of the unique and absolute agent of the History. In this sense the theory of the exemplification of the historical event whose essential traits Pellisson describes puts a final period on simulation as political discourse of the historical to-be-written narrative and on the simulation of its effects of reading as eulogic discourse. The past and self-sufficient narrative of the historical acts of the king—and all his acts are historic—as exemplary acts well defines models of political action, but which foresee the future in the mode of the repetition of a substantial and transcendent permanence of the absolute power of the state-me-ego (*état-moi*), present in a continued and successive manner in each of his acts, exacting therefore, and necessarily, the performance of a hyperbolic eulogic discourse by its narrator.

Lifting the Narrative: The Picture of History

It is therefore not by chance that the ultimate reference of the future historical narrative and its supreme justification should be the painting of history: "History puts all the great things it encounters in a better light through a nobler and more composed style, which encloses a lot in a little space with no wasted words." Why? Because only the picture, through its medium, substance, and the insurpassable constraints of iconic narrative representation, necessarily gives the narrative-to-be-seen as a-chronic model, in the present, in the limited space of its canvas, and in the order of coexistence of its parts.

It is therefore on a picture that the *Project* ends, but one very different from the one that opens the narrative-to-be-written of the king's history:

> If one does not know how to melt and alloy all of this together [the history's "parts"] into a solid body, full of a variety of forces and brilliance, how to paint rather than tell, how to make the imagination see [*faire voir*] everything that is put on paper, how to attract the readers by that, and how to interest them in what is happening, it is no longer History. It is at most a register or chronicle.

The inaugural representation had the function of giving to the *narrative* its beginning and origin in the description of a state of composition of the antagonistic forces that articulated European strategic space. The final representation is the totalization of the narrative, of the ordered ensemble of its successive sequences, in a textual "body," a complex unity present *uno intuitu*, synchronically, to the global gaze of the imagination. It is not a question then, as one would have thought, of a description of the state of Europe, and particularly of the state of the kingdoms of France and Spain, *after* the last war, a description in synchrony of a stasis parallel and symmetrical with the first, where the new equilibrium of the forces would be inscribed after the changes and upheavals provoked by the conflict. No. It is the narrative itself that—because it *will have been* told in a certain manner—will have become the picture. It will not be the relation of the transformation of one state of equilibrium into another state of equilibrium; it is the narrative itself that will be transformed, in its very narrative essence, into a "body," a synchronic structure where the subordinate relationship of the "parts" to the center will explode. But that is not yet saying enough: the "body of the history" is not only an organic structure, "solid and full of variety," it is also and above all "full of force and brilliance"; it is body only through its *effects*. It is even there that history distinguishes itself from registers or chronicles, which servilely obey the linear and chronical form of time. The narrative of history is truly history only through the effects of totality of a manner of writing it, of which the *Project* has established the imperative rules starting from its own center, here named the place of the king: it is in the central place where the true, the only, the unique agent of history bursts forth that the total body of the history finds its solidity, variety, force, and brilliance.

It is, indeed, remarkable that the enumeration of the history's parts made by the author of the *Project* deals with the narrative through preterition. "Circumstances" predominate over the chain of events and over the linearly ordered sequences of the narrative utterances. Final exclusion of the narrative mode? Certainly not, but ultimate transformation of the narrative into picture. From the beginning, Pellisson insists: the narrative, the style of narration, is the general form of the history, its specific enunciative modality; it is indeed narratively that the king's historian must explain the causes of the rupture and the king's just claims; it is narratively that he must place and disperse here and there, with art and diversity, portraits and characters, that he must praise the king everywhere by tearing from the mouth of the reader magnificent epithets and eulogies; it is again to the narrating art that he entrusts the operations of exemplification, amplification, and intensification of the sovereign's acts. And yet all of this—reflections, discourses, harangues, counsels, and descriptions—everything that is lifted from the narrative, once integrated into the body of history, no longer refers back to the narration, to a narrator's telling, but to the work of painting. The ultimate quality of the historical narrative, where history is realized while finding its specific difference from the bad narrative genres, is paradoxically the narrative's negation or, rather, its lifting, its *Aufhebung* in the icon; an ultimate quality that is the culmination of the style of narration or its supreme *figure*, the fiction of presence: the hypotyposis "that *paints* things in such a lively and energetic manner that it puts them in a way before the eyes and *makes* of a narrative an image, a picture or even a living scene."[32] Through this figure and this fiction, narrative representation becomes visible presentation, *subjectio ad adspectum*, and the supposed real reader comes definitively to fill his simulacrum, to enclose himself in his mannequin—progressively constructed, *coup* after *coup*, by strategic calculation, the matrix of the history-to-be-written—to the point of identifying himself with him: "If one does not know . . . how to paint rather than tell, how to make the imagination see everything that is put on paper, *how to attract the readers by that, and how to interest them in what is happening*, it is no longer History. It is at most a register or chronicle."

The construction of the paradigm of history as the infinite totality of the attributes of the royal substance defines and determines the narrative as its translation into time and space. The narrative utterance *produces* the historical event as the inscription of the perfections of the substance of the state-me in the instantaneous *and* continual miracle of its act; as moment of narrative *representation* that is the moment of visible *presentation*, of "basilophanic" manifestation in time and space; where to tell *is to paint* and to narrate is to *make* things *be seen* [*faire voir*] by the spectator's imagination, because this moment of history is the fulgurant and permanent present where the royal substance *makes* its perfections *be seen*.

But these perfections can be seen, present and presented in the imagination, only because the narrator-painter has represented them by all that he has put on paper. Thus the total body of the history is none other than the solar and luminous body of the king, that bursting-brilliance [*éclat-éclatement*] that the *Project* posed strategically in its central place, the point where the formulation of what *will be* the history (the narrative) of all of this last war is reversed in the prescriptive enunciation of what history is *ideally* since always, now and never, and therefore of what *must* be, by logical necessity and by ethico-political obligation, its narrative realization to the extent of the conjuncture of times and places. Thus the narrative of the last war has become the body of the king, and the body of the king, the body of the history. The initial representation, fat in its immobility, with all the storms of the war, has been transformed by the secret virtues and potential powers of a strategy of writing into the omnipotent body of the history, whose terminal effect will be the imaginary picture fascinating the reader with its brilliance and variety.

I recapitulate: (1) the final description or the synchrony of possibles, become real through the conflictual strategies of the historical agents, is definitively effaced and substituted for by (2) the exposition of the definitive success of the strategic calculation of enunciation, which is at the same time (3) the last thrust [*coup*] in this strategy and the *coup de grâce*—that of victory—since it marks the triple identification of the royal body with the body of history, of the body of history with the reader-simulacrum, and finally of the real reader with his mannequin. In other words, the absolute subjugation of the subjects of the king to his absolute power is operated by the manner of writing history; that is to say, of writing the king—of writing his solar body as brilliant body of history and vice versa—and of making the imaginary reader "swallow" this political Host, a reader who is none other than "the reading imaginary" of the real reader: an absolutist manner of writing the absolute history of absolutism.

Interlude
The Discourse of the Flatterer, or the King's Eulogy

Of the three great modes of discourse that Aristotle analyzes in the *Rhetoric*[1] — deliberative, or political, discourse; judiciary, or the advocate's, discourse; and demonstrative, or the discourse of eulogy and censure — it would seem that political power, in its desire for the absolute, can find no representation more adequate than the one offered by the epideictic mode in its positive form of panegyric and praise. It is in this way that "the historical eulogy of the king," an expression that designates a fragment of Racine's and Boileau's royal historiography, constitutes the genre appropriate for the "king's narrative." This narrative, by occupying the place of an absent political discourse, represents its total effectuation in the narrative form of the royal gesture in its actuality. It is a narrative that does not aim to re-present the past by making it present once again but, rather, by insisting on or redoubling the presence of the prince in his immediate action, thereby giving him his essential legitimacy as the brilliant manifestation of his perfections.

Indeed, the king's history, because it is simultaneously actual and history and because it aims toward a representation of the present presence of the prince in his act, unites not only the two dimensions of representation in general but also the two great types of eulogic discourse: the panegyric and the funerary oration. The panegyric, by redoubling the hero's present in the language of a poem, gives him his plenitude and assures him permanence and growth by mirroring his perfections. The funerary oration, by re-presenting with suitable words the past gestures of the deceased hero, makes those who hear it forget their present by allowing them to relive ancient times in a near-hallucinatory or, at the least, imaginary mode. The king's narrative stems from both types: from the first, because it does not aim to represent the past but the present, and from the second, because it is a narrative, the narration of a history that necessarily puts its agent at a distance from the reader in order to provoke his identifying alienation.[2]

But, notably in a monarchical regime, there exists a group of "oratory genres" in which the epideictic, or demonstrative, mode finds a space that is natural for deploying its strategies—thus, with Bary, "panegyrics, funerary orations and ephithalamiums, epitaphs, entrance harangues, letters of civility, congratulations, thanks, and confidence."[3] More precisely, Crevier notes a century later in his *Rhétorique française* that

> Discourses of the first type of demonstrative genre, that is, those whose object it is to praise, are often used among us. We know the Panegyrics of the Saints, the Funerary Orations and Eulogies that are read in the Academies. The gentleness of our mores, on the other hand, makes public invectives very rare, and even so they are directed against vices in general and do not attack persons. . . . In the demonstrative genre can also be included the Harangues used to open the *Compagnies de Judicature* and the Public Lessons in the *Grandes Ecoles*, Compliments to the Powers [*Puissances*], the Speeches that are given at receptions in certain Academies, and others like these.[4]

And Crevier goes on to justify indirectly the preeminence in practice of the demonstrative mode by effacing the deliberative mode, that is, the mode of political discourse:

> Occasions for discourse in the deliberative genre are not common in our usage. Under a monarchical government such as ours, the affairs that were dealt with in Rome and in Athens before the Senate and in the people's Assembly are reserved for a Council at which the king presides, and to which only a small number of Ministers are admitted. There the great ornaments of Eloquence would be misplaced.[5]

In the demonstrative "genre's" own places, the authors of treatises on rhetoric essentially examine the diverse manners of praising and censuring (*laus* and *vituperatio*). Le Gras, for example, in his work of 1671, *La Rhétorique française*, defines the form of praise or censure in terms of increase or decrease, "obtained," he writes,

> through circumstances, as by saying that the person who is being praised did the thing by himself, or that he was assisted by only a small number of persons, or that he is the first to have dared to undertake it.

"The hyperbole," he adds,

> so long as it is not excessive, is the figure best suited to praise, because praise is something free, with the goal only of elevating the subject it speaks about and of showing that it surpasses all others; and, as this hyperbole is made ordinarily by a comparison, this comparison must always be above the thing that is being compared, or, to speak more clearly, the thing being praised must never be compared to something that is lesser or equal, but always to something that is greater.

Naturally, the king's history comes under the rhetorician's pen:

> One compares, for example, the designs and actions of Kings to the designs and works of God: the King's designs can be seen only in his actions, as one sees God's only in his works.

Assuredly, Le Gras's undertaking being fundamentally normative, it is fitting to mark the hyperbole's limits:

> Discretion must be used. . . . Praise must be founded on truth. All the orator can do is elevate his subject, which is what the historian cannot do.

But we have seen how, with Pellisson and Racine or Boileau, historical narrative can become hyperbolic praise when read through the judicious use of litotes in writing the narrative. Le Gras continues:

> A judicious orator will compare the speed of an excellent horse to that of wind or lightning and a private person's beautiful house to a Prince's palace, whereas the flatterer will say the same thing of a common horse and of an ordinary house, or will praise what is not laudable, like the courtier who, seeing Demetrius with a cold, praised him for coughing and spitting in harmony.[6]

As Kibédi Varga remarks, "The demonstrative genre is at once that of praise and of censure. But the passages cited distinctly show that in the eyes of the authors of the treatises, the texts belonging to the demonstrative genre are practically all eulogies."[7] And that for two reasons. First, the eulogy is a work superior to censure because it is more difficult; censuring satisfies a natural bent of the mind, whereas "praising is done at the expense of the pride [*amour-propre*] of the person who praises"[8] and is that much more difficult in that it should never be formulated directly, as is censure. We find again, then, the royal historiographers' strategies of writing, which aimed, through the simple and naive expression of the prince's act, to tear from the mouth of the reader the magnificent epithet that qualifies it. And second, in the hierarchy of literary and oratory genres, "satire, which is the proper domain of censure, is a genre inferior to the ode or the funerary oration, where praise is almost obligatory."[9]

But if, by the admission of the discourse's theoretician, the flatterer's hyper-hyperbole constitutes by itself, as in the anecdote of Demetrius's courtier, the manifest criticism and censure of bad eulogic discourse without the necessity of a development that would make its excess explicit and reveal its ridiculousness, we can then examine some kinds of satire that, still dependent on the epideictic mode, would not be directly identified with *constituted* genres of censure, such as they are *authorized* by the literary and political *institution*. Or to put it another way, we can ask what makes a hyperbole hyperbolic. In Le Gras, the person who says of a common horse that its speed is that of the wind is a flatterer; in return, it is a judicious orator who writes: "The King's designs can be seen only in his actions, as one sees God's only in his works." Without a doubt the inner spring, at once political and literary, of the eulogy resides in the assessment by the person who utters it of the threshhold of acceptability of the person who is its object, whether this assessment is intuitive on the part of the orator or theorized by the rhetorician, or whether it depends narrowly on the "concrete" circumstances of the eulogy's production or flows from the norms, constraints, and exigencies of the institution where it is produced. Also, from this point of view the "unacceptable" eulogy becomes a kind of satire of the accepted eulogy, without however slipping into the institutionalized form of satire.

It is in this way that La Fontaine, in one of his fables,[10] by staging [*mettre en scène*] and narrating [*en récit*] a eulogy whose excess and ridiculousness his public (and he himself, no doubt) perceives immediately, but by showing how easily received it is by him to whom it is destined, simultaneously brings to light the inner springs of the strategy of the eulogy itself and effects its critique by a parody in situ. As we know, the Aesopic fable is a genre even more minor than the satire, to the point of not figuring in the great hierarchical classifications of genres. In this way also Perrault will begin one of his tales with a eulogy of the king that the narrative will take care of converting into censure, to the point of *having* one of his women readers *write* [*faire écrire*] the following verses in his preface:

> There are some Satiric traits in places,
>   But, without bitterness or malignity,
> They give pleasure in reading to all alike.
> Another thing that pleases me in its sweet simplicity
>   Is that it diverts and makes one laugh,
>   Without Mother, Husband, or Confessor
> Being able to find fault with it.[11]

It was therefore tempting to analyze this fable (and this tale), simultaneously eulogy in the utterance and parodic censure in its enunciation, and to confront the mechanisms that it brings to work on these two planes with those of one of the "Speeches that are made at receptions in certain Academies, and others like these," in order to test the political, juridical, and aesthetic effectiveness of the relationship in chiasmus of representation and power and, more precisely, the way in which the king gives himself to be consumed as symbolic body to his subjects, and how these last constitute him such through the discourses they address to him.

The Fox's Tactics

The Crow and the Fox
>Master Crow, perched in a tree,
>> Held in his beak a cheese.
>
>Master Fox, enticed by the smell,
>> Held forth more or less in these words:
>> "Hey! Good day, Sir of the Crow!
>
>How pretty you are! How handsome you look!
>> It's no lie, if your song
>> Is like your feathers
>
>You are the phoenix of the denizens of this wood."
>At these words, the crow was beside himself with joy;
>> And to show his beautiful voice
>
>He opened his large beak, letting fall his prey.
>The fox seized it and said: "My good sir,
>> Learn that every flatterer
>> Lives at the expense of his listeners.
>
>This lesson was well worth a cheese, no doubt."
>> Ashamed and embarrassed, the crow swore,
>> But a little too late, that he would not be taken in again.[1]

What, then, is the discourse of flattery, if it constitutes, as in a famous text of the *Phenomenology of Spirit*, the fundamental mode of exchange and the essential form of "culture" by which the politically powerful aims to fulfill himself as absolute monarch in the celebration of his name by the courtier and by the noble consciousness, and to acquire by this manipulation of language the wealth, the objective essence, that permits him to elevate himself to the consciousness of self?[2]

A fable by La Fontaine, *The Crow and the Fox*, is in a sense a staging of the discourse of flattery. This tale permits us to approach the dialectic of the power of state, of language and wealth, where is unveiled at once the articulation of the desire of power for the absolute and that of the infinity of representation that power gives itself in order to attain that absolute. Before reading, in *this* particular fable, the essential mechanisms of the discourse of flattery, it is appropriate to formulate two working hypotheses concerning the fable that touch directly on the question of power and representation. The first concerns the principal character of fables in general, the *speaking animal*: this fiction preserves of animality the primitive sanction of all "social" behavior, to eat or to be eaten, but keeps of man that which characterizes him essentially, language, through which the going beyond of immediate and singular desire in cultural universality is manifested. The speaking animal of fables is thus like the figure of an origin of language in the devouring of bodies, and the animal's discourse is the figure of this devouring, the fiction of a *clinamen* of verbality in orality. The second hypothesis that I propose is to consider this origin of language to be indiscernible from an origin of power of which the inter-devouring of bodies is, in its turn, the figure. In the fable, to eat (or to be eaten) figures the radical power of discourse in language: to eat the other is the "monstrous" fiction of the power to speak [*pouvoir parler*] (to) the other. Power institutes itself as power only through and in the representation of language, just as the representation of language is effectuated only in the power where it is realized.[3] To eat the other and to speak to the other, to appease one's primitive need in that other and to assure, outside of and beyond one's present exercise, one's force in and through one's power *over* that other, would be another figure of the dialectic of wealth and power of state in the enunication of the "king's discourse," where the king is simultaneously exalted as body of language in the institution of discourse and consumed as economic body in the institution of power.

This fundamental relationship appears from the first verses of the fable in the suggestion of a dynamic equality to be transformed between "holding a cheese" [*tenir un fromage*], food, and "holding (forth in) these words" [*tenir un langage*], discourse: "Master Crow, perched in a tree, / Held in his beak a cheese. / Master Fox, enticed by the smell, / Held forth more or less in these words." The master of the food in the high position possesses, in silence, wealth: immobile time, full duration, the imperfect tense ["*tenait un fromage*"]. Master Crow has the potential of eating; he possesses all the time to eat. He holds power and wealth in a primitive equality; noble consciousness. In return, the fox is initially the figure of inequality and inadequation of the one and of the other. In the low position of need, the signal of the smell points to the instantaneous event of lack, the instant of opportunity. In the flow of the smell, he who will "hold" language appears. But at the same time, at this point precisely, in the utterance of the fable appears the narrative moment, marked by the preterit tense [*"tint ce langage"*], of its introduction into the schema of incidence in the full duration of the imperfect tense.[4] Signs will appear in an instant, within an instant, in the empty place opened up by the need to eat. From that moment on, if the movement of need is launched by indices and traces, if signals indicate the presence of the thing that is good to eat, to speak or hold discourse will not consist of *saying* the indices or of naming the traces but of substituting for the index-signals discreet signs that will all signify something else that is not given here and now: by proferring itself, the discourse *will say* something other than that to which, in fact, it refers. If Master Fox is trapped by the smell of the cheese (the thing itself in the metonymy of its indices), he mounts in his turn another trap, wholly of language, but whose only objective is to obtain, through this detour and excession, the desired thing in order to appease his hunger; a discourse that is the metaphor of the cheese, in the literal sense of this term. It is a metaphor that the term *to hold* [*tenir*] signals and suggests, applied alike to the thing that is good to eat and to the discourse good to speak, but a metaphor that makes a disjuncture appear in the equality: if to hold a thing is to possess it by an essential transitive appropriation, then to hold language is to speak to someone—inescapable transitivity—to transmit signs, to give words. If to hold a cheese is to possess food in potential assimilation to oneself, to hold discourse consists right away of putting oneself outside of oneself, of "estranging" oneself in the potential universality of exchange. While the master of the food, by a substantial metonymy of the body to the cheese through the beak, poses his immobile identity in the *cogito* of the appropriation, "I am what I have," the master of language, through signifying metaphor, presents himself in the dialogic alterity of transport and process: "I am what I put outside toward you, in your direction."

The fox's discourse is that of someone who *has* his share of language to another who *has* food; more exactly, it is the discourse of him who possesses the *savoir-faire* of discourses and who *wants power* [*vouloir le pouvoir*] as wealth, a discourse addressed to the crow, who is precisely the one with the power and wealth.

But the discourse of the fox is authorized a second time by the fox himself in his address to the crow: "'Hey! Good day, Sir of the Crow!'"—exclamation, wish, and nomination. At first, in the guise of an opening, something like a cry, an interjection, or a "phatic" word that serves to call him whom one is addressing, to attract his attention to oneself, to call upon him. "Hey! I'm talking to you!" By calling upon you, I pose myself as initiator of the discourse; the speech [*parole*] comes from me, and the person called upon is placed in the position of listener. But "hey" is also that interjection that serves to give more force to the words that follow it, the discourse addressed by the fox to the crow and of which the crow will be the object. Not only is the crow placed in the position of addressee, but also he cannot not occupy that position.

Now what immediately follows the exclamation is a wish: "Good day." The exclamation and wish on the part of the fox have no other function than to prepare the concrete conditions of discursive legitimation. Now he names his interlocutor, and he names him twice, "Crow." He knows his name and by that declares that he knows him. Maybe the crow does not know Fox, but the reverse is not true, and if Fox knows Crow although the latter does not know him, then by implication Fox signifies to Crow that he is known by many, that he is famous. By naming him after having called upon him, Fox not only speaks but also arrogates to himself the right to speak to Crow.

"Sir of the Crow" [*Monsieur du Corbeau*]: Not only does Fox name Crow, but he gives him a title, he gives him an appellation that classes him in a hierarchy, and that twice. The first situates Crow in the nobility, and by implication Fox declares, through simple civility and courtesy, that he recognizes himself to be his inferior. But there is more. "Crow" is at the same time a proper name in the narrative that the fabulist is giving us, and a common name or noun in the ordinary discourse he shares with his reader, the name given to a species of bird. When the fabulist, with Fox, names and gives the crow the title (the name of the species and the name of the character in the fable) of "Sir of the Crow," the title de-natures the common name by acculturating it, by making it a proper name: "crow" is from that time on the name of a singular individual who names himself Crow and whose title shows that he belongs to an elevated social class.

But Fox does not say "Sir Crow" [Monsieur *de* Corbeau] but literally "Sir *of the* Crow" [Monsieur *du* Corbeau], a new ambiguity. One can no doubt understand it as an appellation, but the partitive *du* subsists in the title: "Sir of the Crow" extracts from the species "crow" this crow here as character of the fable, as *dramatis persona*. By that, the reader discovers that the crow does not have a proper name—it is an individual of a species of bird called crow—but only a title. More precisely, his title is his proper name: deprived of the title that Fox gives him, he would fall back into anonymity as a member of a zoological species. The crow needs the title given by the fox in order to get out of generality and accede to individual identification, in order to recognize himself.

Now the crow knows quite well that he has no right to this title. Nevertheless, he does not disabuse the fox. He accepts the title, but less as a usurped title than as a mark by which the fox recognizes the proper position of his discourse concerning him. Through it, Fox recognizes the place he speaks from: he indirectly qualifies his discourse as discourse from inferior to superior. Moreover the reason the crow does not disabuse the fox is not that he would understand the title as a false title but that it signifies an inferiorizing qualification of the discourse addressed to him. And it is in this way that Fox legitimates his discourse: he makes sure the addressee recognizes it as such. That is the fundamental mechanism of the discourse of flattery, by which the addressor of the eulogy puts the addressee in the position of legitimizing and authenticating the discourse that he addresses to him, that is to say, of recognizing it as a discourse to which he has a right and, at the same time, as a discourse that the addressor has the duty to address to him.

The addressor declares that he supposes that the addressee knows who he himself is, but the addressor does not say *what* the addressee knows about himself. In return, he says what he, the addressor, knows about him. From that point on, the acceptance by the flattered of the flatterer's discourse consists of substituting the image of himself that the flatterer offers him for the image that he has of himself, or, more exactly, of recognizing in this image a truth about himself that he did not know, of recognizing himself in it, of identifying himself with it. But the flatterer's essential strategy for attaining this objective will consist of making the addressee transform a modality of obligation, "I *must* be what you say I am," into an established fact, "I am what you tell me I am," but of which the condition is that "you tell me so." In other words, how and why does the addressee *believe* the addressor? The inner spring of this strategy of the flatterer will consist, then, of making himself be recognized as legitimate and authorized addressor by him whom he addresses.

All of the flatterer's art will consist of saying what the addressor *must be* [*devoir être*] in the mode of *being* [*être*], that is, by noticing and describing (by saying he limits himself to describing) what the addressee is. Nevertheless, these analyses of the effects of discourses of flattery have meaning only because the interlocutors have some *interest* in entering into the exchange. That is what the fiction of the talking animal of fables uncovers with perfect pertinence. The fox has, in effect, a vital problem to resolve, that of the consubstantial relationship of language and food, and having taken the initiative by addressing the crow it is, in the end, in this same problem that he will enclose him. The fox is fasting and is enticed by the odor of the cheese, and if he stops at the foot of the tree where the crow is perched, it is to obtain from him the cheese that he holds in his beak. His vital interest is to eat, and the only means at his disposal is language. Whence the problem to be resolved: How to transform the discourse (that he holds) into food? How to "transubstantiate" the language that he holds into the cheese that the other possesses? How to sing while keeping the cheese? This could be the symmetrical and inverted version of the fox's questions that the crow would have to resolve, if the flatterer's purpose did not have the end of making him forget it while inciting him to sing.

But whatever the problem and the modalities of his position, to speak of transformation necessarily implies a "force" of transforming. For nourishment, to eat entails the ability to transform food into one's own substance, to assimilate it at the price of its destruction: such is need and its appeasement. Master Crow, at the top of the tree, holds a cheese in his beak. He does not eat it, but he could: a force reserved as potential and, for the famished fox at the foot of the tree, a brilliant index of a power. What about language? In what sense does speaking operate, and can it operate, a transformation? Not while speaking of things: words slip, incorporeal, on their surface, without modifying them in any way. In return, to give an order, to promise, or to give a title, these modify a situation, a state of things. Likewise if, through a certain usage of speech by one person, the other is persuaded, convinced, obligated, seduced, or provoked: for better or for worse he can thus be brought to modify his own position in the world. It is in this way that Master Fox operates through his flattering discourse.

The eulogy of flattery, and maybe all eulogy, is at first a provocation: "'How pretty you are! How handsome you look!'" After the interjection, the wish, and the nomination in vocative form that open the discourse, two exclamations: an irresistible thrust of the voice: "'(I am so subjugated by what I see that I cannot prevent myself from saying) how pretty you are!" By that, the fox offers to the crow, as if torn from him in a cry of admiration, the image he has of him. Before provoking the addressee in the challenge, the addressor admits himself to be irrepressibly provoked to speak through and about him. But the two exclamations cannot be reduced to a double cry: with them are articulated two steps of one argumentation. I affirm, me, Fox (1) how pretty you are, and (2) how handsome you look: two declarative propositions whose reference to the uttering subject has simply been elided. But paradoxically the ellipsis adds a supplement that is of the order of voice, of the intonational inflexion where the dimension expressive of locutionary attitude is manifested. In effect, the amplification, in the utterance, of the quality of "pretty" to "handsome" is accompanied by the restriction, in its enunciation, of "being" to "seeming." What was a lesser quality, affirmed irresistibly as true reality, becomes a greater quality, but posed as appearance. It is through this that the flatterer's provocation to speak will turn around to that of the flattered. For the crow, the almost obligatory pragmatic implication of the fox's two exclamations will be to transform the addressor's "opinion" into the addressee's "truth" or, more, to overvalue at once the utterance and the enunciation. Whence the fox's challenge to the crow that immediately follows: "'It's no lie, if your song / Is like your feathers / You are the phoenix of the denizens of this wood.'" True, with the challenge we leave to an extent the discourse of praise, but the fox's tactic brings to light one of the essential frameworks of this discursive mode, namely, the operation by which the addressee of the discourse rushes to identify himself with what the addressor is telling him about himself; and the challenge adds this extreme that the addressee must himself demonstrate the truth of the addressor's opinion: "Although up until now I have thought you handsome, it is you who must let me know [*faire savoir*] that you are such in truth." The crow can make this demonstration, or at the very least he is put in the possibility of making it, since the fox defines the necessary and sufficient proof that he must and can bring: to sing. We will have remarked that the fox does not explicitly qualify the crow's feathers but only lets his interlocutor understand that it is his feathers that tear from him his initial exclamations. He does not tell him, either, that the single fact of showing his voice will suffice in making him a phoenix. In short, he does not ask him to sing but lets him suppose that, if he sings, then will he be a phoenix. Whence the seduction that the challenge implies: to know what he is in truth and to learn it himself the crow must, and it will suffice that he, rush to identify himself with what he supposes the fox is telling him he is.

Sir of the Crow will sing, then, forgetting that he holds power and wealth in his beak; he will sing forgetting that the organ of vocal expression and of the ingestion of food occupy the same place of the body; he will sing to obtain a new title, that of "Phoenix of the Denizens of This Wood," a title that must definitively dissipate the ambiguity that Master Fox's initial address involved, "Sir of the Crow," between the common noun of the animal species and the proper noun of a singular individual. For the phoenix is a unique and singular case in the class of birds: if "Sir of the Crow" is a title to which a common noun is reduced, "Phoenix" is a title that is and can only be the one proper noun in the universe of birds, the absolute of name and the name of the absolute. By challenging the crow to sing in order to become a Phoenix, the fox plays on the desire for the absolute of all holders of power and offers him, with this title, the representation of an absolute where imaginarily power in its desire is fulfilled.

We know indeed that the mythical bird possessed the power to be reborn from its own ashes after having lived more than five hundred years: a symbol of immortality, perpetuity, and infinite continuity and a symbol of royal virginity as well as of the resurrection of Christ. But as Kantorowicz[5] and Giesey[6] have stressed, for the jurists of the church, the emperor, or the king, it is the singularity and uniqueness of the bird that assume the greatest importance. The phoenix indeed represents the exceptional case in which the individual is by itself the whole species, since the species produces only a single individual at one time. Now since the species is immortal and the individual mortal, the mythical bird uncovers a duality in itself: it is at once Phoenix and of the genus phoenix, mortal as individual although immortal as species.[7]

A myth, the phoenix functions well as the juridical model of the "perenniality" of the same royal body in the line of individuals in which it is successively incarnated; when Claudian describes the death-birth of the phoenix, the terms he uses could be applied to the death-enthroning of the king: "To the paternal bird, an identical / But new bird follows: for barely a single moment, / The flame has distinguished the course of these two lives."[8] In a note commenting on the royal token, or medal, for the New Year 1644, on the reverse side of which is a phoenix enflamed by rays from the sun at the top of a mountain, we can read:

> The Phoenix is born and rises from the Ashes of his Father through
> the Influence sent to him by the Heavens and the Sun. Thus the King

has been miraculously given to us from on high, and from the funerary site [*lit funéraire*] of his father he rises to his throne [*lit de justice*].⁹

Theological, juridical, and political paradigm, the Phoenix is thus indeed, as title, the proper name of the absolute and the absolute of the proper name. We understand, in the parodic mode, the stakes of the flatterer's challenge to Master Crow: it is a question of absolute power or, which comes down to the same thing, of the absolute name of power that "phoenix" at once names and represents. But the argumentation in its implications and presuppositions, because it concerns a fable and talking animals, is in a way misplaced in the domain of the body and of substances that are good to eat, in those places of the body where words and food cross each other and are exchanged. The phoenix, without assignable origin because self-reproducing, bird of light and of sun, is made only of brilliant colors and of perfumes. It nests in the spices on which it feeds. But it is a bird without voice; the singular universal bird is silent.¹⁰

Also, when the fox proposes to the crow the decisive experiment of *singing* in order to be the phoenix of the denizens of this wood, he offers him as a compensation for his "antiphoenicity" the ability to exhibit a quality of which the phoenix is deprived, song, and thus to become a "superphoenix." No doubt, but on the condition of forgetting that he possesses none of the other qualities of this extraordinary bird. On the contrary, his smell (that of the cheese) is not a perfume; his black feathers are not a motley of brilliant colors; and his cold and moist food is not made of dry and hot spices. But will he perhaps sing? It would be his privilege with respect to the bird without voice. Such is one of the essential mechanisms of the discourse of flattery: to fix the gaze or the ear of the interlocutor on the identifying *representation* at and in place of the real *presentation* that the former dissimulates and supplements. Certainly, the fox "lies," as do all flatterers, but we cannot help but notice that he lies in the order of representation, not in the order of the real and of life. Who can dispute that for the fasting animal the smell of the cheese is a perfume? that the proprietor of the food is the origin and source of life? The argument of the fox's seductive injunction is the conformity of the song and the feathers, but he qualifies neither the one nor the other. It is precisely here that the dialogic structure of the discourse that the fox holds operates with a maximal efficiency. Just as the fox has been enticed by the smell of the cheese (the order of the real), the crow is drawn by the evocation of his song (the order of representation): "The smell of your cheese appears to me to be as good in what it anticipates for me—food—as the blackness of your feathers seems handsome to you in what it promises you, to be a singing phoenix (the order of representation)."

The whole discursive tactic of the fox at the foot of the tree and the play of his *coups* rest in truth on an unsaid that brings us from the speaking animal, man, to the beast, which is also man. After all, the beast began to speak—and with what skill and power—only to bring to light and reveal *the place of the body where eating (the power of)* and *speaking (the power of)* are situated undecidedly and indiscernably, whether it is called mouth, throat, or beak. So that this place could be, if I may dare say, theoretically revealed, the tactic of the discursive *coups* of him who speaks only to eat had to be practically and pragmatically deployed: "*At these words*, the crow was beside himself with joy; / And to show his beautiful voice . . ." How to transform words into cheese? I asked Master Fox. How, if not by provoking the master with the words and the sly tactic of the discursive potential of him who *needs* to eat? The "master" is he who has no "needs" or who has the durable power to satisfy his need. How, if not by provoking the master in his *desire* to sing, to *show* his beautiful voice? The crow has no *need* to speak or to sing, because he has no *need* to eat. But the fox's words and his argumentation incite the master without need to show his beautiful voice, to occupy the status of "superphoenix" in the aesthetic gratuitousness and finality without end of the beautiful song, which does not aim toward a goal, which does not fulfill an interested need, but which shows itself for the pleasure of it.

Nevertheless, to show his voice in all its beauty the master must necessarily open his beak. To hold the cheese is incompatible with holding discourse. Either the crow keeps his prey but does not sing, or he opens his beak (to sing) but lets it fall. The mouth (beak, throat) is that ambivalent place, the organ of eating *and* of speaking (singing), but not at the same time. Nature and culture are manifested in the same space, but successively: I speak before eating or after having done so. Before, I speak because I have an empty stomach (need), and I hold the discourse of sly violence to transform *my* language into the *other's* cheese. After, I sing because I am no longer hungry, and from that point on I carry out my desire in the finality without end of the pure pleasure of beauty.

Everything begins, then, with this putting in reserve of the cheese, with this potential (of eating) now and in the future, where food is converted into signs and where power is assured for the present time and the future, in a mastery of time. . . . Therefore, as the wafts from the cheese spill into the interval, the fox is found there, famished. He turns up at the foot of the tree and, in the instant of a *kairos*, his linguistic violence takes power in the trap of its desire for the absolute, that is, its desire to have its name, and the only name, the name "Phoenix," where death and life coincide. Why then did the crow not eat the cheese at the instant in which he took it? We must reread Hegel on this point and on the moment of sensible certitude in the *Phenomenology of Spirit*, where immediate devouring is said to be the profound wisdom of the beast.[11]

The crow in the instance of the song—the cheese in reserve in his beak, desiring a name, desiring the absolute—is very much the figure of the origin of all power, and the famished fox, but sly speaker, that of the violence of the discourse of flattery. The fox seizes it and says: "'My good sir, / Learn that every flatterer / Lives at the expense of his listeners."'" The fox seizes the cheese, but he also puts it in reserve to hold forth, a second time, a speech to the crow, but very different from the first. Pragmatic and sly violence is succeeded by moral didacticism; the vocative of admiration, by the enunciation of the unimpeachable maxim of wisdom; pragmatic, hypothetical argumentation, by the indubitable position of the practical rule. In short, one position of power is substituted for another, the former founded, as is the latter, on the transfer of a vital reserve: "Every flatterer / *Lives* at the expense of his listeners"; but also on a delay in the satisfaction of the need. Master Fox takes the time to give a lesson. Master of a certain wisdom, he is animated by the desire to teach [*faire savoir*] *while waiting* for the moment to satisfy his hunger. There is therefore a gap and a primitive accumulation where morality takes the "origin" of its discourse. The mute reserve of the crow at the top of the tree had permitted the desire for the absolute of power to manifest itself in the imaginary rush to a representation of the absolute. The talkative reserve of the fox at the foot of the tree authorizes the fulfillment of the desire to know in the nontemporal present of the lesson. The fox become schoolmaster—the cheese beneath its paw—draws the image of a power of knowing that would be only a reversed violence; a force of discourse in a singular situation of need and urgency has become a reaction reflected in the universality of norms valid in all times and all places. The figure of the genealogy of morals and its authority: "My good sir, / Learn that every flatterer / Lives at the expense of his listeners."

But what is this lesson, this philosophy? What is this knowledge? It is a *vital* lesson. The theory that is uttered in the throat of the magister is the theory of a practice and a pragmatic. Master Fox produces the theory of his practice, flattery. It would be an artist's discourse of representation if there were not, motivating it from one end to the other, the concrete finality, the law of the urgency of vital need; a discourse of parasitism: I do not live by my work, by my hunting or by my gathering. I live at the expense of the person who produces and possesses. I live by consuming the substance of the other, with no other means of existence or of survival than my discourse. A precarious, risky, dangerous life, one thrust at a time, where every discreet instant of a meeting with the powerful and secure other is decisive: devouring or devoured, life or death, all or nothing, law of the jungle, "ferocious," which could mean at once bestial and savage. Reread in order to be convinced of it *The Court of the Lion*, *The Animals Sick from the Plague*, or *The Lion, the Wolf and the Fox* by La Fontaine, among others. And in these risks of every instant there is only one weapon, one discourse where words touch with delicacy, please and satisfy. Yes, in truth . . . this lesson is well worth a cheese.

A strange conclusion, nevertheless, when we think about it, for: (1) Can the "bestial-ferocious" existence—the discourse of flattery—of the parasite of the secure and the strong, by nature or by custom, be the object of a "lesson"? Can the *virtù* of the flatterer be taught? If the temporal structure of the parasite is that of a succession of discreet and singular moments of which life and death are, each time and singularly, the total stakes, can each of these situations where the fox of the fable plays his all be universalized in the maxim that he utters: "Every flatterer lives at the expense of his listeners"? Why not? But then the rule is inapplicable, and the crow will always discover a little too late, always after the fact, that he cannot be a phoenix or an eagle—see *The Crow That Wanted to Imitate the Eagle*. "Ashamed and embarrassed, the crow swore, / But a little too late, that he would not be taken in again." Unless the "lesson," far from being what has been described above, is but an ultimate trap of the sly one, to make his powerful victim believe that his own *virtù* can be taught to him, in order to dispose once again of his credulity and to place him, from now on, in the position of potential victim. (2) Certainly, all lessons and all transmissions of useful knowledge merit a salary, a cheese, for example. But it is the custom that the pupil pay the teacher when the lesson has been given, that is to say, after the pupil finds himself equipped with the knowledge that he did not have before. The strange thing at this juncture is that Master Fox pays himself in advance or, that, more precisely, the salary is none other than the lesson itself, indistinguishable from it. A variant, less perfect, of Protagoras's paradox,[12] but the same temporal structure of moments in discontinuity operates here in order to neutralize the mastery of knowledge, at the very moment when it is affirmed most fully.

The fable in its narrative power is the parody of political power in its discursive representations, a parody that, because it is displaced onto the world of animals and the ferocity of its forces, can exhibit humorously the hidden inner springs of the strategies that animate the political world, the world of power in its desire for the absolute.

Racinian Strategies

After the fable of the crow and the fox, the speech [*discours*] given by Racine welcoming Abbé Colbert to the French Academy.[1] It is indeed a question of a eulogic discourse [*discours*] and of a direct eulogic discourse in which the orator must, according to the rules and norms of the genre, speak positively about the newly elected member, displaying the qualities and virtues that earned him admission into the company, and must speak first of all to the newly elected member himself, to whom the speech is from the first to the last line (or almost) addressed. However, the problem that Racine must resolve on 30 October 1678, when he makes his speech, is how to eulogize the king while eulogizing Colbert. The solution is at first glance easy, or at least its principle: since the abbé is the second son of the minister and the latter is the king's minister, it is necessary and sufficient to ascend the natural line from son to father and the institutional one from servant to master in order to hear the echo of the eulogy of the prince in that of the newly elected member. By this I am pointing out that the manner of expression will have at this juncture as much if not more importance than what will be said, to the extent that, in particular—and there is a difficulty at once supplementary and generic—the king's eulogy has already been made by the abbé in his acceptance speech. How to speak about the one while speaking about the other and only about him? How to speak about the other without repeating what the person being spoken about has said about him?

The general schema of Racine's speech is as follows: The orator at first—and this is fundamental for all eulogic discourse—defines his "place" of discourse, the place of the enunciation, which at once gives him the right to speak and makes his discourse authorized speech [*parole*]. Next, he positions the person he is addressing as the *obligated* addressee of the eulogy that is about to be made. In order to do this, Racine *turns back* to their addressor the thanks that the latter had addressed to the company for having welcomed him into its bosom by thanking him, in the name of the academy, for the honor he does it by entering it.

The avenue is then open for a narrative, its frame traced, its stage erected: the narrative of the life of the eulogy's addressee, his biography. It is a question, therefore, of saying to Abbé Colbert who he is by telling him the story of who he has been and what he has done up until that day. The paradox of such a narrative is evident: why tell young Colbert what he already knows, his own existence? Unless the objective of this narrative is not to make something known [*faire savoir*] but to operate performatively, through and in the discourse, the recognition of the subject as subject fit for the institution that is welcoming him, as de jure subject of legitimate predicates and not as de facto subject of historical qualifications.

And it is precisely at the very moment of the subject's identification that the speech eulogizing the newly elected member is strategically displaced onto that eulogizing the august protector of the academy. There is no subject appropriated to himself who is not appropriated in truth and by right into one of the king's institutions, that is, into one of the institutions of which the king constitutes, in one way or another, the essential function. There is no property autonomous in itself except with respect to him. And from then on the "real" addressee of the eulogy is positioned as proper potential addressor of Louis's eulogy.

Racine can then end his speech with the king's eulogy, a eulogy that will be given only with preterition and mediation or by deferring its effective presentation, all of these procedures constituting, without a doubt, a eulogy of the prince whose effects will have an efficacy infinitely greater than that of a real eulogy. In this way, therefore, as in the fable of the crow and the fox, the eulogy's power lies less in what is said than in what is not said but is supposed to have been said without having been so. The whole framework rests on precise manipulations of vocabulary and syntax but even more, and more precisely, on manipulations of the markers of enunciation, as much on the side of the addressor as on that of the addressee, whether present or represented. In the end the "critical" moment of Racine's eulogic discourse is that of the displacement of the appropriation of the subject, from himself onto the other. He is identified as proper subject only by a double alienation, alienation in his function as praiser of the king and alienation in the familial function of king's servant. Now the academy for which Racine is spokesman is defined, but institutionally, by this same and double function: to praise the king is to serve him, and how would he be served by a service that would not be his praise? The academy in its institutional functioning—of which Racine and Abbé Colbert are temporary cogwheels—is only a relay, *though an essential one*, in the *permanent eulogy* of the king—that is, in the eulogy that the king, through his word, thought, and action, addresses to himself with respect to what he says, thinks, or does: a simple but necessary mediation in the tautology of the absolute monarch.

> Sir, it is a very honorable thing to find myself at the head of this celebrated company, and I owe a lot to chance for having put me in a place where merit would never have elevated me. But this honor, as great as it is, becomes for me, I admit, even more considerable when I think that my first function in this place where I am is to explain to you the sentiments the academy has toward you.

This opening of Racine's speech has no other function than to legitimate and authorize the addressor as addressor of eulogic discourse. In substance, Racine declares that he speaks because he is the director of the academy, not only one of its members (and it is merit that makes someone a member) but also at its head. Nevertheless, the orator's elevation of himself to the pinnacle is immediately diminished in the manner of operating it. Racine is the object (and not the subject) of this exceptional honor, and he owes this honor very much to chance (though not only to chance, and yet the director was drawn by lots), more to chance than to merit (that merit that had been recognized by the company when it chose him). Racine thus has the right to speak, but what he has at first the right to say is only to speak of that right to the newly elected member he addresses. Through that operates the transfer, less to the addressee (Colbert) than to the speech addressed to him, of the honor institutionally vested in the addressor of the speech (Racine).

In other words, the reflection by which the subject of the discourse legitimately poses *himself* as subject of discourse has no other strategic finality than to pose the addressee as legitimate addressee of the discourse. It is by constituting himself as authorized subject of the discourse that Racine poses Colbert as legitimate object of his (Racine's) own discourse. This transfer of right becomes explicit in the last sentence of the text cited, where we discover Racine to be only the spokesman of the institution where the addressee is being received, and his function only that of explaining the sentiments of the academy toward him. We must, therefore, clearly see that the self-legitimation by the subject of the discourse of his right to speak is indeed operated by this same subject in the movement of reflection where he poses and designates himself as subject of speech [*parole*]; but at the same time this reflection is made possible only by the institution to which the subject belongs and that the addressee of his speech is entering. The eulogic discourse is, therefore, a discourse of circumstance in the full sense of the word: the praiser cannot be reflected as an "authentic" subject of speech [*parole*]; he can only authorize himself to praise in the place that the institution defines and on the condition that he declare that he is speaking from that place and from no other place. And if his discourse in its exordium uses the pure language of the institution in general (as the power to speak), it is no doubt to the exact extent that the particular institution he is speaking from is the pure institution of language—the academy.

> You believe you owe it thanks for the honor you say it does you; but it also has to give you thanks: it is obliged to you not only for the honor you do it but also for the honor you have already done the republic of letters.

The transfer of right is completed in a polite exchange; but if to give something is to oblige the person to whom one gives it to return it, and with excess, in order to open up a new obligation for the person who receives it, then the institutionalized assault to which Abbé Colbert and Racine surrender themselves, unless they pursue each other to infinity, can conclude only on the infinite obligation owed by the new member to the institution. It will suffice afterward to displace that institution onto the person who is, at least in appearance, its absolute addressee with no return, the king. Thus the young Colbert believed he was indebted to the academy; he also thought he had paid his debt through his thanks. Racine announces to him that in fact he was not the debtor, that it was the academy that was and that, through his voice, it acquits itself of its debt toward him "a hundredfold." The addressor through his praise places the addressee in the position of being obligated, and that much more surely since the praise liberates him totally from the one debt—that of recognition—that he really has: to have been assimilated by the academy. It is through this exchange that the biographical narrative opens, a narrative that is, as we know, one of the *morceaux de résistance* of the panegyric.

> Yes, Sir, we know how much they [letters] are indebted to you. For a long time now the academy has had its eyes on you; none of your proceedings have been unknown to it; you carry a name that too many reasons have made sacred to men of letters: all that concerns your illustrious house can no longer be unknown or indifferent to them.

It is in the structure of the exchange that the paradox already pointed out, which consists of telling Colbert the younger the story of his own life, finds its solution. Racine gives the abbé the narrative of his own life today only in order to discharge the debt that the republic of letters, which is governed by the academy, has contracted in the past concerning him. The eulogic discourse in the narrative reimburses a debt and, in this fashion, obligates the creditor once more. The payment of the debt does not bring a gain of knowledge to the creditor, however, because he already knows what is going to be said to him. It is therefore not the narrative and the history the narrative takes into account that form the object of the transaction but the fact and manner of saying them: the very act of narrating and the "ornaments" by which the narration will know how to clothe its purpose, ornaments that, as we will see, are essential to the strategy of the eulogic discourse.

"Letters are indebted to you; we know it, and we even know how much," Racine, spokesman of the institution, declares with no other oratory precaution than that he is in the position of telling the story of young Colbert's life. Not only does the academy know it, it knows it very well, more than the newly elected member believes it to be so. There is, in any event, a point that the academy knows and that Colbert did not know about his own life, and that is that since the beginning he was known to it. "For a long time now the academy has had its eyes on you; none of your proceedings have been unknown to it." The praiser puts himself in the position of omnivoyant, and at the same time the praised is declared transparent to his gaze. The academy, as the king's institution, is the relay of the power [*puissance*] of his gaze. Whence a double implication: first of all the narrative that is to follow is at once authentic and complete, and second of all the narration that will be made of it, by giving back to the addressee what properly belongs to him, his life, reimburses the gifts for which letters have long since been indebted to him.

And if the abbé long since has been followed and penetrated by the academy's gaze, it is because of his name and house. The academy finds itself indebted to Colbert the son for the pensions given to (men of) letters by Colbert the father. The transactional passage of the father's gifts to the son's biography finds its reason in the name, by a triple metonymy: of the gifts in the father's name, of the father's name to the son's, and of the son's name to the history that this name names and that the narrative that is going to be made of it must appropriate to this name and give back to the name by giving back the initial gift.

> We considered with attention the progress you made in the sciences; but if you had at first excited our curiosity, you did not delay in exciting our admiration. And what applause did we not give to the excellent philosophy that you have taught publicly . . . ! However, this savant philosophy was just a path for you to lift yourself up to a more noble science, I mean to say to the science of religion. And what progress have you not made in that sacred study? With what marks of estime has the most famous faculty of the universe . . . associated you to its body? The academy has taken part in all your honors and applauded your most celebrated actions; but Sir, since it saw you ascend the pulpit, since it heard you preach the truths of the Gospel, not only with all the force of eloquence but even with all the accuracy and *politesse* of our language, then it judged that you were necessary to it. It chose you, it named you. . . . Yes, Sir, it chose you.

The narrative of Abbé Colbert's life in the universe of knowledge and culture, from science to philosophy and theology, is woven with another narrative, in "under-play," which is that of the narration of the narrative itself, where a whole series of passional qualifiers, from curiosity to admiration, from expressive astonishment to need and desire, modalize and characterize the narrator as simple gaze witnessing the history of the young Colbert. This history, taken up again in the narrative epideixis, is split, therefore, between the narrative of an educative cursus as regards the thing "narrated" [*narré*], culminating in religious predication, and the narrative of a passional cursus as regards the person "narrating" [*narrant*], culminating in the passage from admiration, the passion for knowledge, to desire, the fundamental vital passion. We will remark that the conjunction of the two narratives, that of the history and that of the narrator of that history, is effected in what could be called the order of the discourse: it is at the moment when Abbé Colbert becomes a master of predication that the academy, institution of discourse and language, desires to make him a member of its body. We understand, then, the objective that the biographical and narrational strategy is pursuing. Doubtless, by telling Colbert the abbé the history of his own life, Racine, the academy's spokesman, returns to him what his name and house have given to letters, which are governed by the academy. But this narrative obeys a precise objective: to give to Colbert the son's history the one finality of being chosen by the institution. "It judged that you were necessary to it. It chose you." The necessity of Abbé Colbert's presence at the Academy is equaled only by the freedom of the academy's choice of him. For the addressor (Racine as the academy's spokesman), to be free is to be constrained by a necessity. For the addressee, to be necessary is to be obligated by a freedom. Racine insists:

> Yes, Sir, it chose you; for we do not mind that it be known that
> neither intrigue nor solicitations open the doors of the academy; it
> goes ahead of merit, it saves merit the embarrassment of coming to
> offer itself; it seeks subjects who are suited to it. And who could be
> better suited to it than you?

There again, it is fitting to read beneath the epideixis and the complex play that underpins it and that it manifests in the forms that are its own: the academy is placed in the necessity of returning to the son, in the form of a title and nomination in the institution, the money, pensions, and favors the father has given to the academy and to men of letters. But the epideictic rhetorical problem to be resolved is how to transform the necessity of returning, of liberating oneself from that debt in this fashion, into the freedom to give that nomination, that title, and that quality as the obligatory recompense of merit. How to transform a necessary exchange of different kinds of things (a title and a sign for pensions) between different partners (the father and son) into a gift at once free and obligatory of things of the same nature (a title and a sign for speeches) between similar partners (a company of men of letters and an abbé man of letters)? It is the function of the epideictic narrative of Colbert the younger's life, addressed to him, that, by the play of the narrative of the addressee's life and of that of the narrator-witness of that life (the academy and Racine, who is its voice), it becomes apparent that the finality of Colbert the younger's history is for him to be chosen as academician. This is true, very simply, because the culmination of Abbé Colbert's history is to know how to speak, to know how to "hold" forth the most elevated discourse in the hierarchy of discourses, the predication of the Gospel's truths, and because the academy is that institution of the king that monopolizes all knowledge of language and of discourse. From that point on, the epideictic narration—the narrative of the life of the addressee of the eulogic discourse, and thus of the narrative—operates the identification of the narrated subject, his "appropriation," only in order to equate him with the addressor of the narrative, or with its spokesman: "The academy seeks subjects who are suited to it. And who could be better suited to it than you?" The property of the addressee of the discourse, his identification as fit subject—and is not telling his history that very thing?—consists, then, of being appropriated by the institution whose voice is the addressor of the discourse and of passing entirely, in a tilting movement, into instituted culture.

The eulogic discourse of Colbert the younger by Racine proceeds, then, in an exact parallelism with the fable of the crow and the fox by La Fontaine, except for the manner. We recognized in our preceding analyses the mechanism put forward by the fabulist, the self-legitimating address by the fox to the crow: "'Hey! Good day, Sir of the Crow!'" Here we have arrived precisely at the verse "'You are the phoenix of the denizens of this wood,'" but with an essential difference. In La Fontaine's fable the epideictic narrative is lacking. In its place we have the double exclamation "'How pretty you are! How handsome you look!'" whose objective in the discursive strategy we have analyzed. And if the narrative is lacking, it is because, according to the fox, the crow addressee of the eulogy has not yet proven that he deserves the title of "Phoenix," the unique name of the incomparable bird, while, for Racine, at the end of his "biography" of the king's minister's son, even before his election to the academy, Abbé Colbert had already proven that he was potentially a necessary member of it.

Still, in both cases it is the voice—be it song or predication—that operates the identification of the subject as belonging not to itself but to the other, alienated because extraneous to the other. In La Fontaine's fable it is the voice, his epideixis of the crow's song, that will make the cheese (which is, metonymically, the voice) pass on to the fox. In Racine's discourse it is the pensions given by Colbert the father to men of letters (who are metonymically discourses) that will pass as a title given to Colbert the son, namely, "member of the academy," this title constituting at once his highest identification and his most total alienation.

But the Racinian eulogic discourse does not stop at the point where the fable concludes; the fox's brief lesson to the crow is replaced by a development where the fox's lesson could come in handy, in the end, as veritable moral. Indeed, in the discourse's strategy it is the tilting movement of the identification of oneself with institutional alienation, of singular appropriation with nomination as part of the body, that is going to permit Racine to operate the conversion of the effective narrative of Colbert the younger's history into a "potential" narrative of the king's history. For the speech-narrative of praise for Colbert given by Racine, who recognized him as a necessary member of the academy, transforms him, in the instant of a word, *into being second* to the group of the members of the institution and, precisely, second to Racine, the king's historiographer since the preceding year.

> Who could be better suited to it [the academy] than you? Who could better second us in the design that we have all proposed for ourselves, to work toward immortalizing the great actions of our august protector?

This reversal, this conversion that is the essential moment of the academic eulogy and the inner spring of its dynamic and strategy, is effected for two reasons, one circumstantial and the other structural: Racine is (through chance) director of the academy and (through merit) member of the company, but the latter has an august protector who is, by essence and definition, and who can only be the king. Spokesman of the academy as temporary director, Racine, by essence and definition, only *takes* the floor [*prendre la parole*] in order to *give* it, to offer it as gift to the academy's protector. Such would be the circumstantial reason for speech [*parole*] that is manifested here or there in the institutional circle, in a member of the royal body, and by destination this speech [*parole*] must return to its origin, the prince. Circumstances and chance have made Racine the organ of this voice on the occasion of the reception of Abbé Colbert—another could have spoken, another could have been received. The speech [*parole*] sent as order (in the two senses of the term) had to come back as praise to its source, the king. Thus all circumstance is in the king's space, as structural manifestation: never as the effect of chance but as the expression of necessity. That is why the second reason can only refer back to this necessity: there is no other finality for the cultural institution that is the academy than to praise its protector, the king, and this praise is defined precisely as the narrative of the king's history, "immortalizing the great actions of our august protector." Therefore, the narrative of Colbert the younger's history—finalized by his entrance into the academy, becoming a member of which is his proper identification as proper subject—finds its true meaning, its true end, in the narrative of the history of the person who is the protector of that institution. And from then on the speech of praise addressed to him can only be a speech of praise addressed to the king, where he is the simple relay, the point of rebound.

Three remarks: "the design that *we have all proposed for ourselves.*" The institution reflects and represents itself, and the effect of this reflection is to produce the subject as producer and addressor of the discourse of praise addressed to the king. Similarly, Racine, reflected as the subject of the discourse praising Colbert the younger, institutes himself as subject authorized to speak in his own institutional field, defined as a domain protected by the king, as a place of speech [*parole*] authorized by the king, and as praise of the prince.

"The design that we have all proposed for ourselves, to *work* . . ." To praise the king is an infinite task, an impossible endeavor; or rather it can be realized only by incessant reiteration. The desire inscribed in all words of celebration, which is to make the celebrated person exist [*faire être*] through speech [*parole*] itself, can know only an always deferred fulfillment. In this sense the representation of the prince, which is the royal epideictic discourse, is the work—but infinite—of the mourning of the absolute that is all power. All power desires to be absolute, and no power ever consoles itself for not having been able to be so.[2] The representation of the prince that his own speech [*parole*] offers him and that aims to fill the gap that will always separate him from the absolute monarch is "the design we have all proposed for ourselves, to work toward immortalizing the great actions of our august protector." There is no other form of praise for the king than to tell his history; that narrative will be his immortalization in a monument of signs and utterances that will immobilize his will forever after in the accomplished and represented act, as that kind of cenotaph that representation also is, an empty tomb whose dead body has absented itself in order to pass entirely into the architecture that was to enclose it.[3]

An infinite work in proportion to the infinity of the object it has to forge: Abbé Colbert will not be one too many.

> Who could better help us celebrate this prodigious number of exploits, whose greatness overwhelms us, so to speak, and makes us powerless to express them? We need entire years to write down even one of his actions in a worthy manner.

We will have recognized at once the theme and the manner of royal historiography: the theme, unique, of royal action; the manner, equally homogeneous, the narrative of celebration—but that collides, nevertheless, with a paradoxical obstacle: the acts of the prince that are fit to be praised are prodigious in number, and each action is in itself infinite. From then on the discourse of praise in its very enunciation and in its writing impedes and forbids itself. Speech [*parole*] can only celebrate by falling back on the mutism of astonishment and the silence of admiration. There is an infinite inequality between the expression of the discourse and its object. Still, epideixis finds its essential means in this paradox: by enunciating the essential impossibility of a *representation* of the prince, this discourse *shows* and exhibits its very object; it *presents* it (epideixis) by declaring its radical impotence to *represent* it, and the king's act will, in the end, be expressed as absolute at the very moment when the discourse declares itself to be *infinitely* incapable of expressing its absoluteness, that is, such that no comparison, be it only a description, can equate what is being compared with what it is being compared to. This is the essential tactic that Racine will use in the royal eulogic speech, both to enunciate the celebration of the prince without doing so and to praise Abbé Colbert while praising the king.

> In the meantime each year, each month, and even each day presents us with a throng of new miracles. Astonished by so many triumphs, we thought that arms had brought the glory of this prince to the highest point that it could go. Indeed, after so many provinces so rapidly conquered and so many battles won, the cities captured by assault and the cities saved from pillage, and all those great actions you have painted for us so vividly, could one have imagined that this glory would continue to grow? The peace that he has just given Europe is something even greater than what he did in war. I take care not to assume here the eulogy of this hero after that eloquent speech of yours that we have just heard. Not only have we recognized in it the loftiness of your mind and the sublimity of your thoughts, but above all we see shining that zeal for your prince and that ardent passion for his glory that is the peculiar mark by which we recognize all your illustrious family.

On the one hand, then, we have an infinity of royal acts to tell in the space of one day, indeed of one moment, and every act, be it only an ephemeral gesture, a frowning of the eyebrows, a smile, takes an infinity to express: a double infinity in extension and comprehension to which the infinite work of representation should respond, a representation that, by admitting itself to be extensively infinite, presents the intensive infinity of the king's historical act, the epiphany of its absoluteness. The discourse of celebration, by saying the double infinity that, *de re*, separates the opposed extremes, realizes their conjunction *de dicto*, and for the historical narrative whose completion can only be infinite is substituted the discursive epideixis that enunciates the reasons for this interminable completion. And it is without a doubt in that way that royal praise is an ''epistemological'' reflection of the conditions of possibility or of impossibility of the prince's narrative, a metanarration where this narrative finds a completion, but in an enunciative mode that is heterogeneous to it. Preterition, then, is the figure of discourse used to say the impossibility of saying and the reasons for this impossibility. ''The most skillful praises,'' notes Furetière, ''are made with preterition. . . . I will not say that he is valiant, that he is learned, etc.''[4] A double preterition, at once in the utterance and in its enunciation. In the utterance, it is a question of the king and of the extensive and intensive infinity of the royal act. To say this double infinity with preterition comes back to making of the royal act an absolute, the absolute of the unrepresentable monarch presented. In enunciation, preterition bears not only on the narrative of the king's history but also on the eulogic discourse itself, which is uttered, as we have seen, only to declare the impossibility of that narrative. And it is in this way that Racine can come back to Colbert the younger and to his eulogy in the very eulogy of the king. By declaring that the king's eulogy has already been made, and well made, by the newly elected member, by "pretending not to want to talk about it, all while having already mentioned it," Racine inscribes in his discourse this absent and past eulogy and sets it in his own. He does not repeat "the hero's eulogy," he does not retrace the "vivid painting" of his great actions: by saying that it has been said, by mentioning that it has been done, he frames this painting and this discourse of praise in the paradigm of the king's historical narrative, which is his eulogic discourse by preterition.

From now on the king's praise will proceed, but by a relay, as if the praise of Colbert the son had made it difficult, if not to say impossible, to celebrate the king without mediation or, again, as if the epideictic presentation of the King's eulogy could result only from a representational *mise en abîme*. The king is not known [*connu*] in his presence, but re-cognized [*re-connu*] as present by the sum of the qualities that are necessary to his re-presentation. In the eloquent speech that Abbé Colbert has just given—the eulogy of the hero, the panegyric of the prince—the academy, through the voice of its spokesman, recognizes loftiness of mind and sublimity of thought, the only two qualities that appear in proportion to the king's greatness and to the height to which his glory has climbed. But these qualities are, in their turn, marks of a second kind of recognition: that of the zeal and passion of the praiser for the king. And these qualities in the end refer back to the "house" Colbert the younger comes from, and precisely to its head, the father, the king's minister. The son's speech is marked by loftiness and sublimity only because the father has no other thought or model than the prince's glory.

> While the head of the house, filled with this noble zeal, gives no respite to his indefatigable genius, while he sends a penetrating look even into the least needs of the state, with what ardor, what vigilance, with his children, brothers, nephews, all who belong to him, does he eagerly relieve and support it! . . . I would not finish if I were to put before your eyes everything that is illustrious in your house.

If to praise the minister in his person and lineage is an infinite task, then this endeavor, which a new preterition indicates, can only be the echo, like an extenuation, both of an infinitely infinite task and of the infinity of a representation of another order, that of the master. And just as Colbert the (second) son, the newly elected member whose eulogy is being completed, finds himself in some way absorbed by the glory of his family and father, itself the reverberation of the brilliant light of the prince, Abbé Colbert will in a moment, that of peroration, find himself absorbed into the company that puts all its glory toward serving the glory of its august protector. A passage from the house to the company, from the family to the academy, a passage from one institutional function to another. Better yet, it is by entering the academy that Colbert the son becomes the king's veritable subject. He will find there the same variety of talents and competence as in the Colbert house but also the same unity, the same homogeneity in subjugation to the prince's glory:

> You enter, Sir, a company that you will find full of this same spirit
> and zeal; for, and I repeat, we are all rivals in the passion to
> contribute something to the glory of such a great prince: here
> everyone uses the different talents that Nature has given him.

Unrepresentable narrative representation of the king, that hero, that god who can only be presented, shown, or indicated in the confession of that unrepresentability, such is the essential inner spring of the royal epideixis: a discourse of celebration that can only, in its turn, be effected, in order to approach the permanent epiphany of the prince, with preterition, a manner of saying what one will not say and, by that, saying it with more vivacity and intensity, or by a potentially infinite *mise en abîme* of the representation—which is absent and which can only be absent—of the monarch's absoluteness.

Thus, in pleonasm and hyperbole, the royal representation becomes rarified and extenuated, and that is what shows the power of its presence.[5] The last two sentences of Racine's speech uncover it in a strange fashion:

> That very work that is common to us, that dictionary that in itself
> seems to be such a dry and thorny occupation, we work at it with
> pleasure. All the words of a language [*langue*] and all the syllables
> appear precious to us, because we look at them as so many
> instruments that must serve the glory of our august protector.

What the narrative cannot accomplish except in an infinite endeavor, what eulogy can operate only with preterition, mediation, and *mise en abîme*, in other words, that space where all discourse, sentences, and arrangements of sentences falter in the impossibility of being equal to its object, and where this very faltering shows it, the epideictic frees [*s'affranchir*] itself of these constraints in an ultimate movement by crossing [*franchir*] the borders of the production of meaning. Eulogy descends into the body of a language [*langue*] to its first elements, words, to its nonsignifying parts, syllables, less in order to effectuate itself than to find there its most primitive conditions of possibility. If the cultural institution, the guardian of language [*langage*] and discourse, constituted in the discourse of its spokesman at once the place of legitimacy that authorized it and the ultimate objective that finalized the life of the person who was entering it, it is, in this peroration, language [*langage*] itself, and beyond that the constitutive parts of a language [*langue*] and the small change of the treasure the institution is devoted to maintaining, that gives it its legitimate authority, for the sole reason that words and syllables are instruments that must serve the glory of the institution's august protector. It is indeed at this prediscursive and presignifying level that the transubstantiation of the body of a language [*langue*] into body of power, and of the organs of language [*langage*] into members of the sovereign's body, is mysteriously operated. The king's historic narrative and the prince's eulogic discourse, in their diverse figures and varied strategies, are the rituals that mark the ceremony and designate the meaning of this sacramentary operation at once secret and sacred.

Second Entrance
"This Is My Body,"
or the King of the Sacrament

The Royal Host:
The Historic Medal

Making Someone See or Read

There is a knowing exchange of eye and gaze between the king and his historian: the king, seeing all, acts and is seen only inasmuch as he gives himself to be seen while giving all there is to see; the historian sees everything the king lets him see, and by writing it down he makes it be seen, in its turn, by those who were absent at the time and place of that visibility. At the point where historical narrative *representation* and the *power* of state exchange their power and representation, respectively, in order to constitute the absolute of power in and through the infinity of representation, the motif of visibility appears along with the chiasmus of the two essential modalities of representation: the symbolic one, where representation is constructed by arranging signs of language, terms, and sentences in discourse, and the imaginary one, where representation shows itself by making visible lines, the colors that the lines enclose, figures, and the movements that compose them in the picture. If there is an exchange between the symbolic and the imaginary modalities or a chiasmus between them, this signifies that a boundary has been traced between legibility and visibility, but one that will be continually crossed; pictures are texts that are legible from end to end and images that are resolved into signs; a narrative is in the end a visible image, and history takes on the consistency of a synopsis, map, or panorama to be contemplated. To tell the king's history in a narrative is to show it [*faire voir*]. To show the king's history in his icon is to tell it [*faire raconter*]. Pellisson and Racine vie with Le Brun and Vandermeulen. Read the lecture by the king's first painter, Le

Brun, on Poussin's *La Manne*, and see how all the parts of the picture are subordinated to the exact legibility of the story the picture is telling;[1]—hence the cartoon of the tapestry relating the encounter of the two kings of France and Spain in 1660 at the conclusion of the Peace of the Pyrenees. Reread the end of the *Projet de l'histoire de Louis XIV* by Pellisson, and note that the entire finality of the historical narrative is "how to paint rather than tell, how to make the imagination see everything that is put on paper."[2] Reread again the conclusion of the *Eloge historique du Roi sur ses conquêtes depuis l'année 1672 jusqu'en 1678* by Racine and Boileau: "Some people more particularly zealous for his glory wanted to have in their studies *a précis in pictures* of the prince's *greatest actions*, which prompted this little work that encloses so many marvels in a very small space, so as to put *before their eyes at all times* that which is the dearest occupation of their thoughts."[3] Even though—as it appears—the book was "full of miniature pictures of all the cities in Holland that the King conquered in 1672,"[4] the illustration of the work itself, and, even more so, the insistent reflection by Racine and Boileau on "the pictures of the prince's greatest actions," the occasion of the book, reveal in a significant fashion that the ideal of the historical narrative is indeed the imaginary of a picture where it is condensed and summarized. If, as I have proposed, the raising of the historical narrative is the picture of history, I must point out that, on the contrary, the raising of the picture of history is the narrative that puts it into language. And if the hypotyposis brings the style of narration to its culmination by canceling it out in the fiction of a presence "before their eyes,"[5] we would have to create a specific figure for use by the rhetoric of painting, "narrativism," which, unfolding the one instant represented by the picture in the always coherent diversity of its circumstances, would give to the attentive and competent gaze to read, in this totality at once complex and one, "the moments that preceded it and that would enable it to understand the whole history."[6]

Hypotyposis and narrativism: in both cases it is a question of making someone see or read [*faire voir, faire lire*], at the intersection of the "picture" and the "narrative," at the boundary of the legible and the visible, a "doing" [*faire*] where each of the two finds its most specific and "proper" effect in the domain of the other. The discourses *on* narrative or *on* the painting of history thus *propose* a theory of the effects of reading or of the effects of contemplation that they *suppose*, in both fields, to be the irresistible practice. How is the narrative effect, in reading, a picture? How is the iconic effect, in contemplating, a narrative? More precisely, how are the frameworks of narrative enunciation and iconic representation supposed to produce effects, operate simulations of visibility or legibility, *make* a story be told, and *make* something be seen, to the point at which each of the systems takes them into account—thus by writing in a cartouche the history of which the tapestry shows but an instant, and thus by illustrating with "miniature pictures" the narrative of the war with Holland. In the two fields of the legible and the visible, "doing" signifies a power, but one whose characteristic it is to exist only by virtue of a simulacrum of one of the frameworks in the region of the other: a fictive power, if not imaginary, a representation, in the discourse *on* the narrative or image, of a power the narrative or iconic representation is supposed to possess. To feign a picture of history by representing only an instant of that history is to give oneself the power to make the spectator tell the whole history; to tell the narrative of the history by developing it, sequence by sequence, with all the accidents of the event is to give oneself the power to make the spectator see the whole history as in a picture. By bringing both these theoretical propositions and pragmatic suppositions back to the prince and his history, we understand why and how, through the double imaginary and symbolic effect of the representation of history—whether made of language or of image, of signs (terms linked in sentences, sentences linked in narrative) or of lines and colors (figures constructed in groups, groups put on stage in one moment)—the prince constitutes and completes his absolute power in the infinity of the self-representation, as he constitutes and completes *himself* as unlimited monarch, as "The state is me." For this double effect is supposed to act infallibly on a reader-spectator, the prince's subject, whom the presentation (of language or image) produces at once as the field where its effects appear and as the place of their application. This constitutes, less in the texts and images than in the discourse about them, a theory of their power as effect of the frameworks and systems of representation where the prince finds the fundamental elements of his *own* imaginary (as body and face: portrait) and symbolic (as name) *representation*, whose effect is to constitute him imaginarily (in the picture) and symbolically (in the text) as absolute monarch.

But is it not possible to find an "object" produced that would be situated precisely at the boundary of the legible and the visible, which would realize that very place of contact and exchange, which would operate as such the double inverted and reciprocal effect of one framework in the other, and which would be, because of that, the monumental sign of absolute political power in the infinity of its representation? Such seems to be among other things, while retaining no doubt the very truth of that kind of sign, the king's historical medal.[7]

The Historical Medal

That the royal medal occupies this privileged place of our problematic of political power and its representation, I offer only as first proof and remarkable example a text that is a program of action proposed to King Henry IV, in 1602, taken from the *Discours qui montre la nécessité de rétablir le très ancien et auguste usage public des vraies et parfaites médailles*, by Antoine Rascas de Bagarris, "conservator" of the king's cabinet of medals and antiquities: "Establishing the glory and memory of the great Princes consists principally only of three points. The first lies in forming them in their entirety and perfection, which is done by joining them together; that is, by joining August History with the Living Memory of those Princes from whom glory and memory properly proceed." The objective is then, indeed, to establish and found, in a permanence of memory, the prince's glory—that is, to transform the instantaneous illumination of his act in the exploit or great deed, where a particular divine inspiration bursts upon him, into a narrative that is developed from mouth to ear and transmitted from generation to generation, in short, into a living memory.[8] Antoine Rascas will, moreover, underline it a little further on:

> It is not Wealth, or Power [*Puissance*], or the extent or length of the Princes' command, or other similar things that give them glory or memory, but only two sorts of things: one being the actions, above all heroic, that produce the subject of glory and memory or give them their first being, *but for a time only*; the other sort of thing that gives glory and memory is those actions that establish them or give them their perfect last being, *by perpetuating them after their century*, to posterity. It is impossible to imagine that these things could be other than the Muses, that is, the Sciences and the Arts by their effects, from whose number come the said Monuments I will speak about below.[9]

How, then, *to institute the prince's glory* if not *by constituting a memory* just for him? What would be the means of this constitution, the instruments of this institution? The answer Rascas gives is remarkable: it is fitting, he writes, to "represent" the prince, and "that by the most perfect means, which consists as much of portraiture [*pourtraicture*] as of writing, joined together," a composite means that unifies two sorts of lines, two sorts of imprints, one that makes drawings and the other letters, one that digs the lines and volumes of figures into the material and the other that engraves there the characters of words and sentences: images and names, "portraits" [*pourtraits*] and writings that are all inscriptions. But the inscription of the drawing and the letter is only one means, and there is another even more efficacious. Rascas specifies that it is necessary "to publish and perpetuate them [the August History and the Living Memory], and that by the most perfect Moniment," to which he adds the following commentary to justify the introduction of this neologism:

> The inclusion of the general noun "Moniment"—which comes from the Latin *Monitor* to signify everything that admonishes those absent either from place or time, from the Memory of some subject—into this discourse seems that much more necessary because the other noun, "Monument," has been too restrained by vulgar usage (which is the Master of language) to signify particularly the sepulchers for the dead, which are also made for memory.[10]

The completed form of the prince's glory must, then, be *like* a tomb, but unlike the sepulcher for the dead, which marks, in grandiose fashion, a man's definitive passage into the past by establishing his death by his representation, this form must be *living and present memory*, not the inscription of an old present in the past but the prince's image and name, and the drawing and narrative to his glory presented in the same presence of a representation at once public and perpetual. From that point on it is the prince in the "monument" of his glory who defines the place and time of presence, understood as that transcendental permanence that founds all presence. Also, in the future that is opening up it is not the prince who is absent, lost and dead in a completed past that it is a question of bringing back in representation; the "monument" to glory and memory *must make posterity think itself as being absent from the time and place of the prince* and from the present radiance of his glory that the monument represents, but also as finding in him the stable reference that authorizes it to conceive of itself in the specific time and place of his history. What, then, is this monument if not the monument to the dead? Or rather, what is this monument that, better than the tomb, alerts all those absent from time and place of the perpetual presence of the prince's glory? What is this monument that would articulate the two dimensions of representation, making the absent, the past, and the dead return in a new but *imaginary* presence, and would found *in all legitimacy* the presence of the present and the living by giving it its symbolic dimension, by inscribing it under the regime of the sovereign and the law? It is necessary, then, to construct a living tomb for the prince, that is, a representation that at once tells his glory by showing the image of his exploit, shows his legend by reciting his history and, perhaps even better, simultaneously tells and shows his history by inscribing his face and name.

> Now the only true and perfect Medals, in no other way than by their public usage in all Currencies, in the first place not only contain but alone are capable of containing the aforesaid August History and Living Memory of the great Princes, joined together as much as is necessary for their said glory and memory. In the second place, they also contain the said perfect means of representing the said glory and memory, which means is had as much by portraiture as by writing joined together. And, in the third and last place, the said Medals alone are again the Moniment, the only eternal and the only authentic one and the only one belonging just to the great Princes; and consequently the most perfect for containing, publishing, and eternalizing their said glory and memory, and that for three reasons. First, because the said Medals are alone endowed with all the principal qualities, perfections, and prerogatives necessary for the most perfect moniment to the glory and memory of the Great Princes, in order to contain, publish, and eternalize them. Second, by reason of their rare effects. And third and last, because of the

perfection of their nature and of all they contain in their representation. Therefore, the usage of the said true and perfect Medals in all Currencies, and consequently their reinstatement . . . is absolutely necessary for establishing the glory and memory of the Great Princes.[11]

In these litanies to the prince, in the ornamental rhythm of these repetitions of the same motifs, which gives an insistent presence to the propositions and argumentation of their author, we can nonetheless discern some forceful lines of the theoretical and practical reflection that will be pursued throughout the century on royal medals and the king's metallic history: the medal is perfect representation, that is, complete without lack or fault, because it is entirely *inscription*, portrait and name. The medal as legitimate and authorized representation *contains* the prince in his glory and memory and, by that, dependent on the public domain, it eternalizes him. The medal is a kind of *money*, but a kind, or species, that possesses the truth, perfection, and property of the genre, or genus. This last characteristic, which at once relates medal and money and differentiates them, is fundamental, for the two others to which I have pointed flow from it to a certain extent. The medal must retain the *public* usage of money, its use by a same community, a public usage that makes money at once the instrument of the transactions and exchanges of its members and the standard of the value of things, goods, products, and services; nevertheless, if the medal has a public usage as does money, it is because, like it, it possesses its own "prerogative," the authority that distinguishes it from all other objects and whose sign it carries and whose stamp marks it. The power of the medal, as of money, is an *immediate* effect of the inscription of that authority: it is that imprint that gives to the piece of precious metal, medal, or money its authenticity and its truth. To make medals of all money and, inversely, to make money of all medals—that is a political program necessary to the prince's glory and to his memory, "touching upon all the principal things that consist of fact, actions or figures, all of which could be revoked because of doubt by posterity, since books cannot well represent them by discourse alone or as faithfully as they could be, beyond all reproach."[12] Books, in effect, like all other documents, can be subject to suspicion and criticism; they can be tainted by vice or error. Only medals attest to the truth of the documents they are joined to or constitute; only medals (or money) make the document a monument, because they alone give it authority. It is in this way that inscription as imprint is more than a sign whose referential relationship and alethic function can be questioned; the inscription is for always the index of an unimpeachable presence. With the medal, in it, an origin is engraved, an original is traced that cannot be contested. And with it at the same time, by a sort of short circuit of the discourse, all vices contrary to the history disappear, a history that Rascas defines as truth (since no one can do anything to make what has had a place and time, or what has happened, not so). Why then do medals and money have this prerogative? It is because "they alone carry on their faces and alone are capable of eternally carrying" a double authority, that of the prince, on the one hand, and that of public usage, on the other, which medal-money unifies perfectly as index, icon, symbol, and thing. Medal-money carries, in effect, the prince's mark, the figure of his effigy, or emblem, and the sign of his name and title, and it is this mark that, because it attests to an inalterable value, truth and authenticity, founds the universal acceptance of medal-money in usage. This imprint is thus not only a trace: it is an index that gives to the marked object its own potential, that makes of it an *efficacious sign*, and very precisely a power.

The medal is a representation-power in the primitive sense that—carrying *in* its matter (and not *on its surface* like layers of paint or traces of ink) by imprint, engraving, and inscription the mark of a sovereign authority, indicating by that the legitimate presence of that authority and authorizing that authority—medal-money founds and authorizes itself: it is in itself truth and law.

Conclusion: since "the august usage of moneyed medals" performs the truth of royal history and gives it the permanence and inalterability of a memory living forever,

> the highest, most glorious and most august design, the most
> durable and moreover the most effortless that a great Prince such
> as His Majesty could, and very easily, himself procure in his
> lifetime for the greatness and eternity of his name, without putting
> off the task haphazardly to his successors, would be to reinstate in
> his favor the said very old public usage of history jointly written and
> figured . . . , that of the said true and perfect medals.[13]

The medal—true and perfect—must then institute the prince's glory by erecting his memory as monument. The first foundation of this monument is the engraving of a figure and a writing necessarily joined together in a common inscription; the second foundation is the authority of the sovereign that is marked there by his effigy and name and that founds—by making itself thus unimpeachably recognized, but in the object itself—its public usage. A double relationship that is a double foundation of the monument to memory but that is also the axis of a design for political power that Henry IV's counselor exposes at the beginning of the century. The prince's effigy is the figure of his name and caption as that name and title constitute the signature of his portrait, mark the document with their imprint and, by signing it, raise it to a monument. And the representation that the document also bears, the brief engraved image where the narrative of the great deed is condensed, immediately appropriates an authentic presence; the *fact* of the warrior exploit, of the princely marriage, or of the peace between states acquires in one *coup*, and by that very density, the unimpeachable weight of a juridical, monumental instruction that such signatures authorize, with no private person being able to contest it. We understand, then, in these two fundamental relationships of figure and writing—of history and its subject, on the one hand, and of the sovereign's mark in the product and his indisputable universal recognition, on the other—that the prince's counselor reads the assured inscription and contemplates the majestic figure of political power in its necessary and universal historical truth, the money of its absoluteness that is its memory. Such would be the mystery of medal-money. It would show as thing, marked in its very matter become engraved form, what it signifies as representation, by giving something to be seen and told. In the manner of Eucharistic symbols—but better than them, since it shows whereas they hide—medal-money is the real presence of the power of state, the presence of the absolute monarch in its perpetuity of memory—the historical act of the sovereign agent. Medal-money is the body of the king and of the state present really in their imaginary and symbolic representatives, their portrait and name, just as the sacramental Host also is, at the moment of consecration, a "narrative" reiteration of the historical sacrifice of Jesus Christ and, by virtue of that, the memorial of a history reproduced in presence just as the imprinted cross marks it in the bread of the ritual.[14] But to do that it is appropriate to note the specific difference between both medal and money in their generic quasi-identity and, with that, the operators of the performativity that belongs to it.

Authenticated History

It fell to Abbé Tallemant to do it, after others but in all clarity, a century after Rascas, in the preface he wrote in 1702 for the great work of the "Petite Académie," *Médailles sur les principaux événements du règne de Louis le Grand*:[15]

> No one has been able to clear up until now the difference between money and medals. The opinions on this matter are quite divided. What is most probable is that we must call "Money" that piece of metal that on one side carries the head of the reigning Prince . . . and whose reverse side is always the same; because Money is made to have currency, the people must be able to recognize it easily so as to know its worth. . . . Various marks make the weight or worth of the coin known. What we call the Medals of the Kings of Macedonia, Syria, or Egypt were also apparently money, since we only have one kind for each of these kings. . . . None of these coins marks a particular event. Consequently, they are money. It is not the same case with what has been coined since Julius Caesar. Then there were money and medals. Money ordinarily has on one side the Prince's head and, on the other, the name of the Coinages with these words "*IIIVIR*" (*triumvir*). . . . Medals are coins that mark some memorable event on the reverse side. Medals are lasting monuments

made to transmit great events to posterity. What they represent and say, they must represent and say in a noble and ingenious manner.

On one side, the right side, of medal or money there is an always identical effigy, that of the prince, and the inscription of his name and title.[16] On the other, reverse side, a substitution is operated from money to medal: the indifferent but always identical mark on the coin, an "eagle, galley, victory or divinity, cross, or flower," is replaced by the representation of an event, an inscription of the royal act that is different from one medal to the next and to which all memorable events are reduced—history itself in one of its singular and unique moments, the marvel whose sole agent is the prince. In the coin, a reciprocal guarantee is assured between the right and reverse sides: the figure of the prince and his name, the image of royal authority of which one of the essential marks of sovereignty is the right to coin money, that is, precisely to engrave his face and name on a piece of precious metal; that effigy and name guarantee its permanent value, which is signified on the reverse side by the always identically reproduced marks that authorize its currency, by defining a constant rule of exchange among the prince's subjects.[17] If the medal takes its right side from money, the prince's face and name, in return it inscribes on its reverse side the representation of a unique historical event, the king's great deed, a miracle repeated at each moment and at each moment new. Consequently, the medal cannot have currency like the coin, but it acquires another: it is, as Tallemant writes, "a lasting monument made to transmit great events to posterity." The medal's mystery conceals a secret that is at once a political ruse and a juridical ritual, the secret of a rational magic by which the power of state constitutes its memory in its representation and institutes it in the authority of truth. In this play of identical and different inscriptions, and in the remarkable resemblance of medal and money as form of memory and form of exchange, as value and equivalence, the same permanence, the same identification, the same universally recognized value that are marked on the reverse side of the coin must be ascribed to the historical event represented on the reverse side of the medal. It is in this sense that the medal is *like* the coin, and it is in this sense that Rascas was able, at the beginning of the century, to speak of the reinstatement of medals in the usage of money, indeed of monied medals. But if one supposes that the medal as money has a universally and identically recognized value, the content of this value and identity has changed by the substitution operated on the reverse side, for it is no longer a question of a stable and constant exchange value, the same coin being identically reproduced. It is a question now of a single historical event that *has value in itself*, as *incomparable*, as well as by *its difference* from all others, but whose truth and authenticity and, more directly, forever *memorable* character will find themselves universally and identically recognized by their inscription in a form similar to that of the money-form. The finality of the operation of substitution appears, then, clearly:

the inscription of the historical event as representation on the reverse side of the medal, to the extent that it is and can only be the miraculous act of the king, will have the same validity and receive the same recognition that the sovereign authority gives to the coins marked by its stamp, that it alone has the right to mark because it is the sovereign authority, and that designate it as sovereign authority because it marks them. It is this secret medal's mystery that Rascas reveals to Henry IV:

> The said books, no more than all other monuments except medals, cannot be exempted from vice or error whether in effect, or because one has a suspicion or opinion, or even because one would like to claim, for pretext only, that they have been altered or corrupted by the copyists or printers, whether accidentally or by design and fraud: *vices completely contrary to the soul of history, which is truth, and from which only true medals, that is coins, have always been, are, and always will be free.*[18]

At the end of the century, Tallemant will be more discreet regarding the mechanisms of the medal's functioning, not that they will have changed, but rationality seems indeed to have taken precedence over the magic and aims of simple political propaganda on the ritualization where the mystery of state will be carried out. But the historical medal continues to answer the same questions: How to coin the prince's history? How, by the same juridical act of identification and appropriation that gives currency to a money among peoples, to give currency to the king's history in all times and among all nations? How, if not by striking medals as the king coins money? In both cases it is the same juridical potential, the same sovereign authority that must recognize itself and be recognized such by the production of money and medals: in one case, the legitimate and fixed equivalent for all the transactions of this authority's subjects;[19] in the other, the institution of the subject of the memorable event, the constitution of the universal and absolute agent of history, the erection of the monument to memory and glory that furnishes the true representation, that is, legitimate and authorized, of the historical events to be transmitted to the subjects, present and to come, of the sovereign authority.

The Noble Manner

"The Medal," writes Tallemant, "is a lasting monument made to transmit great events to posterity." He adds: "What it represents and says, it must represent and say in a noble and ingenious manner."[20] Into the ritual and juridical operation of instituting royal memory intervenes in its very mechanism, in order to constitute it, an aesthetic demand that defines the medal's political value. This demand, the necessity of saying and representing the king's marvelous act in the event of history in a "noble and ingenious" manner, characterizes more precisely the substitution of the exchange value of the coin with the value of the public, political, and historical usage of the medal. It is the aesthetic consumption of the medal by posterity that must assure the power of the medal as representation of the king and his act and that must constitute the effect of representation in political power. Unlike the coin, which, as a means of transaction and exchange, is acquired only in exchange with a product and is given only to acquire, the medal is a gift by the king.

But the counterpart to this gift is the contemplation, on its reverse side, of the event of royal history reduced to its matrix of miracle-act and, on its right side, of the subject of this act inscribed in his face and name, a contemplation where recognition—in both the epistemic and ethic senses of the term—is acquired by the beauty of the product; and maybe, beyond contemplation, the counterpart of the gift is the real presence of a fragment of the public and glorious body of the prince, in a "little work that encloses so many marvels in very little space as to put before their eyes [the persons more particularly zealous for his glory] what is the dearest occupation of their thoughts,"[21] exposed in the private place of the subject the king has subjugated by distinguishing. He who has a medal from the king—a medal that represents and contains him and a medal that he gives and in which he gives himself as medal—must therefore recognize the king as subject of the history, recognize the event as the actual manifestation of his power [*puissance*], and recognize the beauty of the manner in which he is represented and the value of the substance in which he is manifested. In this sense the noble and ingenious manner of representing and saying history, and the precious and inalterable matter in which the representation is inscribed and that presents its great political subject, take the place of political and historical "matter-content." The aesthetic effect of beauty constitutes the political power of the medal, and history is instituted in it through the admiration that its representation captures in a eulogic discourse that the product "tears from the mouth of the reader,"[22] who is also its spectator. And Perrault notes in his *Memoirs*:

> Colbert thought it would be necessary to have a quantity of medals struck in order to dedicate to posterity the memory of the great actions the king had already produced and that he foresaw being followed by others even more great and considerable . . . , and that all these things would have to be described and engraved with spirit and understanding so as to pass into foreign countries, where the manner in which they are treated does them hardly less honor than the things themselves.[23]

To transmit the great events of Louis the Great's reign to posterity—or, as the title of the book that collects the engravings of the medals announces, the "principal events." An event is great or principal and worthy of being noticed when the secret commission of five over which Colbert presides decides to mark, engrave, and represent it; and at the same time it is the nobility and ingeniousness of the representation and the discourse, the two aesthetic qualities essential to the device—the type and legend—that lead to greatness and raise to meaning what is represented. Circularity of the representation, and immanent functioning of its framework: by representing the event, representation represents itself in the self-sufficient process by which it is constituted. The reflexive dimension of representation is manifested by its transitive dimension and vice versa, since it is by representing itself that representation makes the event to be represented worthy of being so. The Port-Royal *Logic* introduces this process of reflection in some sense naturally, with its definition of the first operation of the mind: "To conceive means simply to see the thing that presents itself to our mind, as when *we represent to ourselves* a sun, an earth . . . without forming of it any express judgment. And the form in which *we represent* these things *to ourselves* is called 'idea.'"[24] A thing *presents itself* to the mind's gaze, but that gaze is itself reflected to raise the spontaneity of that presence to the idea of that thing, to its representation: a reflection that is simultaneously operation, activity of the mind at the place of its receptivity, and first knowledge of the thing in its idea. The framework produces a subject and an object, a *cogito* and its *cogitatum*.

We find transitivity and reflexivity of representation again with this same complex movement of constituting the event's historicity and instituting the subject, the agent of history, in the act of erecting the monument to memory and glory that is the medal. As the operations of the framework are subject to the law of the framework, similarly, this act is not arbitrary, but legitimated and authorized, all while itself producing the conditions of its legitimacy and authority: what the medal represents and says, it *must* represent and say in a noble and ingenious manner. It *must*. The process of representation and discourse is submitted to rules and norms, those of a way of doing things, those of a "taste" and "style," but the latter are only the manifestation of the law of the power of state, the law of the sovereign with respect to his representation. The sovereign wants his own representation. He wants all the more *to see himself*, as that image of the self is at once the means and the effect of his power. Which is it? He does not know, for this representation could not exist prior to its production. The prince will not know who he is before seeing his portrait. Then will he be able to "enjoy at rest the majestic glory that surrounds him," as Pascal writes with an ironic assimilation of the king to God; then will he be able to contemplate himself in himself and through himself, to be the absolute monarch. Even if the construction of the monument, the constitution of the image, the institution of the portrait is an infinite endeavor in proportion to the infinity of representation, power is power only in and through the representation it gives itself. It is the effect of representation, as representation is the product of power, linked together and caught in the tension of the infinite that characterizes representation and that is the aim of absolute power. Consequently, representing does not refer back to a power that would transcend and be anterior to it, any more than it refers back to an event that would be its reference. No doubt representation makes a departed presence "come back"; but the king's endeavor regarding his glory and memory has a whole other meaning: he aims to constitute his own presence as representation. Also we must not understand the *duty* [*devoir*] of representation as a norm that would transcend it but as itself an infinite process of representation by which the sovereign power institutes his own normativity, erects his own authority, founds his own legitimacy: the process by which he makes himself autonomous. He is his own law: the absolute monarch.

"Monsieur Colbert, who had only great ideas, above all when it was a question of his Master's glory, believed with reason that nothing could better perpetuate the memory of the King's actions than medals on the events of his reign."[25] The expression would be ironic if it were not a question of the king and of Colbert. Thus are we made to feel what Hegel will call the "heroism of flattery":[26] the minister does not and cannot have great ideas or vast designs by himself, he can only really think as high as his king, and the amplitude of his sights is only the reverberation in Colbert's mind of the prince's glory. Produced also as reflections by the monarch's brilliance, great ideas have no other function than to reproduce the brilliance of that glory, and it is in this way that the movement of production and reproduction simultaneously engenders and neutralizes historic time.

The medals that the minister was planning put the event into history as representation: the inscription, the engraving in the metal, marks it and, by this mark, places it in the past. In this way the present passes as event and becomes historic past as re-presented thing; by that, each medal generates a piece of historic time by enclosing it through imprint in its own memory. But that memory, because it is first an unerasable imprint, that piece of precious metal that the inscription transubstantiates into portraiture and writing joined together, is perpetuated in that lasting monument of representation and, if that memory is perpetual, if its matter (gold, silver) and its manner (engraving, inscription) guarantee its duration, it is because it is forever present. The event constituted as past by its inscription is at the same time present but outside of time, in the immobile duration of its monument. Time as passage and as past, be it historic or recollected in memory, is neutralized in the historic monument and by that appropriated, subjugated, and identified in the present presence of the royal glory. Time becomes the king's subject in the memorial of his history: the events of his reign *are* the king's actions *in their medals*, as Tallemant notes it expressly with respect to Colbert's designs. Also, when the minister, "who only had great ideas when it was a question of his Master's glory," thinks of a great metallic history of the reign, then the construction of a memory of the king transcending time is undertaken, his monumental portrait. "So that the medals be sought in all times, this minister resolved to commit the care of composing them to chosen men.'' Sought in the present as the king's signs of recognition and in the future as the noble and ingenious monument of living memory, aesthetic value and political project, artistic creation and ritual juridical form cooperate to give the medals eternal currency.

The Medal and the History Book

Each medal is a historic monument, and their ordered ensemble is that of the king's history, his total and one memory. To take up Pellisson's remark again, the narrative of the history of the reign is constructed as "a solid body, full of a variety of forces and brilliance,"[28] and each one of the royal actions that composes its sequences throughout time is at once a member of the king's historic body and a unique and single copy of that body, just like the sacramental Host of the power of state. This form of history—where the image simultaneously completes its narrative and the narrative its image—was defined from the origins of the great design. In the orders Henry IV addressed to Rascas (no doubt drafted by the latter), the prince commanded him to "draw up the whole of his august history, written as well as figured, not only in the length and continuity of a great volume but also reduced to an abridged form, with separate and divided articles, suitable for application to his medals, and to invent and draw up sketches for the latter based on those of ancient medals" and, for that, "to watch for opportunities or to conveniently generate them so as to establish the said public usage of the true and perfect medals in his favor."[29] It appears, then, that the king's historic narrative has two modes: the written narrative, first, which can eventually be illustrated, but which is a continuous narrative, at full length, in which the time of the history develops linearly as a concatenation of causes and effects, and whose principle of writing is the transcription of change; the writing of the event, the narrative of what happened at a particular moment in time and in a particular place in space, a narrative that successively makes new things appear and gives reason to those things, step by step; in which each sequence of the narrative is at once the consequence of the one that precedes it and the cause, reason, or motive of the one that follows. But the prince also proposes another mode of historical narrative made from the first through abbreviation, separation, and division and destined to constitute the material for the metallic history, ready for the inscription, engraving, and imprint. Each event constitutes, then, a monad of action and glory closed in on itself, endowed with its end and its meaning, a microcosm of history where it is wholly condensed and, with it, the veridical judgment, which by authenticating the event, by identifying and giving it its name and the essential elements of its image, gives it its unique and definitive meaning with its legend, its *legendum*. "Separate and divided articles" sketch a lacunary and punctual historical time, a rosary of discreet and repetitive moments, the king's acts, where the abbreviation and condensation of the narrative has the result of intensifying its effect, *coup* by *coup*, and where the narrative asyndeton has the effect of isolating each sequence as unique and unitary, total in itself, the absolute of the royal act where the infinity of one of his perfections is manifest: in short, a history not to be written but to be inscribed, where each of the events is *through that* lifted to the height, to the intensity, to the sublimity of a total royal epiphany.

But a book—the only one admitted by power[30]—will bring together in 1702 the body of the medals produced throughout the reign, a homogeneous corpus of metallic history totalizing in its volume the glorious body of the king. No doubt the precious matter into which the history has been transubstantiated by imprint gives way to paper, whose fragility and corruptibility Rascas at the beginning of the century, and many others after him, denounced. Nonetheless, a book's volume is not only the easy means of collecting the body of the medals and of showing, all in one vista—the amplitude of the design now realized—what could be a "cabinet" of king's medals; but it is above all the instrument of a vaster diffusion: the medals distributed, year after year, in France and throughout Europe are reengraved in copperplate with, at the bottom of each, a succinct account that displays its subject. Thus the book of the metallic history makes a return to the historic material whose preparation Rascas-Henry IV had suggested with the view of producing medals, those "separate and divided articles," reducing all his august history to an abridged form. Nonetheless, these articles appear in the work at once as a second legend and as an expansion of the exergue's inscription. Tallemant specifies in his preface:

> They even kept to enclosing the account in a number of words that
> never exceed the page, so that the reader could always have the
> medal before his eyes. This constraint on certain occasions prevented
> them from dwelling on the subject as much as it warranted.
> However, they were careful to omit none of the necessary
> circumstances.

We will have noted that, by giving primacy to the narrative's reading, the figured representation's synoptic vision exerts the essential semiotic constraint. The reader must read the history in the optical beam of a same gaze. It is very much the image, and only the image, that defines the instructive space of the truth and authenticity of the historical event that the narrative tells, the field of the legend's reading. The king's historic body, his glorious body, is first a "visible" thing in the political Host that presents it by representing his act. "Thus the readers will see the image of a great event; they will read its abridged detail." The hierarchy of the visible and the legible is explicit, and Tallemant exposes its means: "They will judge the ingenious turn that the invention of the medal presents to the mind; they will find diversity in the designs and legends, and will altogether be able to amuse and instruct themselves."[31] The essential means for capturing the gaze is the ingeniousness of the medal's invention. Its reader sees the image, engraving, and imprint presented to him as great event. But at first he does not know what he is seeing, except that it is an act of the king whose effigy he sees, on the right side, with the immediate recognition demanded by its engraving there and the inscription of his name and title. The image is an enigma, even a riddle, and recognizing the meaning and identifying the truth demand time and reflection. The back-and-forth between the design and the legend, the back-and-forth between the device, the exergue and the narrative, in the place of the page, open up complex, nonlinear paths of reading, where knowledge and affect, injunctions and statements of fact spatialize their contents and effects: amusement and instruction, the two great finalities of discourse in general, are found again there, *delectare* and *docere*, the first the means for the other, which must be well understood as submission and subjugation to the sovereign's law.

The book therefore brings together—and we have seen with what goal—the two modes of writing and engraving of the king's history: on the one hand, the great narrative syntagm of Louis the Great's century; on the other, the noble paradigms in which each of his actions are arranged. "History in length and continuity" is reconstituted imaginarily from the "separate and divided articles" that each medal condenses into image and legend on the reverse side of the prince's portrait and his name. Or, inversely, after reading, once the book is closed again, the series of disconnected narrative segments, all along the line of the time elapsed from the beginnings of the reign until the accession of the duc d'Anjou to the throne of Spain, come to be grouped in the immobile and stable architecture of a promised monument in the imaginary of the reader-spectator, for an eternal duration. Each stone of this monument is made of a medal as before; the same medal is the abridged sequence of a historic narrative—the inscription of a brilliant act of the king, to which this inscription gives the value of model at once in history and outside time. An exemplary book, a book of *exempla*: the narrative that composes it with the succession of succinct accounts at the bottom of each engraving is made only of examples, the devices of each medal; a history book nonetheless, since the inscription to the exergue assures without contest the insertion of the example into a named place of geographic space and a dated moment of chronological time.[32]

Each royal action, on the condition that a device inscribe it on the reverse side of the figure of the king marked in his effigy and name and thus convert his temporary event into a lasting monument, is by that the singular revelation of a universal, an attribute and a perfection of the royal substance. Each medal, from trace to mark, from index to icon, and from icon to sign, reveals this act as the instantaneous and unique point of insertion, in time and space, of a permanent and infinite quality of the king.

The King's reign has furnished ample material for striking medals for him alone, such as all the greats and the good emperors have deserved. *We see* Provinces subjugated in a matter of days; more than three hundred cities taken, and cities that by their fortifications and natural situation were more difficult to conquer than were formerly entire Provinces. *We see* battles won on land and at sea; Allies helped, protected, reinstated; military discipline at its highest point. *We see* the Navy flourishing, ports on both seas, vessels and galleys that make the French colors respected everywhere. In the middle of so many *prodigies* that concern war, we find establishments for the poor, for soldiers, for the nobility, for Men of letters. *We admire* the Prince's prepossessing Goodness, his Justice, Piety, Clemency, Moderation, Liberality, and Magnificence; finally all those glorious things contained in the lives of the Heroes of Ancient Rome.[33]

Thus the narrative of Louis the Great's reign, constituted by the collection in a *book* of the medals struck on the occasion of great events, is "paradigmized" into classes of events (the provinces subjugated, the cities taken, the battles won, and so on) unified by a global vision ("We see . . . , we see . . ."). The reader-spectator, who is the imaginary product and symbolic effect of each medal and of their totalization in the book, attributes each of these paradigms, then, by an epideictic performance at once admiring contemplation and praising discourse, to a quality or perfection of the king (goodness, justice, clemency, and the like) of which each of the remarkable events, because marked on the reverse side of the medals, was the miraculous occasion for revelation.

INTERLUDE
Royal Money and Princely Portrait

I propose to read a fairy tale[1] in which, it seems to me, the network of various problems of representation and political power—of representation as power and of power as representation—are displayed in the narrative form of a peculiar fiction. A narrative at the end of the *Grand Siècle* unfolds in its form and specifies in its uniqueness the real aporias of infinite representation and absolute power, all while surmounting them with the powers characteristic of all fables and the resources they draw from the marvelous. This narrative text is the place of the contradictions of representation in its double relationship to, first, the effect of power of the narrative and the effect of power of the image and, second, to the effect of absolute power and the production of its unlimited subject: the monarch. It is a question of *Peau d'Ane* (Donkey Skin) and of Perrault's rewriting of that oral narrative around 1694.[2]

What *Donkey Skin* tells is a story of power, the story of the desire of all power to be an absolute power in the representation of a king who is also a father. Nonetheless, Perrault takes his precautions in a prologue: How to justify his position as narrator? How to make his taking over of narrative speech and, with it, his taking over of the power to tell a story acceptable? To occupy the place of the master of the narrative is not a matter of course. Thus a double strategy and maybe, with it, a double feint, by which a forceful thrust is dissimulated. He tells the story only to content the reader's wish for a narrative: an author's fiction, but one that permits Perrault to exchange the position of listening to the desire for a tale for one of narrating a story: ''Without fear, then, of being condemned / For badly employing my leisure, / I will, to content your just desire, / Tell you Donkey Skin's entire story." But this operation comes only at the conclusion of another one, which is to respond to these questions: With what right does the storyteller tell? What is the legitimacy of the power to tell a story? What authority founds this law, and by what juridical argumentation does the narrator authorize himself? Now the answer is a forceful *coup*: "As for me, I dare propose that in fact, / At certain moments, the most perfect being / Can love even Puppets without blushing." The mastery of tales is a given—the fact of the writer-prince. The storyteller takes possession of the narrative voice simply by beginning to write. This is the pure *factum* of a potential power that institutes its own right to (re)write, to re-cite, a potential that is itself founded on authorized power and by that constitutes the narrator subject as a subject by right. This fact of mastery— a force that legitimates itself in power—writes only fact, a fact that is the pleasure of the tale and its listeners, the pleasure of the interval of meaning and truth, since "there are times and places / Where what is grave and serious / Is not worth as much as agreeable nonsense." The "pleasure principle" here is a source of right, a *law*, but of which the strangest characteristic is that it is without a decree of application: neither general nor universal, its law is expressed only at certain times and places, for which no criterion can be given. The narrative is written only on the occasion and within the occasion, and the rule of the occasion is pleasure that is without rules; except that pleasure can never be had in the momentary and contingent interruption of the meaning, place and moment, that the writing of the tale by the narrator comes to occupy without striking a blow.

And yet interruption by the pleasure of a tale is not a stranger to the reason and vigilance that characterize it. Pleasure here is not a principle antagonistic to the principle of reason, for the pleasure of the tale is also a pleasure of reason, the one it gets when it goes on vacation and holiday from meaning and truth in the land of fiction. It is the pleasure of regression and, in that regression, of its own "transversion,"[3] a regression not to sleep but to dormancy, not to the sleeper's passive immobility but to being rocked in the arms and voice of the mother who tells a story. Reason lets itself go there, and recreates itself in its childhood with the gentleness of a word that evokes the ogre's threat only to exorcise it with the fairy's omnipotent magic: "Why should we marvel / That the most sensible Reason, / Often weary with too much watching, / Takes pleasure in sleeping, / Ingeniously rocked / By tales of Ogres and Fairies?" Consequently, the power of the storyteller is the power of reason that reason turns back on itself by returning to the reverie and rocking of its childhood, by listening to a voice that is indistinctly its own and one that, while telling, protects against what it itself tells.

Just as the narration of a tale transverts the power of the discourse of reason, the discourse of the law of reality, the discourse of the order of society, by the potential power of the wish and the pleasure of the telling, similarly, what the tale tells, the story it recites, turns the discourse of absolute power against itself by the desire-pleasure for love. In the prologue the writer institutes himself in his legitimate power to tell nonsense only by turning the narrative figure of power, an omnipotent king and a father in love, against itself.

Absolute Power and Its Contradiction

"Once upon a time there was a King . . ." The narrative begins, a tale, which the initial ritual formula obviously marks. But it hesitates suddenly between the *fiction* of a time beyond time and the contemporary *eulogic discourse*: for this king was "The greatest who ever was on Earth. / Amiable in Peace and terrible in War, / He was in the end comparable only to himself."

This marvel of omnipotence with which the narrative begins resembles Louis the Great to the point of being mistaken for his portrait, which, at this moment precisely, the epideixis of the royal person and the monarchical institution erects: "His neighbors feared him, his States were calm / And both Virtues and Fine Arts / Could be seen in all directions, / Flowering in the shade of his palms." The courtier storyteller even finds one of the most remarkable definitions for absolute power, not only with the relative superlative that characterizes its greatness, "the greatest King who ever was on earth," but also in the very mechanism by which power desires to be and poses itself as absolute—since the "external" comparison that measures its power [*puissance*] with respect to that of the other kings on earth assumes itself to be at once dialectically necessary and essentially irrelevant. One compares what can be compared: only the king's self can provide a "comparer" that has the same nature as the compared, the monarch. This tale is a song of praise; the fiction functions politically.

The sphere without fissure of absolute power is instituted at this altitude only to fall from it at once. Nonetheless, the epideixis continues to deploy its figures, but they can say their hyperbolic power only negatively; and far from amplifying its resonance, the effect produced is a lessening, and that in the double dimension of alliance and filiation. For this omnipotent king at once splits into two: "His lovely Half, his faithful Companion, / Was so charming and beautiful, / With a spirit so accommodating and gentle, / That with her he was more / A happy spouse than a happy King." The "scissiparity" of the political absolute in marriage has for consequence that the happiness of the spouse surpasses that of the king. There is a new scission of the absolute in filiation: "Of their tender and chaste Union / A *daughter* was born, / So full of gentleness and charms and with so many virtues, / *That they easily consoled themselves / For not having had a more ample progeny.*" The fragmentation of the absolute accelerates with its fall into the contingencies and chance of nature, since the royal progeny born of the marriage is reduced to a daughter whose very great qualities will not prevent either the line's extinction or the accession to the throne of a son-in-law.

After the king, his sign is suddenly erected, "his rich and vast Palace." The prince's dwelling is in a way the figure by synecdoche of his very power, the present monument, the signifying architecture of his omnipotence. In that palace "There was only magnificence. / It was teeming everywhere with a lively abundance / Of Courtiers and Valets. / In his Stables were / Large and small horses of all kinds, / Covered with beautiful trappings, / Stiff with gold and embroidery." Despite the teeming in the multitude that crowds and ferments, let us note the insistence of a hierarchical order: the courtiers, the servants, the horses. But it is an order that skids in the ironic arrangement of its terms in order to, it seems, point out its extraordinary anomaly, recoil and subversion: "But what surprised everyone upon entering / Was that in the most conspicuous place / A Master Donkey displayed its two large ears." A limit marks the edges of the sovereign's circumference, the boundaries of the sphere of absolute power: a Master Donkey. Recoil: up until now, in the structure of order, we have gone from predecessors to successors and from the predecessor who, not having any himself, has only successor: from the king (his half, his daughter); from his palace (courtiers, valets); from his stables (large, small horses); to the ternary rhythm of the emanations of his omnipotence, $3 \times 3 = 9$, to its most extreme confines, the threshhold of his stables. In this way should be constituted in circularity the sovereign identity of absolute power. In this way should be formulated its imperial tautology. Now— the surprise of the reader equals that of the visitor—this movement is blocked when barely begun and immobilized when barely broached: ready for reverence and prosternation, here we are, readers and visitors, gorgonized: "in the most conspicuous place / A Master Donkey displayed his two large ears. / This injustice surprises you? / But when you know its matchless virtues, / You will not find the honor too great." Injustice, unreason, absurdity? No. For the king comparable only to himself, whom we will not see in the center of the palace, is replaced at his door, in the most conspicuous place, by the animal with the incomparable virtues, and we will see only him. A natural anomaly lends reason, does justice and gives meaning to a cultural anomaly: "So clean had Nature formed it / That it never made any manure, / But rather quite beautiful Crowns with a sun / And Louis of all kinds / That were collected with a golden litter / Every morning at its awakening." Master Donkey is the master, and the donkey, the king very precisely in that it coins money in its own fashion.

$3 + 1 = 4; 3 \times 3 = 9 + 1 = 10$: (the king, his palace, his stables) and the donkey; the king (his half, his daughter); his palace (courtiers and valets); his stables (large and small horses), and the donkey: an instructive numerology for the person who really knows how to read it. Whatever the rule of arrangement adopted, the donkey comes in addition to it (he is the fourth in a ternary order and the tenth in a nonary order), in an unexpected and absurd supplement to the qualitative hierarchy. Everything becomes clear: we understand why "both Virtues and Fine Arts / Could be seen in all directions, / Flowering in the shade of his palms," why "In his rich and vast Palace / There was only magnificence." Master Donkey "never made any manure, / But rather quite beautiful Crowns with a sun / And Louis of all kinds." If the large and small horses in the stables and the valets and courtiers in the palace signify the king figuratively and really, to see the donkey at the door of the stables upon entering the place of the king is to see the figure of the king and to discover the *real* source of his omnipotence.

The donkey-king coins money in his fashion, which is completely natural. He defecates it every morning at his awakening: not manure, but gold-money. *He produces naturally, by way of* [à titre de] *excrement and waste, monetary, culturally precious and powerful entitlements* [titres]. A marvelous metamorphosis: in Master Donkey's waste is inscribed the royal effigy, the head and name that mark it at its value as [à son titre de] gold. He eats his peck of oats and, while eliminating the unassimilable waste of the vegetable nourishment, he produces marvelously—and naturally—the signs of precious metal where that power of the real monarch is marked, where this power is legitimated and its potential realized.[4] In a word, the donkey produces the king of the tale, "the greatest who ever was on Earth," by defecating the money of Louis, the sun king of the storyteller.

A king cut into in the confines of his power, split by alliance, a father disappointed in his descendants and too easily consoled for not having a more ample progeny—here suddenly once again begins the inverse movement of the reconstitution of the absolute after his fall into the contingencies of nature, at the price of the momentary oversight of the fundamental and marvelous condition of his omnipotence, the donkey producer of moneyed gold. The unexpected character of this return to himself has about it, however, something surprising. It is the pure event that intervenes here, deprived of reason but mysteriously realizing what power always desires and, in roundabout ways, fulfilling the secret request of omnipotence, to be alone in itself, identical to itself, the absolute sovereign: "Now Heaven, which sometimes tires / Of making men happy, / And which always mingles some disfavor with its good, / Such as rain with good weather, / Permitted a bitter illness / To suddenly attack the Queen in her prime." First reconstitution of royal omnipotence: the queen, his lovely "half," dies, and the king is a widower, an unhappy, tearful spouse, certainly, but finally king and just a king. That the death of the faithful companion is accompanied by a dangerous play of challenges and oaths, and by reciprocal provocations, is not important to us right away. That play only puts into place the conditions of possibility for the ultimate return to the self of the absolute. The solemn promise requested and made at the queen's death bed to marry only a woman more beautiful, more shapely, and wiser than the deceased, only constructs [bricoler] the trap of the tale, which is not, or not yet, the ruse of the story but only the unexpected figure of power's desire for the absolute. As we know, the king's daughter "alone was more beautiful, / And possessed certain tender charms / That the deceased had not. / The King himself noticed it / And, burning with an intense love, / Foolishly advised himself / That for this reason he must marry her." By returning as spouse to the father, the daughter who, by her birth, had for a moment compromised the royal permanence in the line, permits a new beginning and erases the ultimate exteriority where the absolute of the power had been divided. The search for a replacement for the queen to which the king surrenders himself would show that sufficiently: "He wanted to proceed toward making a new choice, / But it was no easy thing: / He had to keep his oath, / That the new Spouse / Would have more attractions and charms / Than the one who had just been entombed. / Neither the Court rich in beauties, / Nor the Country, nor the City, / Nor the surrounding Kingdoms / Of which the rounds had been made / Could furnish such a one. / The Infanta alone was more beautiful." The rounds of the search, the more and more ample circles of the royal desire in search of its object in exteriority, concentrate finally on the one that had been always already present and given, the infanta.[5] The widower's investigation is a search less for beauty superior to the departed spouse's than for the verification that the daughter present at his side really occupies the place defined by the oath. The circle is reconstituted in genealogical order, since the line of filiation curves back on itself to become the closest alliance to the father and the husband. Figure, did I say? The father's incestuous desire in the fiction of the tale is the figure of another desire, the king's. The erotic is, in its madness, the image of the politic in its will; the intense love with which the king burns for his daughter is the fictive model of the ultimate will for omnipotence that moves the king. Power makes one mad, and absolute power makes one absolutely mad. Thus can the law of the story and its necessary mechanisms express itself in the fiction of the tale and its marvelous frameworks. With it, the king is father; the father is king. Who, then, is the ogre once the mother is deceased?

No less than the major transgression of the prohibition on which all society is founded will do to find the figure suitable for the desire for all power and to describe fictively the drive that animates the political. The father desires to marry his daughter, just as the ogre desires to eat the child and just as the king wants to be the absolute master. But during all this time, in the stables the donkey "works" mysteriously, eating oats and defecating crowns and louis each morning on his litter, the instruments of absolute mastery and its mark — in short, defecating the king at the moment when he desires to gobble up his daughter.

The poor child finds herself doubly cornered: to obey her father is to transgress natural-cultural law; to obey that law is to transgress the father's law. There is only one response possible, the silence of the voice in the body's noise: "But the sad young Princess, / To hear speak of such a love, / Lamented and cried night and day."

Face to face with the ogre, the fairy. Opposite the father and the king, the (metaphoric) mother, the godmother. Opposite the speech [*parole*] of the scandalous order, the wise and sly discourse of advice: "Her heart full of a thousand sorrows, / She went to find her Godmother, / In a secluded grotto far away, /

Richly furnished with Mother of Pearl and Coral. / She was an admirable Fairy / Who never had an equal in her Art."[6] On the one hand, then, is the king, real and symbolic father, omnipotent image of the order of the power whose expressed desires are realized orders. But beneath or behind him, at the limits of the palace, is the donkey, who, marvelously, naturally, produces this omnipotence in the form of manure-money. On the other, the infanta, daughter of the king and the deceased queen, the silent object to be appropriated and reassimilated in order for the monarch to be absolute; and, at her side, behind her, but quite far, apart from the circles of power, "metaphorically" reappeared, the mother, the fairy godmother, endowed with the marvelous potential of her art—incomparable as were the virtues given by nature to the donkey—an art that is at first and essentially that of the discourse of wisdom. In this sense the fairy godmother, the symbolic generator, or producer, of her goddaughter, is, from all points of view, the contrary of the donkey, the fictive producer of the king and of his potential power. She possesses the admirable art of discourse, while the donkey finds himself endowed with a marvelous nature. And the habitually "arbitrary" signs of language, the means of ruse, are the counterpart of the extraordinarily "natural" signs of money, the means of power [*puissance*].

Power's Challenge, or the Game of the Auction

The king-father gives orders that are his desires. The fairy godmother gives advice that is wisdom and knowledge. The infanta does not need to speak: the "mother" knows the worries and pains of her child before she says them: "'I know,' she said, upon seeing the Princess, / 'What makes you come here, / I know the profound sadness of your heart; / But with me you need no longer worry. / Nothing can harm you / So long as you let yourself be led by my advice.'" To accede to the father's foolish demand would be a major error. But neither can one contradict his order, for the good reason, once again, that the king's orders are his desires and his desires, orders. Such is his good pleasure. The principle is laid down, and the law that founds it in its founding is itself nontransgressable, even if the principle is that of transgression, and the law, that of the subversion of all law.

How, then, to refuse without contradicting? The fairy godmother's discourse will be the art of using "transversive" means with respect to the order of the law, of the royal-paternal erotic-politic, without exiting the field that it covers and rules absolutely. Thus will start the auction, the bidding and its successive escalations, the raises of the two players, until the final "carpet" that will be the donkey's skin. The fairy godmother's discourse aims, without bringing into question the desires-orders of the king-father and their well-foundedness, to convey [*émettre*] conditions for their fulfillment. "Conditions" is no doubt saying too much, for it is less a question, in the requests that will be made, of a logic of the necessary, the possible, or the real than of opposing desires to desire and, more precisely, of making of the satisfaction of the former a simple delay in the satisfaction of the latter: a "condition," if you will, but one that, deprived of all logical or ontological rapport with what it conditions, is rather whim or fantasy that plays only on time, on the deferred moment of time. It is in this sense that "resistance" to the desire of the king-father is a challenge or counterchallenge, which can only generate a more elevated challenge. "'Say to him that he must give you, / To satisfy your desires and / Before you abandon your heart to his love, / A Dress that is the color of the Sky.'" A sly discourse, however, for, the stake being supposed too great, the transaction cannot, it seems, take place. The admirable art of the fairy godmother consists in formulating the demands of desire and in having them formulated in terms that are in accordance with the procedures and proceedings of contractual right, and by that in making juridical rules play against the law and principle of desire—by taking the king-father in the double bind of desire and right and, by *saying* desire's *absolute right* to be satisfied in those desires, preventing de facto their satisfaction: "'Despite all his power and wealth, / Though Heaven favors his wishes in all things, / He will never be able to fulfill his promise,'" and by that, his desire. In the end that which the infanta's request of her father and king at once presupposes and provokes is the inadequation of the father's desire and the king's power, by opening up an inequality in the sphere of political omnipotence: desire's power [*puissance*] is shifted away from the desire for power [*puissance*]. Power and desire are not reciprocally convertible terms: the latter's absolute power [*puissance*] does not recover the former's desire for the absolute. The king is not a father from end to end, and vice versa.

Now this calculation of provocation-presupposition reveals itself to be in error. In the match that is engaged in, the amorous father plays the omnipotent king and wins. The simple mouthpiece of the metaphoric mother, the mistress of sly discourse, the infanta, left to that moment without a voice, comes to mumble her request to him, and "The second day had not yet dawned / When the desired Dress was brought. / The most beautiful blue of the Firmament / Is not, when girded with large golden clouds, / Of a color more azure." The azure and gold dress leaves the daughter disconcerted. "The Infanta, penetrated with joy and pain, / Did not know what to say, or how / To escape from her engagement." At that point there was no other alternative than for the godmother to raise the bid: a dress the color of the moon—"The rich dress was made by the appointed day"; a dress the color of the sun—"the industrious worker, / Before the end of the week, / Had the precious work brought. / It was so beautiful, so vivid, so radiant, / That Clymene's blond Lover, / As he moves across the Heavenly vault / In his golden chariot, / Does not dazzle the eyes with a more brilliant splendor." Azure, silver, and gold, the three dresses are each more brilliant, products each more rich of the marvelous art of artisans each more skillful and each more elevated in the hierarchy of the arts, the tailor, the embroiderer, and the lapidarian. The infanta is more and more admiring of the desired clothing and less and less reticent to the foolish demand, even though happily advised by the nearer and nearer godmother: the discourse in the secluded grotto, soft murmurs, and finally the secret inspiration. Three stages of art, beauty, wealth, and brilliance in the requested and received gifts, three moments of a resistance that, weakening, tends toward surrender, three stages of a same discourse that progressively becomes interior voice.[7]

Never two without three—will the third *coup*, the third gift, be it? That would be not to know the godmother very well. She plays a supplementary *coup*, the supreme *coup*, unforeseen: "[She] said in her ear, 'You must not / Pause now after such a good start. / Are they such a great marvel, / These gifts that you have received from him, / As long as he has the Donkey you know about, / That unceasingly fills his purse with gold crowns? / Ask him for the skin of this rare Animal. / As it is his whole resource, / You will not obtain it, or I reason badly.'" One, two, three dresses, the last one made of woven sun and gold, requested and desired in order not to be obtained. At the end of the three bids they are, however, and with them time has been traveled, and night and day, and the entire cosmos, sky, moon, and sun are deployed and inscribed in a "superb cloth," token of "a love without equal." Prey to his incomparable passion, so little master of himself, here is the king master of the universe in three *coups*, three gifts, three dresses, in order to acquire-possess and consume, through alliance, the unique object—his daughter—who is already his by filiation: a power *almost* absolute, a potential *almost* total, a mastery *almost* complete.[8] For her part the daughter, advised by the mother's representative, attempts to escape from the father's and the king's absolute power by turning, with her three requests, the same power against itself: she demands the signs that manifest that power in order to render that same power impotent.

It is in this sense that the "almost" that separates potential from omnipotence, power from absolute power, has an infinite potential: it is an infinitesimal asymptotic gap where, all of a sudden, the curve retraces its steps and becomes in an instant "infinitely" negative. But the father is powerful enough and the king has enough power to carry out successively the daughter's three requests and to disconcert her. And this "enough" is already *almost* "all." In a moment, "enough" *will be* "all." The godmother plays, then, a fourth time, and if I may dare say so, it is not fair play, for according to the rules (of the game, narrative, tale, myth), there cannot be a fourth *coup*, once time, night, day, the sky, moon, and finally the sun are obtained, the sun, "Clymene's blond Lover, / [Who] moves across the Heavenly vault / In his golden chariot," of such a brilliant splendor that it blinds all eyes. Certainly, but the donkey had been forgotten, the donkey who, in the royal stables, in the most conspicuous place upon entering, "worked" during the night while sleeping, so that in the morning on his golden litter quite beautiful crowns with a sun and louis of all kinds could be collected. Master Donkey, in his own way, travels through the cosmic cycle, time and night and day, a burlesque Apollo in the cycle of nutrition between oats and donkey dung, with this one difference that his manure is gold-money, that each morning he coins sun and coins light, making the ringing and stumbling currencies, not in a superb cloth of gold and diamonds but in quite beautiful crowns, each one a little sun reproduced indefinitely. The godmother plays outside of the rules, outside of the game, the donkey against the king, because the donkey is itself outside of the rules and outside of the game, the token that assures, from the beginning, the king's game, order, rules, and law. The godmother, by playing, as we say, all or nothing, plays the absolute thrust against the absolute of the royal power. Do not request any more marvelous *dresses* of art and gold—could one exist, anyway, that was more beautiful than the dress the color of the sun? Ask for the frightful skin of the thing that permitted their production, the donkey's skin. Here the king is trapped: "You will not obtain it, or I reason badly." In a word, what the donkey-*coup* uncovers is that absolute power is absolute only in figure and that, if we look well, here and there, in the past and in the present, we will always find a donkey in a stable somewhere—but political art and artifice are to make one forget about it.

The godmother's fourth *coup*, the supplementary *coup*, brings into play or poses as stake the very supplement of the apparatus of representation: the donkey. With it are then at risk both the figure of powerful reality (moneyed gold) and the figure of the imaginary of power (to have no limit). In Perrault's marvelous narrative the donkey is simultaneously the reality of the royal potential and the essential means of satisfying the desire for unlimited power. But the donkey as narrative character is obviously also the absolute monarch's limit. Omnipotent king, he is subjugated to his marvelous donkey, who provides him marvelously both with the reality of his potential and the means of his desire for the absolute of power. At the level of the narration—for "Donkey Skin's Tale is hard to believe"—the donkey as figure traces the limit of the power to tell a story.[9]

The king, checkmate? No, alas, for his daughter's virtue. The godmother made an error. "This Fairy was quite learned, / And yet she still did not know / That violent love, provided it is satisfied, / Counts silver and gold as nothing. / The skin was gallantly granted as soon as / The Infanta requested it." The godmother was mistaken twice: she took the figure for reality and supposed that her adversary, the king, would not abandon reality for the figure. The calculation was reasonable, but an all-powerful, all-amorous king is not. She supposed that the king would not kill the donkey of the gold-money dung (the reality of his omnipotence) in order to possess his own daughter (the figure of his absolute power). A double error that consisted, after all, in substituting a logic of rational calculation for that of desire, that of time and the project for that of the instant and intensity, the temporal scheme of causes and consequences for the violence of drives and their effects, the juridical matrix of the contract of exchange and transaction by gift and countergift for the reciprocal seduction of confronted desires, where the subjects collapse in the face-to-face as in a mirror of their demands.

Overturn of the overturned: the king-father in a moment, and for a moment, has won: the three dresses are forgotten, and in their place is the freshly flayed skin. Thus, by agreeing to kill his donkey in the game of the supplementary bid, the king suppresses in an instant all limits to the "reality" of both his potential and the satisfaction of his desire. More precisely, he puts himself in the *power* of fulfilling it in the instant when he *is* without the limit of the real, but from then on he will no longer have the *power* to be omnipotent. What Perrault insists on is that the omnipotent and amorous king-father does not reason in terms of power and time. At the instant of the donkey's sacrifice to the infanta's desire, the father's desire is already satisfied, and the loss of the king's potential has not yet occurred. In that instant, the supplement of the representative framework having been suppressed, the latter can function, but only for an instant, completely enclosed, on its own resources, and we notice that power is indeed the effect of representation's framework.

Actually, even if only for an instant, we can ask if representation's framework is ever completely enclosed. The father's desire is no doubt satisfied in an imaginary future, and his omnipotence has not yet passed into a possible or probable future. But from then on, from that very instant, is traced a new limit to the absolute power: it is the limit of the real that is lacking, just as is the erotic reality of his daughter's body that the king does not yet possess, and just as is the economic reality of the donkey's body that the king already no longer possesses. The power is absolute, but it is still and always at the same time *almost* absolute.[10]

After the games of the discourse of sly wisdom and their multiple paths, once all the *coups* have been played and the supreme one, the one where the (figurative) putting to death of the adversary is in fact the occasion of the triumph that was the momentary, certainly, and imaginary, but the absolute triumph of his desire, there is only one way out: the voice [*voix*] of the feint in discourse and the path [*voie*] of the mask for the body, the surfaces of language with a double-entendre, the skin of the disguised flesh. "Her Godmother appeared and showed her [*lui représenta*] / That when we do the right thing, we need never fear, / And that the King must be led to think / That she was entirely disposed / To submit with him to conjugal Law; / But that at the same time, alone and well-disguised, / She must leave for some faraway State / To avoid an evil so near and so certain. / . . . 'The Donkey's skin / Is an admirable mask and will make you unrecognizable. / Hide yourself well in it: / The skin is so frightful that no one will believe / It encloses anything beautiful.' / The Princess thus disguised . . .''

The Path of the Mask and Identification

Change of setting, change of tactic. Actually, the voice of the feint is only the short prologue to the path of the mask: less a discourse than an attitude, less speech [*parole*] than a behavior that "hints" at one intention while another is woven into secrecy. There again, it is not a question of contradicting, of refusing an exigency or a desire of the other, but of presenting herself to him under the aspect of consent, which induces his belief, while keeping her own intention to herself. Not to say no to the king's and father's law, but to let him think yes and at the same time to flee. But since this law is omnipotent and its order absolute, can there be a place that is foreign to it, a corner of the world that is outside of its order? And if to be the daughter of a king is to be disposed by nature and definition to submit to his omnipotent authority, there is no other alternative in order to avoid its application than to no longer be infanta. But how to no longer be that which one is by nature and definition, if not by disguising oneself, by appearing to be other than one is? The infanta escapes by making herself invisible, but as she cannot escape from the eye of the master, she renders herself invisible to him by becoming other than she is. If he—he or his representatives—were to see her, he would see someone else: he would fail to recognize her.

The path of the mask, then. Let us understand "path" in a double sense: the way out, the road where, it seems, there is none, the aporia, in a word, the flight; but also the solution, the resolution of a problem that, it seems, does not allow of any in the imminence that characterizes it. The path of the mask or the displacement of the body in space and its metamorphosis.

Nonetheless, it does not appear to be as obvious that the dead donkey's frightful skin is the living princess's admirable mask. The daughter, on the advice of her metaphoric mother, obtained the donkey's skin; she requested its death and obtained it of the king, her father, of whose power [*puissance*] the donkey was the producing source. Figuratively, by killing the donkey, she kills the king; by having his donkey killed, the king commits suicide. As we have seen, it is by this reasoning that the godmother had articulated her ultimate demand. Murder of the king in his living works, wealth, the foundation of his power [*puissance*]. A metaphoric murder, certainly, in the relay of its figures, but one that has left a remainder, precisely the remains, or the skin, of the donkey; the daughter "had its hide," in the meantime finding her name there. By requesting, after the three dresses, marvels of art, the skin of the marvelous donkey, the princess has indeed obtained a fourth garment, a natural garment, however, a skin that owes its extraordinary character only to the fact that it enveloped the donkey of matchless virtues, but a skin that can become a garment only at the price of the death of that which made its price, for, once this rare animal has been slaughtered and skinned, its skin is only its remains, the same as all other skins.

The skin, become garment, envelops the princess and makes her unrecognizable: "'Hide yourself well in it: / The skin is so frightful that no one will believe / It encloses anything beautiful.'" The skin has become not only a dress (in French we say the "dress" of a horse, so why not that of a donkey?) but also a mask, not only clothing but also a disguise, not only garment but also travesty. The donkey likewise, you will say. Certainly, but each morning, at its awakening, were found the proofs and signs, the witnesses and marks of the marvel. The incomparable virtues of the princess are substituted indeed for those of the donkey under its skin, under the same skin. But the donkey produced the signs of its virtues, it brought their marks to light. The princess, on the contrary, dissimulates those of her princely beauty. Thus, while the whole of the donkey's function is excretion, production, and extraneity (its substance, including its waste, passes into monetary signs and form), the fairy godmother's tactic for the princess is alienation, nonrecognition, and dissimulation. For the living donkey the movement goes from interior to exterior, from internal manure to external minted beauty. In the dead donkey's remains are, on the one hand, the frightful surface, the skin, and, on the other, what it encloses, beauty, without our/one's being able to believe that the first encloses the second, without our/one's being able to pass from one to the other. This is so true that the signs of the daughter's beauty, the exterior marks of her rank, will magically—it is the first time that the godmother is really a fairy—accompany her, enclosed in a large chest that will follow the same path as her, but hidden under the earth. Of course, the fairy's wand is the marvelous vehicle of all of this equipage, as it will be the instrument of its being brought to light at the whim of her desire; but the separation of the princess and her signs thus magically marked has to be underlined. Become invisible, as princess, under the donkey's skin, having lost her signs and her marks, her properties, her titles and even her name, she is then assimilated to the donkey by its skin, enveloped by it, become an animal by the natural garment that encloses her. But it is at that moment that she acquires the power to make herself visible to herself in her signs and first beauty: "'I also give you my Wand. / If you hold it in your hand, / The chest will follow the same path as you / Always hidden under the Earth; / And when you want to open it, / Hardly will my rod have touched the Earth / Than it will offer itself immediately to your sight.'"

The moment is remarkable: it is the moment of omnipotence that has suddenly been passed from the sovereign to the subjugated poles; the wholly narcissistic moment of its constitution as subject in and through the mask she puts on, in and through the travesty that she dons, in and through the disguise she wears. By her mask, travesty, disguise, the infanta is made invisible to all, and first of all to the person who sees everything, the king, the father, who, in the potential of seeing everything, can have everything. Absence from the father of the object of the king's desire, which is first of all the absence of this object divided from itself, in itself, in appearance and being. It is at that moment, however, that the princess acquires the capacity to make her own signs of belonging to the royal sphere visible—but to herself alone—and to make herself visible to herself as infanta, therefore to present herself to herself, to identify herself as subject, in a word, which will be said, to love herself.

And it is also at this moment that the godmother, having for a moment become fairy and relegated her magical power [*puissance*] to her goddaughter—the capacity to identify herself as subject—disappears from the narrative to reappear only on the wedding day. Second—metaphoric—death of the—metaphoric—mother. The princess no longer needs her; she has been identified by herself.

Here are some complementary notes in the form of a demonstration.

1. From the beginning of the narrative the king's daughter has a title: that of princess, or infanta. But she does not have a name of her own. By enveloping herself in Master Donkey's skin, she acquires a garment, any old skin from any old donkey. And at the same time, at least in appearance, she loses her title; she wanders then not only incognito ("'The Donkey's skin / Is an admirable mask and will make you unrecognizable'") but also in the most extreme anonymity ("such a filthy creature . . . a scullery maid"). And when her flight reaches an end, "far, quite far, even farther away . . . at a Farm" where "she was put in a corner at the back of the kitchen," it is then that she acquires a name, "Donkey Skin," a metonymic name from her mask, certainly, but a proper name: "It is . . . Donkey Skin. . . . / And who is called 'Donkey Skin' / Because of the Skin she wears on her neck," a name she keeps to the end of the narrative, until the moment of her triumph, that is, even when at her epiphany she recovers her title. A paradox, but maybe less strange than it seems, of a mask of anonymity that opens right onto a name, which legitimates a nomination. A sur-name, if you like, just as the mask is a sur-body or a sur-face, but I would have to add at once that the use of the mask as surname, and the glorious history attached to it, authorizes and founds its transformation into name. In any case the *coup* of the donkey's skin calculated twice by the godmother permits the princess to acquire a name (a surname) that is at once figuratively a patronym (since the donkey is the figure of the king and the king, that of the donkey), and narratively a matronym (see the fairy godmother's calculation with respect to the donkey and its remains), Donkey [*âne*, a masculine noun] Skin [*peau*, a feminine noun]: a bilinearity traced in the name-surname by the opposed sexes of the two parents, who are at once conjoined and neutralized there, since the name is neither that of the father nor that of the mother. Here in "Donkey Skin" is realized the impossible alliance the father and the king desire, the unnameable transgression of the

law that is the law of his desire and his pleasure, to possess and consum(mat)e his own daughter.

2. Let us take, with the fairy godmother, the inventory of the chest at the start of the journey into exile: "'Here is,' she continued, 'a large chest / Where we will put all your garments, / Your mirror, your toilette, / Your diamonds and your rubies.'" After her arrival at her destination, in the room where Donkey Skin has privacy, on Sunday "She . . . opened her chest, / Set up her toilette properly and / Arranged her little pots upon it. / In front of her large mirror, happy and satisfied, / She would put on now her Moon dress, / Now the one where the Sun's fire shines, / Now the beautiful blue dress / That all the azure of the Sky could not equal." All garments are reduced to the three dresses of the paternal and royal desire. The diamonds and rubies have for the moment disappeared, but the mirror at the departure has become a large mirror where "She liked to see herself young, rosy and white, / And a hundred times more elegant than any other woman. / This sweet pleasure sustained her / And carried her along until the following Sunday." The dresses requested in order not to be obtained, and finally possessed in three times closer imminence to the fulfillment of the desire and order of the king-father, here they are worn, one after the other, on the day of rest, on the Lord's day,[11] as metaphors of satisfied desire and obeyed order. But here they are, above all, represented to her sight in her mirror become large when taken out of the case, seen and contemplated by Donkey Skin, who is cleaned up and become once again for one day, one moment, a princess, thanks to them more beautiful, more elegant "a hundred times more elegant than any other woman." Here they are, in their representation in reflection, gratifying the woman who wears them with the sweet pleasure of identification that, repeated every week, sustains her for seven days. Thus is she sustained "morally" in her trial, but it is appropriate—thus does the narrative develop from the beginning by realizing the metaphors of language, thus must we reread and rewrite it by "appropriating" them, by literalizing them—it is appropriate, then, to read this support literally: to sustain oneself is to nourish oneself, to maintain one's life by means of food that one eats. The sweet pleasure of the subject's identification, the representation of the body in the mirror and in the dresses that envelop it, the sweet narcissistic pleasure of eating with one's eyes one's own and marvelous image. "I represent myself, therefore I am"; read: "I eat myself as representation, in the representation that made me the object of the impossible and refused desire of the king-father, therefore I am really what I am, object-subject of desire, of a 'proper' and innocent desire, of my own desire."[12]

3. The donkey's remains make an admirable mask: so be it, and it is well thus, since "'The skin is so frightful that no one will believe / It encloses anything beautiful.'" But how to don such a travesty? How to envelop oneself in the

donkey's skin? How to wear this mask? I ask this practical question of the tailor or furrier for no other reason than this one: the donkey's skin as garment disappears from the narrative of the poor child's wanderings to reappear only at the moment of the (sur)naming of the princess that she nonetheless disguises: "[She] is called 'Donkey Skin' / Because of the Skin she wears on her neck"; and quite discreetly a last time, preluding her triumph, "when she drew from beneath her black skin / A little hand that seemed of ivory." The skin that encloses her entirely and hides her well at the beginning of the trial has become a stole put on her neck, a distinctive sign and qualifying mark that at once permits and justifies the name she acquires, and finally a simple black glove pulled away from a little hand of ivory for the ring's test and judgment. The mask, stole, glove, the skin-garment, disguise, travesty, is narratively a *peau de chagrin*. In return, at the same time it is the entire body, the hand and the face, that are transformed: "The Infanta . . . pursued her path, / Her face covered with vile scum. / To all Passersby she held out her hand, / Striving to find work as a servant. / But the least delicate and most unhappy of them, / Seeing her so disgusting and full of dirt, / Wanted neither to hear nor bring home with them / Such a filthy creature." "Scum" [*crasse*]—the term comes back several times: dirt that amasses on the skin and that, by "natural" extension, marks a totally inferior social condition. The mask has become a face, the garment a "true" skin, and the infanta's simple travesty made her a disguised person [*travesti*]. Thus the donkey that, in the depths of its body, by the marvelous alchemy of its rare organism, metamorphosed dirt and produced gold-money, here it has metamorphosed, through its skin, the daughter of its king into apparent manure, into scum. At the most prominent place of the palace, it never made any manure: the skin has become, first, a mask—the person who wears it in faraway spaces is seen as disgusting and full of dirt, a person whose sole function will be to clean manure and scum, a "scullery maid."[13] And, second, if this "mask," become distinctive sign and qualifying mark, permits us to properly name her "Donkey Skin," the skin finds itself likewise caught in a constellation of animal appellations that constitute as so many titles her "proper" metonymic name. "'She is the ugliest beast / That can be seen after the Wolf.' . . . 'This Donkey Skin is a black Mole / Even more vile and more of a slattern[14] / Than the dirtiest Scullion.' . . . / Everyone started to laugh, / Crying loudly: 'What is meant / By having that dirty monkey enter here?'" Manure, scum, filth in the order of bodies; wolf, mole, monkey in the order of names; and between the two, between the clean that is dirty and the metaphor that is title, there is "Donkey Skin," which is at once the skin of a body and the metonymy of a name.

The strangest thing however is that these "titles" of the (sur)name "Donkey Skin," these appellations of the person who bears the name and who is no longer anything but that name, not only entitle her name but entitle, in their manner, the qualities of the body, of her body: the wolf names the ugliness of the beast, the mole, its vile blackness, and the monkey, its scummy filth, by a term-for-term correspondance between the qualities of the body and the titles of the name whose two series are ordered by "Donkey Skin," who stems at once from the body and the name. The expression "Donkey Skin" would seem to function, then, as a distributor of connotations or of significations between the order of the signs of discourse and of language [*langage*] and that of marks, attributes, and qualities.

The Princely Medal

Let us take up the narrative again and follow the Ariadne's thread of the narration into the labyrinth of signs and meanings. The princess disguised as donkey leaves, then, "in the early morning dew," the sovereign space of the king her father. With this exit, all of a sudden, she becomes invisible under her mask: "There was no house, no path, no avenue / That was not promptly scoured; / But the agitation was in vain. / No one could guess what had become of her." With the paternal desire and royal order suddenly without consumable object there also fades, at one go, a meal: "No more Wedding, no more Feast, / No more Tarts, no more Sweets. / The Ladies of the Court, completely discouraged, / Did not dine for the most part; / But the sadness of the Priest above all was great, / For he ate quite late, / And what was worse did not get any offering." The father will not consummate, the king will not eat, the court will not dine. A sexual fast and the stomach's fast, and with this double deprivation the universe of absolute power is erased, its order, orders, and hierarchies regulated by all-powerful law.

In its place the line of a pathway, the thread of a transition, the rapid displacement of the narrative and the narration, the princess's wandering: "So she went far, quite far, even farther away." Another space, a space that is other, another world (the other world?), produced by the race and the flight, which is and can only be—for the space of absolute power cannot have a space exterior to itself— a hollowed image, the negative of the one the princess left. One does not flee the royal and paternal universe; one returns there "always already" but while turning it inside out like a glove: "Finally she arrived at a Farm," an agricultural domain and, in this domain, a farm and, in this farm, a kitchen and, at the back of the kitchen, that corner where the farmer's wife (who needed a scullery maid) put her. On the one hand, the king, his palace, his stables; and in the most apparent place, Master Donkey, the producer of gold-money: a simple order and noble hierarchy, without the donkey who comes as supplement to the edifice to assure its foundation. The negative of the royal space is not as regular. Certainly, it also is endowed with a supplement, but it is a question of the almost useless supplement of the scullery maid, accepted in excess by the farmer's wife and, on top of that, this supplement is a double term, whose surname is the indicative (not Master Donkey, but Donkey Skin), body and skin, face and mask, being and disguise, which is divided into two places, the corner at the back of the kitchen and the room at the end of an obscure alley; into two functions, of disgusting work during the week and of ennobling leisure on Sunday; into two places, the one—public, passive, and negative—of exhibition (she was the usual butt of all the valets' teasing and wisecracks), the other—private, active, and positive—of retreat (in private, she opened her chest, set up her toilette properly, arranged her little pots upon it, and so on).

The negatives of the king's palace and stables are assuredly the farm and its menagerie, but there the hierarchic order of the former finds itself remarkably confused and inverted: it is the menagerie that takes the place of the palace, and the farm, that of the stables, but not completely. Those insolent vermin of valets teem in the kitchen, the pigs press themselves around Donkey Skin as she comes to the trough where they eat and which she cleans, while "Hens from Barbary, / Rails, Guinea-Fowl, Cormorants, / Musk Goslings, Petiary Ducks / And a thousand other birds of bizarre kinds, / Almost all of them different from one another" frolic and cackle like courtiers at the royal palace by filling "enviably ten whole courtyards." What a strange court-menagerie is this great farm, since it happens to be all of a sudden ("I forgot to say in passing," intervenes the narrator) the royal property of a magnificent and powerful king. Thus then the king indeed returns in this faraway, very faraway place, to which the infanta disguised as Donkey Skin has fled. He indeed comes back in his negative space, but his court teeming with a living abundance of courtiers and valets has become a menagerie; his courtiers, volatile in bizarre ways, and his valets, vermin: the king of an animal world of birds and beasts with the useless supplement of a scullery donkey, "Donkey Skin," but also wolf, mole, and monkey. To which would be added, if we are to believe Furetière, an ironic impropriety on the part of the narrator, or rather a humoristic lexical displacement, since "menagerie" "is said only with respect to the chateaux of princes and great lords who have them rather by curiosity and magnificence than for profit," and Perrault is within the orthodoxy of the dictionary—but Furetière adds: "It is not said of the courtyards of farms,"[15] and here the storyteller is in danger of false meaning.

After the king, his son, who came often "to this charming abode / When returning from the Hunt, / To rest himself and have a cool drink / With the Lords of his Court. . . . / Donkey Skin from very far away saw him with tenderness. . . . / 'How noble he seems, though indifferently dressed, / And how worthy of love he is,' she said, / 'And how blessed is the beauty / To whom his heart is engaged! / If he had honored me with the least of dresses, / I would have found myself to be more adorned / Than with all those that I have.'" The protagonists of the second story are even now on stage: they find their places in the other space whose double stage has just been erected. The king-father, the faraway proprietor at the vanishing point of an animal and barbarous world of which Donkey Skin, the scullery maid, occupies the back (of the kitchen), but of which as well the exiled princess fills the radiant and secret heart in her room each Sunday in private: a world twice centered, from the bottom (animality, scum, work) and from the top (leisure, cleanliness, celestial and divine brillance). The prince makes his entrance between the two: at one pole, the place of the king his father, at the other, the farm; a hunter-prince, but at rest, more handsome than the handsome Cephalus, between kitchen and bedroom, between Donkey Skin and princess, both invisible to his eyes. What then would a prince do in the back of the kitchen? How, even as son of a king, would he enter the hermetically sealed room? But he has been noticed by both of them: Donkey Skin "recognized by that boldness [of the gaze] / That under her scum and her rags / She still had the heart of a Princess." Invisible in the mask and face, disguise and being, invisible in both of her places and functions, Donkey Skin sees him and speaks.

Her first speech in the narrative is a song of love and desire, modest nonetheless, as is seemly, and resigned, a speech that evokes, to oppose them, the least of dresses, the wished-for sign and mark of the desired and impossible love of the prince-son, and the dresses of great price, the signs and marks obtained from the refused and forbidden love of the king-father. Donkey Skin, adorned with the three marvelous dresses obtained from the father, *sees herself* adorned with a dress given by the prince to the other beauty to whom his heart is engaged. A delicate female narcissism: she contemplates herself as another, she looks at herself and is pleased in her "imaginary." The mirror has moved, it has turned forty-five degrees: a moment ago, invisible, she liked to see herself young, rosy and white, dressed in the three dresses delivered by the father, and this sweet pleasure *nourished* her for a week. Now, just as invisible (from very far away), she sees the prince and likes to see herself *as another* dressed with a dress that he would have given her. "I represent myself, I eat myself (with my eyes) as representation in the representation that made me (in the narrative preterit [the *passé simple*]) the object of the impossible and refused desire of the king-father; therefore I am truly what I am, the object-subject of my own desire" — thus was the behavior of the other Sunday. "I represent myself, that is, I eat (with my eyes) the son (of the) king in the image of the other woman who would have made me the object of the impossible and wished-for desire of the son (of the) king; therefore I am truly what I am, the object-subject of the fictive desire of the other." Invisible because she sees, Donkey Skin *herself* speaks, therefore, for the first time: not words inspired or murmured by the godmother and addressed to the father, not the discourse of a mouthpiece, but that of a subject who expresses her thought and the desire of her heart and who addresses no one else: Donkey Skin speaks *to herself*, the locutor-allocutee in the interior monologue; she identifies with her own voice, she nourishes herself, she who says what she has seen from afar in a gaze.

And here is the event of the gaze and of the eye, the counternarrative, the second great sequence of the story: "One day the young Prince, wandering aimlessly / From courtyard to courtyard, / Entered an obscure alley / Where was Donkey Skin's humble abode.'' I indeed say "event," that is to say, "narrative," but also "chance," the accident of an encounter, the wandering of the prince to the terminal place of the wandering of the unhappy infanta. Descent to the lowest place, to the lowest of the lowly courtyards, but a place that—the extremes touch each other—will be revealed, in the space of a glance, to be the highest place, Donkey Skin's humble abode, the celestial dwelling of a divinity. The beast is a goddess. "By chance he put his eye to the keyhole." In his turn, here is the young prince become invisible, enveloped in the darkness of the obscure alley; but in the shadow at the end of the alley there is a luminous point, a hole that his dissimulated eye comes irresistibly to occupy. "As it was a feast day / She had taken on a rich adornment, / And her superb clothing, / Woven from fine gold and large diamonds, / Equaled the Sun's purest light."

This accident in the story is none other than the necessity of the framework of representation: the keyhole, the place of the point of view and the obscure alley of the lowest courtyard, the dark room of the spectacle. And what, then, does the eye of the prince spectator see, in the break from his wandering, on this holiday, at the hole of the point of view? He sees at first the sun at the vanishing point, the enclosed space of the room entirely illuminated, a light-space and, in this space, in the keyhole, a picture, a portrait, the feast of representation, the glory of the spectacle, the delectation of contemplation. "The Prince, at the mercy of his desire, / Contemplated her, and seeing her / Could only catch his breath with effort, / So much was he overcome with pleasure." Contemplation-desire, gaze, loss of breath, pleasure: in an instant, desire and fulfillment of desire, "theoretical" desire and its immediate satisfaction; the eye at the keyhole and its gaze in contact with the object and yet separated from it by the thickness of the door (of the picture), by the depth of the stage, the imaginary pleasure of representation, the fulfillment of "scopic" desire. In a glance the image of a face, a portrait, takes hold of the prince's heart, once she is imaginarily stripped of her solar dress. "Whatever the garments, the beauty of her face, / Its beautiful turn, its vivid whiteness, / Its fine features, its young freshness / Touched him a hundred times more; / But a certain air of grandeur, / Even more, a wise and modest reserve, / The assured witness of the beauties of her soul, / Took hold of his whole heart." That the representation's effect of pleasure is of an imaginary order, and that the satisfaction of the desire to see is effected in representation, that is to say, simultaneously in the form of a presence from a distance and in the constraint of an interdiction, sufficiently show him to be the ironic description of the heroic conflict between passion and respect, and between violence and contemplation, in which the son of the king is caught: "Three times, in the heat of the fire that transported him, / He wanted to break in the door; / But believing he was watching a Divinity, / He stopped his arm three times in respect."

Thus, after the sacrifice of Master Donkey to the incestuous love of the king-father, the motif of visibility and the framework of representation organize, structure, and regulate the narration, the narrative, the story that is told to us both in the self-identification of Donkey Skin contemplating herself as princess once more in her great mirror and in her amorous relation to the young invisible prince: she sees him from very far away and is not seen by him; invisible, he sees her on the sly, behind a door, through the keyhole. The only thing missing for licit love to be realized and peaceful happiness to be fulfilled is the exchange of two amorous eyes. But we are not yet there. The encounter of the two gazes is deferred by the sequence of the effects of erotic representation in the two bodies. "Communication" will have to go through the play of needs.

There is a double effect of representation at the point of view of the picture in the keyhole; the most immediate, we have seen, is the interruption of breathing, the syncope of voice: "The Prince, at the mercy of his desire, / Contemplated her, and seeing her / Could only catch his breath with effort, / So much was he overcome with pleasure." The second, which prolongs it, is loss of appetite: "To the palace, thoughtful, he retired, / And there night and day he sighed. / He no longer wanted to go to Balls / Even though it was Carnival time. / He hated Hunting, he hated the Theater, / He had no appetite, everything made him ill, / And at the bottom of his illness / Was a sad and mortal languor." Suspension of voice, suspension of hunger, the first negative, neutralizing effects of representation. The third is positive and more powerful yet. That Donkey Skin, neither Nymph nor beautiful, was, in short, "'the ugliest beast / That can be seen after the Wolf,'" he could not believe: "The lines that love had traced, / Always present to his memory, / Would never be erased from it"—the effect of inscription and engraving, the effect of a mark and an imprint, the effect of memory, in the vacancies of the body and of need, of breath and of voice. The moment is of importance.

At the time of its glory, in the most conspicuous place of the royal stables, the donkey defecated, we remember, not manure, "But rather quite beautiful Crowns with a sun / And Louis of all kinds," royal money doubly marked with a sun and the king's profile, the instruments and signs of omnipotence. Upon exiting the keyhole, at the end of the gaze, at the imaginary contact with the (prince's) eye, the solar brilliance of the profile of a "divinity," the luminous splendor of a portrait forever engraved by the lines that love has traced in the prince's memory, a picture, an always present, living, perennial, and unerasable representation, *a medal*: the inscription of a representation, the memorial of love. The crowns and louis, multiplied and reproduced each morning in "the other world" of absolute power, have here become a unique medal, imprinted in a memory, the prince's; the event of a fortuitous encounter at the end of an obscure alley in the lowest of courtyards is transmuted into trace forever unerasable, always present, in indestructible interior monument. The donkey was the alchemical operator of the transformation of the event into royal money. Donkey

Skin is the erotic operator of the transformation of the event into monument, and of the money departed with the royal donkey into medal forever come back in the prince; and she is such only because the donkey has been reduced to its skin and, become an animal because of the skin, the princess is thus able to substitute, *but in representation*, her precious body and her fine and beautiful face for the "real" body of Master Aliboron.[16]

How to Eat a Medal and Reject Its Remainder?

The problem to be resolved, therefore, is the following: how to eat the medal? If royal money is the donkey excrement the king gathers [*recueillir*] in his purse, how to ingest what Donkey Skin produced once and what the prince welcomed [*accueillir*] in his eye, the event of her portraiture, the advent of her image traced forever in the medal of memory?

After the king who came back as proprietor, and after his son who appeared upon returning from the hunt, the queen his mother enters on stage in order to resolve the problem. In the world of absolute power we have the king, the queen his half, alas too soon deceased, and the infanta their daughter so beautiful and so virtuous that the father-king, madly in love, wants to make her the queen his spouse, and coming against this desire the godmother, both metaphoric mother and fairy. In the negative of this world (its other, which is its inverted image) we have the king proprietor of the farm-menagerie, the prince his son, so royal, so martial, and the queen his mother, who has only him for a child. The queen-spouse-half, whom illness took away from that world, comes back in her other as generating mother, as foster mother. We read that the prince her son, without appetite, is prey to a sad and mortal languor, starving for love, with, in his memory, the stigmata of the solar portrait, the imprint of the princely medal. "She pressed him in vain to declare his ill. / He moaned, cried, sighed / And said nothing, except that he desired / Donkey Skin to make him a cake with her own hands; / But his Mother did not know what her Son meant."

We will have noticed that the queen mother, who simultaneously fills the positions of queen-spouse and fairy godmother, displaces and transforms them: not only has the king's half become wholly mother-origin, but also far from holding, like the metaphoric mother, the discourse of counsel plotting—without contradicting him—with the king's absolute power to prevent him in his own desires, she utters the ignorant and blind word of order and power so as to satisfy the unconditioned desire of her son (who finds his voice again only to express that desire). "'Oh Heavens! Madam,' she was told, / 'This Donkey Skin is a black Mole / Even more vile and more of a slattern / Than the dirtiest Scullion.' / 'It does not matter,' said the Queen. 'He must be satisfied / And we must think only of that.'" The son finds the solution, but the mother, by her order, permits its realization: the princess as medal in the prince's memory becomes cake, and precisely *galette*,[17] made by Donkey Skin's hand for the son's stomach. Master Donkey used to make gold-money instead of manure. Donkey Skin is seen as princess by the prince's gaze, and she, become a medal in his memory, will make him a cake to eat instead of her own medal to contemplate. In short, instead of making herself be gazed upon as representation, she will make herself be eaten as cake-symbol. At the end of the chain is the cake that is eaten by the prince (or that he will eat) as "gold-medal" in his stomach; that is, the princess Donkey Skin is none other than the manure defecated by the donkey in "gold-money" with which the father filled his purse. And we will have noticed that the medal-representation of the princess Donkey Skin is the key-operator of this transformation of gold-money, excrement, into cake-symbol, nourishment. The narrator can then intervene and say this long commentary in only two verses: "He would have had gold, so much did this Mother love him, / If he had wanted to eat any."

Nevertheless, for the problem posed to be absolutely resolved and the solution definitive, there must be a remainder, and that remainder must be a sign. The cake must produce in its assimilation, its annihilation as a sensible thing—as Hegel would say—a waste that, different from the waste of all food, is not manure but, like the manure of Master Donkey, a precious sign. A sign, however, that, unlike the crowns that the rare animal of the tale defecates, is not indefinitely reproduced and reproducible, multiple and always similar, a general equivalent of all exchangeable things and by that the instrument of the power of the state, but a unique sign, the single sign of the individual who cannot be compared to any others, the equivalent of one alone, in short, a proper name. Here it is: "It is said that, as she worked, in a little too much of a hurry, / One of her very valuable rings fell by chance / From her finger into the dough. / But those who know the end of this story / Swear that it was put there by her on purpose." Whether it was the accident of a fall, of an *occasus*, or a deliberate intention, we will come back to it; but the result is the same: a strange body deposited-fallen into the dough is going to function as sign and, more precisely, as an indication of recognition and insignia.

Let us read the continuation: "A more dainty morsel was never kneaded, / And the Prince found the cake so good / That it would not have taken a gluttonous hunger / For him to have swallowed the ring as well." From Donkey Skin's industrious hands falls a finger in the form of the ring, a ring-finger, an indication, an "index" in the anatomic sense, in Peirce's sense and in the sense of a deictic, a ring in the form of the index finger, a remainder of the finger, something that is a part of oneself but that is detachable from it, which one renounces or which one loses, but which will permit one to be found, recognized, and reappropriated: at once index and symbol. Now here with the cake, the dainty morsel, is the ring ingurgitated by the starving prince, here is the ring swallowed with the devoured cake, but a foreign body, an inassimilable metal, at once rejected, spat out, and defecated from above (as the crowns with the sun were by Master Donkey from below). "No, it is not good for eating," as Freud would say in *Negation*, but it is good for contemplating, thinking, knowing, and recognizing; no it is not food, it is a sign, and almost already a representation, almost already a judgment. Said otherwise by Charles Perrault: "When he saw its admirable emerald / And the narrow circle of the band [*jonc*][18] of gold / Which showed the form of the finger, / His heart was touched by an unbelievable joy. / He put it under his pillow in the same instant. / His illness still increasing, / And the Physicians wise with experience, / Seeing him grow thinner everyday, / Judged through their great science / That he was sick with love." I pick up all the links of the chain and hook them together: the gold crowns of the king-father defecated by Master Donkey = the gold medal of the infanta Donkey Skin contemplated by the son = the princess Donkey Skin's cake eaten by the son = the princess's golden ring swallowed-spat out by the prince.

Was it the sudden chance of a fall or the deliberate intention of a deposit—an event-accident or a project-design? asked the storyteller with the public and anonymous voice of oral tradition ("It is said that . . ."), as if the art of narrative, the secret maneuver of history that one makes while telling stories was not always to transform the accident into an occasion for a project, the event into a propitious moment for a design. But this very question (or its accident) is seized upon by the storyteller as the occasion for a design that goes beyond the narrative anecdote, in order to reintroduce at this instant the theme of visibility, the framework of representation, not, however, as a scheme organizing the narrative or as a matrix structuring the story, but as a machination of the subject of representation that reveals more perhaps of the framework of representation—the royal picture, the princely portrait—than a long commentary. I have spoken elsewhere of narrative traps,[19] but there are narratives that have no other end than to dismantle traps and, by doing so, to set up others in another place of the discourse. A fortuitous fall, therefore, or a deliberate deposit of the ring in the cake? Perrault leans toward this latter hypothesis: "As for me frankly I would well believe it, / Quite sure that, when the Prince came to her door / And looked at her through the hole, / She noticed it. / On this point women are so quick / And their eyes go so promptly / That one cannot see one for a moment / Before she knows she has been seen."[20] Thus the tactical conclusion: "I am quite sure also, and I would take an oath on it, / That she did not doubt that by her young Lover / The Ring would be well received."

Invisible, Donkey Skin sees (from afar) the prince and is not seen. Invisible, the prince sees (through the hole) the princess, and totally invisible though he is, she sees him. Hence the ring in the dough, the ring in the cake, so certain is she that it will be accepted, but whose deposit passes unobserved by the king's son, or else he would not have almost swallowed it. The ring-deposit (index, symbol, insignia), nearly eaten, at once spit out, is thus, in addition, a trap; it is the trap of representation. It is not, indeed, the prince that the princess sees; he stays hidden behind the door. What she seizes in an instant is his gaze: she sees that he sees her and, if she seizes the prince's gaze, it is because his eye is itself seized in the hole of the well-enclosed room, in the hole of the point of view through which he sees into the little bedroom, a voyeur gorgonized by the spectacle and struck dumb by the fetish. He surprises the beauty in her place by looking through the hole: the hole is a trap; here he is surprised in his own surprise and by her. Gorgonized, thunderstruck, is no doubt saying too much or not enough. Here he is seduced, seized by a glance from the woman his own eye gazes upon. In this accident there is no exchange of gazes and even less of mirrored gazes where the two subjects, reciprocally fascinated by each other's eyes, exhaust themselves. Perrault says it very well: the princess, the woman, knows herself to be seen. Objectified, reified [*chosifié*], as Sartre would say, by the other's gaze? No, but returning the voyeur-gaze back onto itself and seizing it in her own grasp, she stages herself, she puts herself into representation, she constitutes herself promptly as picture or fetish. Thus, pictures or representations are gaze-traps, in this particular sense that a picture always knows itself to be looked at, that is its function and, more than its function, its essence as artifact where it is exhausted, but its spectator knows nothing about it. Thus, I will add, also Perrault the narrator while writing this tale with respect to us as readers, when, stopping for a moment the unwinding of the thread of his narration he constructs, in order to immobilize it in a picture, this brief scene of the invisible prince looking through the keyhole at the princess kneading the dough of her cake. She knew herself to be seen, and the prince did not know that she knew it. That is why the ring that he did not see her depositing in the flour is beyond index, sign, symbol, and insignia, it is a trap (as this scene-picture is the ring-trap that Perrault also deposits in the dainty morsel of his tale), a trap that she put there for her finger to be taken—her hand—in order, in a word, to give her hand to the prince who is asking for it.

A deposit given and received—fallen and almost swallowed—the ring's golden circle is, because of that, a symbol, a *sumbolon* of recognition, certainly (but in the sense in which we can speak of a recognition of a debt), a token of identification, of an identification that is precisely a transaction of identity: one finger and only one fits the ring, and, it follows, one hand, one body, and one person. A double appropriation and double identification of the contracting parts: of the ring by the princess and of the prince by the ring. "Since Marriage, however badly one speaks of it, / Is an exquisite cure for this illness, / It was concluded that he be married. / He made himself be begged for a time, / Then said, 'I will indeed, provided I am given / In marriage the person / This ring will fit.' / At this bizarre request / The Queen and King's surprise was great; / But he was so ill they did not dare say no." The erotic is thus inseparable from the juridical and the political, and it is the narrow circle of the band of gold that, from the moment the prince's request is uttered, possesses the triple potential power of love, right, and power. "So therefore a search was begun / For the one whom the ring, with no concern for blood, / Must place at such a high rank. / There was no one who did not ready herself / To come present her finger, / And no one who wanted to yield her right."

The Quest of a Finger for a Ring

The quest of a finger begins, of a unique finger for the singular ring, and as the circle of the "band of gold" is narrow, "There was finally no maneuver / That a Lady did not apply / To make her finger fit the ring well" — maneuvers preparatory to the trial that soon began. Royal decree instituted the path of a hierarchy and an order similar to the one that reigned in the palace of the king-father that the storyteller had described for us at the beginning, with however this one difference that it regulates the *female*. On the one hand the courtiers, on the other all the noble persons summoned to the palace according to the hierarchy of their titles (princesses, marquises, duchesses, countesses, baronesses, noble persons) "presented their hands in turn, / And presented them in vain." On the one hand valets, on the other grisettes,[21] "Whose pretty and slender fingers, / For some were very shapely, / Seemed to adjust themselves to the ring sometimes." Finally, to the great and small horses in the father's royal stables correspond maids, cooks, lowly servants, poultry keepers . . . all "the riffraff[22] / Whose red and black paws, / No less than the delicate hands, / Hoped for a happy destiny" — the near-animal world of those who lived in the service of the animal, whether it be to raise or prepare it. And just as in supplement to the order of the palace, in the most conspicuous place, a Master Donkey spread out its two large ears, the female order summoned for the royal trial admits of a remainder: "poor Donkey Skin . . . at the back of the kitchen." Everyone knows the end of the story, the triumph of the scullery maid who becomes a princess once more and her glorious solar epiphany that inverts, in a moment, the female hierarchy deployed during the contest for the ring and reestablishes, in normalcy and lawfulness, the initial, anomalous, and monstrous order. In Master Donkey's place, Donkey Skin, but she is, in truth, a royal princess promised, according to genealogical law and the rule of alliances, to the highest rank. The foundation of the king-father's order (the donkey that defecates money in the most conspicuous place) is placed at the top (the princess hidden in the back of the kitchen under the black skin of a donkey, under a surname, is revealed adorned all of gold and sun, the daughter and daughter-in-law of the king), and a happy family is constituted according to the rules of alliance and filiation: "In the joy and the noise of the whole Assembly, / The good King was overwhelmed / To see his Daughter-in-Law in possession of so many charms. / The Queen was alarmed by it, / And the Prince her dear Lover, / His soul overwhelmed by a hundred pleasures, / Gave way beneath the weight of his rapture." I will note only that foolish desire, folly, and death, which had been the "real" lot of the omnipotent king and evil father in the beginning, reappear in this ending but only as hyperbolic metaphors of happiness and love according to order. "Reality" has become a *figure* of language, a way of speaking. This is the price to pay for the licit to become real.

Similarly, the universe of absolute power, following the happy family, is reconstituted; its split into two worlds, of which one was the negative of the other, is repaired; the monarch's sphere is perfect once again—but only for the time of a feast. The internal comparison, by which the absolute of power thinks and posits itself, and the narcissistic movement of reflection onto itself, by which its desire for the absolute is fantastically fulfilled, are once again repeated, but they are also displaced onto the great potlatch of the addressed and accepted universal invitation and onto the sumptuous expense of the marriage banquet. "Everyone at once took the necessary steps for the Marriage. / The Monarch invited all the surrounding Kings / Who, brilliant with various adornments, / Left their States to be present that great day." Even the ogre-kings were at the rendezvous, waiting for the last and most important one to appear, the omnipotent king and evil father, the one who had no other law than that of his absolute power [*puissance*], no other principle than that of his absolute desire, no other rule than that beyond all rules: "Those from Aurora's regions arrived, / Mounted on great Elephants; / From the Moorish shore came some / Who, blacker and uglier still, / Frightened little children; / Finally from all corners of the World / They disembarked, and the Court abounded with them. / But no Prince, no Potentate, / Appeared there with as much brilliance / As the Father of the Bride." In the suspended time of the feast, in the convivial place of the great encounter, is effected the conjunction of the good and the evil king, the good and the evil father. They change into each other in a universal concord whose law could not be transgressed. "As the Father of the Bride / Who, formerly in love with her, / Had with time purified the fires / With which his soul had been burning." The marriage of the prince and princess, the union of two amorous hearts, the conjunction of two happy bodies, is also a political alliance, a strategy born of an occasion, but that much more efficacious, for the future reunion of two powerful houses into only one omnipotent house: "And the future Spouse was delighted to learn / That he was becoming the Son-in-Law of such a powerful King."

The final solution? Why not. And yet there is, in the perfect closure of the circle of absolute power, a remainder, a double remainder, infinitesimal, but large nevertheless with future threats, as if the absolute could not be fulfilled without its crack being drawn or imagined: for in the same hyperbolic figure of discourse we must take into account that the good king, the good father, *was overwhelmed* to see his daughter-in-law possess so many charms. For in the same figure of litotes and diminution we must take into account that the evil king, the evil father, keeps a remainder of his odious flame in his heart and that it is this remainder that "only made his paternal love more vivid." There are no good or evil kings, there is never in power, and that is its very nature, anything but the unconditioned desire—without principle, rule, or law—for the absolute power whose erotic and destructive figure, simultaneously necessary, impossible, and contradictory, is the father in love with his own daughter.

Third Entrance
"A Portrait of Caesar Is Caesar," or the King in His Frame

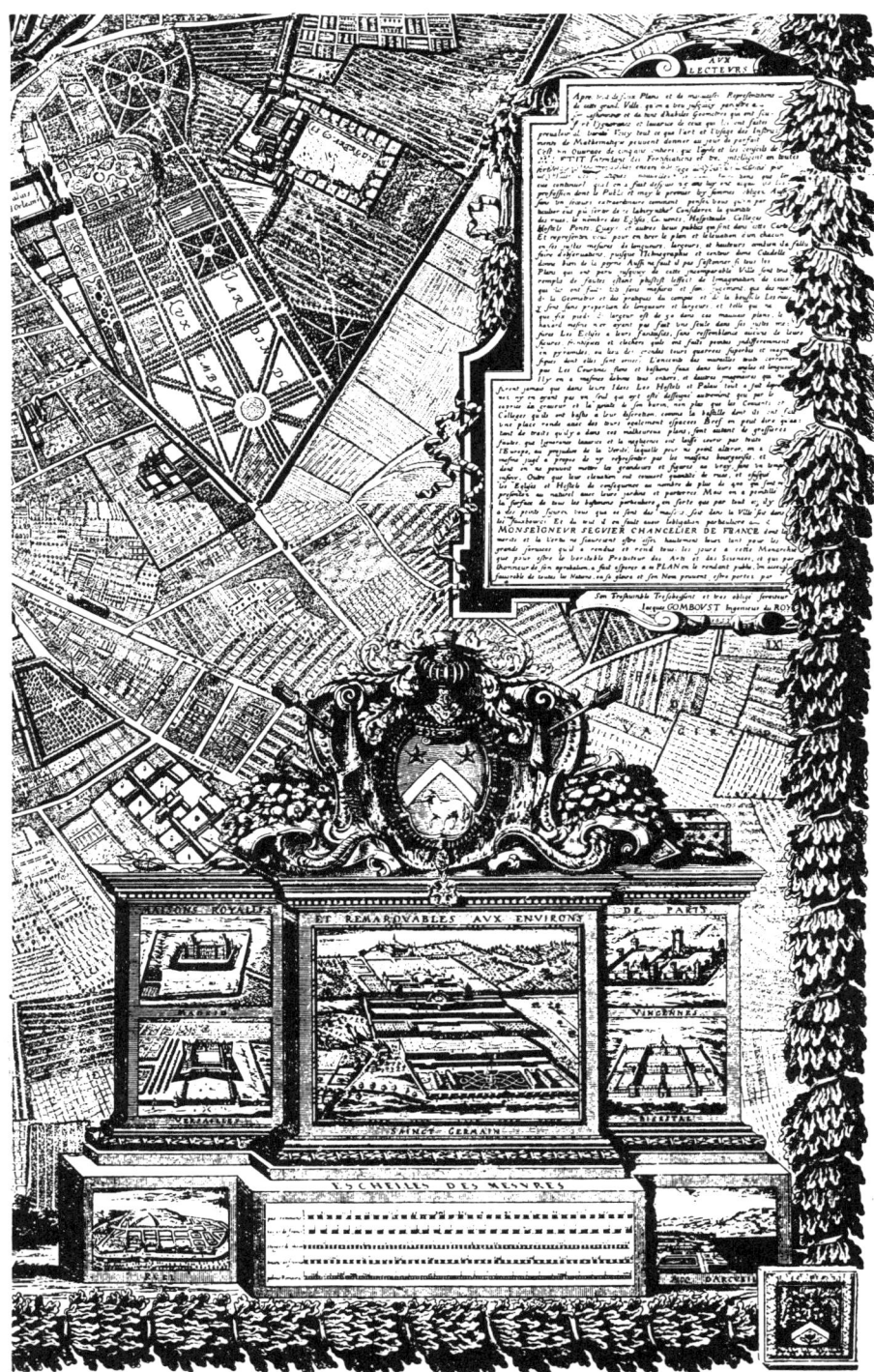

Detail from the plan of Paris by Jacques Gomboust, 1652

The King and His Geometer

Let us consider the map of Paris, surveyed in 1652 by Jacques Gomboust, the king's engineer, with the help of M. Petit, intendant of fortifications—the same who participated in Pascal's experiments on the vacuum in Rouen—and engraved by Abraham Bosse—the too faithful and too punctilious disciple of Gérard Desargues, creator of projective geometry, whose exclusion from the Academy of Painting was obtained by Le Brun some ten years later. The map of Paris: its perfect representation.[1]

On the right side of the map, between the border of oak leaves and the edge of the Luxembourg Gardens, curling up from the parcel of fields, orchards, and kitchen gardens of the Vaugirard plain, a scroll presents a text, addressed "To the Readers." It is not a dedication, but a foreword. Before reading the map while looking at the representation of Paris, we must read the letter that Gomboust, the king's engineer, has written and intended for us:

> After so many false maps and bad representations of this great City that we have seen appear up until now to its disgrace, and after so many able Geometers who have borne those whose ignorance and avarice have prevailed against truth, Here is [*voici*] all that is perfect in what art and the use of Mathematical Instruments can produce. It is the product of five whole years that the help and advice of M. Petit, the Intendant of Fortifications and very knowledgeable in all sorts of belles lettres, have shortened by more than half as much again through the mastery of new practices and rare inventions that he has acquired from their continual use for the past 25 years in this

profession, to which the Public and I above all are obliged. Also, without extraordinary assistance, how do you think that a private person could have emerged from this labyrinth? Consider the quantity of streets and the number of Churches, Convents, Hospitals, Schools, Houses, Bridges, Quays, and other public places that are in this map. And picture to yourself how many observations were necessary to survey the plane and elevation of each in its just measure of length, width, and height, since the ground plan and contour of a citadel give quite a bit of trouble. Also you must not be surprised if all the maps that have appeared until now of this incomparable city are full of mistakes. They have been the product more of the imagination of those who made them, without measurements and without judgment, than of the rules of geometry and the use of the geometer's and mariner's compasses. There the streets are without proportion as to length and width, such that a street of six feet in width is of fifty in bad maps, chance itself not having made any according to its true measure. The Churches are made according to their fantasy, with no resemblance [to the originals] in their appearance, frontispieces or steeples, such that they give them indiscriminately pointed towers instead of the superb and magnificent great squared towers with which they are adorned. The enceinte of the Walls is completely spoiled. The Curtains, flanks, and bastions are false in their angles and lengths. There are even other, imaginary ones that never existed except in their Minds. The Houses and Palaces are totally depraved, there being not even one drawn by other than the whim of the engraver and the point of his chisel, no more than the Convents and Schools, which they render at their discretion, and the Bastille, which they have made round with equally spaced towers. In short, it can be said that there are as many gross errors as there are lines in these miserable maps, which ignorance, avarice, and negligence have let run throughout Europe, to the prejudice of Truth. In order not to alter that Truth, it was judged appropriate not to represent the houses, whose size and appearance could not have been placed correctly without an infinity of time, beyond the fact that their height would have covered many streets and obfuscated the Churches and mansions in the number of more than four hundred, which are realistically represented with their gardens and grounds. But the surfaces of all private buildings have been outlined with dots such that wherever there are dots, picture them as houses, whether in the city or the suburbs. And for all this we must owe a particular obligation to *Monseigneur Séguier*, *Chancellor of France*, whose merit and virtue cannot be praised highly enough both for the great service he has rendered and renders every day to this Monarchy and for being the veritable protector of the Arts and Sciences. He, by the honor of his approbation, has caused this *map*, by making it public, to hope for a favorable welcome by all Nations where his glory and name can be carried by his very humble and obliged servant, Jacques *Gomboust, King's* Engineer, 1652.

"Here is" [*voici*]: "see here" [*vois ici*]: at once an intimation and an order, enveloped by a gesture designating—"on the side" of the text and with the support of its writing—the map of "Lutetia-Paris"; but also a presentation, a show, and already a gift of the author of the work to him who receives it.

See here, reader, . . . you see and you read indissolubly, in the daylight of truth, the product of mathematics applied to the ground you walk on, the streets you travel through, and the houses you live in; you see here the miracle of perfect representation, reality present anew under your attentive gaze, as you have never lived it.

This marvel in its totality is nonetheless only the totalization of a multitude of observations regulated by geometry and made with the geometer's and mariner's compasses. From this text read in the margin of the map as an internal excrescence of the frame, simultaneously space of a reading and site of a lateral point of view that relays the other veritable one that the spectator occupies standing facing the map, the reader is invited to contemplate the ichnographic text that the learned navigators have written of the urban world and the city's spaces. Its inscriptions, marks, and signs, reconstructed patiently for five years, permit him, a simple private person, to leave the inextricable labyrinth of reality for the first time: "Without extraordinary assistance, how do you think a private person could have emerged from *this* labyrinth?" And it is thus that the map entraps its reader, for, upon rereading it, the question is strange. What does the demonstrative designate? Is it the real city where private persons go their way, each toward the duty, business, and loves that summon and call them? Paris the *"grand'-ville,"* or the map of Paris that is displayed "on the side," its representation rigorous? Is it the resident of Paris who would find himself ever lost there? or the reader of the maps of old? or Jacques Gomboust faced with the vast design of giving a faithful portrait of this labyrinth, the impossible design of an exact drawing, were it not for that new, ideal thread of Ariadne traced by the engineer, armed with the geometer's and mariner's compasses and knowing the rules of geometry, which normalize their usage?

Reality or representation? To tell the truth, neither one nor the other or, better, the one and the other: the second slips over the first and covers it at all points, coinciding with it at the price of some regulated transformations in plane and elevation of lengths, widths, and heights. There, both the labyrinth where steps are mistaken and the theoretical labyrinth where ideas are confused become the city contemplated as it never could be, as it never will be, outside of this map, through which a dominant gaze travels freely in all directions. The king's engineer and the intendant of fortifications assure the reader-viewer of this exact coextensivity of reality and representation: they declare the truth of the report they give to be viewed. They must be believed, for they have *science* in hand and in head: "Here is all that is perfect in what art and the use of mathematical instruments can produce." It is for the person who is deprived of it that the map becomes a labyrinth, for the faults are not only errors but also deceptions. The reader-viewer believed he was seeing and recognizing his city. He lost himself in the fantasies of its author, who built in the clouds of the imaginary a mirage city, a lure of representation where such and such a street that was only six feet in width found itself to be a spacious avenue of fifty, where the Bastille was a magnificent round fortress crowned with evenly spaced towers.

Henceforth, on this outspread map, truth *reigns* and, with it, the real, suddenly (after five years of observations) clear and distinct in its representation: the truth of rational knowledge and the whims and fantasies of the imaginary. All the singular routes, their stages and stopping points and crossing points, and all the particular places and the relationships that link them to one another—fortuitous and accidental when a concrete individual occupies, traverses, and traces them— find their ordered arrangement and their true marks through the art and usage of the instrument of science. And what the theoretical eye contemplates is none other than reality itself, which the sensory eye has never seen. He finally knows reality through what learned reason represents of it; even better, it is through this representation that the sensory eye discovers himself able to be theoretical eye, a second eye that he has concealed forever but of which he did not know himself in possession. It was sufficient that a true representation be offered him for him to be constituted subject of knowledge to the measure of the savants' drawing.

He knows himself finally to be theoretical subject. He recognizes himself also in this reasoned order of places and spaces that is the map of the city, because it is strewn with recognizable signs that will fulfill their function even that much better since the rest will be reduced to the monotonous uniformity of abstract elements of geometric space. He finds his bearings there thanks to those signs, which are images exactly resembling "Churches and mansions in the number of more than four hundred, which are realistically represented with their gardens and grounds." The resident of Paris, who has become, in front of the map, reader-viewer, knew them well already: he does not recognize them thanks to the map of Paris in *his* city when he passes through it. He recognizes them *in the map* through the resemblance that these signs bear to the real buildings. What *use* could this resemblance have for him as he makes his way through the city, since he knows them familiarly already? They are not landmarks of his itinerary but landmarks of his reading of the map. These recognizable signs, through their resemblance, are *proofs* of the truth of the representation, the proofs of its demonstration, ostensible "mimetic" proofs, that in each of these places the cartographic representation coincides exactly with real mapped space. In previous false maps and bad representations, one could also see mansions and churches, but made according to fantasy, "with no resemblance [to the originals] in their appearance, frontispieces or steeples, such that they give them indiscriminately pointed towers instead of the superb and magnificent great squared towers with which they are adorned.'' These little pictures were only ideograms, one signifying "a church" and another "a palace," and not, as now, "here is Notre Dame of Paris," "here is the Louvre." The map appropriates the city, and representation, the space of the real, according to the order of knowledge. And that is why, in front of the map of Paris, I can say offhandedly and with no preparation, "This is Paris," and it will be understood that I speak in signification and in figure and that I have the right to speak thus.

The knowledge and science of representation, to demonstrate the truth that its subject declares plainly, flow nonetheless in a social and political hierarchy. The proofs of its "theoretical" truth had to be given, they are the recognizable signs; but the economy of these signs in their disposition on the cartographic plane no longer obeys the rules of the order of geometry and reason but, rather, the norms and values of the order of social and religious tradition. Only the churches and important mansions benefit from natural signs and from the visible rapport they maintain with what they represent. Townhouses and private homes, precisely because they are private and not public, will have the right only to the general and common representation of an arbitrary and institutional sign, the poorest, the most elementary (but maybe, by virtue of this, principal) of geometric elements: the point identically reproduced in bulk. So as not to alter the truth, the two bourgeois savants, Petit and Gomboust, anonymize themselves in the spaces of *their* city. They efface their local and architectural individuality, and that of the people of their "order," in the generality of the demands of the truth of their knowledge. Here is an echo, in the "text" of urban space and of the order of its places, of the rule that the Port-Royal *Logic* gives to the Christian locutor in the ethical field of language and the enunciative order of its discourse:

> Wise people avoid exposing their advantages to the eyes of others as much as they can; they flee from presenting themselves head on and from letting themselves be looked at in private; they seek, rather, to hide themselves in the crowd so as not to be remarked, in order that in their discourse will be seen only the truth they propose.[2]

Through this sly strategy of simulation-dissimulation the true discourse of the wise person is uttered by "no one" to the extent precisely that it is uttered by someone who is the same as everyone else. Truth from that point on seems to propose itself or, which comes down to the same thing, to be declared by a universal utterer.

Similarly Gomboust and Petit, in "the map's discourse," are found to represent the absence of point of view, that is to say, the universal point of view. But this being so, they obey the normative constraints of the social order to which they belong:

> It was judged appropriate not to represent there the townhouses, whose size and appearance could not have been placed correctly without an infinity of time, beyond the fact that their height would have covered many streets, and obfuscated the Churches and mansions . . . , which are realistically represented with their gardens and grounds. But the surfaces of all private buildings have been outlined with dots such that wherever there are dots, picture them as houses, whether in the city or the suburbs

There is a remarkable ambivalence in the terms at play in the order of rational knowledge and in that of religious, social, and political tradition: geometric "size," "shape," and "height" maintain in "scientific" representation a secret complicity with "size," "shape," and "height" in "collective" representation. The general application of the rules of mathematical order to space can entail the subversive obfuscation of the norms of social order. From this follow the constraints of discernment, measure, and judgment where the use of theoretical truth is combined with the asceticism of practical behavior. From this follows the formation of a compromise that is this very measure and judgment, the fiction ("picture them") that reduces all the private buildings to spatially finite surfaces and collections of points, a fiction that is simultaneously the producer of the figure of infinite time, as of the exhaustive representation of the real and of bourgeois individuality, a unit that is indefinitely multiplied and the subject of this representation.

A power enunciates and affirms itself in the map as the effect of a representation or as effect of the representation, that of scientific knowledge and of reason; but it can do so only by playing in the discourse and signs of another power, which is the effect of the force of a tradition, discourse and signs that the map puts also, and that explicitly, in representation.

To the left of the map, in a text matching the address to the readers, Gomboust writes to the king, to whom the completed work is dedicated:

> Sire, here is the map of your incomparable city of Paris, which I dare present to Your Majesty. I believe that this work is not totally unworthy of you and that, representing faithfully the first city of the most flourishing Kingdom of all the earth, it could be favorably received by its King, who is recognized to be the First and most powerful King of all the world. The other maps of this same city that have appeared up to now have been scorned as entirely false, or at least without measure and proportion; there is room to hope that this one, having been made according to the rules of geometry, will be esteemed not only because of the great advantages that can be derived for the very service of Your Majesty but also in order that, in the most distant countries, those who have believed the reputation of Paris to be above the truth may admire its greatness and beauty.

Gesture of homage by the very humble, very faithful, and very obedient servant and subject to his king; gesture of presentation of the very faithful, very exact, and very precise representation made according to the principles of the geometric order, to be given to the principle of the political order, to the prince, to the first who, according to the maximal order of absolute power, has no predecessor and only successors. Thus the city of Paris, the capital of the kingdom, the principal head of the eminent body of the king, cannot be compared to any other capital city but only to its one cartographic representation. It is the first city of the kingdom, the first to be represented as it should be when reasoning with *principles and consequences*: the others *will follow*, and Gomboust, in the same dedication, declares to the king his "design to do the other great cities of the kingdom by the *same method*." First city of the first kingdom of all the earth, whose king is recognized to be "the First and most powerful King in all the world." The order of the enterprise, the order of its rational method, and the political order of the absolute monarchy conspire to the same rhythm in the map. This is the case not only because the work, its methodical design, and its methodological map are instruments of service to His Majesty but also because the representation of Paris, the king's city and the capital of the kingdom, is, according to the science of measures and proportions, such that *at the sight* of this map, which presents reality itself by a correspondence without excess or default, the reputation of the city and the glory of the king will have to be believed true in the most distant countries. *Veritas index sui*: the representation represents itself by offering the marks of its truth. There is no need to seek others, and these marks of truth and of the power of truth are indissolubly those of the truth of power—that is, of all-powerful truth and absolute power. Thus representation according to the *true order* has for effect a *power without limits, that of the absolute monarch*. Thus, inversely, the glory and liberality of the king, as well as his wisdom and omniscience according to political truth, have for effect a faithful and exact representation that is absolute because absolutely *subjugated*, in each of its points and in each of its lines, to its principle, which is the prince.

Gomboust's map solemnly bears the marks of this *chassé-croisé* in chiasmus at its four corners, where it plays the game of the same name. Thus he assigns, without saying or showing it, the twice central center where all his geometry finds its principle and the subject of its representation, his prince, in their proper places and figures. In the upper-left-hand corner there is a panorama, "Paris seen from Mont Martre": the city spreads out in the center of the plain, as if breaking cover from the hills crenellated with windmills, and bounded by a softly undulating horizon, teeming with houses pregnant with ramparts, bristling with churches, towers, and steeples. The Parisian returning from a trip, at the summit of Montmartre, recognizes and names them one by one. The foreigner is surprised and admires their abundance. "A city . . . from far off is a city . . . ; but as one approaches, [it] become[s] houses, trees, tiles, leaves, grass . . . , to infinity. All of this is included in the word [*city*]" (65-115), in the word *Paris*. But Pascal has lost the center of representation—it is everywhere—and its circle—it is nowhere—while in its place, a simple last resort that permits the discourse, a word is said that includes the infinite diversity of things, the indiscernible singularities of the real. Gomboust is wiser: from Montmartre, from the point of view, the incomparable city *appears* in its total profile, girded by ramparts, whose "plane and height" ichnography knows how to erect "in its just measure of length, width, and height" and to construct its exact representation; and as one approaches, the gaze and walk are oriented by its unique principle, its center, the place where the whole city is concentrated and summed up, its *chef*, its capital head, its masterpiece, the place of its prince, his palace, the Louvre, which deploys its majesty in the upper-right-hand corner of the map. There, the "Louvre Gallery," which a legend makes explicit by naming its parts, is contemplated from a respectful distance from the Left Bank of the Seine, which is crowded with boats and ships and crossed by two bridges leading only toward this center. The vast representation of the city—which is methodical and complete and is offered to view enclosed by its frame of oak leaves in the uniqueness of its vertically erect theater and the unity of a totalizing gaze present to all its coexisting parts, according to the order of geometric reason—the representation, then, is from that point on the planifying transformation, according to ruled and measured proportions, of the multiplicity of the pathways from the circumference toward its unique center, from the sub-urbs [*faux-bourgs*] of the city toward the king's palace, pathways of which the two "pictures" offer *one* of the starting points, *one* of the points of view and *the* point of arrival, *the* vanishing point, *the terminus ad quem*. But the reverse would be equally true, for from this unique center it is possible to go toward all the points of the circumference. And the map of Paris in its exact representation is the expansion of the infinite concentration in this place of origin, present presence of the king, imperious and totalizing gaze of his capital city and, from this chief place, his kingdom, his body, and, beyond that, the world: perfect and total reflexivity of representation, without excess or default, reason of state and state of reason, here is the map in its product (the map itself) and its production (the oriented pathways).

Two monuments, in the lower-right-and lower-left-hand corners of the map, exhibit the specific traits of this secret conjunction, this complicity of political and rational power, of the prince and his cartographer. At the top of these monuments are trophies to the glory of arms, on one side, and to the fruits of right and of the arts, surrounding the coats of arms of the king and of his chancellor. Below pictures of the "remarkable royal Houses in the environs of Paris": Fontainebleau on the left, flanked by Monceaux, Villers-Cottret, Chantilly, Limours, Bois-le-Vicomte, and Ecouen; and Saint-Germain on the right, flanked by Madrid, Versailles, Rueil, Vincennes, Bicêtre, and Arcueil. The map expands beyond its visible limits by the depiction of the remarkable royal houses, which beacon the space that is absent from the representation of the capital by an order of places. Its palaces are landmarks that, as in a relay, multiply the Louvre, the central dwelling from which all pathways radiate and where all find their end; more exactly, these are precisely drawn named places of the prince's pathways in the environs of Paris, where all other trajectories find their truth. The king's places, starting with his central place, color with exactitude, *in* the cartographic representation of the capital, his nonrepresented beyond [*son au-delà*], the prince's cosmos, the most flourishing kingdom of all the earth, the very body of the first and most powerful king of the world. But these images have a pedestal that supports them and that provides the châteaux and palaces with the most exact and solid site for their pictures: their foundation in geometric truth; and not only them but also the whole map and its principal center. That pedestal consists of the measuring scales and rules of just measures and rigorous proportions that presided at the observations of the king's engineer and of the intendant of fortifications. The geometer of mapped spaces supports the prince and the places of his power [*puissance*]. The order of metric rule founds the order of norm and law, but it is subjugated to it as well. The first permits knowledge of the second, but the second authorizes the operations of the first through a reciprocity and exchange in which the powers of both are exerted within their just limits.

We must read these measuring scales more precisely, and there we will discover the juridical pretensions of the two powers of the geometer and the prince and the secretly declared exigencies of their right—of the right that representation, between the images of royal places and the figures of geometric expanse, gives itself for a legitimate mastery of the world. The first two scales are identically found in the two "pictures" on the left and right: "common paces" on the first line, "standards of France" on the second, such are the first two rules (of measure, proportion, observation, and representation). Below, on the left, "Spanish feet, English feet, Danish feet"; on the right, "rods of the Rhine, fathoms of Florence, roman hands." Thus the diverse rules that measure space in Spain, England, Denmark, and the diverse countries of the world are convertible. Spaces and their multiple measures, determined by the positivity of particular histories and cultures, find the rules of their reciprocal translatability in Gomboust's map. They are recognized, by their mutual convertibility, to be diverse and equivalent metric representations of a same intelligible space in the homogeneous universality of an identical geometric reason, and to be beyond the accidents that affected the diverse geographic areas according to their particular temporal eras. But in the same gesture "common paces" and "French standards," doubly repeated on the left and the right, are assigned by the king's engineer as the rule of convertibility of the rules. They rule all the others. It is to them that the others refer. They are their general equivalent. The geographic and historic spaces—because the diverse scales that measure them are given—well discover a same space of intelligibility beyond those scales, but this space *com-*

mon to all spaces is, first of all, French. The geometric rationality that underlies the geographic positivities is that of the most flourishing kingdom of all the earth, whose measures of space are at the same time rules like the others and norms for the others. From that point on the king of this kingdom, recognized as the first and most powerful king of all the world, can legitimately claim to develop the network of these places to the confines of the earth: by right and by reason — by *geometric and juridical representation* — he authorizes himself to do so. Is not this network of places already initiated by the ten châteaux of his great subjects on which rests the whole map of Paris, his capital?

We must understand that the accident of an example in the Port-Royal *Logic*, ten to thirty years after the publication of Gomboust's map, associates the geographical map and the prince's portrait when the logicians of the universal art of thinking according to reason want to define the case in which the subject has the right to give to signs the name of the thing signified; that case in which the subject has the right to say offhandedly and without preparation that the map of Paris is Paris, and the king's portrait, the king; the one *and* the other because the one *is* the other and, reciprocally, the representations of the one and the other notifying each other mutually of this rapport.

But, so that the representation be perfect in its self-representation, so that it can found itself legitimately in its power of representing rationally and politically, we, its reader-viewers, must be included as "living," contemplating the incomparable capital of the king and reading its total and unique representation. Oh, marvel! Here we are figured by our most noble representatives, delegates of our theoretical power as subjects and effects of the representation. Look attentively at the lower edge of the map: to the right and left of the Seine there are two hills, one running down toward the river, the other brutally interrupted by a cliff that the eye guesses. On one side there is a gentleman with feathered hat, cape, and sword, on his horse marking time, followed by a valet who is running up, cane in hand; on the other there is a noblewoman accompanied by her governess, a little apart from their maid as it should be, who look at and contemplate, for a moment stopped in their walk, the incomparable city of Louis, their king: Paris, *the real city that they see from within the representation as we reader-viewers contemplate its cartographic representation from the outside*, today marveling at this product of art and mathematical instruments as they do at the first city of the most powerful kingdom of the earth.

In the places where they appear, these five figures (two nobles, a bourgeoise, and two of the people) designate and draw attention to the knot of the chiasmus of the real and representation: *the real city in its moment of history*, Paris in 1652. This city that they look at from the top of the hill, from the place of their point of view — as they would have been able to see it, and as we have seen it in its panoramic profile, if they had been at the summit of Montmartre—and which absents itself definitively in the *past unreality* of the represented map, this city here returns, more than three centuries later, faithful, exact, and rigorous, toward our eye today through our attentive gaze. Figures in their place, which is represented from our point of view of representation, they free it in an instant and at a point of time and space, since just like that we, now, are their figures in the real that we only perceive, in 1981, in the representation that, for five years a long time ago, Gomboust, the king's engineer, built of it. With the gentleman and his valet, the lady of quality, her governess and her maid, in their places of view and contemplation, the past and the present, and the real and its representation, are exchanged and neutralized in this symbolic point of quasi-coincidence. This occurs in the same way as are exchanged, in the map itself, the foreword to the readers and the dedication to the king, the panorama of the city that is carried toward its center, the prince's palace and the map of Paris, its images in their natural state and its collections of arbitrarily significant points, and the pictures of remarkable royal houses and the military engineer's measuring scales: exchanges that are producers of effects, the power of reason and political power. Thus long ago was built and is continually being built the cartographic monument forever present—outside time, outside space—of representation, the memorial monument of the king and of his geometer.

The Prince's Palace

The stage that geometric reason erected on the abstract plane of the map to produce there the portrait of the capital city, "the first city of the most flourishing Kingdom of all the earth," and to present it to its king, "the First and most powerful King of all the world," was, in its very rigor and exactness, a mix. The tight system of representational reasons in the order of truth as celebrated by the geometer, the surveyor-prospector, is articulated, more subtly than it would at first seem, in the less dense, but more strategically disposed, network of imaged references that are pathway beacons for the gaze educated by the old tradition: not only the churches, convents, hospitals, schools, houses, bridges, and other public places that are on this map but also, extracted from the labyrinth that is exhaustively worked by the cartographic text in order to present it in a vignette, we find the king's palace, the Louvre, which makes of Montmartre an ideal perspective from which to see the city. Ideal in truth and in image, for what sufficiently sharpened eye can discern the Louvre from the height of the eminence that dominates the city? What panoramic view, inserted in the real expanse and its concrete sites, can find, in the teeming of the city, the center of its circle, the end of its direction, and the goal of its sense? To present this ideality that orients the map of Paris and, with it, that of the world, an ideality that founds the great political and ideological postulations, the map of the geometer-prospector must admit the ornamentation of the images superimposed on the "theory" of spatial truth and the order of places. It must accept the decor of a multiple landscape of princely architectures: first, at the upper right, the king's palace profiled along the Seine in the heart of the capital; and second, at the two lower corners of the map, on the ground of two hills from which the spectator's delegates contemplate simultaneously both the map and the city that the map represents, we have the two monuments of the arms of the sovereign and those of his chancellor of justice, which carry the images of the "remarkable royal Houses in the environs of Paris." But this decor and these ornaments are neither free nor in excess. It is they, on the contrary, that bring about the unity of the theory of the eye of understanding and prospect that is the office of geometric reason, and the synopsis and aspect of the political gaze that is the office of the power of state. On the map of the king's city, his capital, the head of his kingdom, the portrait of the site of his body, we find the image of the Louvre, multiplied in those of Fontainebleau and Saint-Germain, his members, "and Bois-le-Vicomte and Ecouen and Bicêtre and Vincennes and Rueil . . . ," and that at the very spots of the map where the grisaille of the lines and points of the geometric and bourgeois summary are spread out and where are exposed, like so many demonstrative proofs of truth, the measuring scales. What the sensitive eye cannot immediately perceive on the map of the king's engineer and the intendant of fortifications, and yet that gives to the order of the capital of the most flourishing kingdom of all the earth its true orientation, the decor of the architectural "landscapes" renders explicit to the gaze. Thus *the center of the map and the centered network of the power of state* that is articulated there *frame the cartographic space* with their own images as well as those that repeat and multiply them in the environs of Paris. Thus the geo-graphic expanse where the geometer inscribes his lines and points with the geometer's and mariner's compasses finds itself *subjected* to the network of the king's sites and to his central place, all while giving it its *basis* of truth—in a *chassé-croisé* of the authentic and the legitimate, of right and truth, of the deontic and the alethic, between map and portrait.

The portrait of the Louvre, the king's palace, is extracted from the map of Paris from the "view site" of Montmartre in order to "reproduce" itself in those of the remarkable royal houses in the environs of Paris and, beyond the frame, in those of the houses of the kingdom's great men. With this "abstraction" a second stage is erected, that of the portrait of the king in his site, a portrait that is for the moment only the "landscape" of the prince's palace, until it is to become the map of its face. This gesture of abstraction, which in Gomboust's 1652 map of Paris is completed in the ornament and decor in the form of a decisive superposition of the "portrait-landscape" onto the "plan(e)-map," will be realized in situ some twenty years later with *Versailles*. The house which, beneath the château of Madrid, borders, with Vincennes and Bicêtre, the château of Saint-Germain, will become the first palace of all the earth, that of the first and most powerful king of the world.

> The Louvre is assuredly the most superb palace in the world. . . .
> This house of Versailles has much more to do with Your Majesty's pleasure and diversion than with Your glory. . . . What a pity if the

greatest King were to be judged by Versailles. . . . Your Majesty will also observe that You are in the hands of two men, Louis Le Vau, first architect, and Andre Le Nôtre, first gardener, who hardly know You except at Versailles. The thought that they have to pay court to Your Majesty together with the patronage that they possess means that they will drag Your Majesty from design to design to make these works immortal if You are not guarded against them.[1]

Of this celebrated remonstrance of Colbert's to the king on the subject of Versailles I will retain only the opposition of "palace" and "house" and that of "pleasure and diversion" and "glory." On the one hand, we have the state and its reason, which is simply reason and nothing else, and with it the glory of the king whose palace is the place at the heart of his capital; on the other hand, in the form of diversion, indeed of diversion and of perversion with respect to his duties, we have the pleasure and whims of the prince in a house that offers him a retreat. "Why does he go there, once or twice a week, with very little company?" To "see the buildings that he is having built there; nevertheless, it is said that there is something even sweeter," writes Guy Patin; and Saint-Simon: "To be more in private with his mistress." "The love for La Vallière (which was at first a mystery) gave rise to gallant promenades."[2] We must add to these games of desire and pleasure rudely confronted by the minister at work, and to the effort of glory, the incompatibility of prudence and *political calculations for the future* by a great king surrounded by wise counselors at the Louvre with the *dream of immortality* through works, from project to project, by a too-generous prince besieged by flattering courtiers in the closed place of Versailles. There would then be for Colbert two centers and, dare we say it, two domains, two spaces, and on the outside two persons in the "royal substance": the center of political deliberation and decision, and the eccentric place of pleasure and recreation in the interval between works; the field of the sovereign's glory in his palace and, in an aside of diversion, the domain of the prince's fantasy and whim in his home; the "public" space and the "private" place; Louis's sensitive and impassioned individuality and the historic dignity made of the sovereign's omnipotence and infinite wisdom. Through this discourse of respectful remonstrance we discern the confrontation, in the two faces of king's counselor and prince's courtier, of the minister of finance who administers and increases the fortune of the king and the kingdom and of the creating artists who dissipate it in gardens and buildings, in brief, of the real and rational, on the one hand, and of the imaginary, on the other.

In truth it is the collection of these binary oppositions that the framework of representation invalidates through its multivalent functioning, and not that the king saw further than his minister, nor that the minister resigned himself to his master's wishes, nor that some had triumphed over others in the sovereign's graces. These are all psychological, sociological, or political explanations that, without being wrong, are only the symptoms or effects of operations of another amplitude, that of a system of signs otherwise arranged to produce the symbolic power that, in return, finds there the bases of its legitimacy and the sources of its authority.

It is those operations that we will attempt to grasp in some texts extracted from the *Description sommaire du château de Versailles*, published at the end of 1673 by Félibien.[3] No doubt the work passes itself off as a description, that discourse that "represents and depicts," and by that offers itself as substitute for a gaze and as equivalent to a percept. But if the figure of thought through development, said to be topography—"a description that has for object any one place such as a vale, mountain, . . . house, temple, garden, etc."—has all its effect, its product will never be other in the mind of the reader than an image or a succession of images. Thus, on the condition of reading these pages with all the attention they merit—not as documents giving precious information on the development of architectural constructions and gardens, the dimensions of ornamental waters, and the height of terraces but as political stategies aiming to produce through carefully mounted frameworks of imaginary effects—of seeking not to trace the plans of the palace of Versailles and of its gardens in the 1670s but to build and install their simulacrum in literature, we can catch a glimpse of the half-erased drawing of a phantasmatic of the power of state, discern the first features of a political imaginary of the absolute monarch, extract the elementary pieces of the representation of the king and his place that function to produce them, the one as "the First and most powerful King of the world," and the other as "the first palace of the most flourishing Kingdom of all the earth."

To describe is to represent and to depict: a pen institutes itself as gaze, and a text as picture. But which gaze and which picture? Would it be the synoptic gaze, outside of a point of view, which embraces and comprehends, *uno intuito oculi*, a stable order of places? Or that of a voyage in displacement in the middle of spaces and itineraries, which successively occupies, to cross them, points of view tied one to the other by oriented pathways? Here, then, are litigious strategies and tactics, where space is "the effect produced by the operations that orient, circumstance, and temporalize it and bring it to function as a polyvalent unity of conflictual programs or contractual proximities," where it would arise from a great syntagmatic of plural syntaxes and refer back to notions such as those of pathway, itinerary, or trajectory, whose manifestations in the texts would be of the order of narrative and, in the images, of that of landscape. There, in return, stative taxonomies and classifications—those of the orders according to which elements are distributed in the rapports of coexistence, where it is impossible that two things be at the same place, and those of the structural arrangements of positions, where laws of properties of stable configurations of places arise from a great paradigmatic made of tables with multiple entries and refer back to notions such as that of *map* or of *picture* whose manifest discourse would be precisely that of description.[4] And yet, though Félibien gives to his work the title and name of "description," he often refers to his purpose as "narration." Which gaze, then, and which picture? It is, in effect, easy to perceive that the "narrative," by inscribing a pathway, passes through the "voyage" in all senses of this term: it institutes its moments as notable events of the past and dissipates the mobility of its performance, paradoxically, in the stability of traces that construct the order of places traversed. Thus the narrative constructs a configuration of places as the inscription of a pathway. It is a kind of map, a topography, just as, inversely, the map, which as a configuration of inscribed sites in the proper order of a coexistence without faults implies in its very inscription the virtual syntagmas of narratives insisting in the discreet form of possible pathways.

Places and spaces, to adopt this terminology, constitute, then, the characteristic determinations of description as of narrative: thus the point of departure and that of arrival are, for all narrative, *places* that condition the production of the *spaces* that the narrative's actors unfold in proportion to their movements. And the voyage, which all narrative gives, in one way or another, to be transcribed before "passing" through into it, is first a passage, a clearing or crossing of the border of a domain or dwelling, with all the dangers that such a crossing implies, since the traveler puts himself outside of the law of the place that he is leaving without yet finding that of the place where he is arriving. And if the place is still the place of a law and of an order that defines it as "place" in the immobility of a tradition and memory where the authority that produces it is founded, the narrative, through its voyage and crossing of spaces, is able to appear, on the one hand, as clearing borders and as being put outside of law and, on the other, as expansion of the law of a place and as display of its authority and legitimacy.[5]

All narration, all description integrate in diverse manners operators of spatialization and indicators of location, by implication presupposition, condition, and so on. A map can thus be the possible postulate of an itinerary, and a trajectory, the necessary condition of a local configuration. This is to note that these multiple forms of integration can be diversely modalized. But let us listen to Félibien announce to us his description and narration of Versailles:

> As this House is today the delight of the greatest King on earth, as it
> is visited every day by people of all sorts in France, and as
> Foreigners and those who cannot have the pleasure of seeing it are
> quite pleased to hear tell of its marvels, it was appropriate—while
> waiting for all the things that have been started and that are being
> worked on unceasingly in this royal House to be entirely completed,
> which will then permit an ample and exact description of it—that one
> be written that, while brief and summary, will not fail to give some
> idea of this pleasant abode to those who are remote from it. It could
> even be useful to many people who are going to visit it, for by

having them observe an infinity of things where sight does not ordinarily stop because of the great quantity of objects that dissipate the senses, all of which, nonetheless, deserve to be considered in particular, they will have even less trouble remembering and going over agreeably in their minds what they have seen in order to inform their friends of it.[6]

The presentation that Félibien makes of his work can immediately be read as doubly substitutive: he replaces at once the more ample and exact description that he announces and prepares and the direct vision of the completed palace whose actual house and domain are the abridgment and sketch. The "topographic" text thus occupies a strategic position between an absent object and a desire to see, on the one hand, and, on the other, between a design-drawing that is an existing project and a work to come that is still to be done. But the first "report" must, in its turn, take the place of the other. By giving to the reader's "sight" a place and dwelling that he has not seen, the description is, as it were, completing, in the imaginary of the reading, the construction of the palace that is *in process* in the real: to give to sight the "thing" is to give to reading some "idea" of the thing absent both at Versailles and in the mind of those who cannot go there. The description is therefore twice representation, in the sense that through it and through the operations that arrange its signs in discourse, it makes what is not present *come back*; but it makes it come back, in a manner of speaking, not as something that has been there and that is no longer, that *is past in* the past—it would be the function of the narrative of history to inscribe and give a place to what has taken place and to transform the event into monument—but much rather as something that at once is not yet and will be there, because the reader of the description *will be able* to come see what has been described to him, and because the architectural design-drawing begun *will have to* be completed. Double representation and doubly representative, but with a nuance in this redoubling: the description of the place is the incitement to a *possible* voyage at the end of which the reader will come simultaneously to verify, confirm, authenticate, and legitimate his admiration; but it is also the modalized *presentation* as *devoir être* (simultaneously alethic and deontic, necessary and obligatory) of a program in process of execution. In other words, we find the "topography" that Félibien proposes occupying the "meeting place" of a *possible* narrative discursive program in its terminal sequence (*to be able to* come to Versailles) and of an *ideal* descriptive topic program in its totalized local order (*to have to* complete Versailles).

Still, this strategic position of the topographical representation between a possible spatializing operation and an obligatory localizing indication is simultaneously justified in its principle and founding in its effect, and that from the first lines of the text we are examining. Why write a topography of Versailles? The answer to this question is one with the first gesture of the writing: "This House *is today* the delight of the greatest King on earth." The pleonasm of the present stresses the presence, to some extent *immediate*, of the principle of representation: the king. The representation of "this royal house" represents the presence of the king, just as the place (as dwelling and domain) envelops in its borders the greatest king of all the earth. Through his presence in this limited place, the king's dwelling *is* eminently all the earth. The macrocosm is *in* the microcosm. The representation, in its imaginary reiteration "of absence," stresses, then, a presence that is already there and that also goes for the universe, and it is in this sense that, "justified" by this presence ("as this House is today the delight of the greatest King on earth . . . , it was appropriate [to describe it]"), it legitimates it by representing it, founding it in right and in truth by furnishing it with a text in which it makes itself be seen through being read and, maybe more profoundly, where it can see, recognize, and contemplate itself by reading itself. Thus, then, the strategic position of the "topography" of Versailles finds itself once more "reinforced," since the principle that makes its writing appropriate is founded in the name of an effect through this same writing insofar as it is read. And it is this mirrored duality of the visible and legible, whose virtual reciprocal image brings to light the prince and defines his "portrait," that prolongs and perfects itself in a new "awaitedness" of the topography: "it is visited every day by people of all sorts in France, and as Foreigners and those who cannot have the pleasure of seeing it are quite pleased to hear tell of its marvels, it was appropriate . . ." Representation of the effect, and effect of the representation, if such is the prince in his "topoprosopography," this short circuit is unfolded in the functioning of the system from the pole of the sole addressor (from the text and its object, the king) to the pole of the addressees, for they are two: the subjects of the prince, the French, who, *every day*, *see* (his domain, his dwelling), and the others, those who cannot see, who are by that foreigners, outside of the law and of the king's authority, and who can only *hear*. There are those who visit the royal place and who are immediately taken by its radiance, the charm of a visible that ravishes, transports, and subjects them through admiration and pleasure to him who constitutes himself there as body of delights; and there are those who hear the narrative of the royal marvels, the "legend" of the miracle of his palace. A generalized oral text if one dares say—diffuse noise, rumor of astonishment, universal renown—precedes the one that begins to be written here: the royal description that Félibien proposes authorizes simultaneously the foreign "collective speech," by authenticating and transforming the "said" into a monument of legibility, and represents in an effect of lasting vision and memory, by a "memorial," what the prince's subjects see every day but what each has seen only once, the glory of Versailles.

We must go further, however, and it is here that the description proposed by the courtier-author sees completion as royal instruction. Indeed, not only does the text that Félibien starts to write imaginarily take the place of a monument doubly absent in the real, absent as unfinished and absent for those who cannot have the pleasure of seeing it; not only will it constitute the monument of memory of the royal subjects who have seen it, since "this House . . . is visited every day by people of all sorts; but also it "could even be useful to many people who are going to visit it." The representation of the château and its gardens in his text represents also the *pathway* of those who visit them: it duplicates their itinerary in the king's place with a narration that accompanies it; the discursive map of the site is spatialized in the narrative of a possible trajectory that clears its approach there; and the order of the prince's monument at once conditions a circuit that operates its space while developing itself there through writing, and finds itself through that very circuit constituted as monument of reading by a configuration of legible *topoi*. The circuit is a circular pathway, not because the visitor to Versailles leaves the prince's place by the way he entered, which is not, in fact, the case, but because the monument that provokes the voyage at its beginning and that the voyage implies and presupposes is none other than that circuit that the very voyage builds in the ideal plenitude of its marvels. Tautology? No. In the meantime the château, which is unfinished and being worked on unceasingly at Versailles itself, conquers its topographical ideality, its descriptive perfection and its simulacrum completed in the discourse, and in the same interval—the time of a passing through, the time of a reading, the time of a metamorphosis of an architecture of stone, trees, and water into an architecture of signs, sentences, and figures—the order of the royal places in the topic configuration of their description has become the order of a discourse of instruction determining prescriptively the moments and objects of the gaze. In short, the prince in his topic order has become the order of the king in his discourse. There is a complete reversal without excess or lack: one corresponds to the other, and the latter recovers the first perfectly. The structure is injunctive, and the injunction structural. The topic body of the king is completed in a sovereign word of prescription, and the royal portrait is projected onto the symbolic *topoi* of his body, which is "architectured" on the map.

Even brief and summary, Félibien's topography "could . . . be useful to many people who are going to visit [this royal House]"; for it will have "them observe an infinity of things where sight does not ordinarily stop because of the great quantity of objects that dissipate the senses, all of which, nonetheless, deserve to be considered in particular." It matters, indeed, that the recovery of local order by the "narrative" representation be rigorous, for the place of the king is that of the absolute and the infinite, and neither absolute nor infinite can be seen by a gaze that would only be that of the sensual eye. To the infinite local order must correspond the order of a pathway of observation that would itself be regulated and normativized by an absolute order that is indissolubly that of rational understanding and the prince. On this condition alone the narrative itinerary of the visit can envelop the infinity of the royal marvel in its network. On this condition alone the royal miracle can be manifested. For "aspect," the simple view of things, as Poussin would say, things that, because quantitatively and qualitatively infinite, can only disperse and dissipate the gaze, must be substituted "prospect," the office of reason, which is a particular way of knowing things well, that is to say, of considering them in the ordered hierarchy of their presentation. This would be a "theoretical" trial of reason whose principle is the prince, whose rule is the king, and whose norm is the absolute monarch. The successive syntagmas of the "visit" are the projection in the text of the paradigms that configure places as the articulations of the king's eminent body, thus making explicit the orders of his will and good pleasure so that the miraculous manifestation of his glory will be made perfect.

Two or three pages later when the visitor, who has come from Paris where he goes up the avenue—and it is not surprising, for the capital city comes to the king's château through one of its delegates so that the member of the political body may recognize its head and submit itself to it—crosses the Place Royale, goes through the gates of the palace, penetrates into the forecourt, then the court, and then, just before entering the château, receives from Félibien this instruction:

> It is well to note that as the sun is the King's device and as Poets confound the Sun and Apollo, there is nothing in this superb house that is not in rapport with this divinity; therefore all the figures and ornaments to be seen there have not been placed there by chance, but have a relationship either to the sun or to those places where they have been put.[7]

Nothing is left to chance, whether it be the architecture of the buildings and gardens or their decoration. The principle that regulates them, the norm of their visibility and legibility, is the king, whose body and type is the sun in his device and whose soul is its legend, the very one of the incomparable absolute, *Nec pluribus impar*. The principle of interpretation that furnishes the "narrative voyage" with the instruction of its program ("the sun or Apollo must be read everywhere") is thus rigorously identical to that imperious one that has presided at the construction of the stage and its representation. This identity of necessity and obligation gives to the pathway its *total security* and offers it *its definitive certainty*. Across the topographical representation what is visible is totally legible, and what is legible is visible; image and symbol melt into a same *reality* of discourse and space, that of a perfect simulacrum that manifests an identical prosopography, the portrait of the Sun King.

And we understand how Félibien may see, in this redoubled order of map and portrait, of description and narration, of regulated succession and normativized injunction, that his text does not cease to represent the most assured guarantee of a monumental memory that is simultaneously that of the monarch in the configuration of his place, that of the subject who traverses its space, and finally that of the collective body of the kingdom that gives its head to be seen in an identical shared discourse: "[The summary description of the château of Versailles] could even be useful to many people who are going to visit it. . . . They will have even less trouble remembering and going over agreeably in their minds what they have seen in order to inform their friends of it." In the open space of the French and European macrocosm the topography that Félibien starts to write will return to the orality of collective speech. But the rumor of astonishment that, a while ago, filled one's ears with the marvels of the château will be replaced by the discourse of a pathway and map, ordered and authorized by the master of the places visited—a discourse whose scenario and matrix have been defined by the narrating courtier-(de)scribe(r), and in which the prince in his house at once discovers his portrait on the stage and in the decors that suit him and receives from it his definitive symbolic legitimation. The memorial of the prince in the soul of each of his subjects, the royal château and landscape raised in the interior of the minds, revisited in the imagination, re-presented in the incessant repetition of the voyage and map once completed, are, by their reiterated repetition, the instruments of a society in which the king's subjects would be transformed into members of a same body, communicating and communioning in the glory of its head.

Félibien's text exactly conjugates place indicators and spatial operators so as to trace the progress of a pathway according to the rigorous constraints of the map and, inversely, to project the demands of the local order onto the possibilities of spatial succession. An example:

> What to observe in the little Park. After having considered what pertains to the château, one can see the gardens and what is enclosed in the little Park. But as there are an infinity of objects that attract the eye from all sides, and as one often finds oneself at a loss as to which side to go to, it is good to follow the order I will be marking so as to see each thing in sequence more conveniently and without fatigue.[8]

As early as the subtitle of the work, which introduces the description of the gardens, the anonymized reader-visitor in the collective indefinite of a "one" [*on*] is the object of an order: "Learn what you must do in the little Park." But the first sentence modalizes this order, "You *can see* [*pouvoir voir*] the Gardens," a complex modalization since it is at once a *permission* given by the master of the places and a *possibility* left to the discretion of the visitor. Still, this game is barely begun when permissiveness and possibility are themselves at a loss: the representation of the infinite absolute in its map and in the configuration of its places can only open *a space* of wandering and error for the finite being, for the anonymous subject who enters it by choice. From this comes the order of an order, the obligation of an arrangement that is at once a syntax of the marks in the descriptive text and a system of landmarks in the topical expanse—an order that is offered as a simple instruction of the pathway to render it at once exhaustive and convenient. More precisely, Félibien's narrative topography, his topical narrative, has no other function than to operate, for the use of the king's subjects, the transformation of the infinite into the absolute—the infinite of the diversity of the prince's places into the absolute of an order that regulates its arrangement and normativizes its pathway—and in this sense this touristic guide, between map and itinerary, is also a political text in which (narrative and topographical) representation is power, and power (of the prince and of the describer-narrator of his place) is representation.

On first examination, spatial operators dominate as, introduced by them, do the sequences of an embryonic narrative:

> After having considered what pertains to the Château, one can see the gardens and [all that] is enclosed in the little Park. One can then, from the great terrace that is at the front of the Château and that separates it from the grounds, go down on the side of the Tower. At the beginning, in the first alley, one encounters the Siren's basin, which is across from the Terrace steps. This basin is seventeen fathoms long by seventeen fathoms wide. . . . It is called the Siren's basin because its principal figure in the middle represents a siren that spouts water from a large shell.[9]

Or again,

> When all these different lodgings have been considered, one can leave the Château by the hall that overlooks the middle of the little Court and, by passing under the vaulted galleries, go to the great Terrace that is in the Garden in front of the entire Palace. . . . But before advancing any further into the gardens and the little Park, the great building facade that overlooks the ornamental waters of the grounds and the two sides that are the enclosure of the Château deserve to be well considered as much for the majestic grandeur of all this mass as for the beauty of the stones with which it is built, the care that has been taken to carve them well, and the choice that has been made of the figures and ornaments that embellish it.[10]

"One can go down . . . , go out . . . , one encounters . . . at the beginning . . . , and then . . . , by passing under . . . , before advancing . . ." The pathway descriptors arm the descriptive text with oriented processes, directed movements, and arrowed beacons whose ensemble, in a dynamic network, operates the exhaustive "beat" of the prince's space, and the "encounters" are only the articulation points of successive movements, the crossroads where they change orientation ("on the right," "on the left"). But this network forms only the base frame of the descriptive text. It supports another obstinately recurring network to which it is hierarchically subordinated. This network is constituted by stops, rests, and stases that produce in the "topography" sites, themselves bound together, of a same gaze ("after having considered . . . , one can see [*By looking above, one sees . . . , one considers with pleasure what is worthy of being noticed.*]. . . what deserves to be well considered . . ."). These sights have gradations that can be underlined—from possible vision to actual sight and from attentive gaze to admiring contemplation—gradations that thus draw, in the pathway itself, the stable order of a hierarchy of local values. From that point on the movements and their textual operations are only displacements of points of view and have no other function than to make possible a "theorization" of the traversed spaces and to produce a configuration of places as a hierarchized optic order of gazes. This order is the only order possible, that of absolute visibility through the perfect legibility of the text, that of the visibility of the absolute that regulates and normativizes the cartographic expanse in order to make it the king's prosopography.

This optic order, which the pathway produces and which regulates its progress rigorously, organizes also the configuration of the places that the "voyage" explores. It founds itself on this configuration by transposing it onto topography. Built architecture and gardens are not only offered to the gaze that is regulated by prospect but are also themselves gazes at once in their disposition on the map and in their "visitation" by the trajectory of the "tourist": "The hall . . . overlooks the middle of the little Court . . . at the moment when one can go out of the Château by crossing it. . . . This great building façade . . . overlooks the ornamental waters of the grounds and the two sides that are the enclosure of the Château," at the moment when, before engaging in the visit of the gardens and the little park, one turns around according to the instruction of the "guide" to consider attentively "the majestic grandeur of all this mass" of the palace. There is thus a "theoretical" order of the places that, in their monumental silent immobility, accompany and, even more, perhaps demand from their structural gaze the "theorization" of the spaces that the pathway operates through its displacements of points of view and its stases of contemplation. The one represents the other, and the second performs the first; and the monarch in his palace, visited by his subjects, is like an Argus with a hundred eyes that no gaze can escape; he is at once his château in continuous expansion in space and time and its center, or heart, which gives it its meaning and receives from the structures that scan and articulate this space and time the legitimization of its symbolic reality. What is true of gazes, barely distinguishable relationships between an eye—and its relays—and "theorems" themselves endowed with vision, is also true of matter, as it was, we have seen, of ornament.

> All these places are adorned and enriched by all sorts of marble that the King has had brought from several spots of his Kingdom where, ten years ago, were discovered quarries of marble of various colors and as beautiful as those that in the past were brought from Greece and Italy. One has made sure to use those that were most rare and

precious in those places that are the closest to the King's person, such that as one passes from one room to another, more riches can be seen there.[11]

In its decor and wealth the royal palace, through the diversity of the materials used, is like the condensation of the kingdom, its metaphor; nevertheless, this "microcosm" obeys a rule of order and arrangement that orders their use: the greater or lesser proximity of the king's person defines the principle of a hierarchy, with the result that to realize the representation that Félibien gives of it and to transform it into real presence, one will conclude that the king's person, with respect to his material body, defines in the place it fills the absolutely rare and infinitely precious, a flesh that exists only in the individual and singular state, comparable to no other except to itself, a transfigured flesh, exalted beyond nature, a glorious body whose château in its ordering is in some sense its expansion or its metonymic displacement, such that the degree of the wealth and beauty of the marble used here or there will indicate to the attentive spectator-visitor his exact place in the sovereign's space, his precise position in the configuration of the places that organize it, that is, his "topographic" distance with respect to the center, the place absolutely rare and the point infinitely dense of all the wealth of the kingdom, a distance that is in proportion to his exaltation toward the grace of the local presence or of his erring in the desertlike space of disgrace and absence.

The Magician King, or The Prince's Fête

> The Trianon palace was first looked upon by everyone as an enchantment: for, having been begun only at the end of winter, it was found to be completed in spring as if it had come up out of the ground along with the flowers of the gardens that accompany it and that at the same time appeared laid out such as they are today and filled with all sorts of flowers, orange-trees, and shrubby green trees.[1]

If the construction and development of the royal château seem to be an infinite enterprise proportionate to the absolute that it must enclose while giving it its symbolic place, it is in return another manifestation of the prince's representation and power, of his representation as power and of his power as representation, which no longer consists of unfolding the time of the design toward its completion but, rather, of canceling it out in the quasi-identification of intention and realization. On the one hand, we have the providence of an infinite wisdom, which gives to absolute will its rationality, and rationality, which gives to omnipotent action its direction and meaning; on the other, we have the magic of an imagination without limit, which makes marvelous realities of its whims or dreams at the moment they appear. On the one hand, we have time ordered toward its totalization; and on the other, duration contracted into a brilliant moment. The minister in his remonstrances to the young king had confounded the one and the other by thinking that the political and artistic design of the reason of state was only an ephemeral and costly diversion of the prince's imagination, while the fête, by its *magic* and in that register, represents more clearly than any other domain the phantasms that animate the reason of state in its principle and project. At the end of the century, in the prologue to *Donkey Skin*, the tale of absolute power and of infinite representation, Perrault will be surprised that one can be surprised: "Why should we marvel / That the most sensible Reason / Often weary with too much watching / Takes pleasure in sleeping, / Ingeniously rocked / By tales of Ogres and Fairies?"[2]

In the "topography" of Versailles and its gardens that Félibien writes in 1672, the Trianon is at the edge of the project, that is, of its design of symbolic politics and of the imagination's playful diversion in festivity: between providence and magic. In the text of the description of the king's place is indicated an essential motif of the royal fête along with the apparition of this palace in the gardens of the château: the conjunction of the time of the architectural creation and realization and of that of nature in the cycle of its seasons. Not only do the workings of art in the prince's service unfold at the same rhythm as the geneses of nature; it is as if nature itself had become the servant of his desires:

> It could be said of the Trianon that the graces and Cupids [*Amours*]
> that form that which is perfect in the most beautiful and magnificent
> of art's works, and even that carry out those of Nature, were the
> only architects of this place, and that they wanted to make of it their
> dwelling.[3]

A second feature characterizes the Trianon as the princely fête, a trait that underlines more directly the magic of the enterprise as well as the playful aspect of the architecture of the palace and its gardens: the disproportion between the edifice's end and the means put into action to attain it. Félibien indeed praises the "plan to make a little Palace of extraordinary construction" where Louis could "pass some hours of the day during the summer heat,"[4] an exceptional "creative expense" for some moments of the king's life, the dog days. But whereas the most common trait of an act of magic (in the texts of fairy tales) consists of obtaining extraordinary results with very little means—thus with a wave of the wand to make of an ordinary pumpkin "a beautiful golden carriage" and of six little mice "a handsome team of six horses of a beautiful dappled mouse-gray"[5]—the king puts into action immense means—or at least Félibien's "narration" lets that be understood—no doubt to realize a palace "of extraordinary construction" but one that, in its smallness—for it has only one floor—has no other function than to shelter the king for some hours of the day during the summer's heat. Certainly, magic here makes one image with truth but, by inverting the marvelous relationship between means and ends, the magician-king reveals his omnipotence to be quite beyond what the fairy of *Cinderella* realizes, since the latter, with waves of her wand, aims at the extraordinary result of marrying a scullery maid (Perrault's "Cuçendron," that is, Cinderella) to the king's son and thus of making her a queen, whereas the king, between winter and spring, with the exceptional means of the art of the men at the disposal of his will, has no other end than to pass some moments in a cool place at the far end of his park. The "gratuity" of the end makes a "disinterested" game of the whole enterprise that leads to it, unless some moments of relaxation and of rest for the prince be of so great and high a price that, belonging to an order other than that of an "economic" calculation proportioning end to means, this infinite end devalorizes and reduces to nothing all real means.

Conjugated to art, the magic frame of the work's realization, natural time is finally mastered for the king's pleasure: "one could with reason call the Trianon and its garden *spring's ordinary abode*, for in whatever season one goes there, it is enriched by all sorts of flowers, and the air one breathes there is *always* scented by those of the jasmine and orange trees under which one walks."[6] There is therefore only one season in this retired place, that of renewal, an eternal present in which time has been immobilized in a unique period but which, because it is that of rebirth, assures to this place an inexhaustible variety of pleasures of sight and smell, an infinite variety that reveals to the courtier-(de)scribe(r) the essential impotencies of his discourse. The discourse is the ultimate way of giving to the object described the assurance of its infinity by posing it, in the text, as incomparable, untranslatable—be it by the most exact signs of hyperbole—and unassignable and, therefore, shown and given to sight as absolute.

> But since in all of the diverse seasons extraordinary and surprising changes can be seen there, whether in the diversity of the flowers or in the disposition of the place, one must put off a more precise description to another time and yet let those who will see all of these places judge if any are more delightful or pleasant.[7]

The little palace of Trianon, of extraordinary and convenient construction, constitutes, in the "topography" of the Prince in his château and park of Versailles, an entrance into the universe of the royal fête, be it only through the somewhat affected graces of Félibien's discourse; and in his text it occupies the boundary place, at once of transgression and harmony, of reason and imagination, of the symbolic project and the whim of fantasy, of providence and magic, but maybe even more of space and time. Whereas the visit to the château and park in the "topographic" discourse had permitted bringing into the narration of the pathway the configuration of the prince's places and, with it, the description of the map, this narrative had no other end than to constitute these places in an optic order whose sole principle, rule, and norm were the royal power but which, in return, furnished it with its legitimizing representation. With the fête, it is essentially the places outside the château, the park and the domain, that will be manipulated, represented, remodeled, and very precisely *feigned* in order to form, but *in time*, a second order that is temporary, even ephemeral, and devoted to consumption and destruction; a gratuitous sumptuous "expense" (as was, but more lastingly, the Trianon) in the permanent "immortal" economy, as Colbert reproached in his remonstrance on the king's places. A spectacular framework of air, water, and fire is set in the architectural optic order of stone and earth in order to represent it by metamorphosing it; a framework endowed with its specific time that redoubles and transforms that—repetitive and ceremonial—reigning in the royal space.

If, in the "topography" of the château, the narrative of the "visit" implied a former local order as its postulate and reference and re-produced this same order in the *Divertissements de Versailles*[8] —but valorized and stratified in its symbolic political effects—the "royal miracle" (while waiting for Pellisson to try to write it) is not an expression that turns toward the panegyric or hyperbole of flattery but, rather, one that describes quite exactly the effect of belief that is brought about by the *secrecy* in the decision and the *omnipotence* in the realization:

> One of the things that must be considered fully in the Fêtes and Diversions with which the King entertains his court is the promptness that accompanies their magnificence; for his orders are executed with so much diligence through the care and particular application of those who are its principal stewards that there is no one who does not believe that everything is accomplished there through miracles, so much is one suprised to see in the space of a moment, and without having noticed it, theaters erected, groves adorned and enriched by fountains and figures, collations prepared, and a thousand other things that seem to need a great deal of time and an infinite number of workers. However, most often the Court does not notice the preparations that are made for all these kinds of fêtes, and the many people occupied at these tasks are so unobstrusive that they are not even seen.[9]

Félibien insists on the surprising promptness with which the royal fêtes are organized, the effect of magic consisting here in the disproportion between the magnificence of the realization and the brevity of the time needed to accomplish it. Upon looking at it more closely, however, the rapidity is an effect secondary to a more essential effect, the surprise that strikes the court at the brilliance [*éclat*] of the fêtes no doubt, but above all at their bursting forth [*éclatement*], at the suddenness of their appearance. And it is the eruption of this festive theophany in the places and on the stage of the sovereign that brings along the effect of belief that the term *miracle* summarizes. Everything is accomplished and occurs *as if* through miracles, to the point "that there is no one who does not believe that everything is accomplished there *through* miracles." And Félibien furnishes with precision the reasons for this chain of effects, as Pascal would say. These effects depend essentially, at first, on the *dissimulation of the operation*: the workers in infinite number, in the very places where the court circulates, are kept properly invisible to it; not only does the duration of the enterprise contract (the "Trianon effect"), but its instruments also disappear in contradiction with the rational calculation of the project's execution, the duration of the labor being inversely proportional to the quantitative and therefore visible importance of the means implemented.

But more fundamentally, if the operation itself is hidden in favor of the radiant [*éclatant*] visibility of its result according to the key principle of post-tridentine theology, *ex opere operato*, it is because the intention that presided at the conception has remained *secret*: only the king knows what he ordered the principal executors of his project to do; more precisely, only the king knows the order that his orders, once immediately executed, arrange and organize: the secret order of the diversions whose preparations are dissimulated until the realized will of the king bursts forth in its multiple images. Racine will find its definitive formulas ten years later, but with respect to the king's history:

> In the King's history everything lives, works, and is in action. One has only to follow him, if one can, and study only him well. It is a continuous chain of marvelous deeds that he himself starts, that he himself completes, as clear and as intelligible when they are executed as they were impenetrable before their execution. In a word, the miracle follows closely upon another miracle. Attention is always vivid, and admiration always taut; and one is no less struck by the grandeur and the promptness with which peace is made than by the rapidity with which conquests are made.[10]

Visibly, the diversions of the prince in his château and domain—their narrative shows it—in their conception and execution obey the same principles as do the king's war and peace in the space of Europe and the world. The diversions, in this sense, represent war in the time of the peace that interrupts it, as war is the prince's fête in another field and on another stage. War is the fête continued by other means, as diversion is politics pursued on another register. Thus it could be said that the prince's *coup d'état* is represented in the miracle of the fête; political behavior is dramatized in the playful gesture; and the secrets of power, the *arcana imperii*, are repeated—reproduced and anticipated—according to the intentions of the aesthetic fantasy.[11]

From then on can be glimpsed at once the political reason of the fête in the frame of the château and the ideological reason of its narrative by Félibien, who duplicates its topography. By representing it in the space of the fête and metamorphosing it there up until the dazzle of the destruction, the king puts on stage, mounts in space, and risks ritually and gratuitously the order of his place, the monument of his glory and his symbolic body in the spaces of the royal diversion, as if to give, in and through the spectacular framework that constitutes it, a superpotential to the power of his representation, a superpotential to his representation itself. In this sense the prince's fête is a repetition that founds the king's representation.

The fêtes of 1674, we learn upon reading Félibien, lasted six days, but nearly two months of chronological time elapsed between the first and the last, two months of the royal house's time, the time of the permanence of the order of the places and monuments, the present presence of a "now" of the king, who in this sense is indeed the continuing referent of the other time, that of the diversion. Six days, two months: three Wednesdays, the 4th, 11th and 18th of July; two Saturdays, the 28th of July and the 18th of August; and, to conclude, the night of the Friday to the Saturday of the last day of that month. Here is discontinuous time, then, where the intervals between the days and nights of fête are drawn out, no doubt corresponding to the preparations necessary for a sumptuousness that steadily increased. And yet this time is given to us to read and, in all likelihood, to imagine in the continuity of a duration signaled by the ordering of the days (first, second, and so on), a duration that transcends that of referential time; a duration also marked by the succession of dates that are specific to it (Wednesday the 4th of July, Wednesday the 11th of July, and so on), another duration whose scansion, rhythm, point of departure, and end are "fixed" by the king's design and will. An effect of the narrative representation, one could say; no doubt. It is Félibien's narrative that brings continuity to the six days of fête and that isolates them from their chronological and constant substratum, a simulacrum of time where the months of Caesar and Augustus in 1674 are made up of only six days.

But the representation *in the text* of the diversions is not exhausted in this effect alone, for upon returning from the conquest of the Franche-Comté, the king represents the time of origins with the six days of fête given at the court: the six days of the genesis of the world. By offering six days of playful "creation" the king puts on stage, after the war and his return to rest, the seventh day, Sunday, of which the fêtes of July and August are the temporal synecdoche. It is in this way that the time of the fête operates a metamorphosis of the historical and chronological time of the royal dwelling, a metamorphosis, however, in which the king is posed, *but "as signification and figure," as representation*, as master of time. This is done to the extent precisely that the staging and the scenic products of the spectacular framework at once signify the end of the epic story, the (temporary) end of the king's gesture, and his return from the war to the repose of peace and mimic the origin of the world and the time of the divine gesture of creation *ex nihilo*. One perceives by that how the royal *diversion*, at least that of 1674, occupies a strategic position in the system of representation and in the framework of the power of state, not only because it articulates political reason and aesthetic imagination but also because it furnishes the illusions and feints of the imagination that he orders and puts on stage with a "mysterious" reference—the creation of the world by God. This reference gives to this conduct, in the playful interval of the rational conduct of the affairs of State, at once its symbolic power and its ultimate legitimation: the foundation, suddenly given to sight as "image," of the sovereign authority and of the law that normalizes that power.

The king entertains his court: the latter is the privileged addressee of a gracious gift from the prince. Félibien, describing the fêtes of 1668, notes precisely this point:

> The King, having granted peace at the entreaties of his allies and upon the wishes of all of Europe, and given marks of a moderation and a benevolence without example even in the mightiest of his conquests, thought only to apply himself to the affairs of his Kingdom when, to make up, in a way, for what the Court had lost in the carnival during his absence, he resolved to have a Fête in the gardens of Versailles.[12]

The prince's fête compensates for the king's absence, his past absence from his own place, the château, the domain and *his* house, with his presence now, here, but in another space and above all in another time, which at once redoubles and intensifies it. Present time and places, still marked by his absence as agent of the history that he has just made, are played and represented *as* time and places of origins where all begins and takes shape. By that itself the here and now are recharged in potential power and value. It is as if, by making a gift of these fêtes to the court in his domain and in his own space, of these redoubled and mounted representations, through the metamorphoses of a monumental and permanent order of places in a spectacular ephemeral framework, the king reappropriated his house for himself as symbolic body of glory, the glory of Apollo acquired in the works of Mars.

The king proceeds through the space of the fête and constitutes it as places through the order of his gaze. The frameworks of the diversions throughout all of the six days will function in an analogous manner: a particular space of the gardens or the courts, already regulated by a determined optic and geometric order, is modeled, remodeled, and displaced into another, which transforms it by building on it. The king enthrones this new space with the pathway he makes through it and consecrates it with his gaze, which in the majority of cases completes it in its appearance and apparition as *spectacle* for the court. At the outside, it could be said that Félibien's narrative will at first consist of constructing the permanent and ephemeral double stage that will be the site of the prince's eye and then of telling the gaze of the king, a gaze that produces the diversion by evoking the illusions it is made of and by showing them to the dazzled court. It is in this way that the court is gorgonized, struck dumb by images for a moment real; less, however, by those images in themselves than because all of them reverberate, and each in a specific fashion, the gaze of the master in which and through which they have taken shape. This power of the royal gaze, which in the narrative of its pathway performs for six days during two months the shapes and things of a new world, the other of this world, before the fascinated eyes of the courtiers, will find its point of origin—and this process is itself significant—in the theatrical creation, in order to know its fulfillment in the creation of light. The royal gaze covers with the beam of its fantastic potential power the entire field of visibility, of the spectacular product *in representation* on stage to what makes all possible spectacle visible, to the condition of all vision, transcending vision itself: light as visible even in its invisibility, its secrecy.

It is thus that, for example, Wednesday the 11th of July (the second day of the diversion), we again find the Trianon:

> As in the Château and the park of Versailles there are places where each season of the year seems to have established a particular dwelling, it could be said that it is at the Trianon that one always finds Spring. . . . The King, continuing to entertain the Court, chose this spot to pass the evening and, to this effect, ordered that a comfortable place be prepared there in order to hear the *Eglogue de Versailles*.[13]

Such is the secret moment of intention and design, of choice and decision, the mysterious moment of the order that will be intelligible only after the fact, when the fête is over—or the war, as in the case of Racine—and when Félibien (or Racine) tells its history. Therefore, because the place is the Trianon, spring's abode at Versailles, the spectacle will be the *Eglogue* of Versailles, a pastoral piece in which shepherds and shepherdesses converse in the heat of summer. Such, then, is the first act of the narrative, the secret order of the king.

The second sequence consists of the description of the stage floor in the permanent order of the royal house:

> *Outside the enclosure of the Trianon garden there is a little confined wood* in the large Park, whose tall trees, thick with foliage, *make* an admirable cover. *The principal walk of this wood extends opposite the Palace* such that, *by opening* a gate that *closes* the garden, *this walk makes a perspective that much more pleasant that at the end of it one perceives a hollow of trees and a fountain* whose shade and freshness have something about them that is quite delightful. It is at the end of this walk that *a salon of greenery was erected [on éleva]*.[14]

At the end of the "description"—let us note the "obstinate" recurrence of the present tense—as at the end of the principal walk of the little wood, occurs the narrative event, the execution of the king's order—the preterit [*on éleva*]. On the stage floor, however, made of local exclusions and inclusions, are traced directional processes, operations, movements, and gazes that are at first the fact of things (the walk that extends opposite the palace opens a gate that closes the garden, and makes a perspective), only to culminate in an anonymous gaze in the bosom of the countryside, with no other definition than the constraint of the disposition of the places (*at the end of it, one perceives* a hollow of trees and a fountain).

Henceforth, on the stage floor and starting from the "royal" narrative event, the scenery will be erected (a second stage in the first) with its specific time in the text, the imperfect in the original French. The third sequence, second description:

> This salon *had* two great doors: *one entered* by one door, and by the other, which *was* opposite it, *one saw* a long walk formed on two sides by little arcades. . . . At the end of this walk *was* the basin of a fountain surrounded by tall orange trees and flower pots, in the middle of which *one* saw a large stream of water rising. Beyond the basin *was* a palisade that *formed* a semicircle, where in five large niches *appeared* five figures of satyrs in white marble.[15]

The spectacular framework that is thus constructed, at once in the space of the Trianon and in that of the text, is redoubled exactly into two halves, the one being an ensemble of places (there were . . .), and the other a system of gazes (one saw . . .). It *is instituted* immediately in the reading as the site of the gaze, as the place of the point of view, since the two doors opposite the salon of greenery receive different functions: one *enters* by the one and one *sees* by the other.

Indeed, in the third sequence the spectacular framework of the fête in the permanent order of the places finds its narrative and functional fulfillment with the coming of its great orderer: "The King, having arrived at this salon with all his Court, sat down in a spot that had been prepared for him opposite the walk and the fountain . . . , which formed a very enjoyable decoration in front of him."[16] The king arrives unexpectedly: it is through him, as unique grammatical and semantic subject of the narrative, that history comes about at the end of the little wood's principal walk, outside the Trianon garden's enclosure. His order, as a matter of fact, had preceded him; then followed the execution of his decision with the anonymous "one" [*on éleva*] that had erected the salon of greenery. The king, actor of pathways and narrative subject, limits himself to fulfilling the "program of action" that he himself has defined, that design whose drawing has been traced and realized in a passing pastoral scenography. More precisely, the king consecrates the framework with his presence by re-tracing, through his unidirectional pathway, that of the anonymous gaze that had made a system of gazes of this part of the royal space and of this ensemble of places. Through the movement of his walk the king re-marks the perspective that the walk in the wood makes opposite his Trianon palace once the gate closing the garden has been opened, to its end, to the *entrance* door of the salon of greenery and to its center, where he sits down in a spot that has been prepared for him. The view site of the scenography becomes, then, the seat and throne of his eye, the point of view, the origin of the rectilineal pursuit of his gaze beyond the theatrical stage erected for this Wednesday evening, the 11th of July, through the *exit* door of the gaze, along the length of the walk with the little arcades to the basin of the fountain, its stream of water and its semicircular palisade, to the vanishing point: a large niche and a satyr of white marble that assigns, by its figure at the end of his gaze thus sent back to his immobile eye, the genre of the play that he sees, hears, and gives through that means to be seen and heard by all those who surround him.

The king sees and does; he does and sees; performing, his gaze makes something be [*faire être*] in this precise sense that it is at the moment when he sees that he makes all that is to be seen, be seen [*faire voir*], and that alone. And since in the fête's narrative it is the royal gaze that *inaugurates* the day's diversion and that enthrones and consecrates it, it is as if the gaze of his eye were creating the spectacle *ex nihilo* and as if, emitting its own light, it were also creating the condition of its vision. And this gaze is a pure gaze, no doubt attentive but deprived of all affect: a pathetic gaze, a theoretical gaze, when all is told empty, with no other expression than the spectacle that he causes to appear. In return, all the others, all those who are not the king, though admitted into his presence, in a word, the court, are struck by admiration and stupefied by fear and astonishment: they are seized by all the passions of the gaze. Thus consider from among ten examples these notations of the fifth day, Saturday the 18th of August, 1674: "Their Majesties *descended* to the bottom of the royal walk, from where *they* saw the great ornamental water, which makes the head of the canal, illuminated in a manner that *surprised* everyone." And further on, "It was again a new spectacle that *surprised* those who did not expect it and that made the grandeur and magnificence of the diversion appear to even greater advantage."[17] Finally and above all during the sixth day, the last day of August: "Their Majesties having arrived at Apollo's basin, the whole Court began to see more distinctly the beauty of those fires that surround the Canal."[18] It often suffices, as the preceding examples show, that the king alone, or the royal couple, be placed or seated, indeed attain the end of a movement or stop during his walk, in order for what is to be seen then, and then only, to occur to sight, that is, to the narrative representation that Félibien gives of it.

The fifth and sixth days, in many aspects, attain a peak: they are nights of a creation so total in the imaginary that the only possibility left for the fulfillment of its perfection is its quasi-instantaneous destruction: the unique means of realizing the absolute, since all comparison is forbidden and since the spectacle that took place in a single evening will be comparable only to its memory. Thus the end of the fifth day: fireworks and illuminations organized by Le Brun were lit "when the king had been placed under a great tent that had been set up." Here is the final "bouquet":

> All that was seen in this great stretch of more than three hundred
> fathoms was no longer either fire, air, or water. These elements were
> so mixed together that they became unrecognizable and there
> appeared a new one of a most extraordinary nature. It seemed to be a
> composite of a thousand sparks of fire, which as a thick dust or,
> rather, as an infinity of atoms of gold shone in the middle of a
> greater light.[19]

In the upheaval of the luminous appearance under the king's eyes a new element is created. It is at once *other* than fire, air, and water and the mix that reduces them to unity. He destroys the elements and totalizes them through an astonishing *transmutation* in which the dust of the fire of a thousand sparks (fire, air, and water) becomes an *infinity* of atoms of *gold* shining in a great *light*: a light that is metal, and a metal that is light. The king gives himself here the figure of the great cosmic alchemist, but even more so and inversely, the universal alchemist is the *figure* of the infinite potential power of the king, an infinite potential power or, rather, an infinite desire for absolute power [*puissance*]. Pascal has taught it to us: "desire of domination, universal and outside of its order," "tyranny" is the desire for the homogeneous, for an order unique through the annihilation of all external differences. Thus the new element that appears above the grand canal is at first neither fire nor air nor water.

But this desire is also—continues Pascal—that of wanting to have by one path what can only be had by another. "Tyranny" aims to bring together all differences in the field of its exercise and to recuperate them through totalization in the immanence of its hold. Thus the gold-light created one evening in August is, by transmutation, the sum of the three natural elements. The new element, in the feint of its profuse apparition, is thus indeed the figure of the precious metal gold, tapped by the minister in the coffers of the Sun King. This gold, which permitted the production of the illusion of an element of artifice, is both metaphor of the solar body of the king and metonymy of his power in a representation that is at once the fascinating image of the former and the veracious proof of the latter. And it is exactly the play and the gesture that show to "everyone" that it is only a question of an illusion. It is the playful act of gratuitous expense that will attempt to make of the staged representation an *infinite* presence and, of the potential power that it reserves in the economy of its signs, an *absolute* power. The moment when the framework producer of illusions is discovered is identified with that of its annihilation by fire, the very element whose transmutation into the semblance of a gold-light it had permitted. From then on the simulacrum, in an instant, is turned around and poured back into the real itself, whose consummation is represented in an ultimate spectacle.

> As one also let the whole Machine on the Canal burn along with the
> seven large boats that carried it, this burning was again a new
> spectacle that surprised those who did not expect it and that made the

grandeur and magnificence of the diversion appear to even greater advantage.[20]

The burning of the machine along with the seven boats that carry it is the epiphany of the glorious body of the king in the brief and sudden instant of his real presence, but whose representations and simulacra had to be multiplied so that their conflagration could reveal it. All told, the self-production that founds the royal body through the infinite reflection of the system of representation onto itself, where the absolute monarch was historically, juridically, and politically defined, finds its exact figure, the 18th of August 1674, when "one let the whole Machine on the Canal burn."

The sixth day will be the fulfillment and perfection of the operations I have just described:

> The whole Court was surprised by the novelty and grandeur of the spectacle.... The King, wanting to show [*faire voir*] beauties that had never yet been seen, seemed this time to have been served by Magic itself, so much did the eyes and mind find themselves surprised by the different marvels that charmed them.[21]

Here is the announcement of representation in representation itself, the convocation of the court to the irresistible effect of belief called "miracle" in the hindsight of narration, still a semblance, but in which the king literally gives the glory of his body to be enjoyed.

The functioning of the spectacular framework that we know is repeated: "*His Majesty having left the Château* at about one o'clock at night, the blackest and calmest night there had been in a long time, *one saw* in this great obscurity all the parterres traced with lights." But the lights, as Félibien explains, "marked new parterres and formed figures of fire instead of flowers and greenery."[22] The garden became visible again on the blackest night, but it is *another*, delivered up in a spell for charming the eyes and the mind, to a drawing of flames. Thus, the Sun King remodels *his* space and *his* local monument to the pleasure of the fire light that emanates from his substance: transubstantiation of his own place. And from then on the king's world appears to all those here below and today *as another world, as the other world*.

> It [the Grand Canal] was surrounded on all sides by luminous bodies, but of the soft and private light of the movement and action that one sees in ordinary fire. These fires did not have any shadow. They represented different figures that could be discerned from afar with difficulty and whose images appeared on water that was no less calm than the light itself, such that the profound silence and obscurity where one found oneself then resembled very much what Poets have written about the Elysian Fields, which they depict as a space of country lit by a precious light with its own sun and stars.[23]

Each stage of Félibien's narration, like each moment of the final diversion that the king gives to his court, uncovers how, with perfect precision, the king only constitutes himself in his image and how he only institutes himself *as* his portrait of king of the world because the world of the king is delivered up, for a night, to the infinity of the representation of each of his parts and of each of his places. The result is a generalized "between-representation" where substances as well as orders of reality are overturned and confounded in a universal and incessant reflexivity. A baroque fête, one would say. No doubt, on the condition of not letting oneself be taken in by the spells of the magician-king, that is, on the condition of perceiving that, far from being beyond all these images, as is the illusionist who would play with them, he is himself taken in by the phantasmagoria of the diversion. The infinite reflection of the representation produces him as this "virtual" image, with no other reality than the multitude of luminous refracted rays that come to cross one another there in order to give him an ephemeral and grandiose consistency, that of absolute monarch. It is an image, then, that would find its "veritable reality" only in the *effects of belief* provoked in the imaginations of those who saw, on that night of the 31st of August to the 1st of September 1674, the king of France on the Grand Canal, in the park of his château of Versailles; ephemeral effects as on that night, but to which Félibien's narration gives the monumentality of great history. That is why the absolute monarch is no more and will never be more than his portrait in a brief moment whose text magnifies the effects forevermore:

> A magnificence so rare stopped the eyes of the whole Court for a long time with pleasure. They could not tire of admiring the marvelous effects of these illuminations, whose images still appeared in the depth of the water as other Palaces and other figures larger than the veritable ones. All sorts of Fish seemed to have arranged themselves at the edge of the water to watch the greatest King of the world pass by on their element as in triumph. A multitude of others that were seen in the water seemed to be there as the mute spectators of all the royal pomp with which the Versailles canals were honored during the night. After the King had come back up the length of the Canal and the whole Court had landed at the spot where they had entered the gondolas, His Majesty returned to the Château.[24]

The King's Portrait

In 1671 Félibien published a collection of *Descriptions de divers ouvrages de peinture faits pour le Roi*. It opens with the description of the arch erected on the Place Dauphine for the entrance of the king and queen in 1660 and ends with the account of the fête at Versailles in July 1668. The second description is that of Le Brun's painting, *Les Reines des Perses aux pieds d'Alexandre*; the fourth and fifth are those of the two tapestry hangings made for His Majesty, *Les Quatre Eléments* and *Les Quatre Saisons*. At the center of the group, flanked by the great historical picture and the allegorical tapestries, signified by the former as the new Alexander and symbolized by the latter two in his attributes and perfections, is the king in his portrait, also by Le Brun.[1] In truth, the picture of the portrait is absent from the collection, but in its place there is a text that describes it, the portraiture of a portrait, precisely a prosopography of the king, with the difference that the being described (in his face, body, traits, physical qualities, exterior, bearing, and movements) is not the king but his painted portrait, not a real animated thing, to take up Fontanier's expressions again, but a fictive object, an image. This remark goes for all the other descriptions of the collection, but with the king's portrait it takes on fundamental theoretical and political values. Is it *possible* to describe the king otherwise than in his image? Is it possible to trace him otherwise than by retracing him in his representation, by redrawing him from his portrait? Is the king other than his image? Or, inversely, is the king's image, one and multiple, single and diversely reproduced, not the whole of the king? A positive answer to these questions would imply that the king's portrait was deprived of all reference to other than a portrait. In other words, the little work that Félibien wrote and that he placed at the center of his collection of 1671, the prosopography of a king's portrait, would be the model of all the king's portraits. It would be properly constitutive of the very being of the king, simultaneously as infinite representation and as absolute power.

To write a description of the king's portrait and then address it to the king is not a lesser paradox, inasmuch as the portrait described is in the king's study, disposed for his own always incessantly and immediately possible contemplation. The problem is here, in the apparent ornamental complications of an introduction-dedication: of what "interest" for the king is this written representation of his painted representation that is constantly present to him? What is the function of this supplement? In what way is the reflexivity to infinity of the king's representation—be it at the price of the passage from one substance of expression to another—necessary to the position of the monarch's absoluteness? Félibien has a precedent: he described Le Brun's picture *Les Reines des Perses aux pieds d'Alexandre* and offered the work—his written copy—to the king, who accepted it, "although the original of this picture was in his study."[2] Consequently he hopes for the same favor for the painting he is presenting to him today, since it is more excellent and more noble than the first. The description has become a painting; the representation of a representation, the presentation of a painting; a written copy has duplicated the painted original in the space of an instant only in order to authorize the substitution of the first for the second. The text supplements the image without excess or lack. But that is to acknowledge, at the same time, that the text by that very thing "absents" the image—if I may be permitted this expression. It puts the image in a state of vacancy with respect to itself, unless the text has no other function than to make the mute image speak by saying what it means to say but that it will never say, by giving its implicit spoken discourse and by revealing its secret. Nevertheless, Félibien adds, marking the whole difference between historical pictures and the king's portrait:

> It is true that having to speak about the greatest King in the world is a subject so much beyond my power [*forces*] that my endeavor could be accused of temerity if the subject itself did not serve as an excuse for this endeavor, since I cannot better fulfill my duty than by using all my power to speak about those great qualities that the whole earth admires in your august person and that are painted so mysteriously in the picture that I want to describe.[3]

To speak about the picture of the king's portrait and to transcribe the picture that represents him into writing that speaks him is to speak indissolubly and necessarily about the greatest king in the world, to say *who* the picture represents and to make his portrait in language, signifying two things: on the one hand, that when it is a question of the king, the *portrait is* in some way and in some fashion *the person it represents*; and on the other, that the prosopography of the king's portrait is not so remote as one could have thought it to be from its first object, the king, that the painted portrait it proposes to describe does not introduce a supplementary degree of degeneration with respect to reality, and that, in short, the descriptive *discourse* is, as regards the model, on equal footing and in equivalent competition with the portrait. In front of Le Brun's portrait of the king, Félibien indeed says, as does everyone, "It is the king," but having to write and describe it, he is no longer as certain as the logicians of Port-Royal that he speaks in signification and through figure and therefore, facing this face, opposite this "real presence," the writer with his pen confronts the painter and his brush.

He discovers then, if only by preterition joined to hyperbole, that the subject is beyond his power [*forces*] as writer—the subject, but which one? Let it be noted that it is indeed a question of speaking about the greatest king in the world and not of describing the picture that represents him. The subject is the king and not a picture *of* the king, which represents him as himself and which is his property. But of this weakness Félibien's introductive matter will make a strength: the infinity of the subject to be represented, the king—who would make of any attempt at representation a crime of *lèse-majesté* if it aimed to appropriate that infinity for itself by defining his singular substance—becomes, on the contrary, an absolute exigency of representation, to the point precisely at which representation will show, by its very content, the infinite distance that separates it from its object. In effect, the subject that made of Félibien's endeavor (*to speak about the king*) a desecrating audacity becomes his excuse, since it obliges him, by an absolute duty, to employ all his strengths *to speak about the king's qualities*, "those great qualities that the whole earth admires in your august person." And it is there that the writer returns to the painter and the projected description of the king, and to the picture that portrays his qualities: the king, for the describer as for the portrayer, is accessible only through his qualities. To write them on a page of paper in a book or to paint them on canvas, to transcribe them in signs or to capture them in lines and colors, is to have mysterious access to substance itself in the august person of the king. It is this mystery of the king's portrait and prosopography that it is fitting to explain, the mystery of the king's representation and of the king as representation, and of infinite representation, the image or text, which is the "mystical" foundation of his authority, absolute power.

We must no doubt understand, as Félibien will explain next, that the "greatest painters as well as the most learned philosophers often hide their science and the height of their thoughts under mysterious shapes and figures when they treat extraordinary and elevated subjects";[4] and that is the reason why Le Brun painted, with His Majesty, in the air and on clouds, the three figures of Abundance, Renown, and Victory: "It is under the veil of these figures that the Painter has hidden the great things he planned to represent."[5] Mystery would only aim, then, for allegory. Still, we can ask if figures as stereotyped as Abundance with the horn of plenty, Renown with her trumpets, and Victory with her crown of laurel constitute adequate veils for hiding the extraordinary and sublime subjects he wants to represent. True, mystery does not qualify the allegorical figures per se but, rather, the fact that, having to represent the infinite attributes of the singular substance of the king—at this juncture, his goodness, majesty, and power [*puissance*]—the painter has chosen to detach them in a way from the figure of the king in order to hypostasize them in the three allegorical figures of abundance (goodness), renown (majesty), and victory (power). These figures do not constitute mystery, and they do not signify it symbolically: they indicate it with the distance constitutive of allegory. This gap that the spectator remarks, in the space of the picture between the figure of the king on horseback and the three aerial figures posed on clouds, indicates to him not only the unsoundable depths of the sovereign's attributes but also, and inversely, the mystery of the king's body under its optical-theoretical symbol, its portrait that hides him as "canvas" and uncovers him as symbol. To continue to paraphrase with respect to the king's portrait what the Port-Royal *Logic* writes of the Eucharistic sacrament, it does not matter that the king's body subsists in its own nature, so long as in our senses is excited the image of a body that helps us to conceive in what way the king's body, "so precious and dear to France," as Félibien wrote, is lavished by His Majesty to ensure more and more the happiness and rest of his peoples, and how the subjects are united among themselves in the same political body.[6]

The mystery of the portrait is there: it is the mystery of absolute power in its representation; it is the mystery of a "political" sacrament. Sacrament, the envelope of mystery that it hides as much as reveals; mystery, the spiritual sacrament whose fulfillment produces corporal mystery, secretly effective signification in its apparent sign; as this sign is already, in some manner, the performing force of the signification that hides there, we could say of the king's portrait what theological discourse has elaborated on the Eucharist. The king is himself figured in his visible portrait whose incessant epiphany, in all places and at all times, celebrates the multiple presence; but this portrait-sacrament is equally a memorial of history, it is re-representation of an absent man in the erection of his monument—soma, sema—and, as Rascas de Bagarris had glimpsed, with an exceptional semiotic and political perspicacity, it is this memorial of history that is presence itself, that defines the place and time of the absolute present outside of which all others, in the past and future, will have been or will be absent. This portrait in its sacramentary mystery makes one conceive of the union of subjects in a same collective body whose head is the king, the body of the kingdom whose subjugated members find an identity in the king's name that the portrait inscribes. The king's portrait in its mystery would be this sacramental body that would at once operate the political body of the kingdom in the historical body of the prince and lift the historical body up into the political body.

Immediately after the evocation of the picture's mystery Félibien writes:

I know that it was permitted only to Lysippus and Apelles to work
on Alexander's portrait. But it was not forbidden to all the Greeks to
admire the works of these two excellent men, to preserve their ideas,
and to make, of their originals, copies that were as so many glorious
monuments dedicated to the memory of that great Prince.[7]

A rare portrait and a multitude of copies; for in its near singularity the portrait ceases to be a copy of a model, itself singular, in order to substitute itself for it and become an original whose copies (in truth, copies of copies) would be monuments of memory and tombs of glory. In this hierarchy of representations the first model, Alexander (in flesh and blood, if I may say so), is effaced as at the other end of the chain the last copies become dense and monumental. Alexander's portrait is only a representation, a reminder in images and tombs of the historic body of the deceased prince; it is only a memory.

With Louis XIV the problem of the royal portrait changes nature:

Heaven, which has shed on Your Majesty so many graces and
treasures and which seems to have undertaken in forming you a chef
d'œuvre of its power by giving to the earth a perfect model of the
great King; Heaven, I say, which makes visible in Your person a
complete Monarch, wanted to produce at the same time workers
capable of worthily representing You, and it has shed on the minds
of these learned men such a penetrating enlightenment, [and does
such that] their conceptions [are] expressed in a manner so rare and
so extraordinary that I feel myself gently forced to make a portrait of
Your Majesty's portrait and to give it to the public, not as a mark of
my self-sufficiency but as a witness of my passion and of my respect
for Your sacred person.[8]

We see in what consists the difference between Lysippus or Apelles and Le Brun, and above all between Alexander and Louis the Great: whereas Alexander is only the royal person, the "referent" that Lysippus and Apelles paint and that only they have the right to paint, Louis is *already* before all process of portrayal a "portrait," the *chef d'œuvre of the power* of the divine artist; he is the perfect model of a great king, and he is the unique model only because he is already the portrait of the absolute, the "unique" copy of the king of kings. Even better, to perfect representation corresponds a sublime artist: if Heaven makes of the king its own portrait (the chef d'œuvre of its power) — and we sense that Félibien here brushes against blasphemy through hyperbole — it owes it to him to graciously inspire the artist who will represent him, and it is properly through that same inspiration of divine grace that Félibien feels himself gently forced to take his place in the great chain of inspirations and to make, in his turn, the written portrait of the painted portrait of the king, who himself is neither painted nor written but *is* the living and omnipotent portrait (of God), the chef d'œuvre of Heaven's power. The king *is* from end to end, if I may say so, the self-portrait of the divine artist. Consequently (and this appears particularly in the last sentence of the cited text), to make the king's portrait, that is, to make a copy of the king's portrait, is not only to reproduce and multiply the links of the mimetic chain but also to celebrate, as officiating priest chosen by Heaven, the ritual of the royal mystery of the transubstantiation of the prince's body.

Félibien's prosopography incessantly marks this dimension of the royal mystery in the power of its representation. It is not a question, in order to give to sight and admiration the absolute of power in its infinite representation, of producing a portrait that "would imitate" the absolute and the infinite, of constructing a colossus, as the ancient sculptor who wanted thus to sculpt Alexander, for this excess "would not have given anything to knowledge either of the form of his body or of the qualities of his soul."[9] We can even ask if the perfect imitation that makes a replica of the portrait is a possible and desirable ideal for the king's painter. "Certainly, Alexander took more pleasure when Apelles worked on his portrait and made that image so similar to the original that it appeared to be another Alexander,"[10] to the point at which in some of his pictures the representation made the spectator tremble with fear as the original would have done. But nothing equals the mystery of Le Brun's work, since he not only, as I have said, represented in celestial and mysterious figures the infinite attributes of the king "apart" from his own substance, like secrets, but also "painted the image of Your Majesty on a canvas of average size and enclosed the portrait of a King whose name fills the whole earth in quite an ordinary space."[11] New secret, new sacrament: how can the *quite ordinary* place *of the image* be marked, re-marked, or recognized by *a name that makes itself be named* by all the earth? How can this little piece of ordinary bread, "no different on the outside," contain the infinity and absoluteness of the difference of the king of charity given up in his body for all and eaten by the faithful at the ecclesial banquet? How, in its modest dimension, can the king's portrait be at once infinite representation—such would be the function of the allegorical figures—and absolute name, that of the sole monarch—such would be the function of the recognition of the painted body and face?

What, then, would be, in this ritual of recognition, the role of resemblance, of a mimesis that, as in the case of Alexander and Apelles, would be brought to perfection? Reading the text, we will see that it is not a question of resemblance, and that for a simple reason: the king is inimitable, through writing as well as through image, through the pen as well as through the brush. Félibien's prosopography was certainly able to exceed Le Brun's portrait by enriching it with charms and ornaments, but that was not necessary, for it would not have taught anybody anything. Félibien will enclose his description, then, within the limits of the picture. But even there, how to speak about the king's image?

> After having spoken about those figures that accompany the image of Your Majesty, I must finally speak about that image and, even though I have the opportunity here to say many things that could enrich the painting I want to make, and give it charms and ornaments that could not be represented in the picture whose copy I am making [*no doubt because going beyond the specific means of pictorial figurability*], I will nonetheless not undertake to touch upon them. Everyone knows them: France receives its advantages, and the whole world admires them. I will remain, then, within the terms I have fixed for myself, and I even admit that the Painter who worked to show what is great and majestic in Your person has so far surpassed himself that my pen cannot imitate the strokes of his brush, and I do not have strong enough expressions to properly represent all that is admired in this rare work.[12]

Yet the writer attempts to say what is admired, to represent in words what the painter, in surpassing himself, has represented of the greatness and majesty of the king, and "speaking" the painting, he gives us the criteria for recognizing his model:

> That bearing and that size, so great, noble, and at ease, with which the Ancients formed their demigods . . . are so well imitated in this portrait that there is no one who does not recognize you there, and recognize you as you appear when, at the head of your armies, you inspire a new ardor in the soul of all those who have the honor of following you.[13]

That bearing, *that* size, etc. — the demonstratives in the prosopography point to the bearing and size of the king, since it is they that the portrait imitates so perfectly; but it is not by them, however, that the spectator will recognize *this* portrait as being that of the king of France at the end of the 1660s, but because they are the traits that the Ancients gave to their demigods. The characteristics of the ancient demigod's representation are the criteria for recognizing and attributing the portrait, on the basis of the presupposition that Louis XIV is the living portrait of the ancient demigods, which is another way of saying that the king is inimitable and unrepresentable, since it has already been confided to us that he was the chef-d'œuvre portrait of the power of the Christian Heaven.

Let me add this essential remark in the form of a paradox: Why would Félibien attempt to furnish the spectator with the marks of recognition and attribution of the portrait to its model, since in the king's study it has the privilege of having only one spectator "by right" who is its very model, the king? But maybe the king needs to know that *there* is the king's portrait, or more precisely, by giving him the description of his own portrait that he sees to read, maybe he must, between the legible and the visible, produce or reproduce it — once more — as absolute monarch. For that, one has simultaneously to tell him, he who contemplates his "own" image, "it is the king," to make him believe that it is really him (that he is really as Le Brun has painted him and as Félibien tells him that Le Brun has painted him by describing him in his portrait), but to tell him also, "It is Apollo" or "It is Hercules" and also "It is God in His omnipotence"; in short, to permit him to say simultaneously in front of his portrait these three founding utterances of the theology of art and politics: "This is my body," "It is Louis the Great," and "The state is me." The king's portrait operates their identification and, by that, produces the king as absolute monarch. Certainly, the painter "has represented there [in his picture], as in a very pure mirror, all those great qualities that make you beloved by your subjects, feared by your enemies and admired by the whole world"; but Phidias had an easier task, for he represented gods he had not seen.

> It is not the same thing here. For although the Painter is rich and abounding in beautiful imaginings, he has nonetheless a subject he is obliged to imitate, but a subject so excellent there are no ornaments that can properly represent him.[14]

It remains only to tell the king the effect of that portrait that constitutes him, through and in his representation, in absolute power. The effect is that of fascination; he is one with the irresistible power [*puissance*] over all gaze of an infinite self-resemblance:

> But I admit that, always having my eyes on that Image, I have difficulty pulling them away in order to examine with greater care all the other parts of the picture; and I find so much resemblance in this Portrait that if the works of Apelles provided the opportunity to say formerly that there were two Alexanders, that Philip's son was the Invincible one and that of Apelles the Inimitable one, there are grounds for saying today with more truth that with your Person and your Portrait we have two Kings, both of whom will never have anything comparable to them.[15]

Like the Phoenix, the king is no one's son, neither the son of his father, as Alexander is of Philip — and the fourteenth of the name will quickly become Louis the Great, the unique — nor even less of his painter, Le Brun, the new Apelles. It is this double filiation that compromised the invincibility of Philip's son and the inimitability of that of Apelles. But when the king contemplates his portrait, there are two kings face to face who are comparable to none other than each other, the king to the portrait and the portrait to the king. It is in this way that, under the third-party gaze of the celebrant of the monarchic high mass, the mysterious transubstantiation operates — at the end of which, if the portrait is the king's portrait, the king is no less than the portrait of the portrait.

Also, to paint the king's portrait is to make the portrait of all possible future kings, since in its representation it is the portrait of all the others — as opposed to

Zeuxis, who in order to realize the picture of perfect beauty had to unite in one figure the various characters of the most beautiful girls of Greece: "how much greater happiness it is to today's excellent painter to find in the sole person of Your Majesty the material for making the painting of a King who will be, in the future, the model of all other Kings."[16] And it is thus that, in front of the painted portrait and at the end of the written portrait, the text that Félibien addresses to the king is completed in silence and adoration, for to go further would mean sounding the depths of the royal substance in the "sacramental body" of the portrait: "I could not without temerity undertake to penetrate further into the perfections that fill your sacred person and the heroic virtues that the Painter with all his art and colors would not know how to represent. I must be content with admiring them in veneration."[17]

Finale
The Legitimate Usurper,
or The Shipwrecked Man as King

In 1670, when publishing within his treatise *De l'éducation d'un prince*[1] Pascal's "Three Discourses on the Condition of the Greats,"[2] Nicole—under the pseudonym of the Sieur de Chanteresne—gave them a preface. Their goal would be to remedy three flaws to which greatness itself carries those who are born to it. The first is that "they misunderstand themselves by supposing that all the property they enjoy is due them and like a part of their being, which means that they never look upon the natural equality they have with all other men";[3] in this flaw we recognize not the art of the prince's *coups d'état*, the science of perfect dissimulation from others of the decision made in the secrecy of the king's wisdom and power [*puissance*], but the dissimulation of oneself from oneself, a form of the narcissistic illusion and vanity of a self that makes itself the center of everything. It is thus that the greats—and the prince is in this case only "absolutely great"—look at themselves incessantly and never see themselves, according to the beautiful formula of the treatise *De la connaissance de soi-même*.[4]

The second flaw is that "they fill themselves so much with those exterior advantages of which they happen to be master that they pay no respect to all the more real and estimable qualities and do not try to acquire them . . . , and that they suppose that the sole quality of being great merits all sorts of respect and does not need to be sustained by qualities of mind and virtue"[5]—a flaw that Pascal would call "tyranny," that is, at once "the desire for domination universal and outside of its order" and the desire to "have by one avenue what can only be had by another" (58-332). But doing so, Pascal would give the flaw a different inflection, since it would no longer arise only from the field of spiritual ethics, but from a political and metaphysical anthropology. It is in this way that tyranny is not only an absurd struggle for absolute mastery—"to want to reign everywhere" (58-332)—but also the constituting process of the self, of the subject itself—"In a word, the self has two qualities: it is unjust in itself for making itself the center of everything; it is inconvenient for others in that it wants to subjugate them: for each *self* is the *enemy* and would like to be the *tyrant* of all the others" (597-455).

The third flaw is that "the condition of the greats, being joined to licence and the power to satisfy their inclinations, engages several of these in unreasonable outbursts and base disorders. . . . Instead of putting their greatness to the service of men, they make it consist of treating them with insolence and abandoning themselves to all sorts of excess."[6] Such would be the illegitimate use of force as regards others, the violence of barbarism that is the perhaps inescapable consequence of a hierarchically and institutionally dominant social position, the same one that the politeness and sociability of the libertine's reciprocal obligations attempt to regulate: "The *self* is hateful: you, Miton, cover it up, you do not get rid of it for that; so you are still hateful.—No, for by acting obligingly as we do toward everyone, they no longer have cause to hate us.—This is true, if one only hated in the *self* the displeasure it brings us" (597-455).

Let us not start to believe, however, that Pascal's three discourses aim directly at the three characteristic flaws of the condition of nobility to which Nicole points. To see otherwise it is enough to underline the displacements and distortions to which Nicole, *volens nolens*, submits Pascalian thought: we need only mark the divergences. What in Nicole becomes significant for the aristocratic position—for "court society"—is in Pascal a fundamental anthropological trait, efficaciously revealed in particular by the mechanisms of the *political framework*. Whence the use of a vocabulary of terms or images, of a collection of examples or illustrations of a *political nature* to deal with man in his situation of existence and in his worldly condition. The second divergence: what in Nicole is presented as a flaw, indeed as a vice of a moral and social order susceptible, by ethical exercises and spiritual asceticism, to reformation, is analyzed by Pascal as a mechanism of fact, the functioning of a framework, and the manner alone of addressing the discourse to a determined interlocutor reveals through its pathos his philosophical and religious biases.

But it is remarkable to notice that Pascal in the "Three Discourses," like Nicole in his presentation, defines a great man essentially as a property holder: the great man is a rich man whose having determines his being; thus in Pascal: "Do not imagine that it is by a lesser chance that you possess the wealth of which you happen to be master than that by which that man happens to be king. . . . All the right by which you own your property does not come from nature, but from human establishment";[7] or in Nicole:

Man is compelled in order to love himself to represent himself to himself as other than that which he is in effect; to hide himself from his miseries or from his poverty. . . . Seeing that human wealth and power [*puissance*] are the ordinary means for making oneself master of those objects of concupiscence, the latter begins to look upon them as *great property*, and consequently it judges the *rich and great who possess them* to be happy, and unhappy the poor who are deprived of them.[8]

Therefore, if the great man is a rich man, man in general is a poor man whose desire for wealth and power [*puissance*] dissimulates misery and dispossession. In other words, the philosophical motif of the peculiarity and of the appropriation of the subject to himself, through his qualities (the self), is read directly into the sociological and political motif of the power [*puissance*] and property of the individual and collective person, through his wealth and property — just as, inversely, that of the misery and alienation of the "figure" of the subject is read into the motif of dispossession, deviation, and impotence.

The problem that the "Three Discourses" pose is thus much more a fundamental problem of politics whose fundamental character refers back to the foundation of the statesman in religious anthropology: it is a question of the problem of the prince's authority. What legitimates the prince's power? What is the right — the justice, in Pascalian language — that founds his domination? Let me add right away, to forestall any objection, that the condition of the great man, whose analysis is the subject of the three discourses, is a particular case of the "royal condition" for Nicole, who published the Pascalian discourses after his treatise *On the Education of the Prince*, as it is for Pascal, who explains himself in the third discourse: "You are . . . surrounded by a small number of persons, over whom you reign in your way," writes Pascal, addressing, according to tradition, a great man (Charles-Honoré de Chevreuse, son of the duc de Luynes);

Those persons are full of concupiscence. They request the things of concupiscence from you; it is concupiscence that attaches them to you. You are thus properly a king of concupiscence. Your kingdom is of small expanse; but you are equal, in that, to the greatest kings on earth; they, like you, are kings of concupiscence. . . . Do not aspire to reign by any other avenue than the one that makes you king.[9]

It is, then, a question of the king, of his power as king, of his rights and of the honors due him, of the relationship between the king's power in his authority and legitimacy and God — "God is surrounded by people full of charity, who ask him for the things of charity that are in his power [*puissance*]: thus he is properly the king of charity" — a relationship that is — we notice it in these quotes taken from the third discourse — in exact analogy with the preceding one, but where concupiscence is the rigorous contrary of charity, whence the final practical postulation: "We must scorn concupiscence and its kingdom and aspire to that kingdom of charity where all the subjects breathe only charity and desire only the things of charity."[10]

Pascal's question, in the end, is this one: what is a king? And his answer occurs in the "image" that introduces the first discourse. With this figure, indeed this "figurative" or, rather, this narrative in the form of a parable, Pascal operates—and in a radical manner—the scission of the body of the absolute monarch; but not for all that to come back to the doctrine of the king's two bodies, a duality that the absolute monarch—because monarch and because absolute—had attempted to identify.[11] What Pascal discovers at the end of his radical division, exactly because what is political is only the key to the cipher of what is anthropological, is what Hegel will call the "self-alienated spirit," or "consciousness,"[12] whose first utterances Pascal was then formulating:

> What I am saying to you does not go very far; and if you stay there, you can only lose yourself; but at least you will lose yourself as *honnête homme*. There are people who damn themselves so stupidly. . . . The means that I open up to you are no doubt the most honest; but in truth it is always a great folly to damn oneself; and that is why you must not be satisfied with that. You must scorn concupiscence and its kingdom.[13]

What, then, is a king? He is a king's portrait, and that alone makes him king, and besides that he is also a man. To which it is appropriate to add that the "portrait effect," the effect of representation, *makes the king*, in the sense that everyone believes that the king and the man are one, or that the king's portrait is only the king's image. No one knows that, on the contrary, the king is only his image, and that behind or beyond the portrait there is no king, but a man. No one knows this secret, and the king less than everyone else perhaps.

> To enter into the true knowledge of your condition, consider it in this image. A man is thrown by a storm onto an unknown island, whose inhabitants were at pains to find their king, who was lost; and bearing a strong resemblance in body and face to this king, he was taken for him and recognized as such by the whole population. At first he did not know which part to take; but he resolved himself finally to lend himself to his good fortune. He received all the respects offered him and let himself be treated as king.[14]

Right away, the initial "image" indissolubly ties the political problem to the anthropological question: the new "king" of the unknown island is and is only a man, a naked man, reduced to his body and face, a shipwrecked man, and, in a remarkable symmetry, the previous king of the island is a "lost" king, erring, unfindable—a double echo of a fundamental double theme in the *Thoughts*: "A king without diversion is a man full of misery'' (137-142); "but all of that misery . . . is . . . the misery of a dispossessed king" (116-398). We know that Pascal understood by "king's diversion" all that fills the intervals in the prince's affairs and movements, all that occupies his rest, for rest is the void, and the void, necessarily, is the return onto itself of reflection and, with it, the view of man's misery. If the king's diversion is at once what pulls him out of himself and what is put in the place of the vertiginous void of auto-reflection, it appears indeed as the king's por-trait and *pour-trait* ["for-trait"], his portrait, which characterizes him as such; and inversely, the specific misery of man, the one that characterizes his condition, "proves his greatness. It is the misery of a great lord, the misery of a dispossessed king" (116-398) that defines, in the optical sense of the word, the negative of a lost original or, better perhaps, that of a model that has retired into secrecy. "What is nature in animals we call misery in man; whereby we recognize that his nature being today the same as that of animals, he has fallen from a better nature that was once his own. For who finds himself unhappy not to be king if not a dispossessed king? . . . Perseus was found to be so unhappy at no longer being king because his condition was to be one always, [so much so] that it seemed strange that he could bear to go on living" (117-409). The king without the accompaniments and the *essential* circumstances of diversion, without his kingly portrait, is only a man full of misery, but the miserable man is a dispossessed king. The man is a king who has lost his kingdom, and the king is a man who has become diversion: his portrait.

From these symmetrical and inverted propositions we will deduce that the whole difference between the king and the man is that it is in the very definition of the kingly condition to be representation in representation without end, whereas that of the man is to have lost his royal dignity forever. Also Pascal constructed a fictive proof, a simulated representation, a figure, that of a king who, while being king, would be without diversion; the king, then, is no longer king but only a miserable man (137-142). Still this simulation model is only the mirrored projection, the specular image of a "real" anthropological experience, that of the *dispossession* of the man who has lost his own place, the domain of which he was king; he is a king, but in exile on an earth without borders, wandering in a foreign world, shipwrecked in a space without limits—an erring that Pascal calls, with Christian tradition, "original sin." The "political" fiction of the king without diversion, a man full of misery, is the anthropological figure of the man disappropriated of his own being, a king who has lost his kingdom, a king who is lost. Consequently, the king deprived of his portrait, where the miserable reality of man is revealed, is the *portrait of the dispossessed king*, dispossessed of his dignity as king, which presents the traces and traits of the "native" greatness of man.

Pascal's third letter to the Roannez (in September or October of 1656) will resound with the same echoes, but in other harmonies.[15] At the time of "the persecution that is being prepared not only against individuals (which would be a small thing) but also against truth, it is no lie, God is indeed abandoned'' by his own, but "God has kept hidden servants for himself, as he said to Elijah." Now, in order to discern the just man, that is to say, grace in the worldly event and profane history, God "wants us to judge grace through nature and . . . , just as a prince driven out of his country by his subjects feels profound tenderness for those who have remained faithful to him during the political revolt, it seems that God considers with a particular benevolence those who defend today the purity of religion and morality that is so strongly opposed.''[16] But the analogical parallelism between theology and politics stops there. For "there is this difference between earthly kings and the King of kings, that princes do not make their subjects loyal, but rather they find them that way; [*completely empirical positivity of the political institution and the social bonds that it regulates*] whereas God never finds men other than unfaithful, and when they are faithful, he has made them that way." In other words, the prince's subjects are loyal to him because of the institution (*thesei*) and God's creatures are unfaithful to Him by nature (*phusei*).

However, the consequence that Pascal draws from that is extremely serious, less in the theological register than in the political one: "Such that whereas kings have a signal *obligation* to those who remain obedient to him, it happens, on the contrary, that those who subsist in God's service are themselves *infinitely indebted* to Him."[17] Legitimate power, we will have noted, has a signal obligation to the subjects who remain submissive to it: submission to power is institutional, thus arbitrary, and the subjugation of subjects to the king opens up for the latter a *debt* of recognition and "tenderness." Which signifies precisely also that, if submission to power is institutional—it is civil society—political revolt is natural—it is the state of nature—without its being for all that a right. In return, men, God's creatures, are unfaithful to Him by "postlapsary" nature (or in the state of fallen nature). But in the ecclesiastical institution, in the mystical body, in "the church" outside of which there is only "malediction," God makes them faithful. Meanwhile, this faithfulness, given graciously by the effect of infinite divine mercy, is never "instituted" once and for all. Grace is necessary for the least movement of faithfulness. Man's faithfulness to God creates his infinite obligation toward God, and it is in this way that the king's signal debt toward his subjects in political society is the worldly or profane reverse side of man's infinite debt toward God in the community of faith.

The third letter to the Roannez thus formulates, through a new disproportional proportion, a second approach to the political problem in which the anthropological question is grasped in its relationship to the religious world: from then on the king without diversion—the fictive proof of simulation—has become the king dispossessed of his kingdom by public revolt—a real historical experience—and the latter is not the image of the erring man outside of his own place, not the portrait of a lost greatness, but the figure of God abandoned by His own in the persecution of truth, for God has kept hidden servants for Himself, whom He has graciously maintained in faithfulness. (Pascal writes: "I pray God that we will be well with him and as we should, in spirit and in truth and with sincerity."[18]) For God abandoned by His own is also God who has retired into his secrecy, and the secret servant He has kept for himself is also the one to whom he reveals Himself. And Pascal writes in the following letter to the Roannez (at the end of October 1656): "Let us give Him infinite thanks, for, having hidden Himself in all things for others, He has revealed Himself in all things and in so many ways for us."[19] The figure of the King driven out by his subjects thus functions as a sort of anamorphotic *portrait* of God according to a double point of view: we recognize there either the just man, the true just man abandoned by his own in persecution and, with him, the mystery of Jesus Christ suffering and "in agony until the end of the world"; or the just man, the true just man "who dwelled unknown among men . . . , with no difference on the outside," who retires into secrecy; or—to come back to the first discourse—the shipwrecked man, the lost king.

The rapprochement of these few texts by Pascal with the discourses on the condition of the greats thus makes, in the articulation of the political problem with the anthropological question, on the one hand, and with the theological position, on the other, the portrait and secrecy appear to be fundamental operators of the disproportion of homologies, of the disparity of comparisons, and of the differentiation of structural analogies—the portrait in its relationship to the method of "figuratives," and secrecy in its relationship to that of representations in simulation. With the "image" proposed in the introduction to the first discourse, we have to contend with both of them. It is, in effect, at once a figure, a fiction, and a "figurative": it is a little imaginary narrative that wantonly gives itself its own elements out of sheer caprice, and by that it has a *function of dissimulating* truth, since it does not immediately yield the truth it proposes, the "concept" of the condition of *greatness*, but tells its story, puts it in narrative representation, and provokes the reader to interpretation without, however, being able to be completely satisfied by the one that is given to him ultimately, for the image does not take into interpretive account *all* the elements and *all* the relationships that narrative brings into play.

The "image" is also a fiction. I understand by that an explicative *model* that chooses in the situations of observation some relationships and terms in order to give, through *simulation of "reality,"* a valid general explanation for those particular situations, without being for all that an explanation through simulation that is exportable outside of those situations—the ones that are constituted by a determined social condition, "to be a great man," since the narrative tells the story of the institution of the great man par excellence, the king.

The "image" is finally a figurative in the Pascalian sense of the term, and that is perhaps its most important function, for as figurative it *puts aside a secret*, all while insinuating the marks of that operation essential to all secrecy that consists of *excluding the addressee from the secret message*, from the role of depositee of that secret.[20] The figurative is a cipher with two meanings, as "when coming upon an important letter where a clear meaning is found and where it is nonetheless said that the meaning is veiled and obscured, that it is hidden such that one will see this letter without seeing it, and understand it without understanding" (260-678). It is thus that a figurative carries a secret (a cipher with two meanings), and that in this sense a figurative is a portrait, "a portrait [that] carries absence and presence, pleasure and displeasure." And this image is that much more a portrait [*in the Pascalian sense of the term, at once figurative; a cipher with two meanings, a secret; fiction: an explaining model, a simulation; and figure: a narrative representation, a dissimulation*] and a secret in that what it tells is the history of a portrait, of a portrait-king, of a simulation, of a dissimulation, and of a secret of that portrait.

On the other hand, this "image" is propedeutic and didactic. It is didactic in that it contains, if we consider it attentively, all that is necessary to know the truth of the condition of greatness. It is, then, a question of knowledge, and of true knowledge: of theoretical truth. And yet it is only an illustration: not yet discourse of the concept but narrative of the imagination. More, it is only propedeutic: it is only a question of truly beginning to know the condition of greatness. But this true knowledge through image (thanks to its means and through them) is only the introduction to another activity, which is no longer theoretical knowledge but the practice of knowledge. The propedeutic through image indeed produces a true knowledge, but the latter is, moreover, the indication of a practice whose path it is limited to clearing—a method and knowledge that signify only in order to show. It is said or told only to open the field of an ethical and, more fundamentally, a religious prescription.

These are the three moments marked in the third discourse: that of the exit of propedeutic knowledge through the image ("I want *you to know*, sir, *your true condition*," and no longer, "*To enter into the true knowledge of your condition*, consider it in this *image*") into the true concept, the essential definition of "great lord" ("What does it mean . . . to be a great lord?")—a concept that implies a succession of ethical prescriptions ("Do not aspire then. . . . Content their just desires; alleviate . . . , make it your pleasure to . . . , advance them . . .").[21] But all of this discourse—the speculative propositions and ethical prescriptions that flow from them—is brutally interrupted in order to give way to the space of indication: "What I am telling you does not go very far. . . . You must . . . aspire to that kingdom of charity. . . . Persons other than myself will tell you the way."[22] A doubly ascetic indication: asceticism of the discourse, since it interrupts itself; and discourse of the ascetic, but belonging to others. From this point of view the *Three Discourses on the Condition of the Greats* have, by the very confession of their author, a detouring function, and in two ways: not only because they aim to detour their addressee away "from those brutal lives where I see that several persons of your condition have let themselves get carried away,"[23] but also because they keep the secret of the "kingdom of charity," which is, however, the essential one, whose call is the *secret* that the ethical prescriptions indicate, and which is perhaps, in the end, what the "image" that opens the first discourse—figure, fiction, figurative—indicates by hiding it.

I could certainly find other prescriptive utterances in the first and second discourses, but, like the initial image-narrative, I can analyze them simultaneously as a *screen dissimulating* the other prescription that is not said but only shown, and also as the *space of projection* and regulated transformation *of what the screen dissimulates*. What dissimulates the secret is at the same time the vehicle of the secret, its insinuation, and its "figurative." Indeed, the characteristic of the cipher with two meanings (that can be compared to the anamorphotic portrait) is that the clear meaning, which one reads immediately in the surprise letter, *dissimulates the second meaning but carries it inscribed* in the arrangement of its signs, a hidden second meaning that consists in the utterance clearly signifying that there is a hidden meaning, which is illegible and which "the manifest contrarieties" we find "in the literal sense" indicate. We will note an obvious example of this "double play" of the text as early as the imperative of the first sentence, "To enter into the true knowledge of your condition, consider it in this image," where the pronoun *it* refers back both to "true knowledge" (of your condition) and to "your condition." From then on if the "image" is the condition of fact and of right of true knowledge, it is because the son of the duc de Luynes will have considered the image that he will be able to have enter into true knowledge. There is access to truth only by mediation, detour, and the detouring of images. But at the same time the young duke will be able to see his condition as their very image, as fictive as that image that Pascal constructs at leisure: here is your portrait; it is "your" condition of greatness and the condition of the true knowledge of your condition. Here is the portrait of the king that you are, for you are properly a king (as portrait), but you do not yet know it, since you will have to wait until the end of the third discourse to learn that you are properly a king, of the same kind as the greatest kings of the earth.

Here, then, is the king's portrait. But the portrait is deferred, since the narrative of the shipwreck is beginning or, more exactly, since the portrait is the last sequence of a history that, like all tales with a happy ending, brings the resolution of an initial lack. This is to say that the portrait comes to occupy the place of that lack, to fill it, to hide and dissimulate not something or someone, but an absence. That portrait is not a mask but a re-presentation. Nevertheless it does not happen to the narrative from the outside: it is very precisely the end of the process by which it is constituted. Here is the king's portrait: "Consider your condition and its true knowledge in this narrative that tells the story of how the king's portrait was made in order to dissimulate, by its representation, an absence."

The first sequence is that of a double absence in the spaces of the maritime map and in the place of the island, that of the minimal initial conditions for the process of portraiture to begin. First, a man thrown by the storm onto an unknown island, a shipwrecked man who has lost companions, ship, fatherland, his origin erased in the violent agitation of the natural elements. This man is *pro-tractus*, pulled from the storm out of his own place, pro-duced by the violence of air and water onto an island unknown to him, which does not appear on his navigating map, with no trace or mark in the field of knowledge and which, by virtue of this, is even beyond foreignness. It is indeed in this way, at the end of the seventeenth century and during the following one, that the utopias and allegorical tales of the "statesman" will start. A storm is necessary to break the order of temporal continuity, and the blank of the *terrae incognitae* on the map, to signify the interval of difference itself in the spatial continuity that insularity still accentuates, so that the direct or inverted representation of the perfect society can be constructed: two means in the imaginary of closing off a sociopolitical ideal and of proposing its theory.

But to this first lack, that of the dereliction of the shipwreck, is added a second: for the king of the unknown island has also been lost; he has disappeared, erred from his way, shipwrecked perhaps, and the inhabitants in uneasiness were striving to find him. Two absences, then, but the second is less added to the first than it is, in a way, its specular complement. If the man has been shipwrecked "now," the king had already been lost formerly, and if there is this difference between them, it is because the second is sought painfully by the island's inhabitants—they wish to find (and not to find-again) their lost king—while the first is forgotten, as we say, by God and men. The first three questions of place are thus posed by the narrative's first sequence: A man is thrown onto an unknown island. Although unknown, the island defines the place toward which and in which ends his journey. In return, we do not know where he comes from. The king of the island has been lost. He withdrew from the island where he was king, he absented himself from it. We indeed know from where he left, but to where? With what destination? Is it an exile, a wandering, an error, a loss? The inhabitants who dwell on the island seek their king to occupy its deserted center. They seek him on the island, supposing perhaps that their lost king dwells there, but in hiding. Thus the island of the shipwrecked man is, if I may dare say so, a place with a hole, since it has lost its center. Absent from the mapped spaces of knowledge, it is also institutionally and politically in a state of vacancy. The three "questions" of the place have been posed: *quo*? *ubi*? *unde*? That of the goal, that of the "here," and that of the origin. To each an answer has been given, but fragmentary. Where does the shipwrecked man come from? Where has the king gone in his loss? The "here itself" of the island is a void in its center. In return, there is one question that is excluded: that of the crossing without origin or end, journey in its "pure" state, *qua*? Through where? It is the absent and perhaps the

FINALE: THE LEGITIMATE USURPER □ 225

true question, the question of truth and justice that cannot be asked as such, since it is a matter, in this tale, of instituting and constituting, of making a state, of constructing a power, a king.

A triple spatializing process: the shipwrecked man, the king, the inhabitants; we know that the pathways of space can postulate an order of places, and an order of places can imply a pathway of space. The shipwrecked man is the first operator of pathways whose place of origin is undefined and place of destination unknown (to him). The king is the second operator of pathways whose place of origin is determined (the island, his kingdom) but place of destination undefined: where did he get lost? Between the two, an empty place, the island, which, left empty by the king's disappearance, is found that way by the irruption of the shipwrecked man, and which the inhabitants wish to fill. The *terminus ad quem* of the shipwrecked man's "journey," an *unknown* place, is the *terminus a quo* of the king's "journey," an *empty* place, the place of the island's inhabitants' *desire*. The unknown, the thing absent from knowledge, is the same place as the lack, the thing absent from desire and absent from knowledge, the place unknown to the latter, is going to be hidden by the lure of the desire of others. In truth, it could not be a question of the *same* place, since it appears only at the term of two different processes: a double place of the difference between the lack of a knowledge and the lack of a desire, the island manifests itself, in the place of its identity, not as a being, a geographical, spatial and political reality, but as the constitutive negation of a double difference between knowledge and will (desire) and between anthropology (man) and politics (the king), since: (1) the shipwrecked man *does not know* where he is, and the inhabitants *lack* a king; and (2) the shipwrecked man is a "man full of misery," and the king is a lost king, dispossessed of his kingdom. From now on, the structure of the portrait as lure is inscribed in the insular apparatus that must serve him as frame and support, in the form of a double absence in knowledge and will, in the theoretical (where am I?) and the practical ("I desire a master"), in a place qualified at once by the irruption of the *event hic et nunc*, "a man is thrown by the storm onto an unknown island," and by the memory of a *history*, a kingdom "whose king *had been lost* and whose inhabitants were at pains to find him." The portrait will aim to join in its *semblance* these negative dualities in internal and reciprocal contrarieties — knowing and wanting, anthropology and politics, event and history — and to reconcile them in a representation that is power, in a power that is representation. But it will be only an attempt, an attempt incessantly reiterated to suture the hiatuses, to identify the differences, to unify the dualities, since all the political, ethical, and religious injunctions and prescriptions coming out of the consideration of the portrait will only open them up and make them work.

The second sequence of the narrative is that of the constitution of the portrait as king and of the king as portrait, but in favor of chance, the chance of an accident, that of the profound resemblance of the shipwrecked man's body and face to those of the king who is lost. It is thanks to that chance and that accident that he is taken for the king and recognized in that quality by all the population. We should ask here, and before every other consideration, if this strange coincidence, if this mysterious chance, if this astonishing accident of *resemblance* are not themselves, and all told, a lure of the narrator aiming to detour a too quick interpretation or, maybe even more, a mark of the infinitely destructive irony of all representation in the discourse of the clever man.

For we will agree that chance, that coincidence, that accident greatly weaken the demonstrative, propedeutic, and didactic quality of the parable-image. No doubt Pascal, in the explicit interpretation he proposes to his interlocutor, will insist on chance:

> Do not imagine that it is by a lesser accident that you possess the wealth of which you happen to be the master than that by which that man happens to be king. . . . Is it not by a thousand accidents that your ancestors acquired and preserved it? . . . It is only from this encounter with chance that you were born, by the whim of laws favorable with respect to you that puts you in possession of all those things.[24]

But the accidents that Pascal evokes (the infinity of accidents) concern precisely the *series* of chained chance events of which the last was the birth of Charles-Honoré de Chevreuse, son of the duc de Luynes. For Pascal, it is not enclosed for all eternity in the monad of Charles-Honoré that he will be the son of a duke, at the end of a divine calculation *de maximis* and *minimis*. And the order by which Charles-Honoré de Chevreuse finds himself the proprietor of great property "is only founded on the sole will of the legislators who could have had good reasons, but of which none is taken from a natural right" that he would have to those things: a fantasy of favorable laws with respect to him that chance made the son of a duke.

Also the chance that this explicit interpretation is indeed rather that of the encounter of a shipwrecked man on an island whose inhabitants are at pains to find their king who was lost, the encounter of two independent causal series—as the birth of Charles-Honoré depends "on all the marriages of those you descend from," and those "on a visit made by an encounter, a discourse in the air, a thousand unpredictable accidents," and as his wealth depends on the "encounter with chance that you were born, by the whim of laws favorable with respect to you." In truth, the resemblance of the shipwrecked man and the king is not made by *tuchè*, but as rigorous consequence of *automaton*: it is the hallucination of presence in the representation of desire. The latter, which is the desire for the master, for the lost king as representation, *produces* his resemblance on the object that is only its support. The shipwrecked man does not resemble the lost king, but it is the king who, because lost and because desired to the extent of that loss, resembles himself "onto" the shipwrecked man who arrives unexpectedly. Quite exactly, the portrait does not resemble the king: it resembles itself as king "onto" the shipwrecked man. It is by that and by that alone that the man will be portrait of the king.

The shipwrecked man is not the "double" or "replica" of the lost king. He resembles him very much but not completely. There is between the "resembler" and the "resembled" the vestige of a difference, that existing between "very much" and "totally." Still, that difference between the man and the king is indiscernible, or, at least, only the narrator, who tells and stages this story for us, is capable of discerning it, and not the island's inhabitants who are at pains to find their king, and maybe *because* they are at pains. In other words, the "chance" of the resemblance posed by the narrator is one with the difference indiscernible to the "narrated" (the island's inhabitants) in the sense that the effect of chance of the similarity flows strictly from the reduction of difference to identity through the desire to fill the void in the central place of the island. The desire to have the master *produces* the man who arrives unexpectedly (in all the difference between a shipwrecked man and a king) as the *same* as the lost king, as erasing all possible comparison: incomparable. This comparison is maintained only by the narrator, but at the price of constituting its object as chance: the shipwrecked man resembles the king very much, but only very much. We will note, then, that this difference that can be very small, that must be infinitely small, is at the same time infinite difference, for it is that which makes all the difference that one is not the other, that the shipwrecked man is totally and absolutely different from the king. Through his resemblance undiscerned as resemblance in the lure of an identity, the shipwrecked man "as" king reveals in its truth and efficacity the self-production of infinite representation as absolute power.

The shipwrecked man resembles the king in body and face very much. Pascal distinguishes thus two planes of resemblance, the body and the face, which refer back to two registers constituting the portrait: the portrait of the face and the full-length portrait of the body and face. We will note that there can be no portrait of the body without the face, while the reverse is not true. In representation, the body makes an individual with the face but not without it, while the face makes an individual without the body. Now, in the "real," the body is as individual as the face, like it suspended on the ultimate difference, inconceivable end of an infinite division where individuality itself is constituted, its singular and incomparable identity. A thought, besides, asks the question of the infinite difference of the body, a difference that, in its inexhaustible process, makes of the body a single identity. But in a fashion perhaps less strange than it might appear this thought unifies, in the same analogical approach, body, landscape, and God, on the one hand, and, on the other, the language that attempts to say them: "Diversity.... A man is a substance, but if you dissect him, what would he be? Head [but not the face], heart, veins, stomach, each vein, each bit of vein, each humor of the blood?'' And also: ''Theology is a science, but at the same time how many sciences? . . . A city, a countryside, from far off is a city and a countryside; but as one approaches, they become houses, trees, tiles, leaves, grass, ants, legs of ants, to infinity. All of that is included in the word *countryside*'' (65-115), as above the infinity of sciences under the name of *theology*, and the infinity of the parts and elements of the body under that of *body*; and maybe even more *under the name that is "proper"* to this infinity of singularity, to this infinite comparability that the term that names it ''properly'' poses as absolutely incomparable. ''Jesus Christ'' for theology, *this toponym* for city or countryside, *this name* and also *this face* for the body. Name and face make of the man a *substance* and a substance, *one*, a single and individual substance where both are delegates in the representation of language or image.

It is in this way that the shipwrecked man is taken for the king. He is *gazed upon as* the king by the island's inhabitants. There would be dupery on their part if he were tricking them. But it is they who are tricking themselves. With no intention on his part or deliberate will, he then simulates the king, he feigns to be the person he is not. The error is a mistake for them and an ''objective'' simulation for him. Thus the shipwrecked man, resembling so much the body and face of the king lost and desired that he is taken for him, introduces into the narrative the problem of the sign, that is to say, very precisely that of the portrait.

> When one considers an object in itself and in its own fbeing without bringing to mind what it can represent [*and all objects can represent another, the world of beings and things is potentially representation, but what is this potential, what is this power, and what are the conditions or circumstances of its use?*], the idea one has of it is an idea of a thing, like the idea of the earth, of the sun [*and the earth can be an island, a kingdom, and the sun can be a king, the king*]. But then one looks upon a certain object only as representing another, the idea that one has of it is an idea of sign, and this first object is called ''sign.'' It is in this way ordinarily that one looks at maps and pictures [*but the kingdom-island is not on the map, and the king lost to the extent of his subjects' desire is becoming picture*]. Therefore the sign contains two ideas, one of the thing that represents, the other of the thing represented, and its nature consists of exciting the second with the first [*thus we saw that a shipwrecked man is taken for a king*].[25]

But the story that introduces the first discourse is not the simple illustration of the definition of the sign according to the Port-Royal *Logic* in chapter 4 of the first part, for, since it is a question of the recognition and nomination of one by the others because of his resemblance, this story is also the illustration of the propositions where one can give to signs the name of the things signified under certain conditions that the *Logic* specifies in chapter 14 of the second part:

It is a question of knowing when one has the right to do it principally with respect to institutional signs, for, with respect to natural signs, there is no difficulty, because the visible rapport that there is between those sorts of signs and things marks clearly that when one affirms of the sign the thing signified, one means to say, *not that this sign is really that thing*, but that it is such in signification and in figure. And thus one will say without preparation and offhandedly of Caesar's portrait that it is Caesar, and of a map of Italy that it is Italy.[26]

And at the end of the chapter the logicians introduce, in order to conclude this supplementary remark, that "one must distinguish highly between the expressions where one uses the thing's name to mark the sign, as when one calls a picture of Alexander by the name of Alexander, and those where the sign being marked by its own name or noun (or by a pronoun), one affirms the thing signified by it."[27] For this rule — that the mind of those to whom one is speaking must already look at the sign as sign and be at pains to know what it is the sign of — does not conform to the first kind of expression [*of Caesar's portrait one says very legitimately that it is Caesar*] but only to the second, where one expressly affirms of the sign the thing signified. (Thus, "Daniel answered . . . Nebuchadnezzar that he was the golden head: because he had proposed to him the dream that he had had of a statue that had a golden head and because he had asked him its significance."[28])

The shipwrecked man is a sign of the lost king in the sense that a portrait of Caesar or Alexander is a sign of (dead) Caesar or Alexander and, in front of this "king's portrait," the inhabitants say without preparation and offhandedly that it is the king, but, unlike the example of the Port-Royal *Logic*, in their mistake they do not speak in signification and in figure. Only the shipwrecked man knows it, since he knows that he is not the king that these inhabitants uneasily seek. He knows it, but he says nothing, or, even better, he discovers, precisely at the moment when the inhabitants say, in front of him, "It is the king," that he is only his sign and figure. The inhabitants, who know nothing and who, in their desire to find the king, take him for him, think according to the thing: they think the presence of the being itself; they consider him in himself and in his own being without bringing the mind's eye to what he can represent. The idea they have of him is the idea of their king. The shipwrecked man and the island's inhabitants, through the difference between what one thinks and the others say ("I am the king's portrait," "You are the king"), operate the cleavage of the formula consecrating the Eucharist in Catholic theology: "The Apostles, not looking at the Bread as a sign and not being at pains as to what it signified [*thus the island's inhabitants in front of the shipwrecked man but, as opposed to the Apostles' taking the bread for bread, they take him for their king as shipwrecked man*], Jesus Christ would not have been able to give to the signs the name of the things without speaking against the usage of all men and without tricking them"[29] by saying, "This is my body" in the sense of figure and not in that of reality—thus the inhabitants saying, "This man here is my king" in the sense of reality, as opposed to the man, a true anti-Christ, who will let them say that he is the king when he is only his portrait. Nevertheless, for the island's inhabitants, as opposed to the Eucharistic symbols for the faithful of the Catholic community, the shipwrecked man does not hide the body and face of the king as thing when uncovering him as symbol.[30] For them, the *thing* (bread) has not become *something other* (the body of Jesus Christ) while becoming *sign* (sacramental bread): thing-sign in the mystery of the sacrament while being thing-sign of the spiritual food that is the body of Jesus Christ and the union of the faithful in the mystical body.

The king in his portrait, the king as portrait, the portrait-king, the truth of the infinite representation of political power and the absolute monarch as representation, is a parody of the Eucharistic mystery, the mystic body and the real presence, a parody that the encounter reveals, played and put into representation by Pascal in the place left empty by an absence, between a man thrown by the storm onto an unknown island and the subjects of a kingdom its king has deserted. Thus a king of concupiscence is the inverted image of the king of charity. It is this true knowledge that the author of the discourses will make known, in the third one, to his interlocutor: God "is properly the king of charity. . . . You are . . . properly a king of concupiscence. Your kingdom is of small expanse [*only an island*]; but you are equal, in that, to the greatest kings on earth; they, like you, are kings of concupiscence."[31] What is played at the beginning of the first discourse with the shipwrecked man, the lost king, and the island's inhabitants, what is staged with the constitution of the portrait-king, is at once the founding of political power, its authority and legitimacy as representation and power, and its symptomatic value, its function as indication of truth and justice of which it is the catastrophic inversion; but it is on this reversal that is founded "the economy of the world that he [man] wants to govern. Will it be on the whim of each private person? What confusion! Will it be on justice? He does not know" (60-294).

Also the king who was lost, the true king of the island, the king of charity, is he perhaps not lost, as his subjects think and believe? Maybe he is hidden in

> that strange secrecy God has withdrawn into, impenetrable to men's sight. . . . He stayed hidden under the veil of the nature that covers us until the Incarnation; and when he was to have appeared, he hid himself even more by covering himself with humanity. . . . And finally, when he wanted to fulfill the promise that he made to his Apostles to stay with men until his last coming, he chose to stay there in the strangest and most obscure secrecy of all, which is the species of the Eucharist. . . . There is the last secrecy where he can

be. . . . To recognize him under species of bread belongs only to Catholics: it is only us that God enlightens to that point.[32]

It is thus that Pascal's parable-narrative *stangely* communicates the religious formula of Eucharistic consecration: "this is my body"; the juridical formula of political consecration: "the state is me"; and the rhetorical formula of mimetic consecration: "that is Caesar, that is the king" in front of their portraits.

The shipwrecked man is recognized in the quality of king by the whole population. Not only is he taken for him by the island's inhabitants, but he is recognized. It is not a question of a simple redundancy, of a pure pleonasm. The redoubling marks the distinction between the *fact of the "mistake,"* which is constitutive of the royal portrait and of the portrait-sign as king, and the *legitimation* that juridically founds the portrait-sign in its authority as official portrait, the king in his dignity as King. After the mimetic "forming," here is the moment of the juridical "performing." By that itself, the shipwrecked man who was *like* the king (who was lost) is henceforth like the *King*. We see how Pascal displaces, radically and in a critical fashion, the doctrine of the king's two bodies that was the theologico-political foundation of the king's right until their impossible union, the phantasmatic transubstantiation of one body into the other attempted by the absolute monarch. The distinction between the physical body of the king and the politico-mystical body of the King, or that between the "real" individual body and the body of fictive or representational dignity, finds, in this Pascalian text, a new and "strange" meaning to the extent that one—the physical, individual body—finds its function only in the space of the *mistake* (the sign is taken for the referent, the representative for the being itself) and that the other—the political, mystical, and representative body—finds its own function only in the place of *usurpation*. The person who is not and cannot be king is recognized in that quality by the whole assembled population, a place where the mistake that characterizes the structural potential power of the portrait-sign (structurally, the portrait *is* always in some fashion the person it represents) receives its status as legitimate authority, although wrongly or abusively; in short, representation and its power (the portrait is always in some fashion a *marker of power*).

Yet at the same time it is at that moment that the lost king whom the inhabitants believe has returned is reenthroned as king. Beforehand, he was only shipwrecked, with no insignia or signs other than natural ones—his extreme resemblance in body and face. He is the shipwrecked man taken for the individual king who was lost. The island's inhabitants themselves put into play the doctrine of the king's two bodies (and even more precisely because, for them, the shipwrecked man *is* the king): having recognized in his body and face the shipwrecked man as *the* king who was lost—the first meaning of "to recognize," to know once more by certain signs or marks someone or something one already knows—they recognize him in the quality of *King* that he was before his disappearance—second meaning of "to recognize," to submit oneself to a person's authority. The double process that the narrative marks refers back to the two dimensions of representation in general. With the naked—body and face—shipwrecked man, the inhabitants make the absent, the lost king (but in representation), come back, with the difference that they believe that the image is the thing itself. Come back, the king represents the King, royalty in and by his very presence. He is present as king and has the right to be King. Representation, in this curious story, is at once the imaginary return of the dead man, his resurrection in image, and the symbolic right of his presence, the law of his authority and the authority of his law.

The distinction that the inhabitants make between the two processes of recognition reproduces the bifacial structure of the sign, that portrait-sign the shipwrecked man himself recognized himself to be when, upon seeing him, the inhabitants said without preparation and offhandedly: that is the king. But this structure, which is then already existent (in the narrative and for the man thrown by the storm: "I am the portrait-sign of their king"), is reproduced on another level of the representational framework, that of its legitimation or power and, more precisely, in its juridical institutional dimension: what is has the right to be what it is.

A confirmation of this commentary is given to us by the transformation, introduced by the narrative, of "the islands' inhabitants" into "the whole population." From the first to the second sequence of the tale we have passed from the geographical and social notion—the inhabitants, those who dwell on the island—to the political and juridical notion—the population, the popular body. The island's inhabitants are constituted as political body (of the king) when they recognize the shipwrecked man (whom they take for the king who was lost) in the quality of King. In and through this recognition, whose consensus is total and unanimous, the sum of the inhabitants has become an organic unity at the moment when it is a source of right, the right of the king to be King. It is certainly appropriate that commentary should not exceed the narrative text that is its object, but one will have remarked that the "usurpation" does not appear as an endeavor of the usurper. The taking of power that the narrative describes is not the operation of a tyrant: it does not manifest the "desire for domination, universal and outside of its order," nor the will to "have by one avenue what can only be had by another" (58-332). The taking of power is a mechanism that unfolds all alone, independently of the intentions of the "shipwrecked man's" will or desire. In truth, the taking of power is the fact of the *desire* of those over whom power is exerted, and the king's official portrait, which constitutes and institutes him King, is in some way the image by which the desire is taken on for the subjugation of a whole population aching for a master.

Hence the last sequence of the story itself articulated as two moments, that of hesitation and that of decision: "At first he did not know which part to take; but he resolved himself finally to lend himself to his good fortune. He received all the respects they offered him, and let himself be treated as king."[33] Either to undeceive the people: "I am not the king you are seeking," or else to *laisser faire*, "to let himself be treated as king"—such is the alternative, the source of the hesitation: either to disappoint the desire of all of them, but to be truthful, or else to satisfy a common will, to fill the void with a unanimous desire, but to trick. But the machine is too well mounted to let there be a true choice, and if the wait is prolonged, the private hesitation of the "prince" takes the public figure and appearance of a retreat of majesty into the silence of wisdom and the secrecy of his government.

Consequently, the resolution to lend himself to fortune can only be interior and "all spiritual." Nothing in the situation manifests it on the outside, and the deliberate decision to fall into lying and injustice is indiscernible from what would have been the king's return in the spirit of truth and justice. The usurper has only to let himself be [*laisser être*] by letting the population do [*laisser faire*] in order to enter and maintain himself in the place of usurpation. The simple flow of time simultaneously precipitates him into injustice and founds him in legitimate royalty. For, in truth, what does it mean to be King, if not to be recognized in that quality by the whole population and to receive all the respects that must be paid to the King? What does it mean to be King if not to be treated as King? The King is a King's portrait contemplated with respectful admiration by the unanimous population. It is enough that the portrait resemble itself and that time pass. For if "it is a horrible thing to feel all one possesses drain away" (757-212), on the other hand, there is no possession that the time of usage does not assure.

> One man says that the essence of justice is the legislator's authority, another the sovereign's convenience, another present custom; and it is the most sure: nothing is just in itself *by following reason alone*, everything shifts with time. Custom is the whole of equity, for the sole reason that it is accepted; that is the mystic foundation of its authority. Anyone who tries to bring it back to its principle annihilates it. Nothing is as defective as those laws that correct defects. Anyone who obeys them because they are just is obeying the justice that he imagines, but not the essence of law, which is self-contained; it is law and nothing more. Anyone wanting to examine the motive will find it so feeble and trivial that, if he is not used to contemplating the prodigies of human imagination, he will admire that one century had acquired for it so much pomp and reverence. . . . [The people] must not sense the truth about the usurpation. It was introduced formerly without reason, and it has become reasonable; it must be looked upon as authentic and eternal, and its beginning must be hidden, if one does not want it to come soon to an end (60-294).

What is for the "shipwrecked-king" a beginning is for the assembled people another beginning or, more precisely, the resumption of a continuity, of an instituted tradition, after the momentary accident of a vacancy; and the time of the former's hesitation to lend himself to his good fortune is the double figure at once of the uncertainty and confusion of the origins of all institutions and of the effect of the duration that makes all usurpation not only reasonable but legitimate.

But at the same time the involuntary usurper, by accepting the legitimation of his usurpation through the deception of a whole people, fills their wait, appeases their uneasiness, fulfills their desire for a king: a strange desire and a surprising will. If we believe the fragment we have just cited at length, "the people easily lend an ear" to the critical discourses of established customs that sound "down to their source in order to mark their want of authority and justice. . . . They [the people] shake the yoke as soon as they recognize it, and the great take advantage of it to their ruin and to that of those curious examiners of received customs" (60-294). But the king's disappearance was not the critical examination of the legitimacy of his power. On the contrary, his absence had no other effect than to reinforce the lack to the point of hallucinating his presence, as I have suggested.

Still, that is to describe things and not to give them an explanation. The third discourse brings it. "What does it mean, in your opinion, to be a great lord?"— and the great lord is "properly a king . . . equal . . . to the greatest kings on earth." What does it mean to be a king? "It is to be master of several objects of men's concupiscence and thus to be able to satisfy the needs and desires of several men." And Pascal specifies: "It is those needs and desires that attract them to your side and that make them submit themselves to you: without that they would not even look at you; but they hope, through the services and deference they render you, to obtain from you some share of those things they desire and that they see are at your disposal."[34] It is concupiscence that makes the king's power, that is to say, Pascal goes on to explain, "the possession of those things that men's cupidity desires."[35]

The king, I have said, is a king's portrait contemplated with a respectful admiration by a unanimous population. All together, they draw the prince's portrait, a portrait they present to him—and the presentation of that representation is called respect, love, loyalty—all sentiments that accompany the reiterated position of the institution of right. But they present him with the portrait they have drawn from his body and face only to draw from him wealth and honors, to obtain from him "some share of those things they desire and that they see are at his disposal." The Pascalian analysis of the mechanism of representation and power, of representation as power and of power as representation, joins with what Hegel will say of the absolute monarch: "Considered as it is *in itself*, state power that is reflected into itself, or has become Spirit, simply means that it has become a moment of self-consciousness. That is, it exists only as *super-*

seded . . . essence . . . wealth, into which it is ever changing in accordance with its Notion; but it is a reality whose Notion is just this process of passing over— by way of the service and honor done to it—. . . into its opposite, into the relinquishment of power." He is left only with "the empty name," a name and an exchange; he gratifies their desire for subjugation with the objects of concupiscence of which he is master.[36]

> But, as he could not forget his natural condition, he reflected, at the same time as he was receiving those respects, that he was not the king these people sought and that this kingdom did not belong to him. Thus he had a double train of thought: one by which he acted as king, the other by which he recognized his true state and recognized that it was only chance that had put him in the place where he was. He hid this last train of thought and revealed the other. It was by the former that he dealt with the people and by the latter that he dealt with himself.[37]

End of the story, ultimate sequence, stable institution, foundation of law and authority, legitimate power. Here really is resolved the alternative of usurpation of the one in the deception of the others, or the dereliction of the man and the abandonment of the people, by a double thesis that is not a synthesis of reconciliation or totalization but their tension, where resides all the secrecy of absolute power in the infinity of its representation; and yet this self-alienation appears paradoxically as the resolution of a contradiction between right and fact and between truth and justice, on the one hand, and between lie and iniquity, on the other.

This tension that affects the interior and the exterior, the private and the public, opposes at the same time the hidden thought and the revealed thought, the secret and truest one and the one that is public action but wrong. Consequently, the political domain finds itself split, in immanent fashion, between its own field, which is that of the lie and *piperie* to the subjugated people by the person who governs them, and a section of that domain that, put aside and apart, constituted in secret, is that of the retreat of the political into the ethical, itself defined very generally as reflection of the self onto itself, as position of the self of the subject in reflection. The ethical is obtained by an operation of internal exclusion—if I may dare this expression—of the political; it is the secrecy of the political, or again the retreat of the subject of the political outside of the political itself by reflection onto itself. The ethical is the secrecy of the political in the sense that it is constituted by the place where the political absents itself from itself, the place that is nevertheless that of the substance-subject of the political. Substituted for this retreat, replacement and supplement of this re-traction, there is the king's portrait as the King himself, as the absolute instance of political power in its representation.

What is the content of this ethical reflection that alienates the political through and through while assigning its subject in this self-alienation? It is at first that of a memory, which happens to take the form of the impossibility of a forgetting under pain of stupidity and folly, the necessary negation of negation: "as he could not forget his natural condition . . ." The self-alienated thought, the hidden thought of the self-alienation, is at first a negation of negation and a necessary negation. A memory that is memory itself, since it is that of substantial identity, is thus constituted in this strange detour of a primitive negation of an even stranger negation, a forgetting that would indeed be the mark of a "strange reversal in the nature of man" (427-194). "Is there less of it [stupidity and folly] in persons of condition who live in such a strange forgetfulness of their natural state?"[38] A new reversal: the impossibility of forgetting one's natural condition is the fact of a figure and a figurative in the story, the model and cipher of a shipwrecked man become and recognized king of an unknown island. The necessary negation of negation in fiction is fictive, and reality is indeed that—primitive— of the strange reversal of nature that the double negation in the fiction indicates by inversion.

From then on, if the ethical retreat into the political is marked at first by this "memory," and if this "memory" is a fiction of the figure and the figurative, this indicates inversely that, in the "real," this retreat is not effected and that there is then never anything of the ethical by internal exclusion of the political, that there is never anything of the ethical in/outside of the political, that there is never anything of the ethical but only of the political through and through. Also, what the followers of Machiavelli and Tacitus in that century named the prince's secret, the secrets of state, the *arcana imperii*, in order to characterize the absolute of power,[39] we see how Pascal turns it around and inverts it in the ethical secret, the internal retreat of the political but only as a figure, a fiction of a stranger secret that the third discourse will designate, which is no longer ethical but religious, which is no longer that of an ethical subject *of* the political (the good king, the enlightened despot) but that of the King of kings in his order of charity.

But what is, in its turn, the content of this "memory," the impossible forgetting of his "proper" self? It is the natural condition of man, the shipwrecked man of space without limits in the prison without walls of the unknown island.

> I see the frightening spaces of the universe that enclose me, and I find myself attached to one corner of this vast expanse, without knowing why I have been put in this place rather than in another, or why this little bit of time that is given to me to live is assigned to me at this point rather than at another in all the eternity that has preceded me and in all that follows me. I see only infinities on all sides, which enclose me like an atom and like a shadow that lasts only an instant with no return (427-194).

What, then, is this natural condition? A negation: I am not king, I do not possess this kingdom; that is to say, I am not what I am here and now, a king possessor of a kingdom. I am another, but who, then? This will not be said, except by this negation: my natural condition is to not be this king now; such is my negative certainty, such is the impossible forgetting of a negative identity that "undefines" the being itself and his identification of the subject. Maybe the shipwrecked man was a king whom the storm had dispossessed of his kingdom? Maybe he is destined to find once again his true throne and his legitimate kingdom? One certainty only: "He reflected, at the same time as he was receiving those respects, that he was not the king this people sought and that this kingdom did not belong to him."[40]

Thus the secret of the absolute monarch, the ethical secret, the retreat from the statesman in his portrait, the secret of the all-powerful king, is that he is not so; a hidden thought, never spoken, a thought that is perhaps never thought—and there would be the force of the figure, of the fiction, of the figurative, to think that thought—that of the impossibility of forgetting that he is not what he is. Not narrative or history, project or design: he is not what he is, but he was or will be it. The negative thought of the negation is not taken in time, and the "memory" that constitutes its content would be that of a substantial ontological identity, of a permanence of being, if it were not negation of being and of present condition: "Thus he had a double train of thought: one by which he acted as king, the other by which he recognized his true state. . . . He hid this last train of thought and revealed the other." We must indeed read "double train of thought," and in his instructions to the duke Pascal will repeat the expression: "You must have, like that man . . . a double thought";[41] a secret thought of secrecy (of truth and justice) is the hidden nucleus of the other one by which the king deals with the people and acts externally and publicly as king. And this nucleus is a nothing, a negation of the king-being, an annihilation of the *subject* of the political act and thought, of a political thought that is an external and public act, an annihilation of the king at the very moment he is fulfilled: a "presentification" of the death (of the king) in the performance of the royal act itself. The fragment quoted a little while ago, which seemed pathetically to describe the shipwrecked man of the unknown island, continued thus in effect:

> All I know is that I must soon die, but what I know least is this very death that I cannot avoid. Just as I do not know where I come from, so I do not know where I am going; and I know only that when I leave this world, I will fall forever either into nothingness or into the hands of an irritated God, without knowing which of these two conditions will be my eternal lot (427-194).

From then on, if the monarch is absolute only in the official portrait that his subjects draw of him and that they present in order to draw from him what they desire and what he alone possesses, if the king is only King in his portrait and if his secrecy, the secret thought of his secrecy, so secret that he does not think it, is that he is not what he is, the presence of his absence from himself, then this conjunction of portrait and secrecy which is that of infinite representation and absolute power signifies that the king in his portrait, the absolute monarch, is an empty monument, a cenotaph, a tomb that shelters no body but that is royal body in its very vacuity.

Portrait-secret, double figure: that at first of another tomb found empty one morning by the tearful women, and in the place of the body they had come to anoint in order to institute it in its absent presence of corpse, a message, a word: "He is not here, he is elsewhere, in Galilee where he precedes you as he said he would." But a figure also, the fantastic image of the subjects' desire for subjugation to the absolute power of the monarch, because this image is also the fetish that at once guarantees and ensures the appropriation and consumption of the king's substance by the members of his body in a sort of autophagy, of self-destruction, which reveals in the political and historical body, but while parodying it, the strangest and most obscure secrecy of all, where the King of kings chose to remain until his last coming, still a tomb but also hidden manna and the bread of life of the mystical community of his faithful.

Appendix

Donkey Skin

A Tale

To Madame La Marquise de L***

There are people whose narrow-mindedness
    Beneath an ever-wrinkled frowning brow
    Only bears, approves, or prizes
    The stately and the sublime.
    As for me, I dare propose that in fact,
At certain moments, the most perfect being
Can love even Puppets without blushing
    And that there are times and places
    Where what is grave and serious
    Is not worth as much as agreeable nonsense.
    Why should we marvel
    That the most sensible Reason,
    Often weary with too much watching,
    Takes pleasure in sleeping,
    Ingeniously rocked
    By tales of Ogres and Fairies?

    Without fear, then, of being condemned
    For badly employing my leisure,
I will, to content your just desire,
Tell you Donkey Skin's entire story.

    Once upon a time there was a King,
    The greatest who ever was on Earth.
    Amiable in Peace and terrible in War,
    He was in the end comparable only to himself:

His neighbors feared him, his States were calm,
    And both Virtues and Fine Arts
    Could be seen in all directions,
    Flowering in the shade of his palms.
His lovely Half, his faithful Companion,
    Was so charming and beautiful,
With a spirit so accommodating and gentle,
    That with her he was more
    A happy spouse than a happy King.
    Of their tender and chaste Union
    A daughter was born,
So full of gentleness and charms and with so many virtues
    That they easily consoled themselves
  For not having had a more ample progeny.

    In his rich and vast Palace
    There was only magnificence.
It was teeming everywhere with a lively abundance
    Of Courtiers and Valets.
    In his Stables were
Large and small horses of all kinds,
    Covered with beautiful trappings
    Stiff with gold and embroidery.
But what surprised everyone upon entering
    Was that in the most conspicuous place
A Master Donkey displayed its two large ears.
    This injustice surprises you?
But when you know its matchless virtues,
You will not find the honor too great.
  So clean had Nature formed it
    That it never made any manure,
    But rather quite beautiful Crowns with a sun
    And Louis of all kinds
That were collected with a golden litter
    Every morning at its awakening.

    Now Heaven, which sometimes tires
    Of making men happy,
And which always mingles some disfavor with its good,
    Such as rain with good weather,
    Permitted a bitter illness

To suddenly attack the Queen in her prime.
    Help was sought everywhere,
But the Faculty that studied the Greek doctor
    And the current Charlatans
Together could not stop the fire
Kindled by the steadily growing fever.

    At her last hour
    The Queen said to the King her Spouse:
    "Allow me, before I die,
    To ask one thing of you:
    That if you should feel like
Remarrying when I am no longer here . . ."
    "Ah," said the King, "those cares are superfluous!
    I would never think of it,
    Be at rest on that count."
    "I well believe it," said the Queen,
"If I take your vehement love as witness;
    But to make me more certain of it
    I want to have your oath,
Softened however by this mitigation,
That if you meet a woman more beautiful,
    More shapely, and wiser than I,
You can give your faith to her freely
    And marry her."
    Her confidence in her attractions
Made her view such a promise
  As an oath, obtained with skill,
    To never marry.
His eyes bathed in tears, the Prince swore then
    All that the Queen wanted.
    The Queen died in his arms,
And never did a Husband create such an uproar.
To hear him sob night and day
It was thought that his mourning would not last long,
    And that he cried for his departed Love
Like a man in a hurry to be rid of a burden.

And this proved true. At the end of a few months
He wanted to proceed toward making a new choice,
    But it was no easy thing:
    He had to keep his oath,

That the new Spouse
Would have more attractions and charms
Than the one who had just been entombed.

Neither the Court rich in beauties,
Nor the Country, nor the City,
Nor the surrounding Kingdoms
Of which the rounds had been made
Could furnish such a one.
The Infanta alone was more beautiful,
And possessed certain tender charms
That the deceased had not.
The King himself noticed it
And, burning with an intense love,
Foolishly advised himself
That for this reason he must marry her.
He even found a Casuist
Who judged that the case could be proposed.
But the sad young Princess,
To hear speak of such a love,
Lamented and cried night and day.

Her heart full of a thousand sorrows,
She went to find her Godmother
In a secluded grotto far away,
Richly furnished with Mother of Pearl and Coral.
She was an admirable Fairy
Who never had an equal in her Art.
There is no need to tell you
What a Fairy was in those blessed times,
For I am sure that your Nanny
Will have told you during your earliest years.

"I know," she said, upon seeing the Princess,
"What makes you come here,
I know the profound sadness of your heart;
But with me you need no longer worry.
Nothing can harm you
So long as you let yourself be led by my advice.
Your Father, it is true, would like to marry you.
To listen to his foolish demand
Would be a great mistake indeed,

But without contradicting him you can refuse him.

    "Say to him that he must give you,
       To satisfy your desires and
Before you abandon your heart to his love,
A Dress that is the color of the Sky.
Despite all his power and wealth,
Though Heaven favors his wishes in all things,
He will never be able to fulfill his promise."

    Right away the young Princess
Went trembling to tell her amorous Father.
    In that same moment he gave
       His most important Tailors to understand
That if they did not make for him, without too long a wait,
A Dress the color of the Sky,
They could be sure he would have them all hanged.

  The second day had not yet dawned
    When the desired Dress was brought.
       The most beautiful blue of the Firmament
Is not, when girded with large golden clouds,
       Of a color more azure.
The Infanta, penetrated with joy and pain,
    Did not know what to say, or how
      To escape from her engagement.
        "Princess, ask for one,"
      Said her Godmother softly,
      "Which, more brilliant and less common,
      Is the color of the Moon.
      He will not give it to you."
Scarcely had the Princess made the request
      Than the King said to his Embroiderer,
"The star of Night must have no greater splendor,
And in four days without fail it must be brought to me."

The rich dress was made by the appointed day,
    Just as the King had declared it should be.
In the Sky where Night has unfolded its veils,
The Moon is less stately in its silver robe
Even when, at the middle of its diligent course,
Its most vivid brightness outshines the stars.

The Princess, admiring this marvelous dress,
Was almost resolved to consent;
    But, inspired by her Godmother,
    She said to the amorous Prince,
      "I could not be happy
If I do not have a Dress even more brilliant
    And the color of the Sun."
The Prince, whose love for her was without equal,
Had a rich Lapidarian come right away,
    And ordered him to make it
Of a superb fabric of gold and diamonds,
Saying that, if he failed in well satisfying him,
He would have him die in the midst of torments.

The Prince was spared the trouble,
    For the industrious worker,
    Before the end of the week,
  Had the precious work brought.
    It was so beautiful, so vivid, so radiant,
    That Clymene's blond Lover,
    As he moves across the Heavenly vault
    In his golden chariot,
Does not dazzle the eyes with a more brilliant splendor.

The Infanta, completely disconcerted by these gifts,
No longer knew what to answer her Father and King.
Her Godmother, right away taking her by the hand,
    Said in her ear, "You must not
    Pause now after such a good start.
    Are they such a great marvel,
  These gifts that you have received from him,
  As long as he has the Donkey you know about,
  That unceasingly fills his purse with gold crowns?
Ask him for the skin of this rare Animal.
    As it is his whole resource,
You will not obtain it, or I reason badly."

    This Fairy was quite learned,
    And yet she still did not know
That violent love, provided it is satisfied,
    Counts silver and gold as nothing.

The skin was gallantly granted as soon as
    The Infanta requested it.

    This Skin, when it was brought,
    Frightened her terribly
And made her complain bitterly of her fate.
Her Godmother appeared and showed her
That when we do the right thing, we need never fear
    And that the King must be led to think
    That she was entirely disposed
To submit with him to conjugal Law;
But that at the same time, alone and well-disguised,
She must leave for some faraway State
To avoid an evil so near and so certain.

"Here is," she continued, "a large chest
    Where we will put all your garments,
    Your mirror, your toilette,
    Your diamonds and your rubies.
    I also give you my Wand.
    If you hold it in your hand,
The chest will follow the same path as you
    Always hidden under the Earth;
    And when you want to open it,
Hardly will my rod have touched the Earth
Than it will offer itself immediately to your sight.

    The Donkey's skin
Is an admirable mask and will make you unrecognizable.
    Hide yourself well in it:
The skin is so frightful that no one will believe
    It encloses anything beautiful."
    The Princess thus disguised
Had barely left the wise Fairy
    In the early morning dew,
    When the Prince, who was readying
    The Festivities for his happy Marriage,
Learned with dread his ill-fated destiny.
There was no house, no path, no avenue
    That was not promptly scoured;
    But the agitation was in vain.

No one could guess what had become of her.

Everywhere spread a sad and black grief:
>   No more Wedding, no more Feast,
>   No more Tarts, no more Sweets.
The Ladies of the Court, completely discouraged,
>   Did not dine for the most part;
But the sadness of the Priest above all was great,
>   For he ate quite late,
>   And what was worse did not get any offering.

The Infanta meanwhile pursued her path,
Her face covered with vile scum.
>   To all Passers-by she held out her hand,
Striving to find work as a servant.
But the least delicate and most unhappy of them,
Seeing her so disgusting and full of dirt,
Wanted neither to hear nor bring home with them
>   Such a filthy creature.
So she went far, quite far, even farther away.
Finally she arrived at a Farm
>   Where the Farmer's Wife needed
>   A scullery maid whose abilities
Would include knowing how to wash rags well
>   And clean the Pigsty.
She was put in a corner at the back of the kitchen
>   Where the Valets, insolent vermin,
>   >   Only took pot-shots at her,
>   >   Talked back and jeered at her.
>   They did not tire of playing tricks on her,
>   >   Tormenting her at every opportunity.
>   >   She was the habitual butt
Of all their teasing and wisecracks.

On Sundays she had a little more rest,
For, having done her little jobs in the morning,
She entered her bedroom and in private
Cleaned herself, opened her chest,
>   Set up her toilette properly, and
>   Arranged her little pots upon it.
In front of her large mirror, happy and satisfied,
She would put on now her Moon dress,

Now the one in which the Sun's fire shone,
    Now the beautiful blue dress
That all the azure of the Sky could not equal,
With the sole sorrow that their long trains
Could not be spread out on the short floor.
She liked to see herself young, rosy and white,
And a hundred times more elegant than any other woman.
    This sweet pleasure sustained her
  And carried her along until the following Sunday.

    I forgot to say in passing
    That on this big Farm
    Was the Menagerie
    Of a magnificent and powerful King
    And that there Hens from Barbary,
    Rails, Guinea-Fowl, Cormorants,
    Musk Goslings, Petiary Ducks
And a thousand other birds of bizarre kinds,
    Almost all of them different from one another,
Filled enviably ten whole courtyards.

  The King's son came often to this charming abode
  When returning from the Hunt,
    To rest himself and have a cool drink
    With the Lords of his Court.
    The handsome Cephalus was never like this:
His air was Royal and his mien martial,
Able to make the proudest battalions tremble.
Donkey Skin from very far away saw him with tenderness,
  And recognized by that boldness
    That under her scum and her rags
She still had the heart of a Princess.

    "How noble he seems, though indifferently dressed,
    And how worthy of love he is," she said,
    "And how blessed is the beauty
    To whom his heart is engaged!
If he had honored me with the least of dresses,
    I would have found myself to be more adorned
    Than with all those that I have."

One day the young Prince, wandering aimlessly

From courtyard to courtyard,
Entered an obscure alley
Where was Donkey Skin's humble abode.
By chance he put his eye to the keyhole.
As it was a feast day,
She had taken on a rich adornment,
And her superb clothing,
Woven from fine gold and large diamonds,
Equaled the Sun's purest light.
The Prince, at the mercy of his desire,
Contemplated her, and seeing her
Could only catch his breath with effort,
So much was he overcome with pleasure.
Beyond the garments, the beauty of her face,
Its beautiful turn, its vivid whiteness,
Its fine features, its young freshness
Touched him a hundred times more;
But a certain air of grandeur,
Even more, a wise and modest reserve,
The assured witness of the beauties of her soul,
Took hold of his whole heart.

Three times, in the heat of the fire that transported him,
He wanted to break in the door;
But believing he was watching a Divinity,
He stayed his arm three times in respect.
To the Palace, thoughtful, he retired,
And there night and day he sighed.
He no longer wanted to go to Balls
Even though it was Carnival time.
He hated Hunting, he hated the Theater,
He had no appetite, everything made him ill,
And at the bottom of his illness
Was a sad and mortal languor.

He inquired who was the admirable Nymph
Who dwelled in a courtyard
At the end of a frightful alley
Where nothing was visible at midday.
"It is," he was told, "Donkey Skin, neither Nymph nor beautiful,
And who is called 'Donkey Skin'

Because of the Skin she wears on her neck.
    For Love she is the true cure;
    In a word she is the ugliest beast
    That can be seen after the Wolf.''
  In spite of what was said, he could not believe it:
    The lines that love had traced,
    Always present to his memory,
    Would never be erased from it.

    Meanwhile the Queen his Mother,
Whose only child he was, cried and despaired.
She pressed him in vain to declare his ill.
    He moaned, cried, sighed,
  And said nothing, except that he desired
Donkey Skin to make him a cake with her own hands;
But his Mother did not know what her Son meant.
    ''Oh Heavens! Madam,'' she was told,
    ''This Donkey Skin is a black Mole
      Even more vile and more of a slattern
      Than the dirtiest Scullion.''
''It does not matter,'' said the Queen. ''He must be satisfied
And we must think only of that.''
He would have had gold, so much did this Mother love him,
    If he had wanted to eat any.

    Donkey Skin then took the flour
    That she had sifted on purpose
    To make her dough finer,
    Her salt, butter, and fresh eggs;
    And to make her cake well,
    She closed herself up alone in her little bedroom.

    First she cleaned the scum
    Off of her hands, arms, and face,
And took a silver bodice that she laced up quickly
    To do the work in a worthy manner,
    And she started at once.

It is said that as she worked, a little too hastily,
One of her very valuable rings fell by chance
    From her finger into the dough.

But those who know the end of this story
Swear that it was put there by her on purpose;
And as for me, frankly I would well believe it,
Quite sure that, when the Prince came to her door
    And looked at her through the hole,
    She noticed it.
    On this point women are so quick,
    And their eyes go so promptly
    That one cannot see one for a moment
    Before she knows she has been seen.
I am quite sure also, and I would take an oath on it,
That she did not doubt that by her young Lover
    The Ring would be well received.

A more dainty morsel was never kneaded,
And the Prince found the cake so good
That it would not have taken a gluttonous hunger
    For him to have swallowed the ring as well.
    When he saw its admirable emerald
        And the narrow circle of the band of gold
        That showed the form of the finger,
His heart was touched by an unbelievable joy.
    He put it under his pillow in the same instant.
    His illness still increasing,
    And the Physicians wise with experience
    Seeing him grow thinner every day,
    Judged through their great science
        That he was sick with love.

    Since Marriage, however badly one speaks of it,
Is an exquisite cure for this illness,
    It was concluded that he be married.
    He made himself be begged for a time,
Then said, "I will indeed, provided I am given
    In marriage the person
    This ring will fit."
    At this bizarre request
The Queen and King's surprise was great;
But he was so ill they did not dare say no.

    So therefore a search was begun

For the one whom the ring, with no concern for blood,
> Must place at such a high rank.
> There was no one who did not ready herself
> To come present her finger,
> And no one who wanted to yield her right.

The rumor having spread that to aspire to the Prince
> One had to have quite a thin finger,
All the Charlatans, to be welcomed,
Said that they had the secret of making it slender.
> One woman, following a bizarre whim,
> Scraped it like a turnip.
> Another, with special water,
Made the skin fall off to make it less fat.
> There was finally no maneuver
> That a Lady did not apply
To make her finger fit the ring well.

The trials began with the young Princesses,
> Marquises, and Duchesses;
> But their fingers, though delicate,
> Were too fat and did not go through.
> The Countesses and Baronesses
> And all noble Persons
Like them presented their hands in turn,
> And presented them in vain.
> Then came the Grisettes,
> Whose pretty and slender fingers,
> For some were very shapely,
Seemed to adjust themselves to the ring sometimes.
But the Ring, always too small or too round,
Rebuffed everyone with a nearly equal disdain.

> One had to turn finally
> To the Maids, the Cooks,
> The lowly Servants, the Poultry-Keepers,
> In a word to the riffraff,
> Whose red and black paws,
No less than the delicate hands,
Hoped for a happy destiny.
> Many girls presented themselves
> With a finger, fat and squat,

Which would as scarcely have passed through the Prince's Ring
    As a rope through a needle.

    It was believed finally that it was over,
    For indeed only poor Donkey Skin
Was left at the back of the kitchen.
    But how to believe, it was said,
    That Heaven destined her to reign!
    The Prince said, "And why not?
Have her come here." Everyone started to laugh,
Crying loudly, "What is meant
By having that dirty monkey enter here?"
But when she drew from beneath her black skin
A little hand that seemed of ivory
    Colored by a little blush,
    And when by the fatal Ring
    With an unequaled accuracy
    Her little finger was surrounded,
    The Court was in such a state of surprise
    That it could not be contained.

She was being brought to the King in this sudden transport,
But she asked that before appearing
    In front of her Lord and Master
She be given time to put on another garment.
    To say truly, people were getting ready
    To laugh at these clothes on all sides,
But when she arrived in the Apartments
    And had crossed the rooms
    With her stately clothes,
Whose rich beauty never had an equal;
    When her lovely blond hair
Mingled with diamonds whose vivid light
    Made as so many rays;
    When her blue eyes, big, soft, and oval,
    Which full of a proud Majesty
Never looked without pleasing and wounding;
And when her waist finally so slender and so fine
That one could have taken it in one's two hands
Showed her charms and her divine grace,
All attractions fell away from the Ladies of the Court
    And their adornments.

In the joy and the noise of the whole Assembly
    The good King was overwhelmed
  To see his Daughter-in-Law in possession of so many charms.
    The Queen was alarmed by it,
    And the Prince, her dear Lover,
    His soul overwhelmed by a hundred pleasures,
Gave way beneath the weight of his rapture.

Everyone at once took the necessary steps for the Marriage.
The Monarch invited all the surrounding Kings,
  Who, brilliant with various adornments,
Left their States to be present that great day.
Those from Aurora's regions arrived,
    Mounted on great Elephants;
    From the Moorish shore came some
    Who, blacker and uglier still,
    Frightened little children;
    Finally from all corners of the World
  They disembarked, and the Court abounded with them.

    But no Prince, no Potentate,
    Appeared there with as much brilliance
    As the Father of the Bride
    Who, formerly in love with her,
  Had with time purified the fires
    With which his soul had been burning.
  He had banned from it all criminal desire,
    And the little that remained
    Of that odious flame in his soul
Only made his paternal love more vivid.
  As soon as he saw her, "Heaven be blessed
    For allowing me to see you again,
My dear child," he said, and crying for joy
    He ran to embrace her tenderly.
Everyone was interested in his happiness,
And the future Spouse was delighted to learn
That he was becoming the Son-in-Law of such a powerful King.

    At this moment the Godmother arrived
    And told the whole story,
    And with her narrative succeeded
    In showering Donkey Skin with glory.

It is not difficult to see
That the goal of this Tale is to teach Children
That it is better to expose oneself to the harshest punishment
    Than to fail in one's duty;
    That Virtue can be unfortunate
    But that it is always crowned;

That against a foolish love and its impetuous transports
The strongest Reason is a feeble dike;
  And that there is no treasure so rich
    That a Lover will not spend it all extravagantly;

    That clear water and brown bread
    Suffice to feed
    All young Creatures,
    So long as they have beautiful clothes;
  That under Heaven there is no female
    Who does not imagine herself to be beautiful,
  And who often does not also imagine to herself
That if the famous quarrel among the three Beauties
    Had taken place with her,
    She would have had the golden apple.

Donkey Skin's Tale is hard to believe,
But so long as in this World there are Children,
    Mothers, and Grandmothers,
    Its memory will be kept.

Notes

All of Pascal's *Pensées* will be cited with the two most widely used numbering schemes, Lafuma's being the first, as per his widely available edition of Pascal's *Œuvres complètes* (Paris: Editions du Seuil, 1966), and Brunschvicg's the second (Paris: Librairie Hachette, 1917). Note also that I have used standard transcriptions of Pascal's *Thoughts* in my translations and not Marin's text, which contains discrepancies of greater and lesser magnitude.

Unless otherwise indicated, all translations of foreign-language quotations are my own. —TR.

Notes

Introduction: The Three Formulas

1. Louis Marin, *La Critique du discours: Etudes sur la Logique de Port-Royal et les Pensées de Pascal* (Paris: Minuit: 1975).
2. Ibid., pp. 105-46, 258-69, 365-419.
3. Ibid., pp. 191-205, 275-90.
4. Ibid., pp. 168-90, 290-99.
5. Leon Battista Alberti, *On Painting*, trans. John R. Spencer (New Haven, Conn.: Yale University Press, 1956), p. 63.
6. [This range of definitions for the verb *to represent* are taken from Littré's *Dictionnaire de la langue française*, 4 vols. (Chicago, Paris: Encyclopaedia Britannica, 1974-78). A parallel set can be found in the unabridged *Oxford English Dictionary*. —TR.]
7. See below, pp. 23-26.
8. Charles Dufresne du Cange, *Glossarium . . . latinitatis* [Niort: L. Fauré; Paris: Librairie des Sciences et des Arts, 1938, 5 vols. —TR.], s.v. "representation": "*Honorarius tumulus.*" Littré, *Dictionnaire*, s.v. "representation." Cf. Ralph E. Giesey, *The Royal Funeral Ceremony in Renaissance France* (Geneva: Droz, 1960), pp. 85ff.
9. Ernst H. Kantorowicz, *The King's Two Bodies: A Study in Mediaeval Political Theology* (Princeton, N.J.: Princeton University Press, 1957).
10. Henri de Lubac, *"Corpus mysticum": L'Eucharistie et l'église au moyen âge*. (Paris: Aubier-Montaigne, 1949).
11. G. W. F. Hegel, *Phénoménologie de l'esprit*, trans. Jean Hyppolite (Paris: Aubier-Montaigne, 1946), vol. 2, p. 72. [In the text I have quoted from A. V. Miller's recent English translation, *Phenomenology of Spirit* (Oxford: Oxford University Press, 1977), p. 309. In the French, the English *presumed* is rendered as *signifié*; the word *actual* as *réel*. —TR]
12. Vincent Descombes, *L'Inconscient malgré lui* (Paris: Minuit, 1977), p. 47.
13. René Demoris, "Le Corps royal et l'imaginaire au XVIIe siècle: *Le Portrait du Roi* par Félibien," *Revue des Sciences Humaines* 44, no. 172 (1978): 9-30.

14. Antoine Arnauld and Pierre Nicole, *La Logique, ou l'Art de penser* [commonly referred to as the Port-Royal *Logic*—TR.], 5th ed. (Paris, 1683), p. 204.

15. Pierre Fontanier, *Les Figures du discours* (Paris: Flammarion, 1968), p. 99.

16. Ibid., p. 79.

17. Ibid., p. 87.

18. Gérard Genette, introduction to Fontanier, *Les Figures*, p. 14.

19. Arnauld and Nicole, *Logique*, p. 211.

20. Ibid.

21. Ibid., p. 58.

22. Cf. Otto von Gierke, *Political Theories of the Middle Age*, trans. F. W. Maitland (Cambridge: Cambridge University Press, 1959), chapters 7 and 8, pp. 61-73.

23. Ernst H. Kantorowicz, "Mysteries of State: An Absolutist Concept and Its Late Mediaeval Origins," *Harvard Theological Review* 48 (1955): 65-91.

24. Giesey, *Funeral Ceremony*, pp. 85ff.

25. F.-M. A. Voltaire, *Le Siècle de Louis XIV* (Paris: Garnier- Flammarion, 1966), vol. 1, p. 310.

26. Giesey, *Funeral Ceremony*, pp. 180ff.

27. Michel de Certeau, *L'Invention du quotidien*, vol. 1, *Arts de faire* (Paris: UGE [10-18], 1980), pp. 242-43, 253-56. [Translated as *The Practice of Everyday Life* by Steven F. Randall (Berkeley: University of California Press, 1985).—TR.]

28. Cited by Jacques Truchet, ed., *Politique de Bossuet* (Paris: Armand Colin, 1966), p. 82.

29. Blaise Pascal, *Pensées*, ed. Louis Lafuma, 2nd ed. (Paris: Delmas, 1952). [The best translation is A. J. Krailsheimer's (New York: Penguin, 1966).—TR.]

30. Cf. Marie-Françoise Christout, *Le Ballet de Cour de Louis XIV, 1643-1672. Mises en scène* (Paris: Picard, 1967).

Overture: The King, or Force Justified

1. Cf. Blaise Pascal, "De l'esprit géométrique" and "De l'art de persuader," in *Opuscules et lettres*, ed. Louis Lafuma (Paris: Aubier-Montaigne, 1955), p. 132.

2. Thus, for example, in *Pensées* 84-79 or 977-320, 756-365 or 512-1. The motif of mockery arises from the same semantic field—"To mock philosophy is really to philosophize" (513-4)—which is that of the infinite irony of the "clever man."

3. It is a question, naturally, of the rhetorical order of persuasion and not that of geometry, "useless in its depth" (694-61).

4. See, for example, 784-23, 789-50, 956 para. 3-15.

5. See 681-353.

6. [In "Concerning Interpretation: A Parable of Pascal" (pp. 189-220 in Daniel Patte, ed., *Semiology and Parables: Exploration of the Possibilities Offered by Structuralism for Exegesis* [Pittsburgh: Pickwick, 1976]), Marin states a preference for translating this phrase as "thought in the back of the mind" or as "secret thought" (p. 222), as opposed to the more common rendering, "thought from behind."—TR.]

7. See in "L'Origine de la perspective," *Macula* 5-6 (1979): 113-37, the demonstration that Hubert Damisch makes of this point in the domain of legitimate perspective during the Renaissance.

8. Blaise Pascal, "Les Provinciales" in *Œuvres* (Paris: Gallimard [Pléïade], 1950), p. 576. [Translated as *The Provincial Letters* by A. J. Krailsheimer (New York: Penguin, 1982).—TR.]

9. See also 977-320. On the problems of juridical legitimation of dynastic right in the kingdom of France and, in particular, the famous *droit salique*, see Ralph E. Giesey, "The Juridic Basis of Dynastic Right to the French Throne," *Transactions of the American Philosophical Society* 51 (1961): 3-47.

10. On the relationship of power and belief in the political literature of the first half of the seventeenth century consult, with respect to Retz, Antoine Adam, *Histoire de la littérature française du XVIIe siècle* (Paris: Del Buca, 1948-56), vol. 4, p. 143; and, above all, François de Colomby, *De l'autorité des rois, premier discours* (Paris, 1622, 1631), in the liminary epistle addressed to the king. On Richelieu's ideological politics see Etienne Thuau, *Raison d'état et pensée politique à l'époque de Richelieu* (Paris: Armand Colin, 1966), p. 173.

The King's Narrative

1. Paul Pellisson-Fontanier, *Œuvres diverses* (Paris, 1735), vol. 2, pp. 323-28. [A version of this study appeared under the title "Pouvoir du récit et récit du pouvoir" in *Actes de la Recherche en Sciences Sociales* 25 (1979): 23-43. —TR.]

2. [Marin is referring here to the seventeenth-century ambiguity in the spelling of the words *dessein* and *dessin*, the first meaning "design" in modern French, in the sense of a plan or intent, and the second "drawing." He refers to this ambiguity also in "'Pascal': Du texte au livre," *Social Science Information* 16 (1977): 27-57, on pp. 29 and 52. To translate both words as "design" would have retained the ambiguity of the seventeenth-century French; since Marin makes the distinction in his text, however, so have I. —TR.]

3. [*Histoire* in French means both "story" and "history." In order to indicate that both meanings are intended here, Marin gives its two German translations. A capital "H" seems to indicate just "history" in Marin's text, and a small "h" is used ambiguously for both "story" and "history." I have kept that distinction here. —TR.]

4. Paul Pellisson-Fontanier was born in Béziers in 1624 and died in Paris in 1693. Born into a Protestant family, he was the son of a *conseiller* in the *chambre de l'édit* of Castres, and his mother, Jeanne de Fontanier, who was very learned, took care of his education. He studied law in Toulouse, learned Italian and Spanish, joined the bar, and published in 1645 a Latin paraphrase of the first book of Justinian's *Institutes*. In the course of travels to Paris he made the acquaintance of Conrart, also a Protestant, and these meetings led to the founding of the French Academy. In 1653 Pellisson published an *Histoire de l'Académie française*, a panegyric of the dawning society that brought him the title of *surnuméraire*. He also became an intimate friend of Mlle de Scudéry and figures in her novels under the names of Acante and Herminius. He bought an office [*charge*] as king's secretary in 1652, and Fouquet took him on as first *commis*. *Maître des comptes* in Montpellier in 1659, he was king's *conseiller* in 1660. Obliging and helpful, he obtained a pension for Mme de Maintenon. Entangled in Fouquet's disgrace, he defended him in three *Discours*. Arrested in Nantes in 1661, he was emprisoned in the Bastille, where he stayed five years. He regained his freedom in 1666 and accompanied the king on the expedition into Franche-Comté, of which he wrote an account. He abjured his opinions in 1670 and was named king's historiographer. He entered into orders, became successively *econome* of Saint-Germain-des-Prés and of Saint-Denis, and then administered the *caisse des conversions*. He accompanied Louis XIV in his campaigns until the day when he was replaced by Racine and Boileau in the office of king's historiographer. Note the publication, in 1686-1690, of his *Réflexions sur les différends en matière de religion* and of a *Traité de l'Eucharistie* in 1694.

5. [On the relationship of sign and representation and the function of the mirror image in the semiotics of the Port-Royal *Logic*, see Louis Marin, "Puss-in-Boots: Power of Signs—Signs of Power," *Diacritics* 7, no. 2 (1977): 54-56; and "Toward a Theory of Reading" in *The Reader in the Text: Essays on Audience and Interpretation*, ed. Susan Suleiman and David Crosman (Princeton, N.J.: Princeton University Press, 1980), pp. 299-302. —TR.]

6. Emile Benveniste, *Problèmes de linguistique générale* (Paris: Gallimard, 1974), vol. 2, p. 241. [Translated as *Problems in General Linguistics* by Mary E. Meek (Miami: University of Miami Press, 1973). —TR.]

7. Aristotle, *Rhetoric*, 1358a36-1360b1 and 1366a23-1368a37. See also A. Kibédi Varga, *Rhétorique et littérature, études de structures classiques* (Paris: Didier, 1970), pp. 28-32, 52-55.

8. On the notion of secrecy, here transferred from the sphere of royal power to that of the reader-subject, consult Etienne Thuau, *Raison d'état et pensée politique à l'époque de Richelieu* (Paris: Armand Colin, 1966), pp. 38-54 on Tacitus and pp. 169-77 on the political principle that "to govern is to make believe" [*gouverner, c'est faire croire*].

9. Nicolas Poussin, *Lettres et propos sur l'art*, ed. Anthony Blunt (Paris: Hermann, 1964), pp. 62-63.

10. *Le Bouclier d'Etat et de Justice, contre le dessein manifestement découvert de la monarchie universelle, sous le vain prétexte des prétentions de la Reine de France* (Brussels, 1667) was written by François-Paul de Lisola in response to three pamphlets in favor of the rights of the queen of France: *Dialogue sur les droits de la Reine Très Chrétienne, Traité des Droits de la Reine Très Chrétienne sur divers Etats de la Monarchie d'Espagne*, and *Soixante-et-Quatorze raisons qui prouvent plus clair que le jour que la renonciation faite par la Reine de France est nulle*. Lisola was born in Salins in 1613 and died at the beginning of 1675. He entered the service of the emperor in 1640; in 1643 he was his resident in England and then imperial ambassador to the courts of Poland, Spain, and Portugal. In 1668 he took part in the conclusion of the peace of Aix-la-Chapelle. An excellent publicist and negotiator, he did not leave off denunciating French imperial and imperialist aims in Europe, notably in the *Politique du Temps, ou le conseil fidèle sur les mouvements de la France pour servir d'introduction à la triple alliance* in 1670, and *Le Dénouement des intrigues du temps* at Liège, in 1672. Pellisson read Lisola's book very attentively and seems indeed to have answered him directly when he wrote that "*the Historian and not the lawyer* must explain the causes of the rupture." Lisola had noted in his preface that "it is truly a tiresome thing to see oneself obliged to reduce a dispute of Sovereigns so solemnly decided by a public Treaty, on whose good faith all of Christianity solely founded its peace and quiet, *to terms of chicanery.*" Similarly, when Pellisson indicated that "the King must be praised everywhere . . . by a narrative . . . [that] must appear disinterested," Lisola wrote: "I ask for the disinterested attention of the readers, if, however, they can be without interest in a cause that touches them so closely by an inevitable rebound."

11. On the litotes, see Pierre Fontanier, *Les Figures du discours* (Paris: Flammarion, 1968), pp. 133-35; and more generally on tropes and figures of expression by reflection, see pp. 123-42.

12. For a positive judgment of the *Brevitas* by Tacitus and its relationship to the secrets of power, see, for example, the new collection of Henri-Auguste Loménie de Brienne's *Mémoires* (Paris, 1837), in volume 27 in a series published by Joseph-François Michaud and Jean-Jacques-François Poujoulat, p. 25: "Everything speaks in this history, and I have tried to make each word, following Tacitus's example, enclose some mystery and, in a word, make each period be full of some noteworthy teaching. It is for the readers to judge if I have executed such a noble and daring design well or badly." For a negative judgment, see the *Anonimiana* cited by Bayle: "Tacitus has chosen the most delicate and susceptible actions from the delicacies of the art. . . . In the reign of Tiberius, which is without contest his chef-d'œuvre and the time of his greatest success, he found a kind of government adapted to the character of his genius. . . . A genius too subtle, he sees mystery in all the actions of that Prince." [See Pierre Bayle, *Dictionnaire historique et critique* (Paris: France-Expansion, 1973). Or, in extracts, ed. Alain Niderst (Paris: Editions Sociales, 1974).—TR.]

13. Fontanier, *Les Figures*, p. 133.

14. René Descartes, "Discours de la méthode" in *Œuvres et Lettres*, ed. André Bridoux (Paris: Gallimard [Pléiade], 1964), vol. 3, pp. 154-67. [Translated as *Discourse on Method* by Donald A. Cress (Indianapolis: Hackett, 1980).—TR.]

15. The references to the all-seeing eye of the prince are too numerous to be cited. Note more particularly on the performing character of the royal gaze, Jean de La Bruyère, *Les Caractères, ou les mœurs de ce siècle*, ed. Robert Garapon (Paris: Classiques Garnier, 1962), X, no. 35, or Jean

Racine, "Discours prononcé à l'Académie française, le 2 janvier 1685" in *Œuvres* (Paris: Gallimard [Pléïade], 1966), vol. 2, pp. 343-49.

16. On the semantic value of *on* as simultaneously reader-spectator and actor, see Jean-Claude Chevalier, "Les Entretiens d'Ariste et d'Eugène du Père Bouhours, soit la littérature et l'idéologie," in *Langues et Langages de Leibniz à l'Encyclopédie* (Paris: UGE [10-18], 1977), pp. 30-31.

17. Aristotle, *Rhetoric*, 1358a36-1358b8.

18. On autopsy, see Giuseppe Nenci, "Il motivo dell'autopsia nella storiografia greca," *Studi classici e orientali* 3 (1955): 35-38; Guido Schepens, "Ephore sur la valeur de l'autopsie," *Ancient Society* 1 (1970): 163-82; and Marcel Détienne's remarks in *Dionysos mis à mort* (Paris: Gallimard, 1977), pp. 51-53. [Translated as *Dionysus Slain*, by M. Muellner and L. Muellner (Baltimore, Md.: Johns Hopkins University Press, 1979).—TR.]

19. G. W. F. Hegel, *Leçons sur la philosophie de l'histoire*, trans. Jean Gibelin, 3rd ed. (Paris: Vrin, 1967), "Introduction," pp. 17-19. [Translated as *The Philosophy of History* by J. Sibree (Darby, Pa.: Arden Library, n.d.).—TR.]

20. See Louis Marin, *Le Récit est un piège* (Paris: Minuit, 1978), pp. 69-115.

21. It is to be understood that, real or imaginary, the presence of the historiographer at the king's side is at any rate a fictive position, a simple condition of possibility or, rather, of *authorization* of the prince's historical narrative.

22. One will find, in particular, in a letter by Chapelain to Colbert the acute expression of this impossibility of writing the king's present history: "I come to history, which with great reason, as you have judged, Sir, is one of the principal means of conserving the splendor of the King's enterprises and the detail of his miracles. But history is like those fruits that are good only when kept for the late season. If it does not explain the motives of the things it tells, if it is not accompanied by prudent reflections and documents, history is only a pure account, without force or dignity. To use them also during the reign of the Prince who is its subject would be to expose to the Public the inner workings of the *cabinet*, giving room to enemies for anticipating them or making them useless, and betraying those who would have liaisons with him, which subsist only through secretiveness and in the shadow of a deep silence. Thus I estimate that if you work on the history of His Majesty in the manner in which it should be, it must only be while keeping the product hidden up until the time when the above-noted drawbacks can no longer prejudice either his affairs or those of his Allies." Jean Chapelain, *Lettres* (Paris: Tamizey de Larroque, 1880-83), vol. 1, pp. 272-77.

23. Racine, *Œuvres*, vol. 2, p. 197.

24. Fontanier, *Les Figures*, p. 137.

25. Aristotle, *Rhetoric*, 1358b21-24 and 1359a16-27.

26. Ibid., 1359b19-1360a39.

27. [On La Fontaine's fable "Le Pouvoir des fables" see Marin's "Le Pouvoir du récit" in *Le Récit est un piège*, pp. 17-34; and "La Voix d'un conte: Entre La Fontaine et Perrault, sa récriture," in *Critique* 36, no. 394 (1980): 333-42.—TR.]

28. Cf. Marcel Détienne, *Les Maîtres de la vérité dans la Grèce archaïque* (Paris: Maspero, 1967), p. 23.

29. Pascal, *Pensées*, *liasse* 5, "Raison des effets." [In "Concerning Interpretation," Marin translates this phrase as "The Effects of Meaning."—TR.]

30. Racine, *Œuvres*, vol. 2, p. 350.

31. On the notion of example, see Karlheinz Stierle, "L'Histoire comme Exemple, l'Exemple comme Histoire," *Poétique* 10 (1972): 176-98.

32. Fontanier, *Les Figures*, p. 390.

The Discourse of the Flatterer

1. Aristotle, *Rhetoric*, 1358a36-1359a29.

2. All of the bibliographical and theoretical elements useful to the distinction that I introduce

here from the prologue of the *Theogony* by Hesiod can be found in Nicole Loraux, *L'Invention d'Athènes: Histoire de l'oraison funèbre dans la "cité classique"* (The Hague: Mouton, 1981). I have also consulted Marcel Détienne, *Les Maîtres de la vérité dans la Grèce archaïque* (Paris: Maspero, 1967), pp. 9-27; George Kennedy, *The Art of Persuasion in Greece* (Princeton, N.J.: Princeton University Press, 1963), pp. 152-203; and Emile Benveniste, *Le Vocabulaire des institutions indo-européennes* (Paris: Minuit, 1969), vol. 2.

    3. René Bary, *La Rhétorique française*, new ed. (Amsterdam, 1660), p. 203.

    4. Jean-Baptiste Louis Crevier, *Rhétorique française*, 2 vols. (Paris, 1765), p. 16.

    5. Ibid., p. 19.

    6. Le Sieur Le Gras, *La Rhétorique française* (Paris, 1671), pp. 19-20.

    7. A. Kibédi Varga, *Rhétorique et littérature, études de structures classiques* (Paris: Didier, 1970), p. 55.

    8. Crevier, p. 110.

    9. Varga, *Rhétorique et littérature*, p. 55.

    10. Jean de La Fontaine, *Œuvres complètes* (Paris: Gallimard [Pléïade], 1947-48), vol. 1, p. 32. ["Le Corbeau et le renard."—TR.]

    11. Charles Perrault, *Contes*, ed. Gilbert Rouger (Paris: Classiques Garnier, 1967), p. 7. [Translated as *Perrault's Complete Fairy Tales* by A. E. Johnson (Nashville: Dodd, Mead, 1982). According to Perrault, these verses are taken from a Madrigal written by a "young demoiselle" at the end of a copy of *Donkey Skin* that he had sent to her.—TR.]

The Fox's Tactics

    1. Jean de La Fontaine, *Œuvres complètes* (Paris: Gallimard [Pléïade], 1947-48), vol. 1, p. 32.

    2. G. W. F. Hegel, *Phénoménologie de l'esprit*, trans. Jean Hyppolite (Paris: Aubier-Montaigne, 1946), vol. 2, pp. 57-61, 64-65, 69-76. [*Phenomenology of Spirit*, trans A. V. Miller (Oxford: Oxford University Press, 1977), pp. 306ff. An earlier version of this study was published as "La Bête, l'animal parlant et l'homme," *Traverses* 8 (1977): 36-47.—TR.]

    3. Louis Marin, "L'Animal-fable Esope," *Critique* 34, no. 375-376 (1978): 775-82.

    4. See Käte Hamburger, *Die Logik der Dichtung* (Stuttgart: E. Klett, 1957) [Translated as *The Logic of Literature* by Marilynn J. Rose (Bloomington: Indiana University Press, 1973).—TR.]; and Harald Weinrich, *Le Temps* (Paris: Le Seuil, 1973), pp. 107-29.

    5. Ernst H. Kantorowicz, *The King's Two Bodies: A Study in Mediaeval Political Theology* (Princeton, N. J.: Princeton University Press, 1957), pp. 385-401.

    6. Ralph E. Giesey, *The Royal Funeral Ceremony in Renaissance France* (Geneva: Droz, 1960), chapter 10.

    7. Lactantius, *On the Phoenix*, verse 166-70, cited and translated in Jean Hubaux and Maxime Leroy, *Le Mythe du phénix dans les littératures grecque et latine* (Liège: Faculté de Philosophie et Lettres, Université de Liège, 1939), p. xx.

    8. Claudian, *Phoenix*, verses 101-10 and verses 69-71, in Hubaux and Leroy, *Mythe du phénix*, p. xxvi.

    9. Cited by Kantorowicz, *Two Bodies*, note 332, p. 414. [The author is anonymous; see Bibliothèque Mazarine, MS 4395, folio 4.—TR.] See the reproduction of the *projet de jeton* in Giesey, *The Royal Funeral*. On the *lit funèbre* and the *lit de justice*, see Bernard de La Roche-Flavin, *Treize Livres des Parlements de France* (Geneva, 1621), book 4, section 110, pp. 353ff. See also Kantorowicz, *Two Bodies*, note 334, p. 414.

    10. More precisely, according to certain traditions, it sings only at the moment of dying, that is, of being reborn.

    11. Hegel, *Phénoménologie*, vol. 1, pp. 90-91.

12. On Protagoras's paradox, see Diogenes Laërtius, IX, 55; in Hermann Diels [*Die Fragmente der Vorsokratiker* (Berlin: Weidmann, 1910-1922), 4 vols.—TR.], 80 A 1.

Racinian Strategies

1. Jean Racine, "Discours prononcé à l'Académie française à la réception de M. l'abbé Colbert," in *Œuvres* (Paris: Gallimard [Pléïade], 1966), vol. 2, pp. 341-44.
2. See Andras Zempléni, "Pouvoir dans la cure et pouvoir social," *Nouvelle Revue de Psychanalyse* 8 (1973): 145.
3. On representation as cenotaph as opposed to the effigy in royal medals, cf. Ralph E. Giesey, *The Royal Funeral Ceremony in Renaissance France* (Geneva: Droz, 1960), pp. 85-91.
4. Antoine Furetière, *Dictionnaire universel* (Paris, 1690), s.v. *preterition*. See also Pierre Fontanier, *Les Figures du discours* (Paris: Flammarion, 1968), p. 143: "Preterition, also known as 'pretermission,' consists in feigning to not want to say that which nevertheless one says very clearly and often even with force." He classes this figure among those of expression by opposition with this remarkable commentary, which is an exact description of some of the mechanisms of the discourse of flattery: "To what point do our minds not bring the artifice of discourse! We go to the point of uttering just about the contrary of what we think; or we make as if we were not saying what we could not say any better; or we affect to want to counsel, or even to prescribe what, often, is the furthest from our thoughts; of course in all these cases, by the manner in which we go about it, we take pleasure in interpreting, and the interpretation conforms to our views."
5. On the discourse of flattery, consult the work of Abraham N. Amelot de la Houssaye, *La Morale de Tacite: De la flatterie* (Paris, 1686), as well as his translation with commentary of Baltasar Gracián's *L'Homme de Cour* (Paris, 1687).

The Royal Host

1. Cf. Louis Marin, "La Lecture du tableau d'après Poussin," *Cahier de l'Association Internationale d'Etudes Françaises* 24 (1972): 251-66. [A version of this study appeared under the title "The Inscription of the King's Memory: On the Metallic History of Louis XIV," in *Yale French Studies* 54 (1980): 17-36.—TR.]
2. See above, pp. 86-88.
3. Jean Racine, "Eloge historique du Roi sur ses conquêtes depuis l'année 1672 jusqu'en 1678," in *Œuvres* (Paris: Gallimard [Pléïade], 1966), vol. 2, pp. 207-38, and in particular p. 238.
4. Dangeau, *Journal* (31 December 1684), cited in Racine, *Œuvres*, vol. 2, p. 207, note 1, p. 1046.
5. Pierre Fontanier, *Les Figures du discours* (Paris: Flammarion, 1968), pp. 390-92.
6. Cf. Le Brun's conference on *La Manne*. [This conference was given at the academy in 1667. See Marin's studies of Le Brun and of Poussin's painting "Les Israëlites ramassant la manne dans le désert" of 1639, in "La Lecture du tableau d'après Poussin" and "On Reading Pictures: Poussin's Letter on *Manne*," *Comparative Criticism: A Yearbook* 4 (1982): 3-18.—TR.]
7. The essential tool for the work in this study is the remarkable edition by Josèphe Jacquiot, conservator at the *Cabinet des médailles* of the Bibliothèque Nationale in Paris, of the *Médailles et jetons de Louis XIV d'après le manuscrit de Londres*, 4 vols. (Paris: Imprimerie Nationale, Klincksieck, 1968). Consult also the fine study by Mark Jones, *Medals of the Sun King* (London: The British Museum Publications, Department of Coins and Medals, 1979); and see the catalog of the exhibition at the Hôtel de la Monnaie, *La Médaille au temps de Louis XIV* (Paris: Hôtel de la Monnaie, 1970).
8. Antoine Rascas de Bagarris, "De la nécessité de l'usage des médailles" in Jacquiot, *Médailles et jetons*, vol. 1, p. lxxxvii.

9. Ibid. It would no doubt be fruitful to study and analyze the theoretical and practical functions and the field of application of the model of the mark (imprint, engraving, or seal) in the philosophical and critical discourse of the seventeenth century, and to measure its effects in the field of classical representation, where the models of the *icon* and the *sign* dominate. Two references in passing: René Descartes, "Méditations métaphysiques" in *Œuvres et lettres*, ed. André Bridoux (Paris: Gallimard [Pléïade], 1964), vol. 3, p. 299; "2ème réponse," p. 373, "5ème réponse," pp. 494-95; and Jean de La Fontaine, Preface to the "Recueil de poésies chrétiennes et diverses" (1671) in *Œuvres diverses*, vol. 2 of *Œuvres complètes* (Paris: Gallimard [Pléïade], 1947-48), p. 776.

10. Rascas de Bagarris, *L'Usage des médailles*, p. lxxxv.

11. Ibid.

12. Ibid.

13. Ibid., p. lxxxvi.

14. See on this point the encounter of my analysis with that of René Demoris with respect to the "royal mystery" and the real presence in the Eucharist, in his article "Le Corps royal et l'imaginaire au XVIIe siècle: *Le Portrait du Roi* par Félibien," *Revue des Sciences Humaines* 44, no. 172 (1978): 9-30.

15. Tallemant des Réaux, "Preface" to *Médailles sur les principaux événements du règne de Louis le Grand*, in Jacquiot, *Médailles et jetons*, vol. 1, pp. cxvii-cxxvi and the "Introduction," p. lv. This preface was suppressed and destroyed on the king's order.

16. On the appearance of the prince's head, most often in profile ("a profile fit for a medal"), in the history of money, cf. Jean Babelon, *Le Portrait dans l'antiquité d'après les monnaies* (Paris: Payot, 1942), pp. 45ff., 50-51; and the first part of the catalog of the exhibition *La Monnaie, miroir des rois*, ed. Yvonne Goldenberg (Paris: Hôtel de la Monnaie, 1978), "Les portraits" (pp. 3-190), and, in particular, the study by Anne Jacquemin and Hélène Nicolet, "Présence du portrait royal dans le monnayage grec antique," pp. 3-23.

17. On the question of the mark on the reverse side of a coin, its appearance and signification in Milesian money, cf. Liselotte Weidauer, *Probleme der frühen Elektronenprägung* (Zurich: Typos I; Friburg: Office du Livre, 1975) and, more generally, the article presenting recent research by Olivier Picard, "Les Origines du monnayage en Grèce," *L'Histoire* 6 (1978): 13-20 and the bibliography.

18. Rascas de Bagarris, "L'Usage des médailles," p. lxxxv.

19. On these problems see the first part of Marc Shell, *The Economy of Literature* (Baltimore, Md.: Johns Hopkins University Press, 1978), pp. 11-63, although the objectives of this book and its totality are very different from mine.

20. Tallemant, "Preface," p. cxvii.

21. Racine, "Eloge historique," p. 238.

22. Paul Pellisson-Fontanier, *Œuvres diverses* (Paris, 1735), vol. 2, p. 326.

23. Charles Perrault, "Mémoires de ma vie," extract from *Mémoires de Charles Perrault* (Avignon, 1759), in Jacquiot, *Médailles et jetons*, vol. 1, p. xcv.

24. Antoine Arnauld and Pierre Nicole, *La Logique*, 5th ed. (Paris, 1683), p. 33.

25. Tallemant, "Preface," p. cxviii.

26. G. W. F. Hegel, *Phénoménologie de l'esprit*, trans. Jean Hyppolite (Paris: Aubier-Montaigne, 1946), vol. 2, p. 71. [*Phenomenology of Spirit* (Oxford: Oxford University Press, 1977), p. 310.—TR.]

27. Tallemant, "Preface," p. cxviii.

28. Pellisson, *Œuvres*, p. 328.

29. Rascas de Bagarris, "L'Usage des médailles," p. lxxxvii. Henry IV's first order was taken up again by Colbert.

30. No metallic history made by the academy had been published before the work of 1702. See Jacquiot, *Médailles et jetons*, vol. 1, p. cxix, note 2, and p. cxii, on the differences of the academy

with Père Menestrier. The king forbade the latter to take the following title for his book, *Histoire de Louis le Grand par les Médailles*, and to insert in it medals made by the Company of Jesus.

31. Tallemant, "Preface," p. cxx.

32. As we know, the reverse side of the medal carries a device composed of an inscription called the *legend* and of a drawing called the *type*. The *exergue* is the little space "*hors d'œuvre*" that was put on the same side as the date and place of the event that the medal commemorates. By extension we call that inscription the exergue. It is not without interest to note that the place of insertion of the device in "real" time and space is *ex-ergon*, outside of the work itself, in a margin. Nevertheless, a more precise study of the king's medals would show that, in the architecture of these monuments, the *exergue* is both outside of the work but also the pedestal of the *type* (the figure[s]) whose *legend* (written inscriptions) constitutes the *arch*.

33. Tallemant, "Preface," p. cxxi.

Royal Money and Princely Portrait

1. The essence of this work, which was the object of a course given in the United States in 1974, was written when René Demoris's remarkable study, "Du littéraire au littéral dans *Peau d'Ane* de Perrault," appeared in the *Revue des Sciences Humaines* 43, no. 166 (1977): 261-79. This article cuts across mine at many points and at others brings precious references or essential complements to it, so much is it true that the interpretation of a tale—like that of a dream—is, strictly speaking, endless. I send the reader of this work, then, back to that study, the two texts mutually comforting each other even to their differences in orientation and content.

2. I will cite from the text of *Peau d'Ane* as it appears in Gilbert Rouger's edition of Perrault's *Contes* (Paris: Garnier, 1967), pp. 51-70. [See the complete tale in translation in the Appendix.—TR.]

3. I propose this neologism to avoid the terms *subversion* and *transgression*, for a tale's narration neither subverts nor transgresses the discourse of reason; it approaches it diagonally, crossing it by returning its own constraints against it.

4. See above, pp. 125-27.

5. The fantastically exhaustive character of the king's quest for a "representative" of the deceased queen is a remarkable figure of the infinity of the representation that the royal and paternal desire for marriage with the infanta converts juridically and ritually into absolute power.

6. I skip the powerful connotations of the fairy-godmother's dwelling, "secluded . . . far away," a grotto, a subterranean place, an excavation in the earth, decorated with white mother of pearl and red coral, where we can read the symbolic representation of the maternal womb to which the daughter returns to hear the discourse of counsel, the soft and calming voice of the mother that signals, in the text, the remarkable intervention of the narrator, his discourse to the child who listens to him and, more precisely, his discourse to himself, which speaks his knowledge from childhood, the knowledge he has always had, sitting in his nanny's lap: "There is no need to tell you / What a fairy was in those blessed times, / For I am sure that your Nanny / Will have told you during your earliest years." An intervention that is therefore the mark of the adult, socialized, "literary," and ironic (re)writing of the verbality-orality of the "narrative of origins."

7. The theme of the three dresses is a recurring motif in the universe of the narrative stereotypes of tales or myths, because of at least one essential trait, named by certain folklorists as "the law of threes." Very often, the same action or word is repeated three times. An abundant descriptive literature exists on this subject. An important text by Louis Gernet in his article "Le Temps dans les formes archaïques du droit," *Journal de Psychologie* 53 (1956): 379-406 (taken up again in *Anthropologie de la Grèce antique* [Paris: Maspero, 1965], pp. 282-85), could contribute to the analysis of this trait in *Donkey Skin*, especially as the problem that Gernet studies is that of temporal models in juridical thought in general and in trials in particular. Now the infanta's three requests, inter-

preted to be challenges to power in the form of increasing bids, could be seen as arising from juridical structures regulating processes of exchange and operations of transaction. One of the ideas that supports Gernet's research is that of an efficacy of time, positive or negative, where time "multiplies" or "erases." How will a rational juridical thought be able to integrate this efficacy of time while at once preserving and going beyond its mythical and religious aspect? The other idea is that of a performative potency of the speech [*parole*] of the person who is vested with *auctoritas* and who is thus able to "speak rightly" [*jus dicere*]. Gernet gives several examples of this triplicity conferring juridical effects onto action, gesture, and word, of which two interest us immediately: "a paternal potential power, which would undergo usury by the fact of alienation renewed in the course of time, falls through the fact of three immediately consecutive alienations. . . . The married woman falls under the *manus* of her husband . . . at the end of a year, unless she has interrupted this prescription by sleeping outside the home three nights in a row . . . , a brief period [which] has the reverse but analogous [with that of the preceding example] effect of breaking suddenly and sometimes at the last moment what a duration of prescription was going to realize." The act, gesture, or word repeated three times in succession would condense the duration that legitimates a property. In the present of the completed act or gesture or of the spoken word, not only is a right said but also that which founds that right; a past and a future are concentrated in the present of the word, gesture, or act that is thrice reiterated. In this way is resolved the problem of the legitimation of a power [*puissance*], thanks to its being put into representation in the form of its triple repetition, by which this potential becomes authorized power.

Another direction of analysis, but which would arise from the same structure and juridical manipulation of time, would be to consider the three dresses in the primitive form of *arrhes*, that is to say, as a deposit of three tokens that would possess in themselves—above all because of their consecutiveness (two, four, and six days) and their growing importance—the value of obligation (cf. Gernet, note 39, on the word *arrabon*, whose juridical and philosophical connotations I have studied in a text by Diogenes Laërtius, II, 119, who reports an argumentation of cynical philosophers, Stilpon and Crates, in "Parler, montrer, manger, ou Le Piège du présent," *L'Arc* 64 [1976]: 40-41); on triplicity with respect to Pilate's three questions in the evangelical narratives of the Passion. see my study "Jésus devant Pilate: Essai d'analyse structurale," *Langages* 22 (1971): 70-71.

8. See above, p. 73.

9. I could say that, as much on the level of the narrative as on that of its enunciation, the donkey is the supplement both of the framework of representation whose effect is political power and of the framework of power whose effect is narrative representation. In the narrative the fairy godmother's supplementary thrust brings into play the supplement itself, the donkey, a supplement that makes the representative framework function and thereby provides its limit. But on the part of the king, to bring the donkey into play is to risk the limit, and the very existence of a limit. If the king agrees to kill his donkey to fulfill his kingly desire for the absolute—in order to marry his own daughter—he suppresses the limit posed to his fatherly desire for the absolute, but at the same time he suppresses the "reality" of his omnipotence and, as well, ceases to *be able* to be absolute king. Inversely, if the king refuses to kill his donkey in order to be able to marry his daughter, thus to fulfill his desire for the absolute, he maintains the "reality" of his power [*puissance*] but also its limit. The donkey is indeed the supplement of the representative framework in this new sense that, not only does it make the framework of representation function, but also, in its very operativity, it impedes its functioning at the highest power. It permits the framework's reflexivity, its self-reproduction, but it limits it. One could object that this is true only because the king is the father and the father the king and that there is a contradiction between the father in love with his daughter and the king desiring absolute power. But that is to free-fall into the narrative trap set by the tale by forgetting that the incestuous father is only the erotic figure of the absolute monarch, just as the king desiring the absolute of power is the political figure of the father's desire for the absolute.

10. Perrault's tale therefore presents three limits to absolute power: the first through the denega-

tion of the "real" as the fundamental social *law*, whose figure would be the incestuous king who wants to make his daughter his wife; the second through the fictionalization of the "real" as essential economic *rule*, whose figure would be the donkey who makes golden money out of his excrement; the third through the lack of the "real" as erotic or economic *body*, whose figure would be the infanta disguised as a donkey, who makes an animal of herself by donning its skin.

11. Note that the three dresses were made in two, four, and six days, respectively—the six days of the week during which the infanta "in exile" wears the donkey's skin. This skin was "made" in one moment, the seventh day, by the sacrifice of the donkey to the princess's desire. It is these remains of the seventh day that the king's daughter exchanges against the three dresses, on Sunday, the day of weekly leisure, which is also the Lord's day.

12. Or again: "I preserve myself as myself not by eating every day but by looking at myself once a week"; Donkey Skin, on Sunday, communicates with the image of her own body in princely kind (the dresses), and we will again find the Eucharistic motif of the real presence of the divine body in kinds that are, in the case of the tale, at once metaphorically edible and properly visual.

13. *Souillon*: (1) Person who dirties his or her clothes. (2) Servant employed to do the dishes (here, the dishes of the dirty animal par excellence, the pig) and other base tasks during which one gets very dirty.

14. *Gaupe*: Unclean and disagreeable woman. The fanciful etymologies cited by the Littré dictionary do not lack interest for our purpose. Du Cange traces the word to the Latin *gausape*, which was used in the Middle Ages for a kind of coat and then passed on to the person who wore it, whence the use for a fat woman or fat girl. Diez links it back to the Old English *Wallop*, a piece of fat, and rejects the old High German *Walpa*, she-wolf, which gave us, he says, the word "group." Devic signals *guappa* in Neapolitan dialect, which signifies a hardy woman, and asks if *gaupe* could have come from the Arabic *galiba*, old woman.

15. Antoine Furetière, *Dictionnaire universel* (Paris, 1690), s.v. *ménagerie*.

16. ["Aliboron" means an ignorant man who acts like an expert. By analogy, in French, an "ass."—TR.]

17. As Furetière indicates, s.v. *galette* (cake), "the galette is a little round and flat cake that is made for children and servants when bread is baked at home." He derives it from *galet*, a round and flat polished pebble.

18. *Jonc*: Type of ring without a setting whose circle is the same all round; "makes one think of *jungere*, because it is a bond," writes Littré, s.v. *jonc*.

19. [See Marin's *Le Récit est un piège* (Paris: Minuit. 1978), as an example.—TR.]

20. Here is once more the whole "plot" and dramatic resolution of the story of King Caudale and his confidant Gyges told by Herodotus in Book I of his *Histories*. Cf. my "Le Roi, son confident et la reine, ou Les Séductions du regard," *Traverses* 18 (1980): 25-36.

21. *Grisette*, according to Littré: "Young girl of modest condition, coquette and gallant, thus named because in the past girls of modest condition wore *grisette*, clothing made of gray [*gris*] fabric of little worth." And according to Furetière: "Young woman or girl, dressed in gray. It is said with scorn of all lower-class women and girls, whatever the fabric they wear." The choice of this term manifests the return at this point in the narrative of the motif of the dress, of clothing, whose importance I underlined in the first part and whose ultimate avatar is the donkey's skin, which operates the major narrative transformation in its central place.

22. Littré, *Dictionnaire*, s.v. *fretin*: "Rejected thing of little worth. Is also said of persons; by extension, small fish, but the term also evokes money and, in particular, small coins of little worth."

The King and His Geometer

1. Cf. for a first study but a comparative one (the plan of Merian, 1647, and the plan and panorama of Toledo by El Greco, 1600) Louis Marin, *Utopiques: Jeux d'espaces* (Paris: Minuit, 1973),

pp. 267-90. [Translated as *Utopics: Spatial Play* (Atlantic Highlands, N.J.: Humanities Press, 1984). —TR.] See also another version of this study, "Les Voies de la carte," published in the catalog of the exhibition *Cartes et figures de la Terre* (Paris: Centre Georges-Pompidou, 1980), pp. 47-54.

2. Antoine Arnauld and Pierre Nicole, *La Logique*, 5th ed. (Paris, 1683), pp. 349-50.

The Prince's Palace

1. Cited by Bernard Teyssèdre, *L'Art français au siècle de Louis XIV* (Paris: Librairie Générale Française [Livre de Poche], 1967), p. 46.

2. Ibid., p. 46.

3. André Félibien, *Description sommaire du château de Versailles* (Paris, 1674—privilege from 1671; printing completed 30 December 1673). I will cite the text according to the 1696 edition.

4. For elements of the theoretical and methodological problems posed by description in its relationship to narrative, see my *Utopiques: Jeux d'espaces* (Paris: Minuit, 1973), pp. 257-90 [translated as *Utopics: Spatial Play* (Atlantic Highlands, N.J.: Humanities Press, 1984). —TR.]; but also John Lyons, *Semantics* (Cambridge: Cambridge University Press, 1977), vol. 2, pp. 475-81 ("Locative Subjects"), and pp. 690-703 ("Spatial Expressions"); Charlotte Linde and William Labov, "Spatial Networks as a Site for the Study of Language and Thought," *Language* 51 (1975): 924-39; and Michel de Certeau, *L'Invention du quotidien* (Paris: UGE [10-18], 1980). [Translated as *The Practice of Everyday Life* by Steven F. Randall (Berkeley: University of California Press, 1985).—TR.]

5. On the sociological and historical plane, consult the indispensable Norbert Elias, *La Société de cour*, trans. Pierre Kamnitzer (Paris: Calmann-Lévy, 1974), chapter 1, "Structures et signification de l'habitat." [Translated as *The Court Society* (New York: Pantheon Books, 1983).—TR.]

6. Félibien, *Château*, pp. 275-76.

7. Ibid., p. 279.

8. Ibid., p. 299.

9. Ibid., p. 300.

10. Ibid., p. 292.

11. Ibid., p. 287.

The Magician King

1. André Félibien, *Description sommaire du Château de Versailles* (Paris, 1696), p. 329.

2. Charles Perrault, "Peau d'Ane" in *Contes*, ed. Gilbert Rouger (Paris: Garnier, 1967), p. 57.

3. Félibien, *Château*, p. 329.

4. Ibid., p. 331.

5. Perrault, "Cendrillon" in *Contes*, p. 159.

6. Félibien, *Château*, p. 333.

7. Ibid.

8. André Félibien, *Les Divertissements de Versailles donnés par le Roy à toute la Cour au retour de la conquête de la Franche-Comté en l'année 1674* (Paris, 1674).

9. Ibid., pp. 5-6.

10. Jean Racine, "Lettre à l'Académie française," in *Œuvres* (Paris: Gallimard [Pléïade], 1966), vol. 2, p. 350.

11. On the *arcana imperii*, see Ernst H. Kantorowicz, "Mysteries of State: An Absolutist Concept and Its Late Mediaeval Origins," *Harvard Theological Review* 48 (1955): 65-91 and, in addition to the texts and references already cited, see René Demoris's introduction to his new edition of the discourses of Saint-Réal, *De l'Usage de l'histoire* (Lille, Paris: Université de Lille III, 1981).

12. André Félibien, *Description de divers ouvrages de peinture faits pour le Roy* (Paris, 1671), chapter 6, "Relation de la fête à Versailles de juillet 1668," p. 197.
13. Félibien, *Divertissements*, p. 17.
14. Ibid., pp. 18-19. [The verbs italicized by Marin in this text are in the indicative present with the exception of "opening," which as in English is a present participle, and the last verb, which is in the preterit.—TR.]
15. Ibid., pp. 20-21. [All of the verbs italicized by Marin in this text are conjugated in the indicative imperfect tense in the original.—TR.]
16. Ibid., p. 21.
17. Ibid., pp. 64, 84. [The verbs italicized in these two citations are all in the preterit in the original.—TR.]
18. Ibid., p. 90.
19. Ibid., pp. 80-81.
20. Ibid., pp. 83-84.
21. Ibid., pp. 85-86.
22. Ibid., pp. 87-88.
23. Ibid., p. 89.
24. Ibid., p. 111.

The King's Portrait

1. André Félibien, *Descriptions de divers ouvrages de peinture faits pour le Roi* (Paris, 1671), pp. 85-112.
2. Ibid., p. 85.
3. Ibid., p. 86.
4. Ibid., p. 92.
5. Ibid., p. 107.
6. Antoine Arnauld and Pierre Nicole, *La Logique*, 5th ed. (Paris, 1683), p. 58. Here is the text from the *Logique*: "It is not important that . . . the bread of the Eucharist subsist in its own nature, so long as is stimulated in our minds the image of a loaf of bread that will help us to conceive in what way the body of Jesus Christ is the food of our souls, and how the faithful are united."
7. Félibien, *Ouvrages*, pp. 86-87.
8. Ibid., pp. 87-88.
9. Ibid., pp. 88-89.
10. Ibid., p. 89.
11. Ibid., p. 90.
12. Ibid., pp. 101-2.
13. Ibid., pp. 102-3.
14. Ibid., p. 105.
15. Ibid., p. 110.
16. Ibid., p. 111.
17. Ibid.

Finale: The Legitimate Usurper

1. Pierre Nicole, *Essais de morale* (Paris, 1723-35), vol. 2, pp. 266-330.
2. I will cite the text of Pascal's "Trois discours" from Louis Lafuma's edition of the *Opuscules et lettres* (Paris: Aubier-Montaigne, 1955), pp. 164-71.
3. Nicole, *Essais*, vol. 2, p. 229.
4. Ibid., vol. 3., p. 7.

5. Ibid., vol. 2., p. 229.
6. Ibid., p. 230.
7. Ibid., p. 166.
8. Antoine Arnauld and Pierre Nicole, *La Logique*, 5th ed. (Paris, 1683), p. 92. This chapter was very probably written by Nicole.
9. Pascal, *Opuscules*, pp. 170-71.
10. Ibid., p. 171.
11. This proposition is clearly one of the fundamental theses of my work.
12. G. W. F. Hegel, *Phénoménologie de l'esprit*, trans. Jean Hyppolite (Paris: Aubier-Montaigne, 1946), vol. 2, p. 83. [*Phenomenology of Spirit* (Oxford: Oxford University Press, 1977), pp. 294-95.—TR.]
13. Pascal, *Opuscules*, p. 171.
14. Ibid., p. 165.
15. Blaise Pascal, "Lettres aux Roannez" in *Opuscules*, p. 97.
16. Ibid.
17. Ibid.
18. Ibid.
19. Ibid., p. 99.
20. Cf. Andras Zempléni, "La Chaîne du secret," *Nouvelle Revue de Psychanalyse* 14 (1976): 313-24.
21. Pascal, *Opuscules*, pp. 170-71.
22. Ibid., p. 171.
23. Ibid.
24. Ibid., p. 166.
25. Arnauld and Nicole, *Logique*, p. 55.
26. Ibid., p. 26.
27. Ibid., p. 211.
28. Ibid., p. 207.
29. Ibid., p. 210.
30. Ibid., p. 57.
31. Ibid., p. 170.
32. Pascal, *Lettres*, pp. 98-99.
33. Pascal, *Opuscules*, p. 165.
34. Ibid., p. 170.
35. Ibid., p. 171.
36. Hegel, *Phénoménologie*, vol. 2, p. 73. [*Phenomenology of Spirit*, p. 312.—TR.]
37. Pascal, *Opuscules*, p. 165.
38. Ibid., p. 167.
39. Cf. above, p. 56 and p. 197.
40. Pascal, *Opuscules*, p. 165.
41. Ibid., pp. 165, 167.

Bibliography

Bibliography

Older Works Consulted

Amelot de la Houssaye, Abraham Nicolas. *La Morale de Tacite. De la flatterie.* Paris, 1686.
Arnauld, Antoine. *Œuvres.* 43 vols. Paris-Lausanne, 1775-83.
Arnauld, Antoine, and Claude Lancelot. *Grammaire générale et raisonnée.* Paris, 1660.
Arnauld, Antoine, and Pierre Nicole. *La Logique, ou L'Art de penser.* 5th ed. Paris, 1683.
Aubéry, Antoine. *Des justes prétentions du roi sur l'Empire.* Paris, 1667.
Audin, Prieur de Termes et de la Fage. *Les Fables héroîques imitées de celles d'Esope . . . comprenant les véritables maximes de la politique et de la morale.* Paris, 1660, 1664, 1669.
———. *Histoire de France représentée par tableaux, commençant au règne de Hugues Capet.* 2 vols. Paris, 1647.
Bacon, Francis. *Œuvres philosophiques, morales et politiques.* Translated by J.-A.-C. Buchon. Paris: A. Desprez, 1836. [English original: *Works of Francis Bacon.* 14 vols. Saint Clare Shores, MI: Scholarly Press, 1976.—TR.]
Balzac, Jean-Louis Guez de. *Aristippe, ou De la Cour.* Paris, 1652.
———. *Le Prince.* Paris, 1631.
Bary, René. *La Rhétorique française.* New ed. Amsterdam, 1660.
Benserade, Isaac de. *Œuvres.* 2 vols. Paris, 1696.
Bié, Jacques de. *Les Vrais Portraits des rois de France, tirés de ce qui nous reste de leurs mouvements, sceaux, médailles et autres effigies.* Paris, 1634.
Bodin, Jean. *Les Six Livres de la République.* 3rd ed. Paris, 1578. [Edited and translated by J. P. Mayes, under the title *The Six Books of the Commonweale.* 1962. Reprint. Salem, NH: Ayer, 1979.—TR.]
Bossuet, Jacques Bénigne. *Politique tirée des propres paroles de l'Ecriture sainte.* Edited by Jacques Le Brun. Geneva: Droz, 1967.
Bouhours, Dominique. *Les Entretiens d'Ariste et d'Eugène.* Paris, 1678. (First edition, 1671.)
Ceriziers, René de. *Réflexions chrétiennes et politiques sur la vie des Rois Henri IV et Louis le Juste.* Paris, 1642.

Chapelain, Jean. *Lettres*. 2 vols. Paris: Tamizey de Larroque, 1880-83.
Claude, Jean. *Réponse au livre de M. Arnauld, intitulé "La Perpétuité de la Foi."* Quévilly, Rouen, 1670.
Colbert, Jean-Baptiste. *Lettres, instructions et mémoires*. Edited by Pierre Clément. 9 vols. Paris: Imprimerie Impériale, 1861-82.
Colomby, François de. *De l'autorité des rois, premier discours*. Paris, 1622, 1631.
Crevier, Jean-Baptiste-Louis. *Rhétorique française*. 2 vols. Paris, 1765.
Descartes, René. "Discours de la méthode" and "Méditations métaphysiques." In vol. 3 of *Œuvres et lettres*. Edited by André Bridoux. Paris: Gallimard (Pléïade), 1937. [Translated by Donald A. Cress, under the title *Discourse on Method*. Indianapolis: Hackett, 1980. — TR.]
——————. *Œuvres*. Edited by Charles Adam and Paul Tannery. 13 vols. Paris: Vrin, 1964.
Desmarets de Saint-Sorlin, Jean. *Clovis ou la France Chrétienne, poème revu et augmenté d'inventions et des actions merveilleuses du roi*. 3rd ed. Paris, 1673.
——————. *Les Jeux de cartes des rois de France, des reines renommées, de la géographie et des fables*. Paris, 1664.
——————. *Le Triomphe de Louis et de son siècle*. Paris, 1674.
Du Perron, Cardinal Jacques Davy. *Traité du Saint Sacrement de l'Eucharistie divisé en trois livres. Contenant la réfutation du livre du Sieur du Plessis Mornay contre la messe*. Paris, 1622.
Dupleix, Scipion. *Continuation de l'histoire du règne de Louis le Juste, treizième du nom*. Paris, 1648.
——————. *Histoire de Louis le Juste, XIIIe du nom, roi de France et de Navarre*. Paris, 1635.
Faret, Nicolas. *Des Vertus nécessaires à un prince pour bien gouverner ses sujets*. Paris, 1623.
——————. *L'Honnête homme, ou L'Art de plaire à la Cour*. Paris, 1630.
Félibien, André. *Descriptions de divers ouvrages de peinture faits pour le Roi*. Paris, 1671.
——————. *Description de la grotte de Versailles*. Paris, 1672.
——————. *Description de l'arc de la place Dauphine*. Paris, 1660.
——————. *Description du château de Versailles, de ses peintures et d'autres ouvrages faits pour le Roi*. Paris, 1696.
——————. *Description sommaire du château de Versailles*. Paris, 1674.
——————. *Les Divertissements de Versailles donnés par le Roi à toute sa cour au retour de la conquête de la Franche-Comté en l'année 1674*. Paris, 1674.
——————. *Entretiens sur les vies et sur les ouvrages des plus excellents peintres anciens et modernes*. 5 vols. Paris, 1666-88.
——————. *Recueil de descriptions de peintures et d'autres ouvrages faits pour le Roi*. Paris, 1689.
——————. *"Les Reines de Perse aux pieds d'Alexandre," peinture du Cabinet du Roi*. Paris, 1663.
——————. *Relation de la fête de Versailles du 18 juillet 1668*. Paris, 1668.
Fontanier, Pierre. *Les Figures du discours*. Introduction by Gérard Genette. Paris: Flammarion, 1968.
Furetière, Antoine. *Dictionnaire universel*. Paris, 1690.
Godeau, Antoine. *Catéchisme royal*. Paris, 1650.
——————. *Eloges historiques des empereurs, des rois, des princes, des impératrices, des reines et des princesses qui dans tous les siècles ont excellé en piété*. Paris, 1667.
——————. *L'Institution du Prince chrétien*. Paris, 1644.
Godefroy, Théodore. *Le Cérémonial français*. 2 vols. Paris, 1649.
Gracián, Baltasar. *L'Homme de Cour*. Translated by and with a commentary by Amelot de la Houssaye. Paris, 1687.
Hobbes, Thomas. *Eléments philosophiques du Citoyen, traité politique où les fondements de la société civile sont découverts*. "Traduits en français par un de ses amis [S. Sorbière]." Amsterdam, 1649. [Edited and translated by Howard Warrender, under the title *De Cive: The English Version*. London: Oxford University Press, 1983. — TR.]

—————. *Leviathan, traité de la matière, de la forme et du pouvoir de la République ecclésiastique et civile*. Edited and translated by François Tricaud. Paris: Sirey, 1971. [Originally published as *Leviathan*. Edited by C. B. Macpherson. New York: Penguin, 1982.—TR.]

Jant, Chevalier Jacques de. *La Méduse, bouclier de Pallas, ou Défense pour la France contre un libelle intitulé "Le Bouclier d'Etat" pour ce qui concerne le Portugal*. Paris, 1665.

La Bruyère, Jean de. *Les Caractères, ou Les Mœurs de ce siècle*. Edited by Robert Garapon. Paris: Classiques Garnier, 1962.

La Calprenède, Gautier de Coste de. *Faramond, ou L'Histoire de France*. "Dédié au Roi." Paris, 1652.

La Fontaine, Jean de. *Œuvres complètes*. 2 vols. Paris: Gallimard (Pléïade), 1947-48.

La Mothe Le Vayer, François de. *De l'instruction de Mgr le Dauphin*. Paris, 1640.

—————. *Œuvres*. 2 vols. Paris, 1662.

—————. *La Physique du Prince*. Paris, 1654.

La Roche-Flavin, Bernard de. *Treize Livres des Parlements de France*. Bordeaux, 1617; Geneva, 1621.

La Rochefoucauld, François de. *Maximes, suivies des Réflexions diverses*. Paris: Classiques Garnier, 1967. [Translated as *The Maxims*. Albuquerque, NM: Foundation for Classical Reprints, 1984.—TR.]

La Serre, Jean Puget de. *L'Histoire d'Auguste et le parallèle de cet illustre monarque avec notre grand roi Louis XIV, roi de France et de Navarre*. Paris, 1663.

Le Gras, Le Sieur. *La Rhétorique française*. Paris, 1671.

Le Moyne, Le Père Pierre. *De l'Art de régner*. Paris, 1665.

—————. *De l'Art des devises*. Paris, 1666.

—————. *De l'Histoire*. Paris, 1670.

—————. *Le Portrait du Roi passant les Alpes*. Paris, 1692.

—————. *Saint Louis ou La Sainte couronne reconquise, poème héroïque*. Paris, 1653, 1658, 1666.

—————. *La Vue de Paris, lettre héroïque et morale à Mgr le Chancelier*. Paris, 1659.

Le Vasseur, Jacques. *Les Devises des rois de France, latines et françaises*. Paris, 1619.

Lisola, François-Paul, baron de. *Bouclier d'Etat et de Justice, contre le dessein manifestement découvert de la monarchie universelle, sous le vain prétexte des prétentions de la Reine de France*. Brussels, 1667.

Loménie de Brienne, Henri-Auguste de. *Mémoires*. Edited by Joseph-François Michaud and Jean-Jacques-François Poujoulat. Vol. 27. Paris, 1836-39.

Lortie, André. *Traité de la Sainte Cène . . . où sont examinées les nouvelles subtilités de M. Arnauld sur les paroles: Ceci est mon corps*. Saumur, 1675.

Louis XIV. *Mémoires*. Edited by Jean Longnon. Paris: Tallandier, 1978.

Loyseau, Charles. *Traité des ordres et simples dignités*. Paris, 1613.

Menestrier, Claude-François. *Des décorations funèbres où il est amplement traité des tentures, des lumières, des mausolées, catafalques, inscriptions et autres ornements funèbres*. Paris, 1683.

—————. *Histoire du roi Louis le Grand par les médailles, emblèmes, devises, jetons, inscriptions, armoiries et autres monuments publics recueillis et expliqués*. Paris, 1689.

—————. *Jeu de cartes du blason*. Lyon, 1692.

—————. *La Source glorieuse du sang de l'auguste maison de Bourbon dans le cœur de St Louis roi de France*. Paris, 1687.

—————. *La Statue de Louis le Grand placée dans le Temple de l'Honneur. Dessein du feu d'artifice dressé devant l'Hôtel de Ville de Paris, pour la statue du Roi qui doit y être posée*. Paris, 1690.

Mézeray, François Eudes (dit) de. *Histoire de France depuis Faramond jusqu'à maintenant*. 3 vols. Paris, 1643-51.

Montpensier, duchesse de. *Mémoires*. 4 vols. Paris: Charpentier, 1858-68.
Motteville, Françoise de. *Mémoires pour servir à l'histoire d'Anne d'Autriche, épouse de Louis XIII, roi de France*. 6 vols. Amsterdam, 1739.
Naudé, Gabriel. *Considérations politiques sur les coups d'Etat*. Rome, 1639.
Nicole, Pierre. *Essais de morale*. 13 vols. Paris, 1723-35.
Nicole, Le président Claude. *Au roi, sur sa campagne de Hollande en 1672*. Paris, n.d.
_____. *Le Portrait du Roi*. Paris, 1664.
Pascal, Blaise. *Œuvres*. Paris: Gallimard (Pléïade), 1950.
_____. *Opuscules et lettres*. Edited by Louis Lafuma. Paris: Aubier-Montaigne, 1955. [Translated by A. J. Krailsheimer, under the title *The Provincial Letters*. New York: Penguin, 1982. — TR.]
_____. *Pensées*. Edited by Louis Lafuma. 2nd ed. Paris: Delmas, 1952. [Translated by A. J. Krailsheimer, under the title *Pensées*. New York: Penguin, 1966. — TR.]
Patin, Charles. *Introduction à la science des médailles*. Paris, 1665. With *Introduction à l'histoire par la connaissance des médailles*. Paris, 1665; and *Histoire des médailles, ou Introduction à la connaissance de cette science*. Paris, 1695.
Patin, Guy. *Lettres choisies*. Cologne, 1691.
Pellisson-Fontanier, Paul. *Œuvres diverses*. 3 vols. Paris, 1735.
Péréfixe, Hardouin de Beaumont de. *Histoire du Roi Henri le Grand*. Paris, 1661.
Perrault, Charles. *Contes*. Edited by Gilbert Rouger. Paris: Classiques Garnier, 1967. [Translated by A. E. Johnson, under the title *Perrault's Complete Fairy Tales*. Nashville: Dodd, Mead: 1982. — TR.]
_____. *Mémoires de Charles Perrault de l'Académie Française contenant beaucoup de particularités et d'anecdotes intéressantes du Ministère de M. Colbert*. Avignon, 1759. Extracts, pp. xciv-xcix in vol. 1 of Josèphe Jacquiot, *Médailles et jetons de Louis XIV d'après le manuscrit de Londres*. Paris: Imprimerie Nationale, Klincksieck, 1968.
_____. *Ode au Roi*. Paris, 1693.
_____. *Ode sur la paix*. Paris, 1660.
_____. *Ode sur le mariage du Roi*. Paris, 1660.
_____. *La Peinture, poème*. Paris, 1668.
_____. *Le Siècle de Louis le Grand, poème*. Paris, 1687.
Poussin, Nicolas. *Lettres et propos sur l'art*. Edited by Anthony Blunt. Paris: Hermann, 1964.
Priezac, Daniel de. *Discours politiques*. Paris, 1652-54. (New edition, 1666.)
Racine, Jean. *Œuvres*. Vol. 2, *Prose*. Paris: Gallimard (Pléïade), 1966.
Rascas de Bagarris, Pierre Antoine de. *De la nécessité de l'usage des Médailles dans les monnaies*. Paris, 1602. Extracts, pp. lxxxv-lxxxvii in vol. 1 of Josèphe Jacquiot, *Médailles et jetons de Louis XIV d'après le manuscrit de Londres*. Paris: Imprimerie Nationale, Klincksieck, 1968.
Retz, Jean-François-Paul de Gondi, cardinal de. *La Conjuration du comte Jean-Louis de Fiesque*. Paris, 1666.
_____. *Mémoires*. Edited by Geneviève Bulli. 2 vols. Paris: Librairie Générale Française (Livre de Poche), 1965.
Richelieu, Armand-Jean du Plessis, cardinal de. *Mémoires*. 10 vols. Paris: Société de l'Histoire de France, 1908-31.
_____. *Testament politique*. Paris, 1647.
Rohan, Henri, duc de. *Le parfait capitaine*. With *Traité de l'Intérêt des princes et états de la chrétienté*. Paris, 1638.
Saint-Réal, César Vichard, abbé de. *Conjuration des Espagnols contre la République de Venise en l'année 1618*. Paris, 1674.
_____. *De l'Usage de l'histoire*. Edited by René Demoris and Christian Meurillon. Lille, Paris: Université de Lille III, 1980. (First edition, 1671.)

_____. *Dom Carlos, nouvelle historique*. Paris, 1672.
Saint-Simon, Louis de Rouvroy, duc de. *Mémoires*. Paris: Gallimard (Pléïade), 1947.
Sandras de Courtilz, Gatien de. *Nouveaux Intérêts des Princes de l'Europe*. Cologne, 1685.
Saumaise, Claude. *Traité de l'autorité royale, dédié au Roi*. [Taken from *Defensio Regia pro Carolo I*. n.p., 1649.] Paris, 1691.
Scarron, Paul. *Le Cœur des princes entre les mains de Dieu*. Paris, 1652.
Scudéry, Marguerite de. *La Promenade de Versailles*. Paris, 1669.
Senault, Jean-François. *L'Horoscope de Mgr le Dauphin*. Paris, 1661.
_____. *Le Monarque, ou Les Devoirs du Souverain*. Paris, 1662.
Sirmond, Jacques. *Le Coup d'état de Louis XIII*. Paris, 1631.
Tallemant des Réaux, l'abbé. "Preface" to *Médailles sur les Principaux Evénements du Règne de Louis le Grand*. Paris, 1702. Extracts, pp. cxvii-cxxvi in vol. 1 of Josèphe Jacquiot, *Médailles et jetons de Louis XIV d'après le manuscrit de Londres*. Paris: Imprimerie Nationale, Klincksieck, 1968.
Vauquelin, Nicolas, Seigneur des Yveteaux. *Institution du Prince*. Paris, 1643. (First edition, 1604.)
Voltaire, François-Marie Arouet. *Le Siècle de Louis XIV*. 2 vols. Paris: Garnier-Flammarion, 1966.

Modern Works Consulted

Adam, Antoine. *Histoire de la littérature française du XVIIe siècle*. 5 vols. Paris: Domat, 1948-56.
Alberti, Leon Battista. *On Painting*. Translated by John R. Spencer. New Haven, Conn.: Yale University Press, 1956.
Anderson, Perry. *L'Etat absolutiste: Ses origines et ses voies*. Translated by Dominique Niemetz. 2 vols. Paris: Maspero, 1978. [English original: *Lineages of the Absolutist State*. London: New Left Books, 1974.—TR.]
Ashley, Maurice Percy. *Le Grand Siècle: L'Europe de 1598 à 1715*. Translated by Claire Poole. Paris: Fayard, 1972. [English original: *The Golden Century: Europe, 1598-1715*. New York: Praeger, 1968.—TR.]
Auerbach, E. "Über Pascals politische Theorie." In *Vier Untersuchungen zur Geschichte der französischen Bildung*, 51-74. Bern: A. Francke Ag Verlag, 1951.
Babelon, Jean. *Le Portrait dans l'antiquité d'après les monnaies*. Paris: Payot, 1942.
Bardon, Françoise. *Le Portrait mythologique à la cour de France sous Henri IV et Louis XIII: Mythologie et politique*. Paris: Picard, 1974.
Batiffol, Pierre. *L'Eucharistie, la présence réelle et la transsubstantiation*. 9th ed. Paris: J. Gabalda, 1930. (First edition, 1905.)
Beloff, Max. *The Age of Absolutism, 1660-1815*. New York: Hutchinson, 1954.
Benveniste, Emile. *Problèmes de linguistique générale*. 2 vols. Paris: Gallimard, 1966-74. [Translated by Mary E. Meek, under the title *Problems in General Linguistics*. Miami: University of Miami Press, 1973.—TR.]
_____. *Le Vocabulaire des institutions indo-européennes*. 2 vols. Paris: Minuit, 1969. [Translated by Elizabeth Palmer, under the title *Indo-European Language and Society*. Miami: University of Miami Press, 1973.—TR.]
Bloch, Marc. *Les Rois thaumaturges: Etude sur le caractère surnaturel attribué à la puissance royale, particulièrement en France et en Angleterre*. Strasbourg: Librairie Istra; London: Oxford University Press, 1924.
Bontems, Claude, Léon-Pierre Raybaud, and Jean-Pierre Brancourt. *Le Prince dans la France des XVIe et XVIIe siècles*. Paris: Presses Universitaires de France, 1965.
Bouvy, Eugène. *La Gravure en France au XVIIe siècle: La gravure de portraits et d'allégories*. Paris, Brussels: Les Editions G. van Oest, 1929.
Certeau, Michel de. *L'Ecriture de l'histoire*. Paris: Gallimard, 1975.

———. *L'Invention du quotidien.* Vol. 1, *Arts de faire.* Paris: UGE (10-18), 1980. [Translated by Steven F. Randall, under the title *The Practice of Everyday Life.* Berkeley: University of California Press, 1985. —TR.]
Chevalier, Jean-Claude. "Les Entretiens d'Ariste et d'Eugène du Père Bouhours, soit la littérature et l'idéologie." In *Langues et Langages de Leibniz à l'Encyclopédie.* Paris: UGE (10-18), 1977.
Christout, Marie-Françoise. *Le Ballet de Cour de Louis XIV, 1643-1672. Mises en scène.* Paris: Picard, 1967.
Church, William F. *Richelieu and Reason of State.* Princeton, N.J.: Princeton University Press, 1972.
Couturier, C. "*Sacramentum* et *mysterium* dans l'œuvre de St Augustin," in *Etudes augustiniennes,* edited by H. Rendel, M. Le Landais, A. Lauras, and C. Couturier, 163-274. Paris: Aubier, 1953.
Dainville, François de. *L'Education des Jésuites (XVIe-XVIIe siécles).* Paris: Minuit, 1978.
Damisch, Hubert. "L'Origine' de la perspective." *Macula* 5-6 (1979): 113-37.
Demahis, Etiennette. *La Pensée politique de Pascal: Le milieu, la doctrine et son originalité.* Saint-Amand: Imprimerie R. Bussière, 1931.
Demoris, René. "Le Corps royal et l'imaginaire au XVIIe siècle: *Le Portrait du Roi* par Félibien." *Revue des Sciences Humaines* 44, no. 172 (1978): 9-30.
———. "Du littéraire au littéral dans *Peau d'Ane* de Perrault." *Revue des Sciences Humaines* 43, no. 166 (1977): 261-79.
———, ed. With Christian Meurillon. *De l'usage de l'histoire,* by César Vichard, abbé de Saint-Réal. Lille, Paris: Université de Lille III, 1980.
Descombes, Vincent. *L'Inconscient malgré lui.* Paris: Minuit, 1977.
———. "Introduction." In *De l'usage de l'histoire,* by César Vichard, abbé de Saint-Réal. Lille, Paris: Université de Lille III, 1980.
Détienne, Marcel. *Dionysos mis à mort.* Paris: Gallimard, 1977. [Translated by M. Muellner and L. Muellner under the title *Dionysus Slain.* Baltimore, Md.: Johns Hopkins University Press, 1979. —TR.]
———. *Les Maîtres de la vérité dans la Grèce archaïque.* Paris: Maspero, 1967.
Devyer, André. *Le Sang épuré: Préjugés de race chez les gentilhommes de l'ancien régime, 1560-1720.* Brussels: Editions de l'Université de Bruxelles, 1973.
Duby, Georges. *Les Trois Ordres, ou L'Imaginaire du féodalisme.* Paris: Gallimard, 1978. [Translated by Arthur Goldhammer, under the title *The Three Orders: Feudal Society Imagined.* Chicago: University of Chicago Press, 1980. —TR.]
Dumézil, Georges. *Idées romaines.* Paris: Gallimard, 1969.
Elias, Norbert. *La Société de cour.* Translated by Pierre Kamnitzer. Paris: Calmann-Lévy, 1974. [Translated under the title *The Court Society.* New York: Pantheon Books, 1983. —TR.]
Figgis, John Neville. *The Divine Right of Kings.* New York: Harper and Row, 1965. (First edition, 1896.)
Friedrich, Karl Joachim. *The Age of the Baroque, 1610-1660.* New York: Harper, 1952.
Genette, Gérard. "Introduction." In *Les Figures du discours,* by Pierre Fontanier. Paris: Flammarion, 1968. [Translated by Alan Sheridan, under the title *Figures of Literary Discourse.* New York: Columbia University Press, 1984. —TR.]
Gernet, Louis. *Anthropologie de la Grèce antique.* Paris: Maspero, 1968. [Translated by John D. B. Hamilton and Blaise Nagy, under the title *The Anthropology of Ancient Greece.* Baltimore, Md.: Johns Hopkins University Press, 1981. —TR.]
———. "Le Temps dans les formes archaïques du droit." *Journal de Psychologie* 53 (1956): 379-406.
Gierke, Otto von. *Political Theories of the Middle Age.* Translated by F. W. Maitland. Cambridge: Cambridge University Press, 1959.

Giesey, Ralph E. "The Juridic Basis of Dynastic Right to the French Throne." *Transactions of the American Philosophical Society* 51 (1961): 3-47.
_____. *The Royal Funeral Ceremony in Renaissance France*. Geneva: Droz, 1960.
Goubert, Pierre. *L'Ancien Régime*. 2 vols. Paris: Armand Colin, 1969-73. [Translated by Steve Cox, under the title *The Ancient Régime: French Society 1600-1750*. Scranton, Pa.: Harper and Row, 1974.—TR.]
_____. *Louis XIV et vingt millions de Français*. Paris: Fayard, 1966. [Translated by Anne Carter, under the title *Louis XIV and the Twenty Million Frenchmen*. Westminster, Md.: Random House, 1972.—TR.]
Grabar, André. *L'Empereur dans l'art byzantin*. Strasbourg: Université de Strasbourg, Faculté des Lettres, 1936.
Grosrichard, Alain. *Structure du sérail. La Fiction du despotisme asiatique dans l'Occident classique*. Paris: Editions du Seuil, 1979.
Hamburger, Käte. *Die Logik der Dichtung*. Stuttgart: E. Klett, 1957. [Translated by Marilynn J. Rose, under the title *The Logic of Literature*. Bloomington: Indiana University Press, 1973.—TR.]
Hegel, G. W. F. *Leçons sur la philosophie de l'histoire*. Translated by Jean Gibelin. 3rd ed. Paris: Vrin, 1967. [Translated by J. Sibree, under the title *The Philosophy of History*, 1900. Reprint. Darby, Pa.: Arden Library, n.d.—TR.]
_____. *La Phénoménologie de l'esprit*. Translated by Jean Hyppolite. Paris: Aubier-Montaigne, 1946. [Translated by A. V. Miller, under the title *Phenomenology of Spirit*. London: Oxford University Press, 1977.]
Hautecoeur, Louis. *Louis XIV, Roi-Soleil*. Paris: Plon, 1953.
Hubaux, Jean, and Maxime Leroy. *Le Mythe du phénix dans les littératures grecque et latine*. Liège: Faculté de Philosophie et Lettres, Université de Liège, 1939.
Hyppolite, Jean. *Genèse et structure de la phénoménologie de l'esprit*. With *De Hegel*. Paris: Aubier-Montaigne, 1946. [Translated by Samuel Cherniak and John Heckman, under the title *Genesis and Structure of Hegel's "Phenomenology of Spirit."* Chicago: Northwestern University Press, 1974.—TR.]
Jacquiot, Josèphe. *La Médaille au temps de Louis XIV*. Paris: Hôtel de la Monnaie, 1970. (catalog)
_____. *Médailles et jetons de Louis XIV d'après le manuscrit de Londres*. 4 vols. Paris: Imprimerie Nationale, Klincksieck, 1968.
James, E. D. "The Political and Social Theory of Pierre Nicole." *French Studies* 14 (1960): 117-28.
Jenkins, Marianna Duncan. *The State Portrait, Its Origin and Evolution*. Monographs on Archeology and Fine Arts, 3. New York: College Art Association of America, 1947.
Jones, Mark. *The Art of the Medal*. London: British Museum Publications, Department of Coins and Medals, 1979.
_____. *Medals of the Sun King*. London: British Museum Publications, Department of Coins and Medals, 1979.
Jouanna, Arlette. *Ordre social: Mythes et hiérarchies dans la France du XVIe siècle*. Paris: Hachette, 1977.
Jung, Marc René. *Hercule dans la littérature française du XVIe siècle. De l'Hercule courtois à l'Hercule baroque*. Geneva: Droz, 1966.
Kantorowicz, Ernst H. *The King's Two Bodies: A Study in Mediaeval Theology*. Princeton, N.J.: Princeton University Press, 1957.
_____. "Mysteries of State: An Absolutist Concept and Its Late Mediaeval Origins." *Harvard Theological Review* 48 (1955): 65-91.
_____. *Selected Studies*. New York: J. J. Augustin Publications, 1965.
Kennedy, George Alexander. *The Art of Persuasion in Greece*. Princeton, N.J.: Princeton University Press, 1963.

Lacour-Gayet, Georges. *L'Education politique de Louis XIV.* 2nd ed. Paris: Hachette, 1923. (First edition, 1898.)
Lavisse, Ernest. *Louis XIV, la religion, les lettres et les arts, la guerre, 1643-1685.* Vol. 7 of *Histoire de France.* Paris: Armand Colin, 1906.
Linde, Charlotte, and William Labov. "Spatial Networks as a Site for the Study of Language and Thought." *Language* 51 (1975): 924-39.
Loraux, Nicole. *L'Invention d'Athènes: Histoire de l'oraison funèbre dans la "cité classique."* The Hague, Paris, New York: Mouton, 1981.
Lubac, Henri de. *"Corpus mysticum": L'Eucharistie et l'Eglise au Moyen-Age.* Paris: Aubier-Montaigne, 1949.
Lyons, John. *Semantics.* 2 vols. Cambridge: Cambridge University Press, 1977.
Mandrou, Robert. *L'Europe absolutiste. Raison et raison d'Etat (1649-1775).* Paris: Fayard, 1977.
_____. *Louis XIV en son temps (1661-1715).* Paris: Presses Universitaires de France, 1973.
Marin, Louis. "L'Animal-fable Esope." *Critique* 34, nos. 375-376 (1978): 775-82.
_____. *La Critique du discours: Etudes sur la Logique de Port-Royal et les Pensées de Pascal.* Paris: Minuit, 1975.
_____. *Détruire la peinture.* Paris: Galilée, 1977.
_____. "Jésus devant Pilate. Essai d'analyse structurale." *Langages* 22 (1971): 51-74.
_____. "La Lecture du tableau d'après Poussin." *Cahiers de l'Association Internationale d'Etudes Françaises* 24 (1972): 251-66.
_____. "Parler, montrer, manger, ou Le Piège du présent." *L'Arc* 64 (1976): 28-41.
_____. *Le Récit est un piège.* Paris: Minuit, 1978.
_____. "Le Roi, son confident et la reine, ou Les Séductions du regard." *Traverses* 18 (1980): 25-36.
_____. *Utopiques: Jeux d'espaces.* Paris: Minuit, 1973. [Translated under the title *Utopics: Spatial Play.* Atlantic Highlands, N.J.: Humanities Press, 1984.—TR.]
_____. "Les Voies de la carte." In *Cartes et figures de la Terre*, 47-54. Paris: Centre Georges-Pompidou, 1980. (catalog)
Maumené, Charles, and Louis d'Harcourt. *Iconographie des rois de France.* Paris: Armand Colin, 1928.
Mauro, Frédéric. *L'Expansion européenne, 1600-1870.* 2nd ed. Paris: Presses Universitaires de France, 1967.
Meinecke, Friedrich. *Machiavellism. The Doctrine of Raison d'Etat and Its Place in Modern History.* Translated by Douglas Scott. New Haven, Conn.: Yale University Press, 1957.
Meyer, Jean. *Noblesses et pouvoirs dans l'Europe de l'ancien régime.* Paris: Hachette, 1973.
La Monnaie, miroir des rois. Paris: Hôtel de la Monnaie, 1978. (catalog)
Nenci, Giuseppe. "Il Motivo dell'autopsia nella storiografia greca." *Studi classici e orientali* 3 (1955): 15-46.
Ong, Walter J. "Space, System and Intellect in Renaissance Symbolism." *Bibliothèque d'Humanisme et Renaissance* 18 (1956): 222-39.
Orgel, Stephen. *The Illusion of Power: Political Theater in the English Renaissance.* Berkeley: University of California Press, 1975.
Picard, Olivier. "Les Origines du monnayage en Grèce." *L'Histoire* 6 (1978): 13-20.
Pintard, René. *Le Libertinage érudit dans la première moitié du XVIIe siècle.* 2 vols. Paris: Boivin et Cie., 1943.
Ranum, Orest. *Artisans of Glory: Writers and Historical Thought in Seventeeenth-Century France.* Baltimore, Md.: Johns Hopkins University Press, 1979.
Rothkrug, Lionel. *Opposition to Louis XIV: The Political and Social Origins of the French Enlightenment.* Princeton, N.J.: Princeton University Press, 1965.

Sabatier, Georges. "Imaginaire, état et société: La monarchie absolue de droit divin en France au temps de Louis XIV." *Procès: Cahiers d'Analyse Politique et Juridique* 4 (1979): 36-152.
Schepens, Guido. "Ephore sur la valeur de l'autopsie." *Ancient Society* 1 (1970): 163-82.
Schramm, Percy Ernst. *Die deutschen Kaiser und Könige in Bildern ihrer Zeit: 751-1190.* 2 vols. Leipzig: B. G. Teubner, 1928.
Shell, Marc. *The Economy of Literature.* Baltimore, Md.: Johns Hopkins University Press, 1978.
Stierle, Karlheinz. "L'Histoire comme Exemple, l'Exemple comme Histoire." *Poétique* 10 (1972): 176-98.
Strong, Roy C. *The Cult of Elizabeth: Elizabethan Portraiture and Pageantry.* London: Thames and Hudson, 1977.
Tans, J. A. G. "Les Idées politiques des Jansénistes." *Neophilologus* 40 (1956): 1-18.
Tapié, Victor Lucien. *Baroque et classicisme.* New ed. Paris: Librairie Générale Française (Livre de Poche), 1972.
Taveneaux, René. *Jansénisme et politique.* Paris: Armand Colin, 1965.
Teyssèdre, Bernard. *L'Art français au siècle de Louis XIV.* Paris: Librairie Générale Française (Livre de Poche), 1967.
Thireau, Jean-Louis. *Les Idées politiques de Louis XIV.* Paris: Presses Universitaires de France, 1973.
Thuau, Etienne. *Raison d'Etat et pensée politique à l'époque de Richelieu.* Paris: Armand Colin, 1966.
Truchet, Jacques, ed. *Politique de Bossuet.* Paris: Armand Colin, 1966.
Varga, A. Kibédi. *Rhétorique et littérature, études de structures classiques.* Paris: Didier, 1970.
Vinge, Louise. *The Narcissus Theme in Western European Literature up to the Early 19th Century.* Lund: Gleerups, 1967.
Vivanti, Corrado. "Henri IV, The Gallic Hercules." *Journal of the Warburg and Courtauld Institutes* 30 (1967): 176-97.
Weidauer, Liselotte. *Probleme der frühen Elektronenprägung.* Zurich: Typos I; Friburg: Office du Livre, 1975.
Weinrich, Harald. *Le Temps.* Paris: Le Seuil, 1973.
Willey, Basil. *The Seventeenth-Century Background: Studies in the Thought of the Age in Relation to Poetry and Religion.* New York: Doubleday, 1953.
Wind, Edgar. "'Hercules' and 'Orpheus,' Two Mock-Heroic Designs by Dürer." *Journal of the Warburg and Courtauld Institutes* 2 (1938-39): 206-18.
_____. "Studies in Allegorical Portraiture I." *Journal of the Warburg and Courtauld Institutes* 1 (1937): 138-62.
Yates, Frances A. *Astraea. The Imperial Theme in the Sixteenth-Century.* London: Routledge and Kegan Paul, 1975.
Zempléni, Andras. "La Chaîne du secret." *Nouvelle Revue de Psychanalyse* 14 (1976): 313-24.
_____. "Pouvoir dans la cure et pouvoir social." *Nouvelle Revue de Psychanalyse* 8 (1973): 141-78.

Index

Index

Academy (French), 105-17
Alberti, Leon Battista, 5
Allegory, 208-11
Animals Sick from the Plague, The (La Fontaine), 103
Aristotle, 48-50, 70, 72, 77, 89
Augmentation, 55, 62-64

Bagarris, Antoine Rascas de, 123-30, 134-35, 209
Bary, René, 90
Benveniste, Emile, 47. *See also* Discourse
Boileau-Despréaux, Nicolas, 49, 89, 91, 122
Bosse, Abraham, 169
Bossuet, Jacques Bénigne, 14-15
Le Bouclier d'Etat et de Justice, contre le dessein manifestement découvert de la monarchie universelle, sous le vain prétexte des prétentions de la Reine de France (Lisola), 40, 59-60

Cartography, 169-81, 184-92
Chronicles, 41, 46-48, 86-87
Cinderella (Perrault), 194
Claudian, 100
Clausewitz, Karl von, 7
Colbert, Abbé (son of Jean Baptiste Colbert), 105-17

Colbert, Jean Baptiste: on medals, 131-34; and Pellisson and the king's history, 39-45, 59, 76; and Racine and the Academy, 105, 109, 111, 115; on Versailles, 182
Court of the Lion, The (La Fontaine), 103
Crevier, Jean-Baptiste Louis, 90
Crow and the Fox, The (La Fontaine), 92, 94-104, 106, 111
Crow That Wanted to Imitate the Eagle, The (La Fontaine), 104

De l'éducation d'un prince (Nicole), 215-17
De Lubac, Henri, 9
Demoris, René, 10
Desargues, Gérard, 169
Descartes, René, 67-69
Descombes, Vincent, 10
Descriptions de divers ouvrages de peinture faits pour le Roi (Félibien), 199, 206-14
Description sommaire du château de Versailles (Félibien), 183-95
Discours qui montre la nécessité de retablir le très ancien et auguste usage public des vraies et parfaites médailles (Bagarris), 123-30, 134-35
Discourse: autobiographical, 46; deliberative, 48-49, 77, 89-90; descriptive, 183-92, 195-96, 208; in *Donkey Skin*, 146-49,

164-65; epideictic (demonstrative or eulogic), 9-10, 48-50, 69-71, 76-81, 85, 89-117, 132, 140; and force, 16, 21-23, 26-27, 29, 36; genres of, 48-50; historical narrative, 9, 42, 44-63, 68-70, 76-79; judiciary, 48-49, 61, 70, 85, 89; and justice, 16, 18-21, 27; in *La Logique de Port-Royal*, 3, 8-9; of the map, 173-74, 176; and power, 16, 22-23, 25, 27-36, 61
Discourse on Method (Descartes), 67-69
Les Divertissements de Versailles donnés par le Roy à toute la Cour au retour de la conquête de la Franche-Comté en l'année 1674 (Félibien), 196-205
Donkey Skin (Perrault), 92, 138-65, 194

L'Eloge historique du roi sur ses conquêtes depuis l'année 1672 jusqu'en 1678 (Félibien), 75, 122
Epideictic discourse. *See* Discourse
Eucharist: and the absolute monarchy, 8-14; and medals, 128, 134-35; and portraits, 209, 211, 213-14, 229-31, 238; and representation, 4
Eulogy: and *The Crow and the Fox*, 98-99; and *Donkey Skin*, 140; and historic medals, 131; and historic narrative, 48-50, 61, 69-82, 85, 87, 89-93; and Racine, 105-17

Fables, 78, 94-104. *See also* La Fontaine, Jean de
Félibien, André, 183-214
Fête, 193-205. *See also* Félibien, André
Flattery, 10, 94-104, 133. *See also* Discourse, epideictic
Fontanier, Pierre, 11, 62, 64, 75, 87, 206
Force: in *The Crow and the Fox*, 98-99; and discourse, 16, 21-23, 27, 29, 31, 42-43; and imagination, 33; and justice, 16-23, 25, 33, 36, 60, 82; Pascal on, 17-23, 25-26, 33-34; and power, 6-7, 16, 33-35, 60-61; and signs, 6-7, 21-22, 26-29, 35-36
Freud, Sigmund, 161
Funerary oration, 89-91
Furetière, Antoine, 114, 155

Giesey, Ralph E., 100
Gomboust, Jacques, 169-81. *See also* Cartography

Hegel, G. W. F.: on absolutism, 9-10, 42, 234-35; on consciousness, 218; on flattery, 94-95, 133; on force, 7; on history, 73-74; on the moment of sensible certitude, 102
—*Phenomenology of Spirit*: absolutism in, 9-10, 234-35; consciousness in, 218; flattery in, 94-95, 133; the moment of sensible certitude in, 102
Henry IV, 123-28, 130, 134-35
Historiographer, 39-88, 89-91, 112-13, 121
History: and medals, 121-22, 130-36; narrative, 39-88, 112-13; and portraits, 209
Hobbes, Thomas, 7
Hyperbole, 91-92, 116, 208, 210. *See also* Fontanier, Pierre
Hypotyposis, 87, 122. *See also* Fontanier, Pierre

Image: and appearance, 26; and magic, 205; and mask, 149-56; and medals, 123, 132, 134-36; and palaces, 199; and portraits, 8-9, 206-13, 218, 221-23; power of, 138
Imagination, 29-33, 36
Inscriptions, 126-37, 158
Intensification, 62-64

Journals, 39-41, 46-47, 61,70, 82, 84
Justice, 7, 16-28, 33-36, 59-61, 82

Kantorowicz, Ernest H., 9, 14, 100
King's Two Bodies: A Study in Mediaeval Political Theology, The (Kantorowicz), 9, 14, 100

La Fontaine, Jean de, 78, 92, 94-104, 106,111
La Vallière, Louise de, 182
Le Brun, Charles, 121-22, 169, 202-3, 206-14
Le Gras, 90-92. *See also* Hyperbole
Le Nôtre, André, 182
Le Vau, Louis, 182
"Lettres aux Roannez" (Pascal), 219-21, 230-231
Lion, the Wolf and the Fox, The (La Fontaine), 103
Litotes, 62-64, 91, 164
La Logique de Port-Royal. See La Logique, ou l'Art de penser
La Logique, ou l'Art de penser (*La Logique de Port-Royal*): on discourse, 173; Eucharistic

sign in, 8-12, 209, 228-30; portraits in, 9-12, 208-9; representation in, 3-4, 10-11, 132, 178, 208, 217; signs in, 10-11, 228-30
Louvre, 176-77, 180-82
Lucien, 75

Machiavelli, Niccolò, 7
Magic, 193-97, 204-5
La Manne (Poussin), 122
Map making. *See* Cartography
Médailles sur les principaux événements du regne de Louis le Grand (Tallemant), 128-37
Medals, 9, 100-101, 123-37, 158-61
Mémoires de Charles Perrault (Perrault), 131-32
Memoirs, 39-41, 46-47, 61, 70, 82, 84
Metaphor, 11, 96, 192, 203
Metonymy: in *The Crow and the Fox*, 96, 111; in *Donkey Skin*, 151, 153; in eulogy, 109, 111; and the king's fêtes, 203; and narrative history, 32, 57-58; and palaces, 192; and portraits, 11
Money, 125-31, 141-42, 146-47, 158-61
Monuments, 8, 124-36, 159

Narrative: of *Donkey Skin*, 138-65; epideictic, 69-82, 85, 89-104, 109-10, 114-17, 131, 135; and historical representation, 8-9, 12-14, 41-90, 117, 121-22, 135; power of, 42-45, 62, 65; topographic, 184-205. *See also* Benveniste, Emile; Discourse
Negation (Freud), 161
Nicole, Pierre, 215-17

On Painting (Alberti), 5

Palaces, 176-77, 180-205
Panegyric: of Colbert, 115; and the funerary oration, 89-90; and historical narrative, 48-50, 61, 69-82, 89-90; of Racine, 108. *See also* Discourse, epideictic; *Rhetoric* (Aristotle)
Paradox, 8, 10, 50, 75, 78, 104
Pascal, Blaise: on cities, 175-76; on the Eucharist, 10; experiments of 169; on force and justice, 6-8, 16-36, 82; on images, 221-23; "Lettres aux Roannez," 219-21, 230-31; and *La Logique de Port-Royal*, 3-4; on power, 14-15, 216-20, 225, 236; on representation, 14-15, 132; "Three Discourses on the Condition of the Greats," 215-38; on tyranny, 18-20, 34, 203, 215-16—*Pensées:* on cities, 175-76; on consciousness, 236-38; on force and justice, 17-24, 27-36, 82, 230; on language, 3-4; on representation, 14, 26-29, 175-76, 219, 222, 230, 233; on tyranny, 18-19, 215-16, 232
Patin, Guy, 182
Peau d'Ane. See Donkey Skin
Pellisson-Fontanier, Paul, 39-88, 91, 121-22, 134, 196
Pensées. See Pascal, Blaise
Perrault, Charles, 92, 131-32, 138-65, 194
Petit, M., 169, 173
Phenomenology of Spirit. See Hegel, G. W. F.
Phoenix, 99-102
Plea, 48-49, 58-59, 61, 70
Pleonasm, 58, 116
Portraits, 7-15, 206-14, 218-19, 221-38
Poussin, Nicolas, 57, 122, 188
Power: and discourse, 16, 22-23, 25, 27-32, 61; in *Donkey Skin*, 138, 147-48, 154, 163-64, 194; and epideictic discourse, 89, 95-96, 99-100; and force, 6-7, 16, 33-35; of historical narrative, 42-46, 52-53, 62, 65, 67, 69, 71, 73-82, 85, 88; and imagination, 29-31; and justice, 59-61; of language, 52, 117; of maps, 174-77, 181; and medals, 127-29, 132-34; and palaces, 183, 190, 193, 195-99, 203; Pascal on, 215-20, 225; 236; and portraits, 207-13; and representation, 4-15, 33-36, 42-44, 48, 53, 56, 71, 73, 95-96, 100-104, 121, 123, 127-29, 132-34, 138, 147-48, 174-75, 190, 193, 195-99, 207, 209, 211, 213, 219, 225-27, 230-35, 238
Preterition, 87, 114-16, 208
Project for the History of Louis XIV (Pellisson-Fontanier), 39-88, 122
Protagoras, 104
Provincial Letters, The (Pascal), 25-26

Les Quatre Eléments (Félibien), 206
Les Quatre Saisons (Félibien), 206

Racine, Jean Baptiste: *L'Eloge historique du roi*, 75, 122; eulogy by, 80, 89, 91, 105-17, 197; and the French Academy,

105-17; as royal historiographer, 49, 75, 80, 89, 91, 121-22, 197, 200
Reader: and descriptions, 185-89; of *Donkey Skin*, 162; and historical medals, 135-37; and historical narrative, 45, 51-81, 87-88, 90; and maps, 171-73, 178
Registers, 41, 46-48, 86-87
Les Reines des Perses aux pieds d'Alexandre, (Le Brun), 206-7
Representation: in *Donkey Skin*, 138, 147-48, 156-62, 194; and epideictic discourse, 89, 95-96, 102-3, 113-16; and force, 6-7, 27, 29, 32-33, 35; in *La Logique de Port-Royal*, 3-4; and maps, 169-78, 180; and medals, 121-37; and narrative history, 8, 12-14, 41-42, 45-57, 51-57, 60-88, 121-23; and palaces, 182-85, 189-91, 193, 195-205; and portraits, 7-15, 206-14, 218-23, 226, 231; and power, 4-15, 33-36, 42-44, 48, 53, 56, 71, 73, 95-96, 100-104, 121, 123, 127-29, 132-34, 138, 147-48, 174-75, 190, 193, 195-99, 207, 209, 211, 213, 219, 225-27, 230-35, 238; and sign, 3-6, 8-10, 96, 161
Respect, 28-34
Rhetoric (Aristotle), 48-50, 70, 72, 77, 89. See also Plea
Rhetorical devices: hyperbole, 91-92, 116, 208, 210; hypotyposis, 87, 122; intensification, 62-64; litotes, 62-64, 91, 164; metaphor, 11, 96, 192, 203; pleonasm, 58, 116; preterition, 87, 114-16, 208; synecdoche, 11. See also Discourse; Metonymy
Rhétorique française (Crevier), 90
La Rhétorique française (Le Gras), 90-91

Saint-Simon, Duc de, 182
Sartre, Jean-Paul, 162
Satire, 91-92
Sign: and the Eucharist, 8-12; and force, 6-7, 21-22, 26-29, 31-33, 35-36; in *La Logique de Port-Royal*, 3-4, 228-29; and portraits, 7-12; and power, 183; and representation, 3-10, 96, 161
Simulacrum: and discourse, 31; and history, 44; and medals, 123; and palaces, 183, 187-88, 203-4; of a reader, 45-46, 51-81, 87-88; and representation, 5-6, 8; and time, 198
Simulation: and historical medals and the viewer, 122-23; and portraits, 221-22, 228; of a reader, 45-46, 51-82, 85
Synecdoche, 11

Tacitus, 63
Tallement des Réaux, Abbé, 128-37
Term, 3
"Three Discourses on the Condition of the Greats" (Pascal), 215-37
Topography, 184-92
Transformation: by discourse, 53-55; in *Donkey Skin*, 158-59; in epideictic discourse, 98-99, 102; of force by representation, 6-7, 27; in historical narrative, 62-64, 82-88
Trianon, 193-97, 200-202
Tyranny, 17-22, 34-35, 215-16

Vandermeulen, 121
Varga, A. Kibédi, 91-92
Versailles, 181-205
Voltaire (François-Marie Arouet), 13

Louis Marin is director of studies at L'Ecole des Hautes Etudes en Sciences Sociales in Paris. A scholar of semiotics, discourse analysis, and the seventeenth-century, Marin has also taught at several campuses of the University of California system and at Johns Hopkins University. Two of his books, *Utopics* and *The Semiotics of the Passion Narratives*, have been translated into English.

Martha M. Houle has been an assistant professor of French at the College of William and Mary since 1983. She received her Ph.D. in literary theory and seventeenth-century French literature from the University of California, San Diego. She has published in *Papers in French Seventeenth-Century Literature* and the *American Journal of Semiotics*.

Tom Conley is chair of the department of French and Italian and professor of French at the University of Minnesota. He has been a visiting professor at the City University of New York and the University of California, Berkeley. Conley received his Ph.D. in 1971 from the University of Wisconsin. He has edited special issues of *SubStance* and *L'Esprit Créateur*, and contributes to *Diacritics*, *Revue des Lettres*, *Littérature*, and other journals.